# Study Guide for
# FINANCIAL ACCOUNTING

*Eighth Edition*

## Helen Brubeck
*San Jose State University*

**Pearson Education**

Boston   Columbus   Indianapolis   New York   San Francisco   Upper Saddle River
Amsterdam   Cape Town   Dubai   London   Madrid   Milan   Munich   Paris   Montreal   Toronto
Delhi   Mexico City   Sao Paulo   Sydney   Hong Kong   Seoul   Singapore   Taipei   Tokyo

*AVP/Executive Editor:* Jodi McPherson
*VP/Publisher:* Natalie E. Anderson
*Acquisitions Editor:* Jodi Bolognese
*Director of Marketing, Intro Markets:*
    Kate Valentine
*AVP/Executive Editor, Media:* Richard Keaveny
*AVP/Executive Producer, Media:* Lisa Strite
*Director, Product Development:*
    Pamela Hersperger
*Editorial Project Manager:* Rebecca Knauer
*Editorial Media Project Manager:* Allison Longley
*Editorial Assistant:* Terenia McHenry
*Development Editor:* Karen Misler
*Supplements Development Editor:* Claire Hunter
*Marketing Manager:* Maggie Moylan

*Marketing Assistant:* Justin Jacob
*Senior Managing Editor, Production:*
    Cynthia Zonneveld
*Production Project Manager:* Lynne Breitfeller
*Production Media Project Manager:* John Cassar
*Permissions Coordinator:* Charles Morris
*Senior Operations Specialist:* Diane Peirano
*AV Project Manager:* Rhonda Aversa
*Senior Art Director:* Jonathan Boylan
*Cover Design:* Jonathan Boylan
*Composition:* GEX Publishing Services
*Full-Service Project Management:*
    GEX Publishing Services
*Printer/Binder:* Courier
*Typeface:* New Century Schoolbook 11/13

Credits and acknowledgments borrowed from other sources and reproduced, with permission, in this textbook appear on appropriate page within text.

Dreamtime.com, pp. v, vi

10 9 8 7 6 5 4 3 2 1

**Prentice Hall**
is an imprint of

www.pearsonhighered.com

ISBN-13: 978-0-13-602334-0
ISBN-10: 0-13-602334-7

# Contents for Study Guide

With
*Financial Accounting*
Student Text, Study Resources,
and MyAccountingLab
students will have more
**"I get it!"**
moments!

# Students will "get it" anytime, anywhere

Students understand (or "get it") right after you do a problem in class. Once they leave the classroom, however, students often struggle to complete the homework on their own. This frustration can cause students to quit on the material altogether and fall behind in the course, resulting in an entire class falling behind as the instructor attempts to keep everyone on the same page.

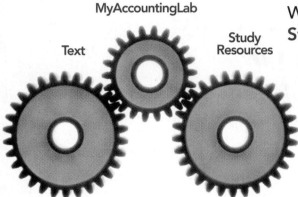

MyAccountingLab

Text

Study Resources

With the *Financial Accounting,* Eighth Edition, **Student Learning System,** all the features of the student textbook, study resources, and online homework system are designed to work together to provide students with the consistency, repetition, and high level of detail that will keep both instructors and students on track, providing more "I get it!" moments inside and outside the classroom.

## Replicating the Classroom Experience with Demo Doc Examples

The Demo Doc examples consist of entire problems, worked through step-by-step, from start to finish, narrated with the kind of comments that instructors would say in class. The Demo Docs are available in the accounting cycle chapters of the text and in the study guide. In addition to the printed Demo Docs, Flash-animated versions are available so that students can watch the problems as they are worked through while listening to the explanations and details. Demo Docs will aid students when they are trying to solve exercises and problems on their own, duplicating the classroom experience outside of class.

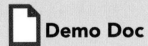

## Demo Doc

### Debit/Credit Transaction Analysis

*Demo Doc: To make sure you understand this material, work through the following demonstration "demo doc" with detailed comments to help you see the concept within the framework of a worked-through problem.*

*Learning Objectives 1, 2, 3, 4*

On September 1, 2008, Michael Moe incorporated Moe's Mowing, Inc., a company that provides mowing and landscaping services. During the month of September, the business incurred the following transactions:

a. To begin operations, Michael deposited $10,000 cash in the business's bank account. The business received the cash and issued common stock to Michael.

b. The business purchased equipment for $3,500 on account.

c. The business purchased office supplies for $800 cash.

d. The business provided $2,600 of services to a customer on account.

e. The business paid $500 cash toward the equipment previously purchased on account in transaction b.

f. The business received $2,000 in cash for services provided to a new customer.

g. The business paid $200 cash to repair equipment.

h. The business paid $900 cash in salary expense.

i. The business received $2,100 cash from a customer on account.

j. The business paid cash dividends of $1,500.

# with the Student Learning System!

**Consistency, Repetition, and a High Level of Detail Throughout the Learning Process**
The concepts, materials, and practice problems are presented with clarity and consistency across all mediums—textbook, study resources, and online homework system. No matter which platform students use they will continually experience the same look, feel, and language, minimizing confusion and ensuring clarity.

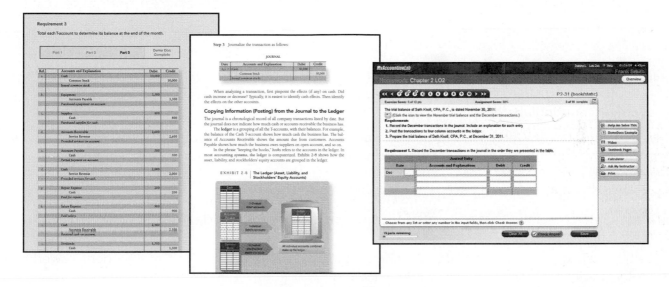

**Experiencing the Power of Practice with MyAccountingLab:** www.myaccountinglab.com
MyAccountingLab is an online homework system that gives students more "I get it!" moments through the power of practice. With MyAccountingLab, students can

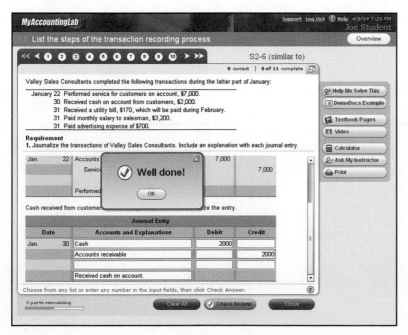

- work on problems assigned by the instructor that are either exact matches or algorithmic versions of the end-of-chapter material.
- use the Study Plan for self-assessment and customized study outlines.
- use the Help Me Solve This for a step-by-step tutorial.
- view the Demo Docs example to see an animated demonstration of where the numbers came from.
- watch a video to see additional information pertaining to the lecture.
- open textbook pages to find the material they need to get help on specific problems.

# Student Resources

**Study Guide and Study Guide CD with Demo Docs**

This chapter-by-chapter learning aid helps students get the maximum benefit from their study time. For each chapter there is an explanation of each Learning Objective; additional Demo Docs; Quick Practice, True/False, and Multiple Choice questions; Quick Exercises; and Do It Yourself questions, all with solutions. Flash-animated Demo Docs are available on the accompanying study guide CD so students can easily refer to them when needed.

www.myaccountinglab.com

MyAccountingLab is Web-based tutorial and assessment software for accounting that gives students more "I get it!" moments. **MyAccountingLab** provides students with a personalized interactive learning environment where they can complete their course assignments with immediate tutorial assistance, learn at their own pace, and measure their progress.

In addition to completing assignments and reviewing tutorial help, students have access to the following resources in **MyAccountingLab**:

- Pearson eText
- Study Guide
- Animated Demo Docs
- General Ledger Student Data Files
- Excel in Practice
- Videos and MP3 files
- Audio and Student PowerPoints
- Working Papers
- Flashcards

**Student Resource Web site: www.pearsonhighered.com/harrison**

- General Ledger Student Data Files
- Working Papers
- Excel in Practice

## Student Reference Cards

 **International Financial Reporting Standards Student Reference Card**

This four-page laminated reference card includes an overview of IFRS, why they matter and how they compare to U.S. standards, and highlights key differences between IFRS and U.S. GAAP.

 **Math for Accounting Student Reference Card**

This six-page laminated reference card provides students with a study tool for the basic math they will need to be successful in accounting, such as rounding, fractions, converting decimals, calculating interest, break-even analysis, and more!

 **Accounting Tips Student Reference Card**

This four-page laminated reference card illustrates the key steps in the accounting cycle.

# 1 The Financial Statements

## WHAT YOU PROBABLY ALREADY KNOW

You want to purchase a cell phone and service plan. It would be easy to visit the closest store and buy the phone and company service plan the salesperson recommends. But would that necessarily be the selection that best services your needs with the least cost? Perhaps not. Before making this decision, it might make sense to

1. gather information from reliable sources,
2. identify the various options and relevant costs,
3. evaluate the cost/benefit relationship of the different plans, and
4. make the decision.

Financial decisions require thoughtful analysis utilizing accurate, reliable, and relevant information. The choice may be finding the best investment for your savings, deciding to purchase or lease a car, or choosing the optimal cell-phone service plan. The process that is undertaken to manage our personal financial lives is the same as that employed by managers and owners of businesses. This chapter will explain the importance of accounting to the many users of financial information and how such data are accumulated and reported.

## Learning Objectives

 **Use accounting vocabulary**

**Accounting** is an information system that measures business activities, processes that information into reports, and communicates the results to decision makers. It is often referred to as the language of business. It's important as you begin your study of accounting to understand the basic accounting vocabulary. Make sure you review the list of interchangeable terms commonly used in accounting. *Review Exhibit 1-1 (p. 4) in the main text to observe the flow of information between accounting and related organizations and users. Compare the four forms of business organization in Exhibit 1-2 (p. 5).*

 **Learn underlying concepts, assumptions, and principles of accounting**

The basic accounting concepts and principles include the entity assumption, the historical cost principle, the going-concern assumption, and the stable-monetary-unit assumption. Make sure you understand these concepts and principles and how they are applied in the business world. These principles also apply to IFRS, International Financial Reporting Standards. The United States is expected to adopt IFRS rules within a few years. While much of U.S. GAAP is already consistent with IFRS, there are a few differences. *Review Global View: International Financial Reporting Standards in the text (pp. 10–12).*

### ③ Apply the accounting equation to business organizations

It is critical to understand each of the basic components of the **accounting equation:**

$$\text{Assets} = \text{Liabilities} + \text{Stockholders' Equity}$$

*Review carefully "The Accounting Equation" section of the main text to understand these important components. Stockholders' equity can be confusing. Pay special attention to Exhibit 1-5 (p. 15), which summarizes the types of transactions that affect Retained Earnings (a part of Stockholders' Equity).*

### ④ Evaluate business operations

Financial statements communicate important information necessary for users to make business decisions. Together the financial statements provide useful information to evaluate business operations.

### ⑤ Use information in financial statements to make business decisions, which are informed by economic, legal, and ethical guidelines

Financial statements include the income statement, statement of retained earnings, balance sheet, and statement of cash flows. The income statement calculates net income, which is used on the statement of retained earnings. The ending retained earnings number is used on the balance sheet. Many numbers from the balance sheet and income statement are used on the statement of cash flows. *Refer to Exhibit 1-11 (p. 27) to see the relationships among the four financial statements.* As the United States moves to adopt IFRS, managers and accountants will be required to place increasing emphasis on professional judgment. The financial statement numbers may become more dependent on these kinds of business decisions. Such decisions are based on economic factors, legal factors, and ethical factors. *Review Ethics in Business and Accounting Decisions (pp. 28–30) for a description of each of these factors.*

# Demo Doc 1

## Basic Transactions

*Learning Objectives 1–5*

After being in operation for one month, Rick's Deliveries, Inc., had the following information on August 31, 2009:

| | |
|---|---:|
| Cash | $2,500 |
| Accounts receivable | 1,700 |
| Supplies | 650 |
| Bicycles | 3,000 |
| Accounts payable | 1,475 |
| Common stock | 6,000 |
| Retained earnings | 0 |
| Dividends | 400 |
| Service revenue | 3,600 |
| Salary expense | 1,800 |
| Rent expense | 850 |
| Utilities expense | 175 |

## Requirements

1. Prepare the income statement, statement of retained earnings, and balance sheet of the business as of August 31, 2009.

2. Write the accounting equation of Rick's Deliveries, Inc.

3. Was the delivery service profitable for the month of August? Given this level of profit or loss, do you think the $400 of dividends paid was appropriate?

4. Rick's Deliveries, Inc., had adjustments to reconcile net income to net cash provided by operations of negative $875. During the month, the bicycles were purchased for cash, the common stock was issued for cash, and the dividends were paid in cash. Rick's cash balance at August 1, 2009, was $0. Prepare Rick's statement of cash flows for the month ended August 31, 2009.

# Demo Doc 1 Solutions

## Requirement 1

①  Use accounting
vocabulary

②  Learn underlying
concepts, assumptions, and principles
of accounting

⑤  Use information in
financial statements
to make business
decisions, which are
informed by economic,
legal, and ethical
guidelines

**Prepare the income statement, statement of retained earnings, and balance sheet of the business as of August 31, 2009.**

Remember that financial statements communicate important information necessary for users to make business decisions. An overview of the financial statements is as follows:

- **Income Statement**—Lists the revenues and expenses to determine net income or net loss for a period. Net income results if revenues exceed expenses; the reverse results in a net loss.

- **Statement of Retained Earnings**—Shows the changes in retained earnings during the period. Net income increases retained earnings; dividends and net losses decrease retained earnings.

- **Balance Sheet**—Lists the assets, liabilities, and stockholders' equity at a point in time, usually at the end of a month.

- **Statement of Cash Flows**—Report of cash receipts (inflows) and cash payments (outflows) for a period of time. (The statement of cash flows is covered in Chapter 12.)

The income statement is the first statement that should be prepared because the other financial statements rely on the net income (or loss) number calculated on the income statement.

The income statement lists all revenues and expenses. It uses the following formula to calculate net income:

$$\text{Revenues} - \text{Expenses} = \text{Net income (or Net loss)}$$

So, to create an income statement, we only need to list the revenue accounts and then subtract the list of expense accounts to calculate net income.

Rick's has Service Revenue of $3,600. Rick's expenses are Rent Expense of $850, Salary Expense of $1,800, and Utilities Expense of $175. These amounts are listed on the income statement.

<table>
<tr><td colspan="3" align="center">Rick's Deliveries, Inc.<br>Income Statement<br>Month Ended August 31, 2009</td></tr>
<tr><td>Revenue:</td><td></td><td></td></tr>
<tr><td>Service revenue.................</td><td></td><td>$3,600</td></tr>
<tr><td></td><td></td><td></td></tr>
<tr><td>Expenses:</td><td></td><td></td></tr>
<tr><td>Salary expense..................</td><td>$1,800</td><td></td></tr>
<tr><td>Rent expense....................</td><td>850</td><td></td></tr>
<tr><td>Utilities expense ..............</td><td>175</td><td></td></tr>
<tr><td>Total expenses.................</td><td></td><td>2,825</td></tr>
<tr><td></td><td></td><td></td></tr>
<tr><td>Net income..........................</td><td></td><td>$ 775</td></tr>
</table>

Net income is used on the statement of retained earnings to calculate the new balance in the Retained Earnings account. This calculation uses the following formula:

Beginning retained earnings
+ Net income
− Dividends
= Ending retained earnings

Again, we just have to recreate this formula on the statement:

<table>
<tr><td colspan="2" align="center">Rick's Deliveries, Inc.<br>Statement of Retained Earnings<br>Month Ended August 31, 2009</td></tr>
<tr><td>Retained earnings, August 1, 2009.................</td><td>$ 0</td></tr>
<tr><td>Add: Net income for month ...........................</td><td>775</td></tr>
<tr><td></td><td>775</td></tr>
<tr><td>Less: Dividends ............................................</td><td>(400)</td></tr>
<tr><td>Retained earnings, August 31, 2009...............</td><td>$ 375</td></tr>
</table>

The ending retained earnings number is used on the balance sheet. The balance sheet is just a listing of all assets, liabilities, and equity, with the accounting equation verified at the bottom:

**Rick's Deliveries, Inc.**
**Balance Sheet**
**August 31, 2009**

| Assets | | Liabilities | |
|---|---|---|---|
| Cash | $2,500 | Accounts payable | $1,475 |
| Accounts receivable | 1,700 | | |
| Supplies | 650 | **Stockholders' Equity** | |
| Bicycles | 3,000 | | |
| | | Common stock | 6,000 |
| | | Retained earnings | 375 |
| | | Total stockholders' equity | 6,375 |
| | | Total liabilities and | |
| Total assets | $7,850 | stockholders' equity | $7,850 |

## Requirement 2

① Use accounting vocabulary

② Learn underlying concepts, assumptions, and principles of accounting

③ Apply the accounting equation to business organizations

**Write the accounting equation of Rick's Deliveries, Inc.**
The accounting equation is:

$$\text{Assets} = \text{Liabilities} + \text{Stockholders' Equity}$$

It is critical to understand each of these basic components:

- **Assets** are economic resources that should benefit the business in the future. Common examples of these would be cash, inventory, equipment, and furniture.

- **Liabilities** are debts or obligations to outsiders. The most common liability is an account payable, an amount owed to a supplier for goods or services. A note payable is a written promise of future payment and usually requires the payment of interest in addition to the repayment of the debt, unlike accounts payable.

- **Stockholders' equity** represents the stockholders' interest in the business. It is the amount remaining after subtracting liabilities from assets.

Rick's assets are Cash, Accounts Receivable, Supplies, and Bicycles. Total assets are:

Cash of $2,500 + Accounts Receivable of $1,700 + Supplies of $650 + Bicycles of $3,000 = Total Assets of $7,850

Rick's has only one liability: Accounts Payable of $1,475. So total liabilities = $1,475.

Rick's equity consists of common stock and retained earnings. Total equity is:

Common Stock of $6,000 + Retained Earnings of $375 = Total Equity of $6,375

So Rick's accounting equation is:

Assets of $7,850 = Liabilities of $1,475 + Stockholders' Equity of $6,375

## Requirement 3

**Was the delivery service profitable for the month of August? Given this level of profit or loss, do you think the $400 of dividends paid was appropriate?**

Evaluating business performance is critical to making sound business decisions. For example, reviewing the income statement shows the results of operations, how much the business generated in net income, or if it incurred a net loss. The statement of retained earnings indicates what caused the change in retained earnings for the period. The balance sheet is a statement of financial condition or financial position, which includes the ending stockholders' equity. The statement of cash flows would identify the cash receipts and cash payments from operating, investing, and financing activities.

From the income statement prepared in Requirement 1, we can see that the delivery service earned $775 of profit during the month of August. The $400 of dividends seems like it might be high given that it is more than half the amount of profit earned during the month.

① Use accounting vocabulary

② Learn underlying concepts, assumptions, and principles of accounting

④ Evaluate business operations

## Requirement 4

**Rick's Deliveries, Inc., had adjustments to reconcile net income to net cash provided by operations of negative $875. During the month, the bicycles were purchased for cash, the common stock was issued for cash, and the dividends were paid in cash. Rick's cash balance at August 1, 2009, was $0. Prepare Rick's statement of cash flows for the month ended August 31, 2009.**

The first component of a statement of cash flows is the net cash provided by operating activities. This number is found by taking net income and adding or subtracting various adjustments. You will learn more about these adjustments, and how they are calculated, in Chapter 12.

④ Evaluate business operations

⑤ Use information in financial statements to make business decisions, which are informed by economic, legal, and ethical guidelines

We know from preparing the income statement that net income is $775, and the question tells us that the necessary adjustments are negative $875. So,

> Net Cash Provided by Operating Activities = Net Income + Adjustments
>
> Net Cash Provided by Operating Activities = $775 − $875 = $(100)

Next on the statement of cash flows is cash used for investing activities. Investing activities deal with the purchase and sale of assets that will be in use for many years. In this question, the only investing activity is the purchase of the bicycles for cash of $3,000. Because purchasing assets uses up cash, this is a negative number. So, net cash used for investing activities = $(3,000).

The last component of cash flow is net cash provided by financing activities. This includes taking out debt (as well as paying it off), issuing common stock, and paying dividends. In this question, the company issued common stock for $6,000 cash (which would increase cash flow) and paid dividends of $400 (which would decrease cash flow). So, net cash provided by financing activities = $6,000 − $400 = $5,600.

Combining these three amounts gives us cash flow. If we add the cash flow to the beginning Cash balance (which, in this case, is $0), then we can calculate the Cash balance at the end of the period.

**Rick's Deliveries, Inc.**
**Statement of Cash Flows**
Month Ended August 31, 2009

| | |
|---|---:|
| Net cash used by operating activities...................... | $  (100) |
| Net cash used by investing activities....................... | (3,000) |
| Net cash provided by financing activities ............... | 5,600 |
| | |
| Net increase in cash (cash flow) ............................. | 2,500 |
| Beginning cash balance........................................... | 0 |
| Ending cash balance................................................ | $ 2,500 |

Notice that the ending Cash balance is $2,500, which is the same number reported on the balance sheet.

### DEMO DOC COMPLETE

# Quick Practice Questions

## True/False

_____ 1. Financial accounting produces financial information and reports to be used by managers inside a business.

_____ 2. A partnership can have two or more owners.

_____ 3. In a Limited Liability Company (LLC) the owner is personally liable for the company's debts.

_____ 4. Most companies and many individuals have established standards for themselves to behave in an ethical manner.

_____ 5. A corporation's owners are called shareholders.

_____ 6. An advantage of a corporation is that it is a separate legal entity.

_____ 7. Accounts payable are amounts owed to other entities.

_____ 8. The entity assumption separates business transactions from personal transactions.

_____ 9. A business has a net loss when total revenues are greater than total expenses.

_____ 10. The statement of cash flows reports the cash coming in and going out.

_____ 11. The most commonly used accounting practices under U.S. GAAP are essentially the same under IFRS.

_____ 12. The three factors that influence business and accounting decisions are equality, legal, and ethical.

# Multiple Choice

1. **What is the private organization that is primarily responsible for formulating accounting standards?**
   a. The Internal Revenue Service
   b. The Securities and Exchange Commission
   c. The American Institute of Certified Public Accountants
   d. The Financial Accounting Standards Board

2. **Which accounting assumption or principle assumes that the entity will remain in operation for the foreseeable future?**
   a. The entity assumption
   b. The going-concern assumption
   c. The historical cost principle
   d. The stable-monetary-unit assumption

3. **Financial accounting provides financial statements and financial information that are intended to be used by whom?**
   a. Management of the company
   b. Potential investors
   c. Employees of the company
   d. The board of directors

4. **What is the purpose of financial accounting information?**
   a. Help managers plan and control business operations
   b. Comply with the IRS rules
   c. Help investors, creditors, and others make decisions
   d. Provide information to employees

5. **Which accounting assumption or principle allows accountants to ignore inflation when preparing financial statements?**
   a. The entity assumption
   b. The going-concern assumption
   c. The historical cost principle
   d. The stable-monetary-unit assumption

6. **Sue Mason owns a bagel shop. Sue includes her personal home, car, and boat on the books of her business. Which of the following is violated?**
   a. The entity assumption
   b. The continuity (going-concern) assumption
   c. The historical cost principle
   d. The stable-monetary-unit assumption

7. **Which of the following is the accounting equation?**
   a. Assets – Liabilities = Stockholders' equity
   b. Assets + Liabilities = Stockholders' equity
   c. Assets = Liabilities + Stockholders' equity
   d. Assets + Liabilities = Net income

8. **If the assets of a business are \$410,000 and the liabilities total \$200,000, how much is the stockholders' equity?**
   a. $150,000
   b. $160,000
   c. $210,000
   d. $610,000

9. **Which financial statement shows revenues and expenses?**
   a. Balance sheet
   b. Statement of retained earnings
   c. Income statement
   d. Statement of cash flows

10. **What is the claim of a business owner to the assets of the business called?**
    a. Liabilities
    b. Stockholders' equity
    c. Revenue
    d. Dividends

11. **What is a major difference between U.S. GAAP and IFRS?**
    a. Use of LIFO is disallowed under IFRS.
    b. U.S. GAAP is more "rules-based," while IFRS is more "professional judgment based."
    c. U.S. GAAP uses the historical cost principle to value most assets, while IFRS uses the fair value approach.
    d. All of the above.

12. **What is the factor influencing business decisions that recognizes that legal and profitable actions may not always be right?**
    a. The economic factor
    b. The legal factor
    c. The ethical factor
    d. The political factor

## Quick Exercises

**1-1. Fill in the statements that follow with the correct type of business organization.**

a. A _____ is a separate legal entity approved by the state.

b. A _____ is an entity with one owner where the business, and not the owner, is liable for the company's debts.

c. A _____ is an entity with two or more owners who are personally liable for the company's debts.

**1-2. Match the following terms with the best description.**

a. Entity assumption
b. Faithful representation
c. Historical cost principle
d. Continuity (going-concern) assumption
e. Stable-monetary-unit assumption

_____ 1. An organization or part of an organization is separate from other organizations and individuals.

_____ 2. An item should be recorded at the actual amount paid.

_____ 3. An entity is expected to remain in business in the future.

_____ 4. Assumption that the dollar's purchasing power is constant.

_____ 5. Accounting data should be neutral, unbiased information that can be confirmed by others.

**1-3. Determine the missing amounts:**

a. Assets = $50,000; Liabilities = $30,000; Stockholders' Equity = _____?

b. Liabilities = $35,000; Stockholders' Equity = $75,000; Assets = _____?

c. Assets = $105,000; Stockholders' Equity = $50,000; Liabilities = _____?

**1-4. On which of the following three financial statements would you expect to find the items (a)–(f)?**

Income Statement (IS)
Balance Sheet (BS)
Statement of Cash Flows (CF)

a. _____ Office supplies

b. _____ Service revenue

c. _____ Collections from customer

d. _____ Utilities expense

e. _____ Payments to suppliers

f. _____ Accounts payable

# Do It Yourself! Question 1

Jennifer Hill incorporated Jennifer's Laundromat, Inc., on October 1, 2011. Jennifer had the following information on October 31, 2011.

| | |
|---|---|
| Cash...................................... | $ 4,350 |
| Accounts receivable................ | 1,450 |
| Supplies.................................. | 500 |
| Furniture................................ | 9,000 |
| Accounts payable ................... | 3,350 |
| Common stock........................ | 10,000 |
| Retained earnings.................. | 1,000 |
| Dividends............................... | 1,000 |
| Service revenue...................... | 6,200 |
| Salary expense........................ | 1,500 |
| Rent expense.......................... | 1,000 |
| Utilities expense .................... | 750 |

## Requirements

1. Prepare the income statement, statement of retained earnings, and balance sheet of the business as of October 31, 2011.

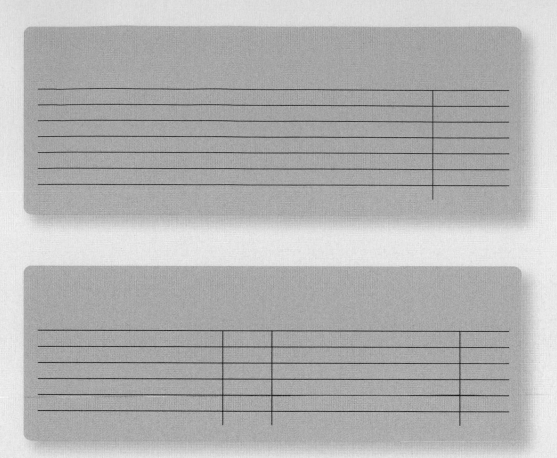

2. Write the accounting equation of Jennifer's Laundromat, Inc., at October 31, 2011.

# Quick Practice Solutions

## True/False

F    1. Financial accounting produces financial information and reports to be used by managers inside a business.

       False—Financial accounting produces information for people *outside* the company. (p. 4)

T    2. A partnership can have two or more owners. (p. 5)

F    3. In a Limited Liability Company (LLC) the owner is personally liable for the company's debts.

       False—The business (and not the owner) is responsible for the company's debts in a Limited Liability Company. (p. 6)

T    4. Most companies and many individuals have established standards for themselves to behave in an ethical manner. (p. 29)

T    5. A corporation's owners are called shareholders. (p. 6)

T    6. An advantage of a corporation is that it is a separate legal entity. (p. 6)

T    7. Accounts payable are amounts owed to other entities. (p. 23)

T    8. The entity assumption separates business transactions from personal transactions. (p. 8)

F    9. A business has a net loss when total revenues are greater than total expenses.

       False—A business has *net income* when total revenues are greater than total expenses. (p. 15)

T    10. The statement of cash flows reports the cash coming in and going out. (p. 24)

T    11. The most commonly used accounting practices under U.S. GAAP are essentially the same under IFRS. (p. 11)

F    12. The three factors that influence business and accounting decisions are equality, legal, and ethical.

       False—The three factors that influence business and accounting decisions are *economic*, legal, and ethical. (p. 29)

# Multiple Choice

1. **What is the private organization that is primarily responsible for formulating accounting standards?** (p. 7)
   a. The Internal Revenue Service
   b. The Securities and Exchange Commission
   c. The American Institute of Certified Public Accountants
   d. The Financial Accounting Standards Board

2. **Which accounting assumption or principle assumes that the entity will remain in operation for the foreseeable future?** (p. 9)
   a. The entity assumption
   b. The going-concern assumption
   c. The historical cost principle
   d. The stable-monetary-unit assumption

3. **Financial accounting provides financial statements and financial information that are intended to be used by whom?** (p. 4)
   a. Management of the company
   b. Potential investors
   c. Employees of the company
   d. The board of directors

4. **What is the purpose of financial accounting information?** (p. 4)
   a. Help managers plan and control business operations
   b. Comply with the IRS rules
   c. Help investors, creditors, and others make decisions
   d. Provide information to employees

5. **Which accounting assumption or principle allows accountants to ignore inflation when preparing financial statements?** (p. 8)
   a. The entity assumption
   b. The going-concern assumption
   c. The historical cost principle
   d. The stable-monetary-unit assumption

6. **Sue Mason owns a bagel shop. Sue includes her personal home, car, and boat on the books of her business. Which of the following is violated?** (p. 8)
   a. The entity assumption
   b. The continuity (going-concern) assumption
   c. The historical cost principle
   d. The stable-monetary-unit assumption

7. **Which of the following is the accounting equation?** (p. 13)
   a. Assets − Liabilities = Stockholders' equity
   b. Assets + Liabilities = Stockholders' equity
   c. Assets = Liabilities + Stockholders' equity
   d. Assets + Liabilities = Net income

8. **If the assets of a business are $410,000 and the liabilities total $200,000, how much is the stockholders' equity? (p. 13)**
   a. $150,000
   b. $160,000
   c. $210,000
   d. $610,000

9. **Which financial statement shows revenues and expenses? (p. 16)**
   a. Balance sheet
   b. Statement of retained earnings
   c. Income statement
   d. Statement of cash flows

10. **What is the claim of a business owner to the assets of the business called? (p. 13)**
    a. Liabilities
    b. Stockholders' equity
    c. Revenue
    d. Dividends

11. **What is a major difference between U.S. GAAP and IFRS? (pp. 11–12)**
    a. Use of LIFO is disallowed under IFRS.
    b. U.S. GAAP is more "rules-based," while IFRS is more "professional judgment based."
    c. U.S. GAAP uses the historical cost principle to value most assets, while IFRS uses the fair value approach.
    d. All of the above.

12. **What is the factor influencing business decisions that recognizes that legal and profitable actions may not always be right? (p. 29)**
    a. The economic factor
    b. The legal factor
    c. The ethical factor
    d. The political factor

# Quick Exercises

**1-1. Fill in the statements that follow with the correct type of business organization. (pp. 5–6)**

a. A <u>corporation</u> is a separate legal entity approved by the state.

b. A <u>limited-liability company</u> is an entity with one owner where the business, and not the owner, is liable for the company's debts.

c. A <u>partnership</u> is an entity with two or more owners who are personally liable for the company's debts.

**1-2. Match the following terms with the best description. (pp. 7–9)**

a. Entity assumption
b. Faithful representation
c. Historical cost principle
d. Continuity (going-concern) assumption
e. Stable-monetary-unit assumption

| | |
|---|---|
| _____a_____ | **1.** An organization or part of an organization is separate from other organizations and individuals. |
| _____c_____ | **2.** An item should be recorded at the actual amount paid. |
| _____d_____ | **3.** An entity is expected to remain in business in the future. |
| _____e_____ | **4.** Assumption that the dollar's purchasing power is constant. |
| _____b_____ | **5.** Accounting data should be neutral, unbiased information that can be confirmed by others. |

**1-3. Determine the missing amounts: (p. 13)**

a. Assets = $50,000; Liabilities = $30,000; Stockholders' Equity = $20,000   ($50,000 − $30,000)

b. Liabilities = $35,000; Stockholders' Equity = $75,000; Assets = $110,000   ($35,000 + $75,000)

c. Assets = $105,000; Stockholders' Equity = $50,000; Liabilities = $55,000   ($105,000 + $50,000)

**1-4. On which of the following three financial statements would you expect to find the items (a)–(f)? (pp. 16–24)**

Income Statement (IS)
Balance Sheet (BS)
Statement of Cash Flows (CF)

| | | |
|---|---|---|
| **a.** | BS | Office supplies |
| **b.** | IS | Service revenue |
| **c.** | CF | Collections from customer |
| **d.** | IS | Utilities expense |
| **e.** | CF | Payments to suppliers |
| **f.** | BS | Accounts payable |

# Do It Yourself! Question 1 Solutions

1. Prepare the income statement, balance sheet, and statement of stockholders' equity of the business as of October 31, 2011.

**Jennifer's Laundromat, Inc.**
**Income Statement**
**Month ended October 31, 2011**

| | | |
|---|---|---|
| Revenue: | | |
|     Service revenue................. | | $6,200 |
| | | |
| Expenses: | | |
|     Salary expense.................. | $1,500 | |
|     Rent expense.................... | 1,000 | |
|     Utilities expense .............. | 750 | |
|     Total expenses................. | | 3,250 |
| | | |
| Net income........................... | | $2,950 |

**Jennifer's Laundromat, Inc.**
**Statement of Retained Earnings**
**Month ended October 31, 2011**

| | |
|---|---|
| Retained earnings, October 1, 2011 ............... | $ 1,000 |
| | |
| Add: Net income for month ........................... | 2,950 |
| | 3,950 |
| | |
| Less: Dividends ............................................. | (2,000) |
| | |
| Retained earnings, October 31, 2011 ............. | $ 1,950 |

## Jennifer's Laundromat, Inc.
## Balance Sheet
## October 31, 2011

| Assets | | Liabilities | |
|---|---|---|---|
| Cash......................................... | $ 4,350 | Accounts payable ............................ | $ 3,350 |
| Accounts receivable................ | 1,450 | | |
| Supplies.................................... | 500 | **Stockholders' Equity** | |
| Furniture................................ | 9,000 | | |
| | | Common stock................................ | 10,000 |
| | | Retained earnings............................ | 1,950 |
| | | Total stockholders' equity .............. | 11,950 |
| | | | |
| | | Total liabilities and | |
| Total assets............................. | $15,300 | stockholders' equity ................... | $15,300 |

**2. Write the accounting equation of Jennifer's Laundromat, Inc., at October 31, 2011.**

Total Assets = $4,350 + $1,450 + $500 + $9,000 = $15,300

Total Liabilities = $3,350

Total Equity = $10,000 + $1,950 = $11,950

Assets of $15,300 = Liabilities of $3,350 + Equity of $11,950

# The Power of Practice

For more practice using the skills learned in this chapter, visit MyAccountingLab. There you will find algorithmically generated questions that are based on these Demo Docs and your main textbook's Review and Assess Your Progress sections.

Go to MyAccountingLab and follow these steps:

1. Direct your URL to www.myaccountinglab.com.
2. Log in using your name and password.
3. Click the MyAccountingLab link.
4. Click Study Plan in the left navigation bar.
5. From the table of contents, select Chapter 1, The Financial Statements.
6. Click a link to work tutorial exercises.

# 2 Transaction Analysis

## WHAT YOU PROBABLY ALREADY KNOW

If you have a checking account, you know that once a month you receive a statement from the bank. The statement shows the beginning cash balance, increases, decreases, and the ending cash balance. The account balance is the amount that the bank *owes* you, its customer. Your balance represents a *liability* to the bank. The deposits you make *increase* the bank's liability to you. The withdrawals or checks you write *decrease* that liability. Instead of using the terms *increase* and *decrease*, businesses have used a system of accounting for over 500 years with debits and credits. Either a debit *or* a credit may signify an increase to the account, *depending upon the type of account:* **asset**, **liability**, or **stockholders' equity**. Your checking account balance is a **liability** to your bank; does a debit or credit indicate an increase? When you take money out of the bank, it *decreases* the bank's liability to you because you've received back a portion of your account balance and it is shown as a *debit* on the bank statement. When you deposit money into your account, it *increases* the bank's liability to you and it is reflected as a *credit* on the bank statement. So, you can see that you probably already know that the rule for a liability account is that increases are shown as credits and decreases as debits.

## Learning Objectives

 **Analyze transactions**

A business **transaction** is an event that can be measured and affects any of the components of the accounting equation: assets, liabilities, or stockholders' equity. Use the accounting equation to record the effects of each business transaction. **Make sure that the amount of the increase or decrease on the left side of the equation (assets) is the same as that on the right side (liabilities and stockholders' equity.)** *This is a simple but crucial concept to understand.*

 **Understand how accounting works**

A business transaction affects two or more specific accounts. There are two sides to an account: the left (debit) side, and the right (credit) side. Remember that *debit only means left* and *credit only means right*. Increases are recorded on one side and decreases on the other. Depending on the type of account, a debit may indicate an increase **or** a decrease. Assets are on the left side of the equation; they increase on the left (debit) side. Liabilities and Stockholders' Equity are on the right side of the equation; they increase on the right (credit) side. *This is a basic concept, but crucial to understand. Review Exhibit 2-7 (p. 80) for the debit and credit rules.*

### ③ Record transactions in the journal

An event that impacts an entity's accounting information is called a *transaction*. These transactions are recorded using journal entries and the debit/credit system. You will practice recording transactions in Demo Doc 1. The more you practice this, the easier it will be to understand.

### ④ Use a trial balance

After transactions are recorded in the journal and posted to the ledger, a trial balance is prepared. The trial balance is a listing of all of the accounts with their balances. In a manual accounting system, it is useful as a check to determine that the total debits equal the total credits. If they are unequal, an error has been made and must be investigated before proceeding. *Review the trial balance in Exhibit 2-12 (p. 88).*

### ⑤ Analyze transactions using only T-accounts

Once you understand how the accounting system works, you will be able to use the information presented in T-accounts and on trial balances for use in daily business decision making.

# Demo Doc 1

## Debit/Credit Transaction Analysis

*Learning Objectives    1–4*

Knight Airlines, Inc., provides private plane transportation for businesspeople. Knight had the following trial balance on April 1, 2009:

**Knight Airlines, Inc.**
**Trial Balance**
**April 1, 2009**

| Account Title | Balance Debit | Balance Credit |
|---|---|---|
| Cash.......................................... | $50,000 | |
| Accounts receivable............... | 8,000 | |
| Accounts payable.................... | | $16,000 |
| Common stock........................ | | 12,000 |
| Retained earnings................... | | 30,000 |
| Total ...................................... | $58,000 | $58,000 |

During April, the business had the following transactions:

a. **Purchased a new airplane for $50,000. Knight paid $10,000 down and signed a note payable for the remainder.**

b. **Purchased supplies worth $1,000 on account.**

c. **Paid $5,000 on account.**

d. **Transported customers on its planes for fees totaling $25,000. The amount of $7,500 was received in cash with the remainder on account.**

e. **Received $18,000 on account.**

f. **Paid the following in cash: interest, $1,200; rent, $2,300; salaries, $7,000.**

g. **Received a bill for airplane repair costs of $3,500 that will be paid next month.**

h. **Knight paid its shareholders $6,000 of cash dividends.**

## Requirements

1. **Open the following accounts, with the balances indicated, in the ledger of Knight Airlines, Inc. Use the T-account format.**

   • **Assets**—Cash, $50,000; Accounts Receivable, $8,000; Supplies, no balance; Airplanes, no balance

   • **Liabilities**—Accounts Payable, $16,000; Notes Payable, no balance

- **Stockholders' Equity**—Common Stock, $12,000; Retained Earnings, $30,000; Dividends, no balance

- **Revenues**—Service Revenue, no balance

- **Expenses**—(none have balances) Interest Expense, Rent Expense, Salary Expense, Repairs Expense

2. **Journalize each transaction. Key journal entries by transaction letter.**

3. **Post to the ledger.**

4. **Prepare the trial balance of Knight Airlines, Inc., at April 30, 2009.**

# Demo Doc 1 Solutions

**Open the following accounts, with the balances indicated, in the ledger of Knight Airlines, Inc. Use the T-account format.**

- **Assets**—Cash, $50,000; Accounts Receivable, $8,000; Supplies, no balance; Airplanes, no balance

- **Liabilities**—Accounts Payable, $16,000; Notes Payable, no balance

- **Stockholders' Equity**—Common Stock, $12,000; Retained Earnings, $30,000; Dividends, no balance

- **Revenues**—Service Revenue, no balance

- **Expenses**—(none have balances) Interest Expense, Rent Expense, Salary Expense, Repairs Expense

Remember, an **account** is a record showing increases, decreases, and the balance of a particular asset, liability, or stockholders' equity. A T-account is a visual diagram of the additions and subtractions made to the accounts.

Opening a T-account simply means drawing a blank account (the "T") and putting the account title on top. To help find the accounts later, they are usually organized into assets, liabilities, stockholders' equity, revenue, and expenses (in that order). If the account has a starting balance, it *must* be put in on the correct side.

Remember that debits are always on the left side of the T-account and credits are always on the right side. This is true for *every* account.

The correct side for the balance is the side of *increase* in the account (unless you are specifically told differently in the question). This is because we expect all accounts to have a *positive* balance (that is, more increases than decreases).

For assets, an increase is a debit, so we would expect all assets to have a debit balance. For liabilities and stockholders' equity, an increase is a credit, so we would expect all of these accounts to have a credit balance. By the same reasoning, we expect revenues to have a credit balance and expenses and dividends to have a debit balance.

The balances listed in Requirement 1 are simply the amounts from the starting trial balance. We actually did not need to be told how much to put in each account because we could have read the numbers directly from the April 1 trial balance.

① Analyze transactions

② Understand how accounting works

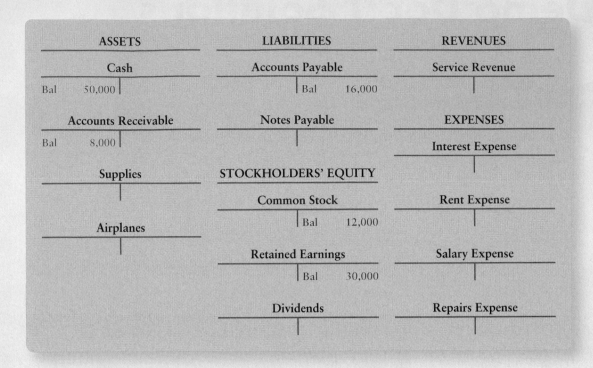

| ASSETS | LIABILITIES | REVENUES |
|---|---|---|
| **Cash** | **Accounts Payable** | **Service Revenue** |
| Bal 50,000 | Bal 16,000 | |
| **Accounts Receivable** | **Notes Payable** | **EXPENSES** |
| Bal 8,000 | | **Interest Expense** |
| **Supplies** | **STOCKHOLDERS' EQUITY** | |
| | **Common Stock** | **Rent Expense** |
| **Airplanes** | Bal 12,000 | |
| | **Retained Earnings** | **Salary Expense** |
| | Bal 30,000 | |
| | **Dividends** | **Repairs Expense** |

## Requirement 2

① Analyze transactions

② Understand how accounting works

③ Record transactions in the journal

⑤ Analyze transactions using only T-accounts

### Journalize each transaction. Key journal entries by transaction letter.

Feel free to reference Exhibit 2-7 (p. 80 in text) for help in completing this exercise.

Business transactions are recorded in chronological order in a **journal**. Similar to journaling that you may do for a class or at home, it provides a history of events that have taken place over a period of time. The recorded data in the journal are copied into the two or more specific accounts affected by the business transaction.

Remember, the steps to analyzing a transaction are (1) specify the accounts affected and the type of account, and (2) determine whether the account is increased or decreased and apply the rules for debits and credits.

After you've done this analysis, the third and final step to record transactions in the journal is to (3) enter the debit account followed by indenting the credit account in the journal. Include a brief explanation of the transaction below the journal entry.

### a. Purchased a new airplane for $50,000. Knight paid $10,000 down and signed a note payable for the remainder.

The accounts involved are Airplanes, Cash, and Notes Payable. The airplane cost $50,000 and $10,000 was paid in cash, so that means that the note payable was for $50,000 – $10,000 = $40,000.

Airplanes (an asset) is increased, which is a debit. Cash (an asset) is decreased, which is a credit. Notes Payable (a liability) is increased, which is a credit.

| | | | |
|---|---|---|---|
| a. | Airplanes | 50,000 | |
| | Cash | | 10,000 |
| | Notes Payable (50,000 – $10,000) | | 40,000 |
| | *Purchased airplane.* | | |


28 Chapter 2 | Demo Doc 1 Solutions

## b. Purchased supplies worth $1,000 on account.

The accounts involved are Supplies and Accounts Payable. Supplies (an asset) is increased, which is a debit. Accounts Payable (a liability) is increased, which is a credit.

| b. | Supplies | 1,000 | |
|---|---|---|---|
| | Accounts Payable | | 1,000 |
| | *Purchased supplies.* | | |

## c. Paid $5,000 on account.

The accounts involved are Accounts Payable and Cash. Accounts Payable (a liability) is decreased, which is a debit. Cash (an asset) is decreased, which is a credit.

| c. | Accounts Payable | 5,000 | |
|---|---|---|---|
| | Cash | | 5,000 |
| | *Paid on account.* | | |

## d. Transported customers on its planes for fees totaling $25,000. Cash of $7,500 was received with the remainder on account.

Knight's business is flying customers to where they want to go. This means that transporting customers is "performing services" and the business earned service revenue. The other accounts involved are Cash (because cash was received) and Accounts Receivable (because some customers charged to their accounts). The total revenue was $25,000 and $7,500 was paid in cash. This means that $25,000 – $7,500 = $17,500 was charged to the customers' accounts.

Service Revenue (revenues) is increased, which is a credit. Cash (an asset) is increased, which is a debit. Accounts Receivable (an asset) is increased, which is a debit.

| d. | Cash | 7,500 | |
|---|---|---|---|
| | Accounts Receivable | 17,500 | |
| | Service Revenue | | 25,000 |
| | *Performed services on account and for cash.* | | |

## e. Received $18,000 on account.

The accounts involved are Cash and Accounts Receivable. Cash (an asset) is increased, which is a debit. Accounts Receivable (an asset) is decreased, which is a credit.

| e. | Cash | 18,000 | |
|---|---|---|---|
| | Accounts Receivable | | 18,000 |
| | *Received cash on account.* | | |

**f. Paid the following in cash: interest, $1,200; rent, $2,300; salaries, $7,000.**

The accounts involved are Interest Expense, Rent Expense, Salary Expense, and Cash.

Interest Expense, Rent Expense, and Salary Expense (all expenses) are all increased, which are debits. Cash (an asset) is decreased, which is a credit.

| | | | |
|---|---|---|---|
| f. | Interest Expense | 1,200 | |
| | Rent Expense | 2,300 | |
| | Salary Expense | 7,000 | |
| | Cash | | 10,500 |
| | *Paid expenses.* | | |

**g. Received a bill for airplane repair costs of $3,500 that will be paid next month.**

Repairs are not billed until *after* they have been performed. So the bill received was for repairs made *in the past*. This means that it is a *past* benefit and should be recorded as an expense. So the accounts involved are Repairs Expense and Accounts Payable.

Repairs Expense (an expense) is increased, which is a debit. Accounts Payable (a liability) is increased, which is a credit.

| | | | |
|---|---|---|---|
| g. | Repairs Expense | 3,500 | |
| | Accounts Payable | | 3,500 |
| | *Received repair bill.* | | |

**h. Knight paid its shareholders $6,000 of cash dividends.**

The accounts involved are Dividends and Cash. Dividends is increased, which is a debit. This results in a *decrease to stockholders' equity,* which is a debit. Cash (an asset) is decreased, which is a credit.

| | | | |
|---|---|---|---|
| h. | Dividends | 6,000 | |
| | Cash | | 6,000 |
| | *Cash dividends paid.* | | |

## Requirement 3

**Post to the ledger.**

The entire group of accounts is called the **ledger**. A manual system would have a book of account pages and a computerized system would have a printout of all of the accounts.

All amounts in the journal entries are put into the individual ledger T-accounts. Debits go on the left side and credits go on the right side.

To add up a T-account, total the debit/left side and total the credit/right side. Subtract the smaller number from the larger number and put the difference on the side of the larger number. This gives the *balance* in the T-account (the *net* total of both sides combined).

For example, with Accounts Receivable, the two numbers on the left side total $8,000 + $17,500 = $25,500. The credit/right side totals $18,000. The difference is $25,500 − $18,000 = $7,500. We put the $7,500 on the debit side because that was the side of the larger number of $25,500.

Another way to think of computing the balance of T-accounts is

① Analyze transactions

② Understand how accounting works

③ Record transactions in the journal

⑤ Analyze transactions using only T-accounts

> Beginning balance in T-account
> + Increases to T-account
> − Decreases to T-account
> _____
> T-account balance (total)

| ASSETS | | | | LIABILITIES | | | | REVENUES | | | |
|---|---|---|---|---|---|---|---|---|---|---|---|
| **Cash** | | | | **Accounts Payable** | | | | **Service Revenue** | | | |
| Bal | 50,000 | | | | | Bal | 16,000 | | | d. | 25,000 |
| | | a. | 10,000 | | | b. | 1,000 | | | Bal | 25,000 |
| | | c. | 5,000 | c. | 5,000 | | | | | | |
| d. | 7,500 | | | | | g. | 3,500 | **EXPENSES** | | | |
| e. | 18,000 | | | | | Bal | 15,500 | | | | |
| | | f. | 10,500 | | | | | **Interest Expense** | | | |
| | | h. | 6,000 | **Notes Payable** | | | | f. | 1,200 | | |
| Bal | 44,000 | | | | | a. | 40,000 | Bal | 1,200 | | |
| | | | | | | Bal | 40,000 | | | | |
| **Accounts Receivable** | | | | | | | | **Rent Expense** | | | |
| Bal | 8,000 | | | **STOCKHOLDERS' EQUITY** | | | | f. | 2,300 | | |
| d. | 17,500 | | | | | | | Bal | 2,300 | | |
| | | e. | 18,000 | **Common Stock** | | | | | | | |
| Bal | 7,500 | | | | | Bal | 12,000 | **Salary Expense** | | | |
| **Supplies** | | | | | | | | f. | 7,000 | | |
| b. | 1,000 | | | **Retained Earnings** | | | | Bal | 7,000 | | |
| Bal | 1,000 | | | | | Bal | 30,000 | | | | |
| | | | | | | | | **Repairs Expense** | | | |
| **Airplanes** | | | | **Dividends** | | | | g. | 3,500 | | |
| a. | 50,000 | | | h. | 6,000 | | | Bal | 3,500 | | |
| Bal | 50,000 | | | Bal | 6,000 | | | | | | |

② Understand how
accounting works

④ Use a trial balance

**Prepare the trial balance of Knight Airlines, Inc., at April 30, 2009.**

Knight Airlines, Inc.
Trial Balance
April 30, 2009

| Account Title | Balance | |
|---|---|---|
| | Debit | Credit |
| Cash........................................ | $ 44,000 | |
| Accounts receivable................ | 7,500 | |
| Supplies.................................... | 1,000 | |
| Airplanes................................. | 50,000 | |
| Accounts payable ................... | | $ 15,500 |
| Notes payable ......................... | | 40,000 |
| Common stock........................ | | 12,000 |
| Retained earnings................... | | 30,000 |
| Dividends................................ | 6,000 | |
| Service revenue....................... | | 25,000 |
| Salary expense......................... | 7,000 | |
| Repairs expense....................... | 3,500 | |
| Rent expense........................... | 2,300 | |
| Interest expense...................... | 1,200 | |
| Total ...................................... | $122,500 | $122,500 |

All of the debits and credits are now listed for the **trial balance**. A trial balance is a list of all of the account titles with their balances at the end of an accounting period. Review the illustration of a trial balance in Exhibit 2-12 (p. 88) of the main text. Again, the accounts are listed in the order of assets, liabilities, equity, revenues, and expenses for consistency.

**DEMO DOC COMPLETE**

# Quick Practice Questions

## True/False

_____  1. A ledger is a chronological record of transactions.

_____  2. A T-account is shaped like the letter "H."

_____  3. A liability is an economic resource that will benefit the business in the future.

_____  4. A note receivable is a written pledge that the customer will pay a fixed amount of money by a certain date.

_____  5. Posting is the process of transferring information from the trial balance to the financial statements.

_____  6. Salaries incurred are listed as expenses on the income statement.

_____  7. When a stockholder receives cash dividends from the business, assets and stockholders' equity increase.

_____  8. When a business makes a payment on account, assets decrease and liabilities increase.

_____  9. Every transaction affects only two accounts.

_____  10. T-accounts help to summarize transactions.

# Multiple Choice

1. **A business transaction is first recorded in which of the following?**
   a. T-account
   b. Journal
   c. Ledger
   d. Trial balance

2. **A trial balance is which of the following?**
   a. A record holding all the accounts
   b. A detailed record of the changes in a particular asset, liability, or stockholders' equity account
   c. A chronological record of transactions
   d. A list of all the accounts with their balances

3. **Which sequence of actions correctly summarizes the accounting process?**
   a. Prepare a trial balance, journalize transactions, post to the accounts
   b. Post to the accounts, journalize the transactions, prepare a trial balance
   c. Journalize transactions, post to the accounts, prepare a trial balance
   d. Journalize transactions, prepare a trial balance, post to the accounts

4. **Which of the following accounts increase with a credit?**
   a. Cash
   b. Common Stock
   c. Accounts Payable
   d. Both (b) and (c) increase when credited.

5. **A business makes a cash payment of $12,000 to a creditor. Which of the following occurs?**
   a. Cash is credited for $12,000.
   b. Cash is debited for $12,000.
   c. Accounts Payable is credited for $12,000.
   d. Both (a) and (c)

6. **Assets are which of the following?**
   a. Debts or obligations owed to creditors
   b. Economic resources that will benefit the entity in the future
   c. Stockholders' claim to the assets of the business
   d. Amounts earned by providing products or services

7. **Which account would normally have a credit balance?**
   a. Accrued Liabilities
   b. Notes Receivable
   c. Salary Expense
   d. Accounts Receivable

8. **Which of the following is the correct journal entry for a purchase of equipment for $50,000 cash?**

|    | Accounts | Dr | Cr |
|----|----------|-----|-----|
| a. | Equipment | 50,000 | |
|    | Cash | | 50,000 |
| | | | |
| b. | Equipment | 50,000 | |
|    | Retained Earnings | | 50,000 |
| | | | |
| c. | Accounts Receivable | 50,000 | |
|    | Equipment | | 50,000 |
| | | | |
| d. | Cash | 50,000 | |
|    | Equipment | | 50,000 |

9. **Which of the following is the correct journal entry for purchasing $5,000 worth of supplies on account?**

|    | Accounts | Dr | Cr |
|----|----------|-----|-----|
| a. | Supplies | 5,000 | |
|    | Cash | | 5,000 |
| | | | |
| b. | Accounts Payable | 5,000 | |
|    | Supplies | | 5,000 |
| | | | |
| c. | Supplies | 5,000 | |
|    | Accounts Payable | | 5,000 |
| | | | |
| d. | Cash | 5,000 | |
|    | Supplies | | 5,000 |

10. **Which of the following is the correct journal entry for providing $20,000 worth of consulting services for cash?**

|    | Accounts | Dr | Cr |
|----|----------|-----|-----|
| a. | Service Revenue | 20,000 | |
|    | Cash | | 20,000 |
| | | | |
| b. | Accounts Receivable | 20,000 | |
|    | Service Revenue | | 20,000 |
| | | | |
| c. | Accounts Receivable | 20,000 | |
|    | Cash | | 20,000 |
| | | | |
| d. | Cash | 20,000 | |
|    | Service Revenue | | 20,000 |

## Quick Exercises

**2-1. Indicate whether a debit or credit is required to record an increase for each of these accounts.**

| | |
|---|---|
| _____ Cash | _____ Furniture |
| _____ Accounts Payable | _____ Notes Payable |
| _____ Salary Expense | _____ Dividends |
| _____ Service Revenue | _____ Utilities Expense |

**2-2. Write a brief explanation for the following transactions:**

| | | Accounts | Dr | Cr |
|---|---|---|---|---|
| a. | | Cash | 10,000 | |
| | | Common Stock | | 10,000 |

| | | Accounts | Dr | Cr |
|---|---|---|---|---|
| b. | | Supplies | 500 | |
| | | Accounts Payable | | 500 |

| | | Accounts | Dr | Cr |
|---|---|---|---|---|
| c. | | Cash | 3,000 | |
| | | Service Revenue | | 3,000 |

| | | Accounts | Dr | Cr |
|---|---|---|---|---|
| d. | | Accounts Receivable | 2,000 | |
| | | Service Revenue | | 2,000 |

| | | Accounts | Dr | Cr |
|---|---|---|---|---|
| e. | | Accounts Payable | 300 | |
| | | Cash | | 300 |

**2-3. Identify each of the following as an asset, liability, stockholders' equity, revenue, or expense account. Also indicate the normal balance as a debit or credit.**

| | | Account | Normal Balance |
|---|---|---|---|
| a. | Building | _____ | _____ |
| b. | Accounts Payable | _____ | _____ |
| c. | Cash | _____ | _____ |
| d. | Accounts Receivable | _____ | _____ |
| e. | Notes Payable | _____ | _____ |
| f. | Supplies | _____ | _____ |
| g. | Utilities Expense | _____ | _____ |
| h. | Retained Earnings | _____ | _____ |
| i. | Dividends | _____ | _____ |

**2-4.** Journalize the following transactions for Ryerson, Inc., using these accounts: Cash, Accounts Receivable, Notes Receivable, Supplies, Accounts Payable, Notes Payable, Common Stock, Dividends, Service Revenue, Salaries Expense, Rent Expense, Utilities Expense.

**Mar 1**      Ryerson, Inc., received $50,000 cash from Sam Ryerson and issued common stock.

| Date | Accounts | Debit | Credit |
|------|----------|-------|--------|
|      |          |       |        |
|      |          |       |        |

**Mar 2**      Paid $3,000 for March rent.

| Date | Accounts | Debit | Credit |
|------|----------|-------|--------|
|      |          |       |        |
|      |          |       |        |

**Mar 4**      Purchased $825 of supplies on account.

| Date | Accounts | Debit | Credit |
|------|----------|-------|--------|
|      |          |       |        |
|      |          |       |        |

**Mar 5**      Performed $12,000 of services for a client on account.

| Date | Accounts | Debit | Credit |
|------|----------|-------|--------|
|      |          |       |        |
|      |          |       |        |

**Mar 8**      Paid salaries of $2,500.

| Date | Accounts | Debit | Credit |
|------|----------|-------|--------|
|      |          |       |        |
|      |          |       |        |

**Mar 15**     **Paid a $1,800 utilities bill.**

| Date | Accounts | Debit | Credit |
|------|----------|-------|--------|
|      |          |       |        |
|      |          |       |        |
|      |          |       |        |

**Mar 20**     **Signed a bank note and borrowed $15,000 cash.**

| Date | Accounts | Debit | Credit |
|------|----------|-------|--------|
|      |          |       |        |
|      |          |       |        |
|      |          |       |        |

**Mar 25**     **Received $10,000 from customers on account. (See the March 5 entry.)**

| Date | Accounts | Debit | Credit |
|------|----------|-------|--------|
|      |          |       |        |
|      |          |       |        |
|      |          |       |        |

**2-5.** Find the errors in the trial balance shown here and prepare a corrected trial balance using the form provided.

Coleman Copy Centers, Inc.
Trial Balance
March 31, 2011

| Account Title | Balance Debit | Balance Credit |
|---|---|---|
| Cash | $30,000 | |
| Accounts receivable | | $ 2,000 |
| Supplies | 600 | |
| Land | 50,000 | |
| Accounts payable | 2,600 | |
| Notes payable | | 35,000 |
| Common stock | | 20,000 |
| Retained earnings | | 22,550 |
| Dividends | | 2,400 |
| Service revenue | | 9,300 |
| Salary expense | | 2,500 |
| Rent expense | | 1,200 |
| Interest expense | | 500 |
| Utilities expense | | 250 |
| Total | $83,200 | $95,700 |

Coleman Copy Centers, Inc.
Trial Balance
March 31, 2011

| Account Title | Balance Debit | Balance Credit |
|---|---|---|
| Cash | | |
| Accounts receivable | | |
| Supplies | | |
| Land | | |
| Accounts payable | | |
| Notes payable | | |
| Common stock | | |
| Retained earnings | | |
| Dividends | | |
| Service revenue | | |
| Salary expense | | |
| Rent expense | | |
| Interest expense | | |
| Utilities expense | | |
| Total | | |

# Do It Yourself! Question 1

## Debit/Credit Transaction Analysis

Ted's Repair Shop, Inc., had the following trial balance on September 1, 2011:

### Ted's Repair Shop, Inc.
### Trial Balance
### September 1, 2011

| | Balance | |
|---|---|---|
| Account Title | Debit | Credit |
| Cash............................................ | $6,000 | |
| Accounts receivable................ | 1,200 | |
| Accounts payable .................... | | $ 700 |
| Common stock......................... | | 4,500 |
| Retained earnings.................... | | 2,000 |
| Total ........................................ | $7,200 | $7,200 |

## Requirements

1. Journalize each of the following transactions. Key journal entries by transaction letter.

a. **Performed repairs for customers and earned $800 in cash and $1,500 of revenue on account.**

| Date | Accounts | Debit | Credit |
|---|---|---|---|
| | | | |
| | | | |
| | | | |

b. **Paid $200 cash for supplies.**

| Date | Accounts | Debit | Credit |
|---|---|---|---|
| | | | |
| | | | |
| | | | |

**c. Borrowed $2,000 cash from City Bank.**

| Date | Accounts | Debit | Credit |
|------|----------|-------|--------|
|      |          |       |        |
|      |          |       |        |
|      |          |       |        |

**d. Paid $3,000 cash to purchase repair tools.**

| Date | Accounts | Debit | Credit |
|------|----------|-------|--------|
|      |          |       |        |
|      |          |       |        |
|      |          |       |        |

**e. Paid the following in cash: interest, $75; rent, $825; salaries, $1,000.**

| Date | Accounts | Debit | Credit |
|------|----------|-------|--------|
|      |          |       |        |
|      |          |       |        |
|      |          |       |        |

**f. Received a telephone bill of $100 that will be paid next month.**

| Date | Accounts | Debit | Credit |
|------|----------|-------|--------|
|      |          |       |        |
|      |          |       |        |
|      |          |       |        |

**g. Paid $500 on account.**

| Date | Accounts | Debit | Credit |
|------|----------|-------|--------|
|      |          |       |        |
|      |          |       |        |

**h. Received $1,100 on account.**

| Date | Accounts | Debit | Credit |
|------|----------|-------|--------|
|      |          |       |        |
|      |          |       |        |
|      |          |       |        |
|      |          |       |        |

**i. Cash dividends of $1,300 were paid to the stockholders.**

| Date | Accounts | Debit | Credit |
|------|----------|-------|--------|
|      |          |       |        |
|      |          |       |        |
|      |          |       |        |
|      |          |       |        |

2. Open the following accounts, with the balances indicated, in the ledger of Ted's Repair Shop, Inc. Use the T-account format. Use the blank T-accounts set up for you in part 3 of this question.

- **Assets**—Cash, $6,000; Accounts Receivable, $1,200; Supplies, no balance; Repair Tools, no balance

- **Liabilities**—Accounts Payable, $700; Notes Payable, no balance

- **Stockholders' Equity**—Common Stock, $4,500; Retained Earnings, $2,000; Dividends, no balance

- **Revenues**—Service Revenue, no balance

- **Expenses**—(none have balances) Interest Expense, Rent Expense, Salary Expense, Utilities Expense

### 3. Post all transactions in Requirement 1 to the ledger.

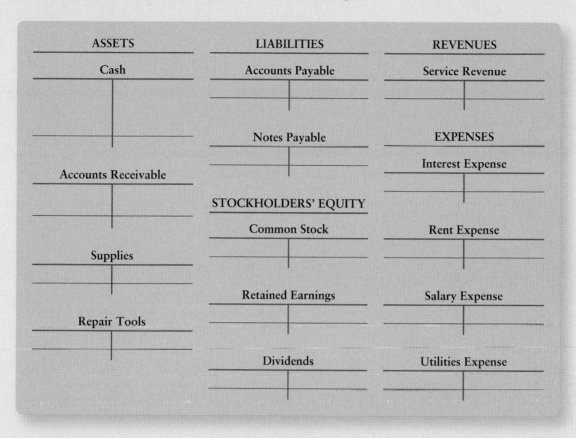

### 4. Prepare the trial balance of Ted's Repair Shop, Inc., at September 30, 2011.

Ted's Repair Shop, Inc.
Trial Balance
September 30, 2011

| Account Title | Balance | |
|---|---|---|
| | Debit | Credit |
| | | |
| | | |
| | | |
| | | |
| | | |
| | | |
| | | |
| | | |
| | | |
| | | |
| | | |
| | | |
| | | |
| | | |

# Quick Practice Solutions

## True/False

F    1. A ledger is a chronological record of transactions.

False—A journal contains a chronological record of transactions. A ledger is a collection of the accounts and summarizes their balances. (p. 81)

F    2. A T-account is shaped like the letter "H."

False—A T-account is shaped like the letter "T." (p. 77)

F    3. A liability is an economic resource that will benefit the business in the future.

False—An *asset* is an economic resource that will benefit the business in the future. (p. 66)

T    4. A note receivable is a written pledge that the customer will pay a fixed amount of money by a certain date. (p. 65)

F    5. Posting is the process of transferring information from the trial balance to the financial statements.

False—Posting is the process of transferring information from the *journal to the ledger.* (p. 81)

T    6. Salaries incurred are listed as expenses on the income statement. (p. 67)

F    7. When a stockholder receives cash dividends from the business, assets and stockholders' equity increase.

False—When a stockholder receives cash dividends from the business, assets and stockholders' equity *decrease.* (p. 71)

F    8. When a business makes a payment on account, assets decrease and liabilities increase.

False—When a business makes a payment on account, assets *decrease* and liabilities *decrease.* (p. 70)

F    9. Every transaction affects only two accounts.

False—Every transaction affects *at least* two accounts. Watch the wording here! Notice that the question uses the word *only* instead of *at least.* Can you describe a transaction that affects more than two accounts? (pp. 70, 77, 84)

T    10. T-accounts help to summarize transactions. (p. 77)

# Multiple Choice

1. **A business transaction is first recorded in which of the following? (p. 80)**
   a. T-account
   b. Journal
   c. Ledger
   d. Trial balance

2. **A trial balance is which of the following? (p. 87)**
   a. A record holding all the accounts
   b. A detailed record of the changes in a particular asset, liability, or stockholders' equity account
   c. A chronological record of transactions
   d. A list of all the accounts with their balances

3. **Which sequence of actions correctly summarizes the accounting process? (pp. 82, 88)**
   a. Prepare a trial balance, journalize transactions, post to the accounts
   b. Post to the accounts, journalize the transactions, prepare a trial balance
   c. Journalize transactions, post to the accounts, prepare a trial balance
   d. Journalize transactions, prepare a trial balance, post to the accounts

4. **Which of the following accounts increase with a credit? (p. 80)**
   a. Cash
   b. Common Stock
   c. Accounts Payable
   d. Both (b) and (c) increase when credited

5. **A business makes a cash payment of $12,000 to a creditor. Which of the following occurs? (p. 85)**
   a. Cash is credited for $12,000.
   b. Cash is debited for $12,000.
   c. Accounts Payable is credited for $12,000.
   d. Both (a) and (c)

6. **Assets are which of the following? (p. 65)**
   a. Debts or obligations owed to creditors
   b. Economic resources that will benefit the entity in the future
   c. Stockholder's claim to the assets of the business
   d. Amounts earned by providing products or services

7. **Which account would normally have a credit balance? (p. 91)**
   a. Accrued Liabilities
   b. Notes Receivable
   c. Salary Expense
   d. Accounts Receivable

8. **Which of the following is the correct journal entry for a purchase of equipment for $50,000 cash? (p. 83)**

| | | Accounts | Dr | Cr |
|---|---|---|---|---|
| a. | | Equipment | 50,000 | |
| | | Cash | | 50,000 |
| | | | | |
| b. | | Equipment | 50,000 | |
| | | Retained Earnings | | 50,000 |
| | | | | |
| c. | | Accounts Receivable | 50,000 | |
| | | Equipment | | 50,000 |
| | | | | |
| d. | | Cash | 50,000 | |
| | | Equipment | | 50,000 |

9. **Which of the following is the correct journal entry for purchasing $5,000 worth of supplies on account? (p. 83)**

| | | Accounts | Dr | Cr |
|---|---|---|---|---|
| a. | | Supplies | 5,000 | |
| | | Cash | | 5,000 |
| | | | | |
| b. | | Accounts Payable | 5,000 | |
| | | Supplies | | 5,000 |
| | | | | |
| c. | | Supplies | 5,000 | |
| | | Accounts Payable | | 5,000 |
| | | | | |
| d. | | Cash | 5,000 | |
| | | Supplies | | 5,000 |

10. **Which of the following is the correct journal entry for providing $20,000 worth of consulting services for cash? (p. 84)**

| | | Accounts | Dr | Cr |
|---|---|---|---|---|
| a. | | Service Revenue | 20,000 | |
| | | Cash | | 20,000 |
| | | | | |
| b. | | Accounts Receivable | 20,000 | |
| | | Service Revenue | | 20,000 |
| | | | | |
| c. | | Accounts Receivable | 20,000 | |
| | | Cash | | 20,000 |
| | | | | |
| d. | | Cash | 20,000 | |
| | | Service Revenue | | 20,000 |

# Quick Exercises

**2-1. Indicate whether a debit or credit is required to record an increase for each of these accounts. (p. 80)**

| | | | |
|---|---|---|---|
| _Dr_ | Cash | _Dr_ | Furniture |
| _Cr_ | Accounts Payable | _Cr_ | Notes Payable |
| _Dr_ | Salary Expense | _Dr_ | Dividends |
| _Cr_ | Service Revenue | _Dr_ | Utilities Expense |

**2-2. Write a brief explanation for the following transactions: (pp. 82–86)**

| | Accounts | Debit | Credit |
|---|---|---|---|
| a. | Cash | 10,000 | |
| | Common Stock | | 10,000 |

**a.** Issuance of common stock.

| | Accounts | Debit | Credit |
|---|---|---|---|
| b. | Supplies | 500 | |
| | Accounts Payable | | 500 |

**b.** Purchased supplies on account.

| | Accounts | Debit | Credit |
|---|---|---|---|
| c. | Cash | 3,000 | |
| | Service Revenue | | 3,000 |

**c.** Received cash for services performed.

| | Accounts | Debit | Credit |
|---|---|---|---|
| d. | Accounts Receivable | 2,000 | |
| | Service Revenue | | 2,000 |

**d.** Performed services on account.

| | Accounts | Debit | Credit |
|---|---|---|---|
| e. | Accounts Payable | 300 | |
| | Cash | | 300 |

**e.** Paid cash on account.

**2-3. Identify each of the following as an asset, liability, stockholders' equity, revenue, or expense account. Also indicate the normal balance as a debit or a credit. (pp. 65–67, 91)**

| | Account | Normal Balance |
|---|---|---|
| a. Building | *Asset* | *Debit* |
| b. Accounts Payable | *Liability* | *Credit* |
| c. Cash | *Asset* | *Debit* |
| d. Accounts Receivable | *Asset* | *Debit* |
| e. Notes Payable | *Liability* | *Credit* |
| f. Supplies | *Asset* | *Debit* |
| g. Utilities Expense | *Expense* | *Debit* |
| h. Retained Earnings | *Stockholders' Equity* | *Credit* |
| i. Dividends | *Stockholders' Equity* | *Debit* |

**2-4. Journalize the transactions for Ryerson, Inc., using these accounts: Cash, Accounts Receivable, Notes Receivable, Supplies, Accounts Payable, Notes Payable, Common Stock, Dividends, Service Revenue, Salaries Expense, Rent Expense, Utilities Expense. (pp. 82–86)**

**Mar 1**     **Ryerson, Inc., received $50,000 cash from Sam Ryerson and issued common stock.**

| Date | Accounts | Debit | Credit |
|---|---|---|---|
| Mar 1 | Cash | 50,000 | |
| | Common Stock | | 50,000 |

**Mar 2**     **Paid $3,000 for March rent.**

| Date | Accounts | Debit | Credit |
|---|---|---|---|
| Mar 2 | Rent Expense | 3,000 | |
| | Cash | | 3,000 |

**Mar 4**     **Purchased $825 of supplies on account.**

| Date | Accounts | Debit | Credit |
|---|---|---|---|
| Mar 4 | Supplies | 825 | |
| | Accounts Payable | | 825 |

**Mar 5**     **Performed $12,000 of services for a client on account.**

| Date | Accounts | Debit | Credit |
|---|---|---|---|
| Mar 5 | Accounts Receivable | 12,000 | |
| | Service Revenue | | 12,000 |

**Mar 8**     **Paid salaries of $2,500.**

| Date | Accounts | Debit | Credit |
|---|---|---|---|
| Mar 8 | Salary Expense | 2,500 | |
| | Cash | | 2,500 |

**Mar 15**    **Paid a $1,800 utilities bill.**

| Date | Accounts | Debit | Credit |
|---|---|---|---|
| Mar 15 | Utilities Expense | 1,800 | |
| | Cash | | 1,800 |

**Mar 20**    **Signed a bank note and borrowed $15,000 cash.**

| Date | Accounts | Debit | Credit |
|---|---|---|---|
| Mar 20 | Cash | 15,000 | |
| | Notes Payable | | 15,000 |

**Mar 25**    **Received $10,000 from customers on account. (See the March 5 entry.)**

| Date | Accounts | Debit | Credit |
|---|---|---|---|
| Mar 25 | Cash | 10,000 | |
| | Accounts Receivable | | 10,000 |

**2-5. Find the errors in the trial balance and prepare a corrected trial balance. (p. 88)**

**Coleman Copy Centers, Inc.**
**Trial Balance**
**March 31, 2011**

| Account Title | Debit | Credit |
|---|---|---|
| Cash | $30,000 | |
| Accounts receivable | 2,000 | |
| Supplies | 600 | |
| Land | 50,000 | |
| Accounts payable | | $ 2,600 |
| Notes payable | | 35,000 |
| Common stock | | 20,000 |
| Retained earnings | | 22,550 |
| Dividends | 2,400 | |
| Service revenue | | 9,300 |
| Salary expense | 2,500 | |
| Rent expense | 1,200 | |
| Interest expense | 500 | |
| Utilities expense | 250 | |
| Total | $89,450 | $89,450 |

# Do It Yourself! Question 1 Solutions

## Debit/Credit Transaction Analysis

### Requirements

1. **Journalize each of the following transactions. Key journal entries by transaction letter.**

| a. | Cash | 800 | |
|---|---|---|---|
| | Accounts Receivable | 1,500 | |
| | Service Revenue | | 2,300 |
| | *Performed services on account and for cash.* | | |

| b. | Supplies | 200 | |
|---|---|---|---|
| | Cash | | 200 |
| | *Purchased supplies.* | | |

| c. | Cash | 2,000 | |
|---|---|---|---|
| | Notes Payable | | 2,000 |
| | *Borrowed from bank.* | | |

| d. | Repair Tools | 3,000 | |
|---|---|---|---|
| | Cash | | 3,000 |
| | *Purchased repair tools.* | | |

| e. | Interest Expense | 75 | |
|---|---|---|---|
| | Rent Expense | 825 | |
| | Salary Expense | 1,000 | |
| | Cash | | 1,900 |
| | *Paid expenses.* | | |

| f. | Utilities Expense | 100 | |
|---|---|---|---|
| | Accounts Payable | | 100 |
| | *Received utility bill.* | | |

| g. | Accounts Payable | 500 | |
|---|---|---|---|
| | Cash | | 500 |
| | *Paid on account.* | | |

| h. | Cash | 1,100 | |
|---|---|---|---|
| | Accounts Receivable | | 1,100 |
| | *Received cash on account.* | | |

| i. | Dividends | 1,300 | |
|---|---|---|---|
| | Cash | | 1,300 |
| | *Cash dividends paid.* | | |

2. **Open the following accounts, with the balances indicated, in the ledger of Ted's Repair Shop, Inc. Use the T-account format (See solution to Requirement 3).**

- **Assets**—Cash, $6,000; Accounts Receivable, $1,200; Supplies, no balance; Repair Tools, no balance

- **Liabilities**—Accounts Payable, $700; Notes Payable, no balance

- **Stockholders' Equity**—Common Stock, $4,500; Retained Earnings, $2,000; Dividends, no balance

- **Revenues**—Service Revenue, no balance

- **Expenses**—(none have balances) Interest Expense, Rent Expense, Salary Expense, Utilities Expense

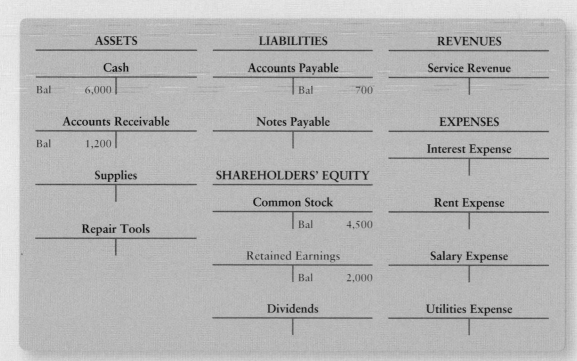

**3. Post all transactions in Requirement 1 to the ledger.**

## ASSETS

### Cash

| | | | |
|---|---|---|---|
| Bal | 6,000 | | |
| a. | 800 | | |
| | | b. | 200 |
| c. | 2,000 | | |
| | | d. | 3,000 |
| | | e. | 1,900 |
| | | g. | 500 |
| h. | 1,100 | | |
| | | i. | 1,300 |
| Bal | 3,000 | | |

### Accounts Receivable

| | | | |
|---|---|---|---|
| Bal | 1,200 | | |
| a. | 1,500 | | |
| | | h. | 1,100 |
| Bal | 1,600 | | |

### Supplies

| | | |
|---|---|---|
| b. | 200 | |
| Bal | 200 | |

### Repair Tools

| | | |
|---|---|---|
| d. | 3,000 | |
| Bal | 3,000 | |

## LIABILITIES

### Accounts Payable

| | | | |
|---|---|---|---|
| | | Bal | 700 |
| | | f. | 100 |
| g. | 500 | | |
| | | Bal | 300 |

### Notes Payable

| | | |
|---|---|---|
| | c. | 2,000 |
| | Bal | 2,000 |

## STOCKHOLDERS' EQUITY

### Common Stock

| | | |
|---|---|---|
| | Bal | 4,500 |
| | Bal | 4,500 |

### Retained Earnings

| | | |
|---|---|---|
| | Bal | 2,000 |

### Dividends

| | | |
|---|---|---|
| i. | 1,300 | |
| Bal | 1,300 | |

## REVENUES

### Service Revenue

| | | |
|---|---|---|
| | a. | 2,300 |
| | Bal | 2,300 |

## EXPENSES

### Interest Expense

| | | |
|---|---|---|
| e. | 75 | |
| Bal | 75 | |

### Rent Expense

| | | |
|---|---|---|
| e. | 825 | |
| Bal | 825 | |

### Salary Expense

| | | |
|---|---|---|
| e. | 1,000 | |
| Bal | 1,000 | |

### Utilities Expense

| | | |
|---|---|---|
| f. | 100 | |
| Bal | 100 | |

**4. Prepare the trial balance of Ted's Repair Shop, Inc., at September 30, 2011.**

**Ted's Repair Shop, Inc.**
**Trial Balance**
**September 30, 2011**

| Account Title | Debit | Credit |
|---|---|---|
| Cash........................................ | $ 3,000 | |
| Accounts receivable............... | 1,600 | |
| Supplies................................... | 200 | |
| Repair tools............................ | 3,000 | |
| Accounts payable ................... | | $ 300 |
| Notes payable ........................ | | 2,000 |
| Common stock....................... | | 4,500 |
| Retained earnings................... | | 2,000 |
| Dividends............................... | 1,300 | |
| Service revenue....................... | | 2,300 |
| Salary expense........................ | 1,000 | |
| Rent expense.......................... | 825 | |
| Utilities expense .................... | 100 | |
| Interest expense...................... | 75 | |
| Total ....................................... | $11,100 | $11,100 |

# The Power of Practice

For more practice using the skills learned in this chapter, visit MyAccountingLab. There you will find algorithmically generated questions that are based on these Demo Docs and your main textbook's Review and Assess Your Progress sections.

Go to MyAccountingLab and follow these steps:

1. Direct your URL to www.myaccountinglab.com.
2. Log in using your name and password.
3. Click the MyAccountingLab link.
4. Click Study Plan in the left navigation bar.
5. From the table of contents, select Chapter 2, Transaction Analysis.
6. Click a link to work tutorial exercises.

# 3 Accrual Accounting & Income

## WHAT YOU PROBABLY ALREADY KNOW

When you receive your car insurance bill, the period of coverage is always in the future. The bill may indicate that your payment must be received no later than 12:01 a.m. on the day after your current coverage expires to maintain your policy. Your payment is actually a *prepayment*, Prepaid Insurance. Prepaid Insurance is an asset because the insurance coverage is a future benefit. But every day that the car is protected by the insurance policy, part of the benefit is used up. When an asset is used up, it becomes an expense. Technically, every day you are incurring an expense of 1/365 of your annual premium. Assume that you paid $730 for an annual insurance policy in December 2010 for the period covering January 1–December 31, 2011. Each day beginning January 1, you are using up $2 ($730/365 days) of the prepaid insurance and incurring an expense or benefit of $2. At the end of January 1, what is your future benefit? It is $728 because you've benefited from the insurance coverage service you received that day. Technically, you have prepaid insurance with a reduced value of $728 and an expense of $2; the total $730 payment is split between the two accounts.

Each day there is an additional $2 expense and $2 less future value in the asset account. Although it would be too cumbersome to "adjust" these accounts on a daily basis, businesses will make adjustments to their records whenever financial statements are prepared.

## Learning Objectives

 **Relate accrual accounting and cash flows**

Consider this example: Assume that you have a pet care business; you care for pets in their owners' absence. You had a customer who went away the last week of December and returned on January 1. You charge $140 for the weekly service and are paid on January 1.

- If you are using **cash-basis accounting**, how much revenue would you record in December? In January? Because the cash is **received** in January, $140 would be recorded as revenue in January and none in December.
- If you are using **accrual-basis accounting**, how much revenue would you record in December? In January? Because the revenue is **earned** in December when you performed the services, that is the month you would record $140 of revenue; you wouldn't record any in January.

Review pages 139–140 in the text to reinforce the difference between the two methods of accounting.

 **Apply the revenue and matching principles**

Consider this example: Assume that the Cool Clothing store opened for business on May 15 and pays employees on the 1st and 15th of each month. Employees who worked May 15–31 will be paid on June 1; no payroll payments are made in May. Does this mean that there should be no wage or salary expense for the month of May? Is it fair that Cool Clothing reports the revenue from selling clothing without the related payroll expense? Customers would not be able to view and purchase the clothing without employees to stock the shelves and check out the customers. It makes sense to **match** the payroll expense for the month of May with the sales revenue. *This is a basic concept that is crucial to understand. See Exhibit 3-1 (p. 141) in the text for a sample business transaction illustrating the appropriate revenue recognition timing. Exhibit 3-2 (p. 142) illustrates the matching principle.*

 **Adjust the accounts**

Adjusting entries fall into one of three categories: deferrals, depreciation, or accruals. Each type of entry must adjust either a revenue or an expense account.

If you have determined that revenue needs to be credited, then an asset account must be debited (increased) or a liability account must be debited (decreased). If you have determined that an expense needs to be debited, then an asset account must be credited (decreased) or a liability must be credited (increased). **WATCH OUT:** For now, cash will **NEVER** be included in an adjusting journal entry. *Read pages 143–155 carefully for a review of the adjusting journal entry process.*

 **Prepare the financial statements**

Follow the flow of data from the adjusted trial balance in Exhibit 3-9 (p. 157) to the financial statements in *Exhibits 3-10 through 3-12 (p. 158).*

 **Close the books**

The revenue, expense, and Dividends accounts are temporary accounts; the account balances are zeroed (closed) out at the end of the year to get ready for journalizing transactions in the new year. The closing process also updates the ending retained earnings balance for the net income or net loss and dividends during the year. *Review pages 165–166 and Exhibit 3-13 (p. 166) to enhance your understanding of the closing process.*

 **Use two new ratios to evaluate a business**

The current ratio (p. 170) is a key liquidity measure. It indicates the amount of current assets that is available for each dollar of current liabilities. A higher ratio is usually considered to be preferable.

The debt ratio (p. 170) is an indicator of the entity's ability to pay its debt. It measures the portion of assets that is financed with debt.

# Demo Doc 1

## Adjusting Entries for Accrual Accounting

*Learning Objectives*    *1–6*

Woodson, Inc.'s, December 31, 2012 (year-end) trial balance (before adjustments) is as follows:

### Woodson, Inc.
### Trial Balance
### Year Ended December 31, 2012

| Account Title | Balance Debit | Balance Credit |
|---|---:|---:|
| Cash | $10,600 | |
| Accounts receivable | 14,000 | |
| Supplies | 1,200 | |
| Prepaid rent | 3,000 | |
| Furniture | 15,000 | |
| Accumulated depreciation—furniture | | $ 4,500 |
| Accounts payable | | 2,600 |
| Salary payable | | 0 |
| Common stock | | 10,000 |
| Retained earnings | | 30,000 |
| Dividends | 11,500 | |
| Service revenue | | 24,000 |
| Rent expense | 5,000 | |
| Salary expense | 10,000 | |
| Depreciation expense | 0 | |
| Supplies expense | 800 | |
| Total | $71,100 | $71,100 |

## Requirements

1. Open the T-accounts and enter their unadjusted balances.

2. Journalize the following adjusting entries at December 31, 2012. Key the entries by letter.

a. Employees are paid $200 every Friday for the previous five days of work. December 31, 2012, is a Monday.
b. Depreciation on the furniture is $1,500 for the year.
c. Supplies on hand at December 31, 2012, are $400.
d. Six months of rent ($3,000) was paid in advance on November 1, 2012. No adjustment has been made to the Prepaid Rent account since then.
e. Accrued revenue of $1,800 must be recorded.

3. Post the adjusting entries.

4. Would any of these entries be made under the cash basis of accounting? Why or why not?

5. Prepare an adjusted trial balance.

6. Prepare the income statement, statement of retained earnings, and balance sheet for Woodson, Inc.

7. Journalize and post the closing entries.

8. Calculate Woodson's current and debt ratios.

# Demo Doc 1 Solutions

## Requirement 1

Open the T-accounts and enter their unadjusted balances.

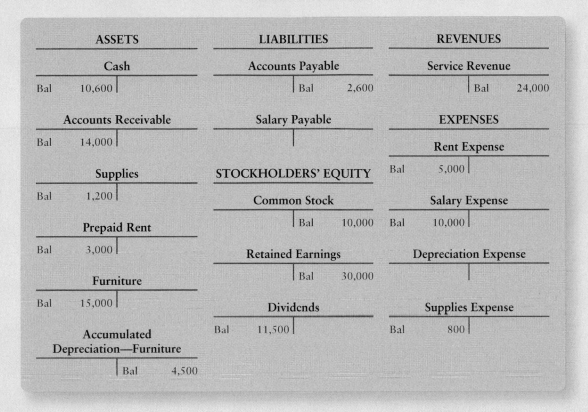

| ASSETS | LIABILITIES | REVENUES |
|---|---|---|
| **Cash** | **Accounts Payable** | **Service Revenue** |
| Bal 10,600 | Bal 2,600 | Bal 24,000 |
| **Accounts Receivable** | **Salary Payable** | **EXPENSES** |
| Bal 14,000 | | **Rent Expense** |
| **Supplies** | **STOCKHOLDERS' EQUITY** | Bal 5,000 |
| Bal 1,200 | **Common Stock** | **Salary Expense** |
| **Prepaid Rent** | Bal 10,000 | Bal 10,000 |
| Bal 3,000 | **Retained Earnings** | **Depreciation Expense** |
| **Furniture** | Bal 30,000 | |
| Bal 15,000 | **Dividends** | **Supplies Expense** |
| **Accumulated Depreciation—Furniture** | Bal 11,500 | Bal 800 |
| Bal 4,500 | | |

## Requirement 2

**Journalize the following adjusting entries at December 31, 2012. Key the entries by letter.**

There are five general types of adjusting entries.

- **Prepaid expenses** are assets that are paid for in advance and will be used up in the future, such as supplies, prepaid rent (see transaction **d**), and insurance. As the asset is used up, the asset account is reduced and an expense is recorded.
- **Depreciation** is the allocation of the plant asset cost over its useful life (see transaction **b**). All plant assets used in the operation of the business, except land, are depreciated. The asset loses usefulness over time and its value is reduced. The cost of the plant asset is not reduced directly. Accumulated Depreciation, a contra asset account, is used to record the loss of asset usefulness. Depreciation expense matches the revenue generated from sales made possible from the use of these assets that are depreciated.
- **Accrued expenses** are expenses the business has incurred but not yet paid. Common examples may be salaries (see transaction **a**) and utilities.

- **Accrued revenue** is revenue that has been earned but not collected in cash (see transaction **e**).
- **Unearned revenue** is a liability that results from receiving cash before earning it. The company owes the customer a product or a service in the future. When the product is delivered or the service is performed, the liability is reduced and the revenue is earned.

**a.  Employees are paid $200 every Friday for the previous five days of work. December 31, 2012, is a Monday.**

② Apply the revenue and matching principles

③ Adjust the accounts

If employees are paid $200 for five days of work, then they are paid $200/5 = $40 per day. By the end of the day on Monday, December 31, the employees have worked for one day and have not been paid. This means that Woodson owes employees $40 × 1 = $40 of salary at December 31.

If the salaries have not been paid, then they are pay*able* (or in other words, they are *owed*). This means that they must be recorded as some kind of payable account. Normally, we might consider using Accounts Payable, but this account is usually reserved for *bills* received. The employees do not send Woodson a bill. They simply expect to be paid and Woodson knows that the salaries are owed. This means that we put this into another payable account. In this case, Salary Payable is most appropriate.

Because salary is not owed until work is performed, we know that Woodson's employees have already worked. This is a *past* benefit, which means that we need to record an expense (in this case, Salary Expense).

There is an increase to Salary Expense (a debit) and an increase to the liability Salary Payable (a credit) of $40.

| a. | 2012 | Salary Expense (1 day × $200/5 days) | 40 | |
|---|---|---|---|---|
| | Dec 31 | Salary Payable | | 40 |
| | | *To accrue salary expense.* | | |

**b.  Depreciation on the furniture is $1,500 for the year.**

③ Adjust the accounts

The entry to record depreciation expense is *always* the same. It is only the *number* (dollar amount) in the entry that changes. There is always an increase to Depreciation Expense (a debit) and an increase to the contra asset account of Accumulated Depreciation (a credit). Because we are given the depreciation expense of $1,500, we simply write the entry with that amount.

| b. | 2012 | Depreciation Expense | 1,500 | |
|---|---|---|---|---|
| | Dec 31 | Accumulated Depreciation—Furniture | | 1,500 |
| | | *To record depreciation expense.* | | |

### c. Supplies on hand at December 31, 2012, are $400.

Before adjustments, there is $1,200 in the Supplies account. If only $400 of supplies remains, then the other $800 must have been used ($1,200 − $400 = $800).

Supplies are an asset, a *future* benefit to Woodson. Once the supplies are used, they are a *past* benefit. This means that they are no longer assets, so the Supplies asset must be decreased by $800 (a credit). *Past* benefits are expenses, so Supplies Expense must be increased (a debit).

② Apply the revenue and matching principles

③ Adjust the accounts

| c. | 2012 | Supplies Expense ($1,200 − $400) | 800 | |
|----|------|----------------------------------|-----|-----|
| | Dec 31 | Supplies | | 800 |
| | | *To record supplies used.* | | |

### d. Six months of rent ($3,000) was paid in advance on November 1, 2012. No adjustment has been made to the Prepaid Rent account since then.

Woodson prepaid $3,000 for six months of rent on November 1. This means that Woodson pays $3,000/6 = $500 a month for rent. At December 31, two months have passed since the prepayment, so two months of the prepayment have been used. The amount of rent used is 2 × $500 = $1,000.

When something is prepaid, it is a *future* benefit (an asset) because the business is now entitled to receive goods or services. Once those goods or services are received (in this case, once Woodson has occupied the building being rented), this becomes a *past* benefit and, therefore, an expense. This means that Rent Expense must be increased (a debit) and Prepaid Rent (an asset) must be decreased (a credit).

② Apply the revenue and matching principles

③ Adjust the accounts

| d. | 2012 | Rent Expense (2 months × $3,000/6 months) | 1,000 | |
|----|------|-------------------------------------------|-------|-------|
| | Dec 31 | Prepaid Rent | | 1,000 |
| | | *To record rent expense.* | | |

### e. Accrued revenue of $1,800 must be recorded.

Accrued revenue is another way of saying "accounts receivable" (or payment in the future). If accrued revenue is recorded, it means that accounts receivable is also recorded (that is, customers received goods or services from the business, but the business has not yet received the cash). The business is entitled to these receivables because the revenue has been earned.

Note that not all revenue is *accrued* revenue. This is *only* the revenue that is earned but not immediately received from the customer (that is, the accounts receivable). Revenues that are earned and received immediately in cash are *not* accrued revenues.

② Apply the revenue and matching principles

③ Adjust the accounts

Service Revenue must be increased by $1,800 (a credit) and the Accounts Receivable asset must be increased by $1,800 (a debit).

| e. | 2012 | Accounts Receivable | 1,800 | |
|----|------|---------------------|-------|-------|
| | Dec 31 | Service Revenue | | 1,800 |
| | | *To accrue revenue earned.* | | |

## Requirement 3

**Post the adjusting entries.**

### ASSETS

**Cash**

| Bal | 10,600 | |
|-----|--------|--|

**Accounts Receivable**

| | 14,000 | |
|-----|--------|--|
| e. | 1,800 | |
| Bal | 15,800 | |

**Supplies**

| | 1,200 | | |
|-----|-------|-----|-----|
| | | c. | 800 |
| Bal | 400 | | |

**Prepaid Rent**

| | 3,000 | | |
|-----|-------|----|-------|
| | | d. | 1,000 |
| Bal | 2,000 | | |

**Furniture**

| Bal | 15,000 | |
|-----|--------|--|

**Accumulated Depreciation—Furniture**

| | | | 4,500 |
|-----|--|-----|-------|
| | | b. | 1,500 |
| | | Bal | 6,000 |

### LIABILITIES

**Accounts Payable**

| | | Bal | 2,600 |
|--|--|-----|-------|

**Salary Payable**

| | | a. | 40 |
|--|--|-----|----|
| | | Bal | 40 |

### STOCKHOLDERS' EQUITY

**Common Stock**

| | | Bal | 10,000 |
|--|--|-----|--------|

**Retained Earnings**

| | | Bal | 30,000 |
|--|--|-----|--------|

**Dividends**

| Bal | 11,500 | |
|-----|--------|--|

### REVENUES

**Service Revenue**

| | | | 24,000 |
|--|--|-----|--------|
| | | e. | 1,800 |
| | | Bal | 25,800 |

### EXPENSES

**Rent Expense**

| | 5,000 | |
|-----|-------|--|
| d. | 1,000 | |
| Bal | 6,000 | |

**Salary Expense**

| | 10,000 | |
|-----|--------|--|
| a. | 40 | |
| Bal | 10,040 | |

**Depreciation Expense**

| b. | 1,500 | |
|-----|-------|--|
| Bal | 1,500 | |

**Supplies Expense**

| | 800 | |
|-----|-------|--|
| c. | 800 | |
| Bal | 1,600 | |

## Requirement 4

**Would any of these entries be made under the cash basis of accounting? Why or why not?**

Cash-basis accounting *only* records a journal entry when cash is involved. This means that there must be a line for cash in the journal entry in order for it to be recorded under the cash basis of accounting.

① Relate accrual accounting and cash flows

Because none of these adjusting entries deal with cash, none of them are relevant (that is, none of them would be recorded) under the cash basis of accounting.

On the other hand, accrual-basis accounting records revenue when it is earned and expenses when they are incurred. Revenue is earned when services are performed or goods are sold. Expenses are incurred when the service is received or the asset is used up. This method is in accordance with generally accepted accounting principles.

## Requirement 5

③ Adjust the accounts

**Prepare an adjusted trial balance.**

| Account Title | Trial Balance Dec 31, 2012 Debit | Credit | Adjustments Debit | Credit | Adjusted Trial Balance Dec 31, 2012 Debit | Credit |
|---|---|---|---|---|---|---|
| Cash | $10,600 | | | | $10,600 | |
| Accounts receivable | 14,000 | | e. $1,800 | | 15,800 | |
| Supplies | 1,200 | | | c. $ 800 | 400 | |
| Prepaid rent | 3,000 | | | d. 1,000 | 2,000 | |
| Furniture | 15,000 | | | | 15,000 | |
| Accumulated depreciation—furniture | | $ 4,500 | | b. 1,500 | | $ 6,000 |
| Accounts payable | | 2,600 | | | | 2,600 |
| Salary payable | | 0 | | a. 40 | | 40 |
| Common stock | | 10,000 | | | | 10,000 |
| Retained earnings | | 30,000 | | | | 30,000 |
| Dividends | 11,500 | | | | 11,500 | |
| Service revenue | | 24,000 | | e. 1,800 | | 25,800 |
| Rent expense | 5,000 | | d. 1,000 | | 6,000 | |
| Salary expense | 10,000 | | a. 40 | | 10,040 | |
| Depreciation expense | 0 | | b. 1,500 | | 1,500 | |
| Supplies expense | 800 | | c. 800 | | 1,600 | |
| Total | $71,100 | $71,100 | $5,140 | $5,140 | $74,440 | $74,440 |

## Requirement 6

**Prepare the income statement, statement of retained earnings, and balance sheet for Woodson, Inc.**

④ Prepare the financial statements

| Woodson, Inc. Income Statement Year Ended December 31, 2012 | | |
|---|---|---|
| Revenue: | | |
| Service revenue........................ | | $25,800 |
| | | |
| Expenses: | | |
| Salary expense......................... | $10,040 | |
| Rent expense............................ | 6,000 | |
| Supplies expense ..................... | 1,600 | |
| Depreciation expense .............. | 1,500 | |
| Total expenses......................... | | 19,140 |
| | | |
| Net income.................................. | | $ 6,660 |

Remember, the one account that has not yet been updated is Retained Earnings. The amount of $30,000 in this account is the amount from the beginning of the year (January 1). To update the account, we need to prepare the statement of retained earnings.

| Woodson, Inc. Statement of Retained Earnings Year Ended December 31, 2012 | |
|---|---|
| Retained earnings, January 1, 2012..................... | $ 30,000 |
| | |
| Add: Net income for year.................................... | 6,660 |
| | 36,660 |
| | |
| Less: Dividends ................................................. | (11,500) |
| | |
| Retained earnings, December 31, 2012 .............. | $ 25,160 |

We use this updated retained earnings amount on the balance sheet.

## Woodson, Inc.
## Balance Sheet
## December 31, 2012

| Assets | | | Liabilities | | |
|---|---|---|---|---|---|
| Cash | | $10,600 | Accounts payable | | $ 2,600 |
| Accounts receivable | | 15,800 | Salary payable | | 40 |
| Prepaid rent | | 400 | Total liabilities | | $ 2,640 |
| Supplies | | 2,000 | | | |
| Furniture | $15,000 | | **Equity** | | |
| Less: Accumulated | | | | | |
| depreciation | (6,000) | $ 9,000 | Common stock | | $10,000 |
| | | | Retained earnings | | 25,160 |
| | | | Total equity | | $35,160 |
| Total assets | | $37,800 | Total liabilities and equity | | $37,800 |

## Requirement 7

### Journalize and post the closing entries.

There are two reasons to prepare closing entries. First, we need to clear out the revenue, expense, and Dividends accounts to a zero balance. This is because they need to begin the next year empty. Second, we need to update the Retained Earnings account.

⑤ Close the books

In Chapter 1, we discussed the formula to calculate the balance in Retained Earnings:

> Beginning retained earnings
> + Net income (or − net loss)
> − Dividends
> = Ending retained earnings

| Retained Earnings | |
|---|---|
| | Beginning Retained Earnings |
| | Net Income |
| Dividends | |
| | Ending Retained Earnings |

This formula is the key to preparing the closing entries. We will use this formula, but we will do it *inside* the Retained Earnings T-account.

What is in Retained Earnings right now? From the trial balance given in the problem, we can see that there is a balance of $30,000. But where did that balance come from? It is the ending balance from last period.

So we have an advantage: The first component of the formula (beginning Retained Earnings) is already in the T-account.

The next component is net income. This is *not* already in the Retained Earnings account. We do not have a T-account with net income in it, but we know that net income is part of Retained Earnings.

We will place all the components of net income into the Retained Earnings T-account and come out with the net income number at the bottom. From Chapter 1, remember the formula for net income:

$$\text{Revenues} - \text{Expenses} = \text{Net income}$$

This means that we need to get all of the revenues and expenses into the Retained Earnings account.

Let's look at the Service Revenue T-account:

| Service Revenue | |
|---|---|
| | Bal        25,800 |

Remember the first reason to prepare closing entries: We need to clear out the income statement accounts so that they are empty to begin the next year. What do we need to do to bring the Service Revenue account to zero? It has a *credit* balance of $25,800, so to bring that to zero, we need to *debit* $25,800.

This means that we have part of our first closing entry:

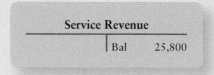

| 1. | Service Revenue | 25,800 | |
|---|---|---|---|
| | ??? | | 25,800 |

What is the credit side of this entry? The reason we were looking at Service Revenue to begin with was to bring net income into Retained Earnings. So the other side of the entry must go to Retained Earnings:

| 1. | | | | |
|---|---|---|---|---|
| | Service Revenue | | 25,800 | |
| | Retained Earnings | | | 25,800 |

**Service Revenue**

| | | 25,800 |
|---|---|---|
| 1. | 25,800 | |
| | Bal | 0 |

The next part of net income is the expenses. In this case, we have four different expenses:

**Rent Expense**

| Bal | 6,000 | |
|---|---|---|

**Depreciation Expense**

| Bal | 1,500 | |
|---|---|---|

**Salary Expense**

| Bal | 10,040 | |
|---|---|---|

**Supplies Expense**

| Bal | 1,600 | |
|---|---|---|

Each of these expenses has a *debit* balance. In order to bring these accounts to zero, we must *credit* them. The balancing debit will go to the Retained Earnings account:

| 2. | | | | |
|---|---|---|---|---|
| | Retained Earnings | | 19,140 | |
| | Rent Expense | | | 6,000 |
| | Salary Expense | | | 10,040 |
| | Depreciation Expense | | | 1,500 |
| | Supplies Expense | | | 1,600 |

**Rent Expense**

| | 6,000 | | |
|---|---|---|---|
| | | 2. | 6,000 |
| Bal | 0 | | |

**Depreciation Expense**

| | 1,500 | | |
|---|---|---|---|
| | | 2. | 1,500 |
| Bal | 0 | | |

**Salary Expense**

| | 10,040 | | |
|---|---|---|---|
| | | 2. | 10,040 |
| Bal | 0 | | |

**Supplies Expense**

| | 1,600 | | |
|---|---|---|---|
| | | 2. | 1,600 |
| Bal | 0 | | |

The last component of the Retained Earnings formula is dividends. There is already a Dividends account that exists:

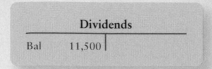

| Dividends | |
| --- | --- |
| Bal 11,500 | |

What do we need to do to bring the Dividends account to zero? It has a *debit* balance of $11,500, so to bring that to zero we need to *credit* $11,500. The balancing debit will go to Retained Earnings:

| 3. | Retained Earnings | 11,500 | |
| --- | --- | --- | --- |
| | Dividends | | 11,500 |

This subtracts the dividends from Retained Earnings.
Retained Earnings now has the following transactions:

| | | | **Retained Earnings** | | |
| --- | --- | --- | --- | --- | --- |
| | | | | 30,000 | Beginning Retained Earnings |
| | | | 1. | 25,800 | Revenue ⎱ |
| Expenses | 2. | 19,140 | | | Net Income |
| Dividends | 3. | 11,500 | | | |
| | | | Bal | 25,160 | Ending Retained Earnings |

The formula to update Retained Earnings has been recreated inside the Retained Earnings T-account.

| | Dividends | | |
| --- | --- | --- | --- |
| | 11,500 | | |
| | | 3. | 11,500 |
| Bal | 0 | | |

| | Retained Earnings | | |
| --- | --- | --- | --- |
| | | | 30,000 |
| | | 1. | 25,800 |
| 2. | 19,140 | | |
| 3. | 11,500 | | |
| | | Bal | 25,160 |

Notice that all temporary accounts (that is, the revenue, the expense, and the Dividends accounts) now have a zero balance.

## Requirement 8

### Calculate Woodson's current and debt ratios.

Current assets are assets whose benefit will be realized within one year (or reporting period, whichever is longer). Typical current assets include cash, accounts receivable, prepaid expenses, and inventory. In this problem, the current assets are:

⑥ Use two new ratios to evaluate a business

$$\text{Total current assets} =$$
$$\text{Cash} + \frac{\text{Accounts}}{\text{Receivable}} + \text{Supplies} + \frac{\text{Prepaid}}{\text{Rent}} =$$
$$\$10{,}600 + \$15{,}800 + \$400 + \$2{,}000 = \$28{,}800$$

Current liabilities are liabilities that will be paid (that is, obligations met) within one year (or reporting period, whichever is longer). In this problem, the current liabilities are:

$$\text{Total current liabilities} =$$
$$\frac{\text{Accounts}}{\text{Payable}} + \frac{\text{Salary}}{\text{Payable}} =$$
$$\$2{,}600 + \$40 = \$2{,}640$$

$$\text{Current ratio} = \frac{\text{Current assets}}{\text{Current liabilities}}$$
$$= \frac{\$28{,}800}{\$2{,}640} = 10.91$$

$$\text{Debt ratio} = \frac{\text{Total liabilities}}{\text{Total assets}}$$
$$= \frac{\$2{,}640 + \$0}{\$28{,}800 + \$9{,}000}$$
$$= \frac{\$2{,}640}{\$37{,}800} = 6.98\%$$

## *DEMO DOC COMPLETE*

# Quick Practice Questions

## True/False

1.  _____ Revenue is recorded when it is earned, usually when a good or service has been delivered to the customer.

2.  _____ The time-period concept provides for periodic reporting at regular intervals.

3.  _____ The revenue principle requires that a cash deposit for future construction should not be recorded as revenue.

4.  _____ Adjusting journal entries are made at the beginning of the period.

5.  _____ The income statement is the first financial statement that should be prepared.

6.  _____ Every adjusting journal entry affects at least one income statement account and at least one balance sheet account.

7.  _____ An accrual is an expense that is recorded after it is paid.

8.  _____ Accumulated Depreciation is a liability account.

9.  _____ Unearned Service Revenue appears on the income statement.

10. _____ Retained Earnings, revenues, expenses, and Dividends are closed out at the end of the year.

11. _____ A lower debt ratio is preferable to a higher debt ratio.

12. _____ Temporary accounts include revenue and expenses.

# Multiple Choice

1. **What items should be matched according to the matching principle?**
   a. Debits with credits
   b. Assets with liabilities
   c. Expenses with revenues
   d. Accruals with prepaids

2. **When is revenue recorded under the cash-basis system of accounting?**
   a. When cash is received
   b. When revenue is earned
   c. When cash is received only if related expenses have been incurred
   d. In the period the related expenses are paid

3. **What do adjusting entries properly measure?**
   a. Cash flow for the period
   b. The amount of cash reported on the balance sheet
   c. Both a and b
   d. Neither a nor b

4. **Which of the following entities would most likely have an Unearned Revenue account?**
   a. A local pizza store
   b. An accounting firm
   c. A department store
   d. A magazine publisher

5. **Georgia Industries paid $48,000 for two years of insurance coverage on July 1, 2011. The company prepares financial statements on July 31, 2011. What is the amount of insurance expense on July 31?**
   a. $48,000
   b. $ 2,000
   c. $24,000
   d. $46,000

6. **Using the information from question 5, what is the adjusted balance in Prepaid Insurance on December 31, 2011?**
   a. $36,000
   b. $24,000
   c. $12,000
   d. $38,000

7. *Sports Illustrated* receives $120,000 on September 1, 2011, for one year's worth of magazine subscriptions for the year beginning September 1, 2011. What is the journal entry to record the prepaid subscriptions?

| | | Accounts | Debit | Credit |
|---|---|---|---|---|
| a. | | Accounts Receivable | 120,000 | |
| | | Unearned Subscription Revenue | | 120,000 |
| b. | | Cash | 120,000 | |
| | | Subscription Revenue | | 120,000 |
| c. | | Cash | 120,000 | |
| | | Unearned Subscription Revenue | | 120,000 |
| d. | | Accounts Receivable | 120,000 | |
| | | Subscription Revenue | | 120,000 |

8. **Which of the following accounts is depreciated?**
   a. Building
   b. Land
   c. Supplies
   d. Prepaid Insurance

9. **What is accumulated depreciation?**
   a. The sum of all the depreciation recorded for the asset
   b. The cost of the depreciable asset
   c. The cost of the depreciable asset divided by the useful life
   d. A liability account with a credit balance

10. **Mason, Inc., has a weekly payroll of $5,000. Wages are paid every Friday for the work performed Monday through Friday of that week. Assuming that the accounting period ends on a Tuesday, what amount of Wages Expense should be recorded on that date?**
    a. $1,000
    b. $2,000
    c. $3,000
    d. $4,000

11. **Which of the following accounts is closed?**
    a. Accumulated Depreciation
    b. Land
    c. Depreciation Expense
    d. Common Stock

Use the following account balances for Philip's Rentals, Inc., as of December 31, 2011, to answer questions 12–13:

| | | | |
|---|---|---|---|
| Cash | $10,300 | Prepaid rent | $ 3,600 |
| Accounts payable | 7,800 | Equipment | 15,000 |
| Accumulated depreciation | 2,000 | Supplies | 1,200 |
| Retained earnings | 9,300 | Unearned revenue | 1,600 |
| Dividends | 2,200 | Notes payable (due 12/31/2015) | 7,500 |

12. **What is the current ratio for Philip's Rentals, Inc.?**
    a. 1.61
    b. 1.03
    c. 1.29
    d. 1.38

13. **What is the debt ratio for Philip's Rentals, Inc.?**
    a. 0.60
    b. 0.73
    c. 0.67
    d. 1.16

# Quick Exercises

**3-1.** Sanderson University received $1,200,000 in tuition from students in August 2011. The tuition is for the four-month semester, September–December 2011. What is the amount of revenue that should be recorded for the month of September?

    a. $_____ assuming the cash basis of accounting.
    b. $_____ assuming the accrual basis of accounting.

**3-2.** For each of the following situations, indicate if an expense or revenue should be recorded and the amount of the adjustment at the end of the month on January 31, 2011.

| | Revenue or Expense | Adjustment Amount |
|---|---|---|
| a. $1,500 of supplies is purchased during January. On January 31, $800 of supplies remain. | _____ | _____ |
| b. The five-day weekly payroll is $6,000. Employees worked the last two days of January and have not been paid by January 31. | _____ | _____ |
| c. $750 of Unearned Revenue has been earned in January. | _____ | _____ |
| d. Depreciation on equipment is $3,600 for the year. | _____ | _____ |
| e. Services of $2,300 were performed on January 31 and have not been recorded. | _____ | _____ |

**3-3.** Journalize the required adjusting journal entries using the information in 3-2.

a.

| Date | Accounts | Debit | Credit |
|---|---|---|---|
| | | | |
| | | | |

b.

| Date | Accounts | Debit | Credit |
|---|---|---|---|
| | | | |
| | | | |

c.

| Date | Accounts | Debit | Credit |
|---|---|---|---|
| | | | |
| | | | |

**d.**

| Date | Accounts | Debit | Credit |
|------|----------|-------|--------|
|      |          |       |        |
|      |          |       |        |

**e.**

| Date | Accounts | Debit | Credit |
|------|----------|-------|--------|
|      |          |       |        |
|      |          |       |        |

**3-4. Following is the trial balance for Coleman Copy Center:**

Coleman Copy Center
Trial Balance
March 31, 2010

| Account Title | Balance Debit | Balance Credit |
|---------------|-------|--------|
| Cash | $30,000 | |
| Accounts receivable | 2,000 | |
| Supplies | 600 | |
| Land | 50,000 | |
| Accounts payable | | $ 2,600 |
| Note payable | | 35,000 |
| Common stock | | 15,000 |
| Retained earnings | | 27,550 |
| Dividends | 2,400 | |
| Service revenue | | 9,300 |
| Salary expense | 2,500 | |
| Rent expense | 1,200 | |
| Interest expense | 500 | |
| Utilities expense | 250 | |
| Total | $89,450 | $89,450 |

**1. Prepare (a) an income statement and (b) a statement of retained earnings for the year ending March 31, 2010.**

Coleman Copy Center
Income Statement
Year Ended March 31, 2010

Coleman Copy Center
Statement of Retained Earnings
Year Ended March 31, 2010

**3-5. Using the trial balance for Coleman Copy Center in 3-4, prepare the balance sheet at March 31, 2010.**

| Coleman Copy Center | | | |
|---|---|---|---|
| Balance Sheet | | | |
| March 31, 2010 | | | |
| | | | |
| | | | |
| | | | |
| | | | |
| | | | |
| | | | |
| | | | |
| | | | |

**3-6. Given the following adjusted account balances, journalize the closing entries for Tires Unlimited on December 31, 2011.**

| | |
|---|---|
| Retained earnings........................................ | $ 90,000 |
| Service revenue............................................ | 104,400 |
| Depreciation expense—building............... | 3,000 |
| Salary expense.............................................. | 28,000 |
| Supplies expense.......................................... | 8,500 |
| Interest revenue.......................................... | 15,400 |
| Rent expense................................................ | 15,000 |
| Dividends...................................................... | 2,000 |

| Date | Accounts | Debit | Credit |
|------|----------|-------|--------|
|      |          |       |        |
|      |          |       |        |
|      |          |       |        |

| Date | Accounts | Debit | Credit |
|------|----------|-------|--------|
|      |          |       |        |
|      |          |       |        |
|      |          |       |        |
|      |          |       |        |

| Date | Accounts | Debit | Credit |
|------|----------|-------|--------|
|      |          |       |        |
|      |          |       |        |

# Do It Yourself! Question 1

Angela's Business Services Corp. has the following balances on its December 31 (year-end) trial balance (before adjustments):

**Angela's Business Services Corp.**
**Trial Balance**
**December 31, 2010**

| Account Title | Debit | Credit |
|---|---|---|
| Cash | $ 40,400 | |
| Prepaid insurance | 4,800 | |
| Supplies | 13,000 | |
| Office equipment | 25,000 | |
| Accumulated depreciation—equipment | | $ 7,500 |
| Accounts payable | | 5,300 |
| Salary payable | | 0 |
| Unearned revenue | | 6,800 |
| Common stock | | 20,000 |
| Retained earnings | | 40,000 |
| Dividends | 8,000 | |
| Service revenue | | 80,000 |
| Insurance expense | 13,200 | |
| Salary expense | 45,000 | |
| Depreciation expense | 0 | |
| Supplies expense | 10,200 | |
| Total | $159,600 | $159,600 |

## Requirements

1. Open the T-accounts and enter the unadjusted balances (see Requirement 3 for T-account setup).

2. Journalize the following adjusting entries at December 31, 2010. Key the entries by letter.

a. Only $1,500 of the unearned revenue remains unearned.

| Date | Accounts | Debit | Credit |
|---|---|---|---|
| | | | |
| | | | |

**b. Depreciation on the office equipment is $2,500 for the year.**

| Date | Accounts | Debit | Credit |
|------|----------|-------|--------|
|      |          |       |        |
|      |          |       |        |
|      |          |       |        |

**c. Employees earned salaries of $4,000 that have not been paid.**

| Date | Accounts | Debit | Credit |
|------|----------|-------|--------|
|      |          |       |        |
|      |          |       |        |
|      |          |       |        |

**d. $5,100 of supplies have been used.**

| Date | Accounts | Debit | Credit |
|------|----------|-------|--------|
|      |          |       |        |
|      |          |       |        |
|      |          |       |        |

**e. Four months of insurance ($4,800) was paid in advance on December 1, 2010. No adjustment has been made to the Prepaid Insurance account since then.**

| Date | Accounts | Debit | Credit |
|------|----------|-------|--------|
|      |          |       |        |
|      |          |       |        |
|      |          |       |        |

**3. Post the adjusting entries.**

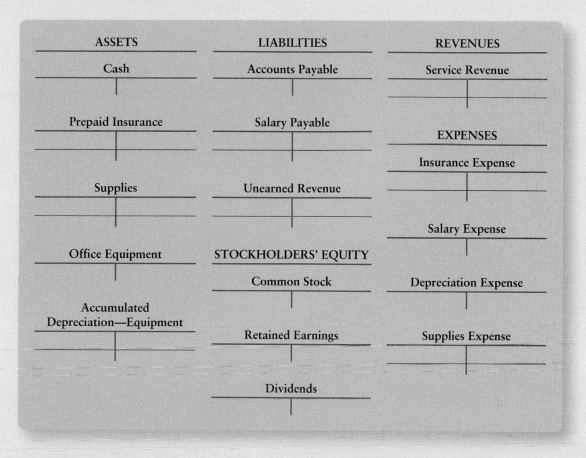

| ASSETS | LIABILITIES | REVENUES |
|--------|-------------|----------|
| Cash | Accounts Payable | Service Revenue |
| Prepaid Insurance | Salary Payable | EXPENSES |
| | | Insurance Expense |
| Supplies | Unearned Revenue | |
| | | Salary Expense |
| Office Equipment | STOCKHOLDERS' EQUITY | |
| | Common Stock | Depreciation Expense |
| Accumulated Depreciation—Equipment | Retained Earnings | Supplies Expense |
| | Dividends | |

**4. Prepare an adjusted trial balance.**

**5. Prepare the income statement, statement of retained earnings, and balance sheet for Angela's Business Services Corp.**

# Do It Yourself! Question 2

This question continues from the Angela's Business Services Corp. problem given in Do It Yourself! Question 1.

Use the data from Angela's Business Services Corp.'s adjusted trial balance at December 31, 2010:

**Angela's Business Services Corp.**
**Adjusted Trial Balance**
**December 31, 2010**

| Account Title | Adjusted Trial Balance | |
|---|---|---|
| | Debit | Credit |
| Cash | $ 40,400 | |
| Prepaid insurance | 3,600 | |
| Supplies | 7,900 | |
| Office equipment | 25,000 | |
| Accumulated depreciation—equipment | | $ 10,000 |
| Accounts payable | | 5,300 |
| Salary payable | | 4,000 |
| Unearned revenue | | 1,500 |
| Common stock | | 20,000 |
| Retained earnings | | 40,000 |
| Dividends | 8,000 | |
| Service revenue | | 85,300 |
| Insurance expense | 14,400 | |
| Salary expense | 49,000 | |
| Depreciation expense | 2,500 | |
| Supplies expense | 15,300 | |
| Total | $166,100 | $166,100 |

## Requirement

1. Journalize and post the closing entries.

| Date | Accounts | Debit | Credit |
|---|---|---|---|
| | | | |
| | | | |

| Date | Accounts | Debit | Credit |
|------|----------|-------|--------|
|      |          |       |        |
|      |          |       |        |
|      |          |       |        |

| Date | Accounts | Debit | Credit |
|------|----------|-------|--------|
|      |          |       |        |
|      |          |       |        |

# Do It Yourself! Question 3

Everly Industries is preparing its financial statements for the year ended March 31, 2011. Three accounting issues have been discovered.

## Requirement

1. Make the necessary adjusting entry for each situation.

a. **Employees work five days a week (Monday through Friday) and are paid $7,500 for the previous week of work each Friday. March 31, 2011, falls on a Thursday.**

| Date | Accounts | Debit | Credit |
|------|----------|-------|--------|
|      |          |       |        |
|      |          |       |        |
|      |          |       |        |

b. **The T-account for supplies shows an unadjusted balance of $1,000. However, only $350 of supplies are on hand at March 31, 2011.**

| Date | Accounts | Debit | Credit |
|------|----------|-------|--------|
|      |          |       |        |
|      |          |       |        |
|      |          |       |        |

c. **The company has forgotten to record four months of interest expense ($80 per month) that has been incurred but not yet paid.**

| Date | Accounts | Debit | Credit |
|------|----------|-------|--------|
|      |          |       |        |
|      |          |       |        |
|      |          |       |        |

## Do It Yourself! Question 4

Krake Theaters, Inc., has the following data for 2011:

| | |
|---|---|
| Total revenues................................ | $10,000 |
| Total expenses................................ | 13,000 |
| Dividends declared and paid .......... | 1,600 |

Retained Earnings had a balance of $8,200 at January 1, 2011.

### Requirement

1. **Journalize and post the closing entries.**

| Date | Accounts | Debit | Credit |
|---|---|---|---|
| | | | |
| | | | |
| | | | |

| Date | Accounts | Debit | Credit |
|---|---|---|---|
| | | | |
| | | | |
| | | | |

| Date | Accounts | Debit | Credit |
|---|---|---|---|
| | | | |
| | | | |
| | | | |

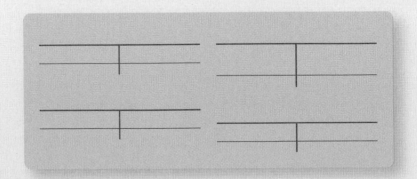

# Quick Practice Solutions

## True/False

|   |   |   |
|---|---|---|
| T | 1. | Revenue is recorded when it is earned, usually when a good or service has been delivered to the customer. (p. 140) |

__T__    **1.** Revenue is recorded when it is earned, usually when a good or service has been delivered to the customer. (p. 140)

__T__    **2.** The time-period concept provides for periodic reporting at regular intervals. (p. 140)

__T__    **3.** The revenue principle requires that a cash deposit for future construction should not be recorded as revenue. (pp. 140–141)

__F__    **4.** Adjusting journal entries are made at the beginning of the period.

        False—Adjusting journal entries are made at the *end* of the period. (p. 143)

__T__    **5.** The income statement is the first financial statement that should be prepared. (pp. 157, 159)

__T__    **6.** Every adjusting journal entry affects at least one income statement account and at least one balance sheet account. (p. 154)

__F__    **7.** An accrual is an expense that is recorded after it is paid.

        False—An accrual is an expense that is recorded *before* it is paid. (p. 150)

__F__    **8.** Accumulated Depreciation is a liability account.

        False—Accumulated Depreciation is a *contra asset* account. (p. 149)

__F__    **9.** Unearned Service Revenue appears on the income statement.

        False—Unearned Service Revenue is a liability and appears on the *balance sheet.* (pp. 152, 153)

__F__   **10.** Retained Earnings, revenues, expenses, and Dividends are closed out at the end of the year.

        False—The revenues, expenses, and Dividends accounts are closed out at the end of the year. *Retained Earnings* is a permanent account and is not closed out. (p. 165)

__T__   **11.** A lower debt ratio is preferable to a higher debt ratio. (p. 171)

__T__   **12.** Temporary accounts include revenue and expenses. (p. 165)

# Multiple Choice

1.  **What items should be matched according to the matching principle? (p. 141)**
    a. Debits with credits
    b. Assets with liabilities
    c. Expenses with revenues
    d. Accruals with prepaids

2.  **When is revenue recorded under the cash-basis system of accounting? (p. 139)**
    a. When cash is received
    b. When revenue is earned
    c.. When cash is received only if related expenses have been incurred
    d. In the period the related expenses are paid

3.  **What do adjusting entries properly measure? (pp. 143, 154)**
    a. Cash flow for the period
    b. The amount of cash reported on the balance sheet
    c. Both a and b
    d. Neither a nor b

4.  **Which of the following entities would most likely have an Unearned Revenue account? (pp. 152–153)**
    a. A local pizza store
    b. An accounting firm
    c. A department store
    d. A magazine publisher

5.  **Georgia Industries paid $48,000 for two years of insurance coverage on July 1, 2011. The company prepares financial statements on July 31, 2011. What is the amount of insurance expense on July 31? (p. 145)**
    a. $48,000
    b. $ 2,000
    c. $24,000
    d. $46,000

6.  **Using the information from question 5, what is the adjusted balance in Prepaid Insurance on December 31, 2011? (pp. 145–146)**
    a. $36,000
    b. $24,000
    c. $12,000
    d. $38,000

7. *Sports Illustrated* receives $120,000 on September 1, 2011, for one year's worth of magazine subscriptions for the year beginning September 1, 2011. What is the journal entry to record the prepaid subscriptions? (p. 153)

| | | Accounts | Debit | Credit |
|---|---|---|---|---|
| a. | | Accounts Receivable | 120,000 | |
| | | Unearned Subscription Revenue | | 120,000 |
| | | | | |
| b. | | Cash | 120,000 | |
| | | Subscription Revenue | | 120,000 |
| | | | | |
| c. | | Cash | 120,000 | |
| | | Unearned Subscription Revenue | | 120,000 |
| | | | | |
| d. | | Accounts Receivable | 120,000 | |
| | | Subscription Revenue | | 120,000 |

8. **Which of the following accounts is depreciated? (p. 147)**
   a. Building
   b. Land
   c. Supplies
   d. Prepaid Insurance

9. **What is accumulated depreciation? (pp. 148–149)**
   a. The sum of all the depreciation recorded for the asset
   b. The cost of the depreciable asset
   c. The cost of the depreciable asset divided by the useful life
   d. A liability account with a credit balance

10. **Mason, Inc., has a weekly payroll of $5,000. Wages are paid every Friday for the work performed Monday through Friday of that week. Assuming that the accounting period ends on a Tuesday, what amount of Wages Expense should be recorded on that date? (pp. 150–151)**
    a. $1,000
    b. $2,000
    c. $3,000
    d. $4,000

11. **Which of the following accounts is closed? (p. 165)**
    a. Accumulated Depreciation
    b. Land
    c. Depreciation Expense
    d. Common Stock

Use the following account balances for Philip's Rentals, Inc., as of December 31, 2011, to answer questions 12–13:

| | | | |
|---|---|---|---|
| Cash | $10,300 | Prepaid rent | $ 3,600 |
| Accounts payable | 7,800 | Equipment | 15,000 |
| Accumulated depreciation | 2,000 | Supplies | 1,200 |
| Retained earnings | 9,300 | Unearned revenue | 1,600 |
| Dividends | 2,200 | Notes payable (due 12/31/2015) | 7,500 |

12. **What is the current ratio for Philip's Rentals, Inc.? (p. 170)**
   a. 1.61
   b. 1.03
   c. 1.29
   d. 1.38

13. **What is the debt ratio for Philip's Rentals, Inc.? (p. 170)**
   a. 0.60
   b. 0.73
   c. 0.67
   d. 1.16

# Quick Exercises

**3-1.** Sanderson University received $1,200,000 in tuition from students in August 2011. The tuition is for the four-month semester, September–December 2011. What is the amount of revenue that should be recorded for the month of September? (pp. 139, 152–153)

a. $ 1,200,000  assuming the cash basis of accounting.
b. $    300,000  assuming the accrual basis of accounting.

**3-2.** For each of the following situations, indicate if an expense or revenue needs to be recorded and the amount of the adjustment at the end of the month on January 31, 2011. (pp. 145–154)

| | Revenue or Expense | Adjustment Amount |
|---|---|---|
| a. $1,500 of supplies is purchased during January. On January 31, $800 of supplies remain. | Expense | $700 |
| b. The five-day weekly payroll is $6,000. Employees worked the last two days of January and have not been paid by January 31. | Expense | $2,400 |
| c. $750 of Unearned Revenue has been earned in January. | Revenue | $750 |
| d. Depreciation on equipment is $3,600 for the year. | Expense | $300 |
| e. Services of $2,300 were performed on January 31 and have not been recorded. | Revenue | $2,300 |

**3-3.** Journalize the required adjusting journal entries using the information in 3-2. (pp. 145–154)

**a.**

| Date | Accounts | Debit | Credit |
|---|---|---|---|
| 1/31/11 | Supplies Expense | 700 | |
| | Supplies | | 700 |

**b.**

| Date | Accounts | Debit | Credit |
|---|---|---|---|
| 1/31/11 | Salary Expense | 2,400 | |
| | Salary Payable | | 2,400 |

**c.**

| Date | Accounts | Debit | Credit |
|---|---|---|---|
| 1/31/11 | Unearned Revenue | 750 | |
| | Service Revenue | | 750 |

**d.**

| Date | Accounts | Debit | Credit |
|---|---|---|---|
| 1/31/11 | Depreciation—Equipment | 300 | |
| | Accumulated Depreciation—Equipment | | 300 |

**e.**

| Date | Accounts | Debit | Credit |
|---|---|---|---|
| 1/31/11 | Accounts Receivable | 2,300 | |
| | Service Revenue | | 2,300 |

## 3-4. Following is the trial balance for Coleman Copy Center:

**Coleman Copy Center**
**Trial Balance**
**March 31, 2010**

| Account Title | Balance Debit | Balance Credit |
|---|---|---|
| Cash | $30,000 | |
| Accounts receivable | 2,000 | |
| Supplies | 600 | |
| Land | 50,000 | |
| Accounts payable | | $ 2,600 |
| Note payable | | 35,000 |
| Common stock | | 15,000 |
| Retained earnings | | 27,550 |
| Dividends | 2,400 | |
| Service revenue | | 9,300 |
| Salary expense | 2,500 | |
| Rent expense | 1,200 | |
| Interest expense | 500 | |
| Utilities expense | 250 | |
| Total | $89,450 | $89,450 |

**1. Prepare (a) an income statement and (b) a statement of retained earnings for the year ending March 31, 2010.** (p. 158)

**Coleman Copy Center**
**Income Statement**
**Year Ended March 31, 2010**

| Revenue: | | |
|---|---|---|
| Service revenue................ | | $9,300 |
| | | |
| Expenses: | | |
| Salary expense................ | $2,500 | |
| Rent expense................... | 1,200 | |
| Interest expense.............. | 500 | |
| Utilities expense ............. | 250 | |
| Total expenses................ | | 4,450 |
| | | |
| Net income........................... | | $4,850 |

**Coleman Copy Center**
**Statement of Retained Earnings**
**Year Ended March 31, 2010**

| | |
|---|---|
| Retained earnings, March 31, 2009 .............. | $27,550 |
| | |
| Add: Net income for year.............................. | 4,850 |
| | 32,400 |
| | |
| Less: Dividends :........................................... | (2,400) |
| | |
| Retained earnings, March 31, 2010 .............. | $30,000 |

**3-5. Using the trial balance for Coleman Copy Center in 3-4, prepare the balance sheet at March 31, 2010.** (p. 158)

## Coleman Copy Center
## Balance Sheet
## March 31, 2010

| Assets | | Liabilities | |
|---|---|---|---|
| Cash | $30,000 | Accounts payable | $ 2,600 |
| Accounts receivable | 2,000 | Note payable | 35,000 |
| Supplies | 600 | Total liabilities | $37,600 |
| Land | 50,000 | | |
| | | **Equity** | |
| | | Common stock | $15,000 |
| | | Retained earnings | 30,000 |
| | | Total equity | $45,000 |
| Total assets | $82,600 | Total liabilities and equity | $82,600 |

**3-6. Given the following adjusted account balances, journalize the closing entries for Tires Unlimited on December 31, 2011.** (p. 166)

| | |
|---|---|
| Retained earnings | $ 90,000 |
| Service revenue | 104,400 |
| Depreciation expense—building | 3,000 |
| Salary expense | 28,000 |
| Supplies expense | 8,500 |
| Interest revenue | 15,400 |
| Rent expense | 15,000 |
| Dividends | 2,000 |

| 12/31/11 | Service Revenue | 104,400 | |
| | Interest Revenue | 15,400 | |
| | Retained Earnings | | 119,800 |
| | *To close revenue accounts into Retained Earnings.* | | |


| 12/31/11 | Retained Earnings | 54,500 | |
| | Depreciation Expense—Building | | 3,000 |
| | Salary Expense | | 28,000 |
| | Supplies Expense | | 8,500 |
| | Rent Expense | | 15,000 |
| | *To close expense accounts into Retained Earnings.* | | |


| 12/31/11 | Dividends | 2,000 | |
| | Retained Earnings | | 2,000 |
| | *To close Dividends into Retained Earnings.* | | |

# Do It Yourself! Question 1 Solutions

1. Open the T-accounts and enter the unadjusted balances.

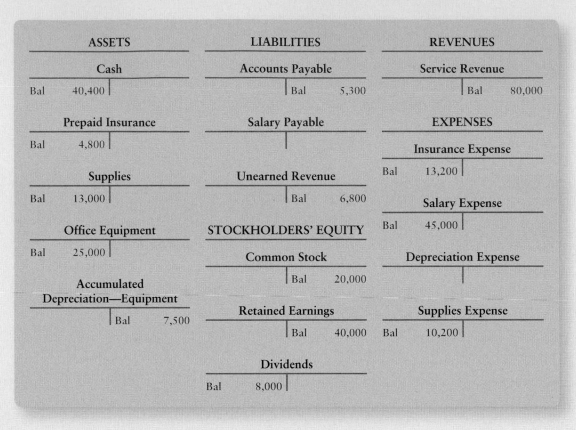

| ASSETS | | LIABILITIES | | REVENUES | |
|---|---|---|---|---|---|
| **Cash** | | **Accounts Payable** | | **Service Revenue** | |
| Bal 40,400 | | | Bal 5,300 | | Bal 80,000 |
| **Prepaid Insurance** | | **Salary Payable** | | **EXPENSES** | |
| Bal 4,800 | | | | **Insurance Expense** | |
| **Supplies** | | **Unearned Revenue** | | Bal 13,200 | |
| Bal 13,000 | | | Bal 6,800 | **Salary Expense** | |
| **Office Equipment** | | **STOCKHOLDERS' EQUITY** | | Bal 45,000 | |
| Bal 25,000 | | **Common Stock** | | **Depreciation Expense** | |
| **Accumulated Depreciation—Equipment** | | | Bal 20,000 | | |
| | Bal 7,500 | **Retained Earnings** | | **Supplies Expense** | |
| | | | Bal 40,000 | Bal 10,200 | |
| | | **Dividends** | | | |
| | | Bal 8,000 | | | |

2. Journalize the following adjusting entries at December 31, 2010. Key the entries by letter.

a. Only $1,500 of the unearned revenue remains unearned.

| a. | Unearned Revenue ($6,800 − $1,500) | 5,300 | |
|---|---|---|---|
| | Service Revenue | | 5,300 |
| | *To record service revenue collected in advance.* | | |

b. Depreciation on the office equipment is $2,500 for the year.

| b. | Depreciation Expense | 2,500 | |
|---|---|---|---|
| | Accumulated Depreciation—Equipment | | 2,500 |
| | *To record depreciation expense.* | | |

**c. Employees earned salaries of $4,000 that have not been paid.**

| c. | Salary Expense | 4,000 | |
|---|---|---|---|
| | Salary Payable | | 4,000 |
| | *To accrue salary expense.* | | |

**d. $5,100 of supplies have been used.**

| d. | Supplies Expense | 5,100 | |
|---|---|---|---|
| | Supplies | | 5,100 |
| | *To record supplies used.* | | |

**e. Four months of insurance ($4,800) was paid in advance on December 1, 2010. No adjustment has been made to the Prepaid Insurance account since then.**

| e. | Insurance Expense (1 month × $4,800/4 months) | 1,200 | |
|---|---|---|---|
| | Prepaid Insurance | | 1,200 |
| | *To record insurance expense.* | | |

## 3. Post the adjusting entries.

### ASSETS

**Cash**

| | | | |
|---|---|---|---|
| Bal | 40,400 | | |

**Prepaid Insurance**

| | | | |
|---|---|---|---|
| | 4,800 | | |
| | | e. | 1,200 |
| Bal | 3,600 | | |

**Supplies**

| | | | |
|---|---|---|---|
| | 13,000 | | |
| | | d. | 5,100 |
| Bal | 7,900 | | |

**Office Equipment**

| | | | |
|---|---|---|---|
| Bal | 25,000 | | |

**Accumulated Depreciation—Equipment**

| | | | |
|---|---|---|---|
| | | | 7,500 |
| | | b. | 2,500 |
| | | Bal | 10,000 |

### LIABILITIES

**Accounts Payable**

| | | | |
|---|---|---|---|
| | | Bal | 5,300 |

**Salary Payable**

| | | | |
|---|---|---|---|
| | | c. | 4,000 |
| | | Bal | 4,000 |

**Unearned Revenue**

| | | | |
|---|---|---|---|
| | | | 6,800 |
| a. | 5,300 | | |
| | | Bal | 1,500 |

### STOCKHOLDERS' EQUITY

**Common Stock**

| | | | |
|---|---|---|---|
| | | Bal | 20,000 |

**Retained Earnings**

| | | | |
|---|---|---|---|
| | | Bal | 40,000 |

**Dividends**

| | | | |
|---|---|---|---|
| Bal | 8,000 | | |

### REVENUES

**Service Revenue**

| | | | |
|---|---|---|---|
| | | | 80,000 |
| | | a. | 5,300 |
| | | Bal | 85,300 |

### EXPENSES

**Insurance Expense**

| | | | |
|---|---|---|---|
| | 13,200 | | |
| e. | 1,200 | | |
| Bal | 14,400 | | |

**Salary Expense**

| | | | |
|---|---|---|---|
| | 45,000 | | |
| c. | 4,000 | | |
| Bal | 49,000 | | |

**Depreciation Expense**

| | | | |
|---|---|---|---|
| b. | 2,500 | | |
| Bal | 2,500 | | |

**Supplies Expense**

| | | | |
|---|---|---|---|
| | 10,200 | | |
| d. | 5,100 | | |
| Bal | 15,300 | | |

## 4. Prepare an adjusted trial balance.

**Angela's Business Services Corp.**
**Preparation of Adjusted Trial Balance**
**Year Ended December 31, 2010**

| Account Title | Trial Balance Debit | Trial Balance Credit | Adjustments Debit | Adjustments Credit | Adjusted Trial Balance Debit | Adjusted Trial Balance Credit |
|---|---|---|---|---|---|---|
| Cash | $ 40,400 | | | | $ 40,400 | |
| Prepaid insurance | 4,800 | | | (e) $ 1,200 | 3,600 | |
| Supplies | 13,000 | | | (d) 5,100 | 7,900 | |
| Office equipment | 25,000 | | | | 25,000 | |
| Accumulated depreciation—equipment | | $ 7,500 | | (b) 2,500 | | $ 10,000 |
| Accounts payable | | 5,300 | | | | 5,300 |
| Salary payable | | 0 | | (c) 4,000 | | 4,000 |
| Unearned revenue | | 6,800 | (a) $ 5,300 | | | 1,500 |
| Common stock | | 20,000 | | | | 20,000 |
| Retained earnings | | 40,000 | | | | 40,000 |
| Dividends | 8,000 | | | | 8,000 | |
| Service revenue | | 80,000 | | (a) 5,300 | | 85,300 |
| Insurance expense | 13,200 | | (e) 1,200 | | 14,400 | |
| Salary expense | 45,000 | | (c) 4,000 | | 49,000 | |
| Depreciation expense | 0 | | (b) 2,500 | | 2,500 | |
| Supplies expense | 10,200 | | (d) 5,100 | | 15,300 | |
| Total | $159,600 | $159,600 | $18,100 | $18,100 | $166,100 | $166,100 |

**5. Prepare the income statement, statement of retained earnings, and balance sheet for Angela's Business Services Corp.**

### Angela's Business Services Corp.
### Income Statement
### Year Ended December 31, 2010

| | | |
|---|---|---|
| Revenue: | | |
| Service revenue.......................... | | $85,300 |
| | | |
| Expenses: | | |
| Salary expense.......................... | $49,000 | |
| Supplies expense ...................... | 15,300 | |
| Insurance expense ................... | 14,400 | |
| Depreciation expense .............. | 2,500 | |
| Total expenses.......................... | | 81,200 |
| | | |
| Net income.................................. | | $ 4,100 |

### Angela's Business Services Corp.
### Statement of Retained Earnings
### Year Ended December 31, 2010

| | |
|---|---|
| Retained earnings, January 1, 2010..................... | $40,000 |
| | |
| Add: Net income for year..................................... | 4,100 |
| | 44,100 |
| | |
| Less: Dividends .................................................. | (8,000) |
| | |
| Retained earnings, December 31, 2010 .............. | $36,100 |

## Angela's Business Services Corp.
## Balance Sheet
### December 31, 2010

| Assets | | | Liabilities | | |
|---|---|---|---|---|---|
| Cash | | $40,400 | Accounts payable | | $ 5,300 |
| Prepaid insurance | | 3,600 | Salary payable | | 4,000 |
| Supplies | | 7,900 | Unearned revenue | | 1,500 |
| Office equipment | $ 25,000 | | | | |
| Less: Accumulated | | | Total liabilities | | $10,800 |
| depreciation | (10,000) | $15,000 | | | |
| | | | **Equity** | | |
| | | | Common stock | | $20,000 |
| | | | Retained earnings | | 36,100 |
| | | | Total equity | | $56,100 |
| Total assets | | $66,900 | Total liabilities and equity | | $66,900 |

# Do It Yourself! Question 2 Solutions

1. Journalize and post the closing entries.

| 1. | | Service Revenue | 85,300 | |
|---|---|---|---|---|
| | | Retained Earnings | | 85,300 |

| 2. | | Retained Earnings | 81,200 | |
|---|---|---|---|---|
| | | Insurance Expense | | 14,400 |
| | | Salary Expense | | 49,000 |
| | | Depreciation Expense | | 2,500 |
| | | Supplies Expense | | 15,300 |

| 3. | | Retained Earnings | 8,000 | |
|---|---|---|---|---|
| | | Dividends | | 8,000 |

**Service Revenue**

| | | | 85,300 |
|---|---|---|---|
| 1. | 85,300 | | |
| | | Bal | 0 |

**Depreciation Expense**

| 2,500 | | |
|---|---|---|
| | 2. | 2,500 |
| Bal | 0 | |

**Dividends**

| 8,000 | | |
|---|---|---|
| | 3. | 8,000 |
| Bal | 0 | |

**Insurance Expense**

| 14,400 | | |
|---|---|---|
| | 2. | 14,400 |
| Bal | 0 | |

**Supplies Expense**

| 15,300 | | |
|---|---|---|
| | 2. | 15,300 |
| Bal | 0 | |

**Retained Earnings**

| | | | 60,000 |
|---|---|---|---|
| | | 1. | 85,300 |
| 2. | 81,200 | | |
| 3. | 8,000 | | |
| | | Bal | 56,100 |

**Salary Expense**

| 49,000 | | |
|---|---|---|
| | 2. | 49,000 |
| Bal | 0 | |

# Do it Yourself! Question 3 Solutions

1. Make the necessary adjusting entry for each situation.

a. **Employees work five days a week (Monday through Friday) and are paid $7,500 for the previous week of work each Friday. March 31, 2011, falls on a Thursday.**

$7,500/5 days = $1,500 salary per day of work
Monday through Thursday = 4 days of work
4 × $1,500 = $6,000

| a. | Salary Expense (4 days × $7,500/5 days) | 6,000 | |
|---|---|---|---|
| | Salary Payable | | 6,000 |
| | *To accrue salary expense.* | | |

b. **The T-account for supplies shows an unadjusted balance of $1,000. However, only $350 of supplies are on hand at March 31, 2011.**

$1,000 − $350 = $650 of supplies used

| b. | Supplies Expense ($1,000 − $350) | 650 | |
|---|---|---|---|
| | Supplies | | 650 |
| | *To record supplies used.* | | |

c. **The company has forgotten to record four months of interest expense ($80 per month) that has been incurred but not yet paid.**

4 months × $80 per month = $320

| c. | Interest Expense (4 months × $80) | 320 | |
|---|---|---|---|
| | Interest Payable | | 320 |
| | *To accrue interest expense.* | | |

# Do It Yourself! Question 4 Solutions

1. Journalize and post the closing entries.

| 1. | | Revenues | 10,000 | |
|----|--|----------|--------|--|
|    |  | Retained Earnings | | 10,000 |

| 2. | | Retained Earnings | 13,000 | |
|----|--|-------------------|--------|--|
|    |  | Expenses | | 13,000 |

| 3. | | Retained Earnings | 1,600 | |
|----|--|-------------------|-------|--|
|    |  | Dividends | | 1,600 |

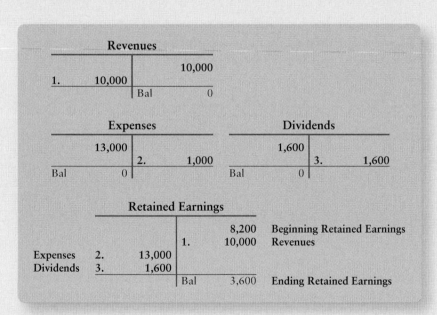

**Revenues**

| | | | 10,000 |
|--|--|--|--------|
| 1. | 10,000 | | |
| | | Bal | 0 |

**Expenses**

| | 13,000 | | |
|--|--------|--|--|
| | | 2. | 1,000 |
| Bal | 0 | | |

**Dividends**

| | 1,600 | | |
|--|-------|--|--|
| | | 3. | 1,600 |
| Bal | 0 | | |

**Retained Earnings**

| | | | 8,200 | Beginning Retained Earnings |
|--|--|--|-------|------------------------------|
| | | 1. | 10,000 | Revenues |
| Expenses | 2. | 13,000 | | |
| Dividends | 3. | 1,600 | | |
| | | Bal | 3,600 | Ending Retained Earnings |

# The Power of Practice

For more practice using the skills learned in this chapter, visit MyAccountingLab. There you will find algorithmically generated questions that are based on these Demo Docs and your main textbook's Review and Assess Your Progress sections.

Go to MyAccountingLab and follow these steps:

1. Direct your URL to www.myaccountinglab.com.
2. Log in using your name and password.
3. Click the MyAccountingLab link.
4. Click Study Plan in the left navigation bar.
5. From the table of contents, select Chapter 3, Accrual Accounting & Income.
6. Click a link to work tutorial exercises.

# 4 Internal Control & Cash

## WHAT YOU PROBABLY ALREADY KNOW

When you shop in a department store, you have probably noticed that there are electronic tags on some of the goods. The cashier will remove the tag upon purchase so that an alarm does not sound when you exit the store through the security gates. You may also have noticed that fine jewelry is likely displayed in a locked case that can only be opened by an employee. The employee will stay with you until the item is returned to the case and locked or purchased. Cartons of cigarettes are also usually secured behind locked doors or cabinets.

If you work as a cashier, it's likely that you have your own cash drawer. Periodically there may be times when cash is collected and deposited in a safe or taken to the bank. At the end of the shift, the cash is counted and compared to the sales rung up for the period to determine that the appropriate amount of cash is in the drawer. These observations are just a few of the procedures and policies that businesses employ to achieve a good system of internal control.

## Learning Objectives

 **Learn about fraud and how much it costs**

Fraud is an intentional misrepresentation of facts for the purpose of causing injury or damage to another party. In business, fraud is usually perpetrated for financial gain. It is important to be aware of the various aspects of fraud in order to learn how to prevent it, as well as to detect it more quickly and easily. Review the Fraud Triangle in Exhibit 4-1 (p. 235).

 **Set up an internal control system**

The components of internal control can be remembered using the mnemonic SCALP:

*S: Smart hiring practices and segregation of duties*

Background checks should be performed for all employees, and new employees need to be properly trained. Once employees are working for the company, they need to be properly supervised. Employees should work only with asset handling, record keeping, or transaction approval, not more than one of these. This is called **segregation of duties**, and it helps minimize employee opportunities to commit fraud.

*C: Comparisons and compliance monitoring*

Monitoring of employees is an important component of fraud prevention. No person or department should be able to completely process a transaction from beginning to end without being cross-checked by another person or department. Compliance can also be effectively managed by the use of **operating budgets** and **cash budgets**. Even after a company's year-end, an audit can validate the accounting records and monitor compliance with company policies.

*A: Adequate records*

Accounting records provide details of business transactions and so it is important to ensure that all major groups of documents are supported by hard copy or electronic records.

*L: Limited access to assets and records*

To help prevent fraud, company policy should limit access to assets only to persons or departments who have custodial responsibility.

*P: Proper approvals*

No transaction should be processed without approval. The larger the amount of the transaction, the stricter the approval process should become. *Review the "Internal Control" section of the text carefully. This topic is critical for business owners and managers.*

 **Prepare and use a bank reconciliation**

*Review the format of the bank reconciliation in Exhibit 4-8, Panel B (p. 250).* Take note that the ending "Adjusted bank balance" and "Adjusted book balance" are the same amount. **These amounts represent the correct book balance**, the amount of Cash that will appear on the balance sheet. As you review Exhibit 4-8, think about the objective of the bank reconciliation, which is to arrive at the correct book balance. This focus should help you to understand the rationale for why the various items are added to or subtracted from the balance per bank and the balance per books. When these balances differ, journal entries record all the items that appear between those two amounts to obtain the correct balance. *Continue to review the journal entries related to Exhibit 4-8.*

 **Apply internal controls to cash receipts and cash payments**

The assignment and separation of employee responsibilities is important for handling cash. Cashiers should each use a separate drawer. The cash should be counted and checked against the sales register information. Remittances that are mailed in are opened and the checks and source documentation are forwarded to two separate individuals. A third party verifies that the amount deposited agrees with the source documentation. *Review the cash receipt and cash payments controls in Exhibits 4-11 and 4-12 (pp. 257–258).*

Three documents are required to be in agreement and approved before a check will be disbursed: receiving report, purchase invoice, and purchase order. Separate individuals must be responsible for approving the purchase, verifying that the services or goods have been received, and approving the invoice for payment. *Review the documents shown in Exhibit 4-13 (p. 259).*

## ⑤ Use a budget to manage cash

A budget helps a company manage cash by planning receipts and payments during a future period. The company can use the budget to determine if it will have the cash it needs for future operations. *Review the steps to preparing a cash budget on p. 260 of the text.*

# Demo Doc 1

## Bank Reconciliations

*Learning Objectives*     *1–5*

Hunter Corp. has the following information for July 2009:

| Cash | | | |
|---|---|---|---|
| Jul 1 | Bal 2,100 | | |
| | | Jul 8 | 400 |
| Jul 14 | 300 | | |
| | | Jul 25 | 900 |
| Jul 29 | 120 | | |
| | | Jul 30 | 500 |
| Jul 31 | Bal 720 | | |

| Bank Statement for July 2009 | | |
|---|---|---|
| Balance, July 1, 2009 ........................................................................ | | 2,100 |
| Deposits | | |
| July 14 ................................................................................... | | 300 |
| Checks | | |
| July 8 ...................................................................................... | 400 | |
| July 10 .................................................................................... | 230* | |
| July 25 .................................................................................... | 900 | (1,530) |
| Other items: | | |
| NSF check from Jim Andrews ............................................................. | | (150) |
| Interest on account balance ............................................................... | | 25 |
| EFT—collection of installment payments from customers ................ | | 800 |
| EFT—monthly rent expense ................................................................ | | (700) |
| Service charges .................................................................................. | | (75) |
| Balance, July 31, 2009 ....................................................................... | | 770 |

*The July 10 check was *not* written by Hunter. It was written by another bank customer and taken from Hunter's account in error.

Hunter deposits all cash receipts and makes all payments by check.

### Requirements

1. Prepare Hunter's bank reconciliation at July 31, 2009.

2. Journalize any entries required by Hunter and update Hunter's Cash T-account. Explanations are not required.

3. The employee at Hunter who opens the mail and physically collects the cash is the same person who updates the cash receipts journal and prepares the bank reconciliation. Is this a good internal control system?

4. In addition to this bank account, Hunter has certificates of deposit worth $200 at July 31, 2009. What amount would be reported for cash on Hunter's July 31, 2009, balance sheet? How would this amount be described?

5. During the month of August, Hunter expects to collect $1,000 of cash from customers, and pay for $600 of expenses in cash. Hunter also expects to purchase new long-term assets for $150 cash. How much cash should Hunter expect to have at August 31? Will Hunter have enough cash available at the end of August if its budgeted cash balance is $800?

# Demo Doc 1 Solutions

## Requirement 1

**Prepare Hunter's bank reconciliation at July 31, 2009.**

When you receive a monthly bank statement, the cash balance on your records is often different from the amount on the bank statement. The bank reconciliation reconciles, or brings into agreement, the checking account balance on the depositor's records and the bank's records.

In this case, to prepare the bank reconciliation we need to add reconciling items to both the bank balance and Hunter's cash balance. First, we must determine what these adjustments are. To more easily calculate the impact of these adjustments, we begin with a work sheet.

Make three columns: one for Hunter, one for the bank, and one for reconciling items in the middle. Begin with the balance both sides have for cash at July 31, 2009.

| Hunter | Reconciling Items | Bank |
|--------|-------------------|------|
| 720 | July 31 Balance | 770 |

A reconciling item arises because a valid transaction has not been recorded by both parties. For example, if the bank records service charges and Hunter does not, a reconciling item is required to bring Hunter's cash balance to the correct amount.

For each reconciling item, we will describe it in the Reconciling Items column and add it to or subtract it from the column of the party that has *not* yet recorded that transaction/entry.

### Deposits in Transit

According to the Cash T-account, Hunter made two deposits.

| | Cash | | |
|---|---|---|---|
| Jul 1 | Bal 2,100 | | |
| | | Jul 8 | 400 |
| Jul 14 | 300 | | |
| | | Jul 25 | 900 |
| Jul 29 | 120 | | |
| | | Jul 30 | 500 |
| Jul 31 | Bal 720 | | |

The two deposits are:

| | |
|--------|-----|
| July 14 | 300 |
| July 29 | 120 |

However, the bank statement only shows one (the July 14 deposit for $300). The July 29 deposit for $120 has not yet been recorded by the bank. This is a <u>deposit in transit</u> and will *increase* the bank account when the bank processes and records the deposit.

## Outstanding Checks and Bank Error

According to the Cash T-account, Hunter wrote three checks.

| Cash | | | |
|---|---|---|---|
| Jul 1 | Bal 2,100 | | |
| | | Jul 8 | 400 |
| Jul 14 | 300 | | |
| | | Jul 25 | 900 |
| Jul 29 | 120 | | |
| | | Jul 30 | 500 |
| Jul 31 | Bal 720 | | |

The three checks are:

| July 8 | 400 |
|---|---|
| July 25 | 900 |
| July 30 | 500 |

The bank statement shows three checks; however, only two (the July 8 check for $400 and the July 25 check for $900) are valid.

The July 10 check for $230 shown on the bank statement is a bank error and does not relate to Hunter. This error needs to be corrected by the bank (it would be a good idea for Hunter to contact the bank to confirm that it is correcting this mistake). This is an *increase* to Cash on the bank's side.

The bank statement does not show the third valid check: The July 30 check for $500 has not yet been recorded by the bank. This is an <u>outstanding check</u> and will *decrease* the bank account when it is recorded. The bank will record this check in the (near) future when it is cashed.

## NSF Check

A check deposited by Hunter for $150 was returned to the bank for insufficient funds. Hunter has not yet recorded the return of this customer check.

The $150 the customer owed has *not* been paid because Hunter was unable to cash the customer's check. The account receivable must be reinstated and Hunter's Cash account must be *decreased*.

## Interest Earned

Interest revenue of $25 has been earned on Hunter's bank balance but has not yet been recorded by Hunter. This will *increase* Hunter's Cash account.

## Installment Payments Received

Installment payments from customers of $800 have been collected by the bank via EFT but have not yet been recorded by Hunter. This will *increase* Hunter's Cash account.

### Rent Expense

The rent payment of $700 was made by the bank (on Hunter's behalf) but has not yet been recorded by Hunter. This will *decrease* Hunter's Cash account.

### Service Charges

Service charges of $75 have been incurred with the bank but have not yet been recorded by Hunter. This will *decrease* Hunter's Cash account.

Put all of these reconciling items into the work sheet.

Notice that the only items showing in the bank's column are deposits in transit, outstanding checks, and bank errors. Generally, these are the only reconciling items that will be on the bank's side of the reconciliation. Almost all other items will be on the company's side of the reconciliation. It is easier to remember potential reconciling items for the bank with the acronym DOE:

D  **D**eposits in Transit
O  **O**utstanding Checks
E  Bank **E**rrors

| Hunter | Reconciling Items | Bank |
|---|---|---|
| 720 | July 31 Balance | 770 |
|  | Deposits in Transit | 120 |
|  | Outstanding Checks | −500 |
|  | Bank Error (July 10 check) | 230 |
| −150 | NSF Check |  |
| 25 | Interest Earned |  |
| 800 | Installment Payments Collected |  |
| −700 | Rent Payment |  |
| − 75 | Service Charges |  |
| 620 | Total | 620 |

Notice that both columns in the work sheet have the same total. This is a good check to ensure that all calculations are correct. If these totals were not the same, there would be an error and/or some data would be missing.

We can now take these reconciling items and prepare the formal bank reconciliation. We list all additions and subtractions required for the bank and Hunter.

```
                          Hunter Corp.
                        Bank Reconciliation
                          July 31, 2009

 1  Bank:
 2  Balance, July 31, 2009 ..........................................................   $  770
 3  Add: July 29 deposit in transit...........................................          120
 4      Bank Error (July 10 check not belonging to Hunter)............          230
 5                                                                               1,120
 6
 7  Less: July 30 outstanding check.........................................         (500)
 8
 9  Adjusted bank balance, July 31, 2009....................................      $  620
10
11  Books:
12  Balance, July 31, 2009 ..........................................................   $  720
13  Add: Bank collection of installment payments.........................          800
14      Interest earned on account ..........................................           25
15                                                                               1,545
16  Less: Rent payment .............................................   $700
17      NSF check........................................................    150
18      Service charges ...............................................     75      (925)
19
20  Adjusted book balance, July 31, 2009....................................     $  620
```

## Requirement 2

**Journalize any entries required by Hunter and update Hunter's Cash T-account. Explanations are not required.**

**3** Prepare and use a bank reconciliation

Any reconciling items on Hunter's side for the bank reconciliation should be journalized. Usually, these entries are made in the order in which they appear on the bank reconciliation.

### Installment Payments

Cash increases (a debit) and Accounts Receivable decreases (a credit) by $800.

| Jul 31 | Cash | 800 | |
|--------|------|-----|---|
| | Accounts Receivable | | 800 |

### Interest Earned

Cash increases (a debit) and Interest Revenue increases (a credit) by $25.

| Jul 31 | Cash | 25 | |
|--------|------|-----|---|
| | Interest Revenue | | 25 |

### Rent Payment

Cash decreases (a credit) and Rent Expense increases (a debit) by $700.

| | | | |
|---|---|---|---|
| Jul 31 | Rent Expense | 700 | |
| | Cash | | 700 |

### NSF Check

Cash decreases (a credit) and Accounts Receivable increases (a debit) by $150.

| | | | |
|---|---|---|---|
| Jul 31 | Accounts Receivable—J. Andrews | 150 | |
| | Cash | | 150 |

### Service Charges

Cash decreases (a credit) and Misc. Expense increases (a debit) by $75.

| | | | |
|---|---|---|---|
| Jul 31 | Misc. Expense | 75 | |
| | Cash | | 75 |

Post these adjustments to the Cash T-account:

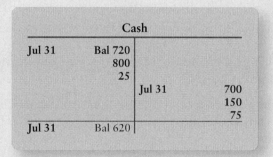

The final cash balance is $620, which is also the total on the bank reconciliation. Both totals must agree, so this is a good check to make sure that everything was done correctly.

① Learn about fraud and how much it costs

② Set up an internal control system

④ Apply internal controls to cash receipts and cash payments

### Requirement 3

**The employee at Hunter who opens the mail and physically collects the cash is the same person who updates the cash receipts journal and prepares the bank reconciliation. Is this a good internal control system?**

If an employee collects the cash *and* records the receipt of the cash *and* performs the bank reconciliation, then there is an opportunity for fraud.

The employee could steal the cash and delay recording the cash receipt or perhaps never record the cash receipt. The employee could hide his or her act for a long period of time by manipulating the bank reconciliations.

To avoid this problem, most internal control systems require separation of duties; that is, the employees who handle cash (both receipts and payments) are *not* the same employees who maintain the accounting records and prepare the bank reconciliations.

## Requirement 4

**In addition to this bank account, Hunter has certificates of deposit worth $200 at July 31, 2009. What amount would be reported for cash on Hunter's July 31, 2009, balance sheet? How would this amount be described?**

⑤ Use a budget to manage cash

The certificates of deposit are considered to be cash equivalents. The $200 of certificates would be added to Hunter's cash balance of $620, for a total balance of $820 on the balance sheet. This amount would be described as "Cash and Cash Equivalents."

## Requirement 5

**During the month of August, Hunter expects to collect $1,000 of cash from customers, and pay for $600 of expenses in cash. Hunter also expects to purchase new long-term assets for $150 cash. How much cash should Hunter expect to have at August 31? Will Hunter have enough cash available at the end of August if its budgeted cash balance is $800?**

⑤ Use a budget to manage cash

Budgeted cash for the end of the month is calculated as:

Beginning Cash + Cash Expected to be Received − Expected Cash Payments = Expected Ending Cash

In this problem, beginning cash is the Cash T-account balance at July 31, which is $620 (as seen in the T-account from Requirement 2). Expected cash increases are the receipts from customers of $1,000. Expected cash payments are the $600 of expenses and $150 for long-term asset purchases. This gives:

Expected Ending Cash = $620 + $1,000 − $600 − $150 = $870

Given this expected balance, Hunter will have $870 − $800 = $70 available at the end of August for additional investments. Following is Hunter's cash budget for the month of August:

| Hunter Corp. Cash Budget For the Month Ended August 31, 2009 | | |
|---|---|---|
| Cash balance, July 31, 2009.................................... | | $ 620 |
| Estimated cash receipts: | | |
| Collections from customers................................. | | 1,000 |
| | | 1,620 |
| Estimated cash payments: | | |
| Payment of operating expenses .......................... | $600 | |
| Purchases of long-term assets ............................. | 150 | (750) |
| Cash available....................................................... | | 870 |
| Budgeted cash balance, August 31, 2009................ | | 800 |
| Cash available for additional investments .............. | | $ 70 |

**DEMO DOC COMPLETE**

# Quick Practice Questions

## True/False

_____ 1. A deposit in transit has been recorded by the bank but not by the company.

_____ 2. An NSF check would be recorded on the books by debiting Accounts Receivable.

_____ 3. The three corners of the fraud triangle consist of motive, opportunity, and rationalization.

_____ 4. The Sarbanes-Oxley Act requires only auditors to issue an internal control report.

_____ 5. Different people should perform various accounting duties to minimize errors and the opportunities for fraud.

_____ 6. A budget is a financial plan that helps coordinate business activities.

_____ 7. The person who prepares checks for payment would be a suitable employee to reconcile the bank account.

_____ 8. Encryption helps to secure confidential information in e-commerce.

_____ 9. Outstanding checks would include only those checks written for the current month that have not cleared or been canceled by the bank.

_____ 10. It is a good control to have just one person open the checks and deposit them in the bank.

# Multiple Choice

1. **Which of the following is not an objective of internal control?**
   a. Help safeguard the assets a business uses in its operations
   b. Guarantee a company will not go bankrupt
   c. Encourage adherence to company policies
   d. Promote operational efficiency

2. **Which of the following items used to reconcile cash requires an adjusting entry?**
   a. Bank service charge
   b. Outstanding check
   c. Bank error
   d. Deposits in transit

3. **Which of the following statements about bank reconciliations is correct?**
   a. Should not be prepared by an employee who handles cash transactions
   b. Is required by Sarbanes-Oxley
   c. Is a formal financial statement
   d. Both (a) and (b) are correct

4. **Which of the following items does not cause a difference between the cash balance per bank and book?**
   a. NSF checks
   b. Deposits in transit
   c. Outstanding checks
   d. Canceled checks

5. **The following data are available for Wonder Boutique for October:**

   | | |
   |---|---|
   | Book balance, October 31 | $5,575 |
   | Outstanding checks | 584 |
   | Deposits in transit | 2,500 |
   | Service charges | 75 |
   | Interest revenue | 25 |

   **What is the adjusted book balance on October 31 for Wonder Boutique based on the preceding data?**
   a. $5,500
   b. $5,525
   c. $5,550
   d. $7,466

6. **The bank statement lists a $70 deposit as $700. On a bank reconciliation, this will appear as which of the following?**
   a. Addition to the book balance
   b. Deduction from the book balance
   c. Addition to the bank balance
   d. Deduction from the bank balance

7. **Which of the following is the first step in preparing a cash budget?**
   a. Add budgeted cash receipts and subtract budgeted cash payments.
   b. Compare the ending cash balance to the budgeted cash balance at the end of the period.
   c. Determine the company's cash balance at the beginning of the period.
   d. Take the beginning balance, add receipts, and subtract payments to give the expected cash balance at the end of the period.

8. **For which items must journal entries be prepared?**
   a. Any errors made on the books revealed by the bank reconciliation
   b. Any errors made by the bank revealed by the bank reconciliation
   c. All items on the bank's side
   d. Only outstanding checks

9. **Which of the following is *not* a control over petty cash?**
   a. Keeping an unlimited amount of cash on hand
   b. Supporting all fund disbursements with a petty cash ticket
   c. Replenishing the fund through normal cash disbursement procedures
   d. Designating one employee to administer the fund

10. **What are the most common reconciling items that will be on the bank's side of the reconciliation?**
    a. Interest earned, deposits in transit, and outstanding checks
    b. Deposits in transit, outstanding checks, and electronic fund transfers
    c. NSF checks, outstanding checks, and deposits in transit
    d. Outstanding checks, bank errors, and deposits in transit

11. **Which of the following is *not* an objective of internal control?**
    a. Encourage employees to follow company policy
    b. Encourage employees to come to work on time each day
    c. Safeguard assets
    d. Encourage employees to comply with legal requirements

12. **If a manager is convicted of fraud, he or she could be subject to which of the following?**
    a. Fines
    b Payment of monetary damages
    c. Imprisonment
    d. All of the above

## Quick Exercises

**4-1.** Classify each of the following reconciling items of the Bread and Butter Company as one of the following:

**a.** An addition to the bank balance
**b.** A deduction from the bank balance
**c.** An addition to the book balance
**d.** A deduction from the book balance
**e.** Not a reconciling item

_____ 1. Collection of note receivable plus interest revenue by bank

_____ 2. Bookkeeper recorded check #849 as $557 instead of the correct amount of $755

_____ 3. Bank service charges

_____ 4. Bank credited the account for interest revenue

_____ 5. Bank added deposit to Bread and Butter's account in error

_____ 6. Deposits in transit

_____ 7. Bank withdrew $1,270 from Bread and Butter's account for a check written for $12,700

_____ 8. Bookkeeper failed to record a check that was returned with the bank statement

_____ 9. Check deposited and returned by the bank marked NSF

_____ 10. Outstanding checks

**4-2.** Using the following information, record the journal entries that would be necessary after preparing the bank reconciliation for Storm, Inc., on May 31, 2011. Some items may not require an entry.

**a.** Outstanding checks total $2,600.

| Journal | | | | |
|---|---|---|---|---|
| Date | Accounts and Explanation | | Debit | Credit |
| | | | | |
| | | | | |
| | | | | |

**b.** The bookkeeper recorded a $12,300 check as $1,230 in payment of the current month's rent.

| Journal | | | | |
|---|---|---|---|---|
| Date | Accounts and Explanation | | Debit | Credit |
| | | | | |
| | | | | |
| | | | | |

**c.** A deposit of $300 from a customer was credited to Storm, Inc., for $3,000 by the bank.

| Journal | | | |
|---|---|---|---|
| Date | Accounts and Explanation | Debit | Credit |
| | | | |
| | | | |
| | | | |

**d.** A customer's check for $1,380 was returned for nonsufficient funds.

| Journal | | | |
|---|---|---|---|
| Date | Accounts and Explanation | Debit | Credit |
| | | | |
| | | | |
| | | | |

**e.** The bank service charge based on the bank statement is $50.

| Journal | | | |
|---|---|---|---|
| Date | Accounts and Explanation | Debit | Credit |
| | | | |
| | | | |
| | | | |

**4-3.** The following data have been gathered for Batter Company to assist you in preparing the September 30, 2011, bank reconciliation:

**a.** The September 30 bank balance was $5,460.
**b.** The bank statement included $30 of service charges.
**c.** There was an EFT deposit of $1,800 on the bank statement for the monthly rent due from a tenant.
**d.** Checks #541 and #543, for $205 and $420, respectively, were not among the canceled checks returned with the statement.
**e.** The September 30 deposit of $3,800 did not appear on the bank statement.
**f.** The bookkeeper had erroneously recorded a $500 check as $5,000. The check was payment for an amount due on account.
**g.** Included with the canceled checks was a check written by Bitter Company for $200, which was deducted from Batter Company's account.
**h.** The bank statement included an NSF check written by Tate Company for a $360 payment on account.
**i.** The Cash account showed a balance of $2,925 on September 30.

**1. Prepare the September 30, 2011, bank reconciliation for Batter Company.**

---

**Batter Company**
**Bank Reconciliation**
**September 30, 2011**

**Bank:**
Balance, September 30, 2011 ......................................
Add:


Less:



Adjusted bank balance, September 30, 2011 ...............

**Books:**
Balance, September 30, 2011 ......................................
Add:



Less:



Adjusted book balance, September 30, 2011 ...............

**4-4.** The following data have been gathered for Ragpicker Company. Calculate the correct cash balance on February 29, 2012, by performing the part of the bank reconciliation beginning with the balance per bank as shown. NOTE: Not all of the following information may be needed.

**a.** The service charges for February amount to $90.

**b.** Outstanding checks amount to $650.

**c.** The bank erroneously credited Ragpicker Company's account for $300 for a deposit made by another company.

**d.** Check #665 for $3,000 for the cash purchase of office equipment was erroneously recorded by the bookkeeper as $2,080.

**e.** A deposit ticket correctly prepared for $975 appeared on the bank statement as a deposit for $795.

**f.** A customer's check for $560 was returned with the bank statement and stamped NSF.

**g.** Check #650 for $125 for utilities expense was erroneously recorded by the bookkeeper as $1,250.

Ragpicker Company
Bank Reconciliation
February 29, 2012

Bank:
Balance, February 29, 2012............................................... $7,975
Add:

Less:

Adjusted bank balance, February 29, 2012 .......................

## Do It Yourself! Question 1

## Bank Reconciliations

Quint, Inc., has the following information for May 2011:

| Cash | | | |
|---|---|---|---|
| May 1 | Bal 4,500 | | |
| | | May 4 | 900 |
| May 9 | 600 | | |
| | | May 12 | 2,300 |
| May 18 | 1,000 | | |
| | | May 22 | 1,500 |
| May 28 | 700 | | |
| | | May 30 | 500 |
| May 31 | Bal 1,600 | | |

| Bank Statement for May 2011 | | |
|---|---|---|
| Balance, May 1, 2011 ............................ | | 4,500 |
| Deposits | | |
| May 9 ................................................. | 600 | |
| May 18 ............................................... | 1,000 | 1,600 |
| Checks | | |
| May 4 ................................................. | 900 | |
| May 12 ............................................... | 2,300 | |
| May 22 ............................................... | 1,500 | (4,700) |
| Other items: | | |
| EFT—payment of mortgage ................... | | (1,300) |
| NSF check from Bennet Smith................ | | (400) |
| Service charges ....................................... | | (100) |
| EFT—monthly rent revenue ................... | | 1,200 |
| Interest on account balance.................... | | 50 |
| Balance, May 31, 2011 ........................... | | 850 |

The mortgage payment includes principal of $950 and interest of $350.

The rent collection is from tenants leasing extra space in Quint's office building.

Quint deposits all cash receipts and makes all payments by check.

## Requirements

1. Prepare Quint's bank reconciliation at May 31, 2011.

```
            Reconciling Items



            Total
```

2. **Journalize any entries required by Quint and update Quint's Cash T-account. Explanations are not required.**

| Date | Accounts and Explanation | Debit | Credit |
|------|--------------------------|-------|--------|
|      |                          |       |        |
|      |                          |       |        |

| Date | Accounts and Explanation | Debit | Credit |
|------|--------------------------|-------|--------|
|      |                          |       |        |
|      |                          |       |        |

| Date | Accounts and Explanation | Debit | Credit |
|------|--------------------------|-------|--------|
|      |                          |       |        |
|      |                          |       |        |

| Date | Accounts and Explanation | Debit | Credit |
|------|--------------------------|-------|--------|
|      |                          |       |        |
|      |                          |       |        |

| Date | Accounts and Explanation | Debit | Credit |
|------|--------------------------|-------|--------|
|      |                          |       |        |
|      |                          |       |        |

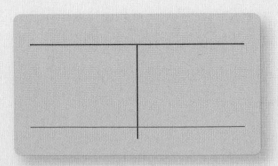

# Quick Practice Solutions

## True/False

___F___  1. A deposit in transit has been recorded by the bank
          but not by the company.

   False—A deposit in transit has been recorded by the *company*, but
   not by the bank. (p. 249)

___T___  2. An NSF check would be recorded on the books by debiting
          Accounts Receivable. (p. 251)

___T___  3. The three corners of the fraud triangle consist of motive,
          opportunity, and rationalization. (p. 235)

___F___  4. The Sarbanes-Oxley Act requires only auditors to issue an
          internal control report.

   False—The Sarbanes-Oxley Act requires reports from both management and the auditor. It requires management to issue a
   report on internal controls similar to Exhibit 4-2 (p. 237), and also
   requires auditors to audit the system and issue their own report
   on the soundness of those internal controls. (p. 237)

___T___  5. Different people should perform various accounting duties to
          minimize errors and the opportunities for fraud. (pp. 239–240)

___T___  6. A budget is a financial plan that helps coordinate business
          activities. (p. 260)

___F___  7. The person who prepares checks for payment would be a suitable
          employee to reconcile the bank account.

   False—Responsibilities for custody, approval, and accounting
   should be held by *separate* employees. (pp. 239–240)

___T___  8. Encryption helps to secure confidential information in
          e-commerce. (p. 244)

___F___  9. Outstanding checks would include only those checks written for
          the current month that have not cleared or been canceled by
          the bank.

   False—Outstanding checks include *all* checks written that have
   not cleared the bank. They could be from the *current month or
   previous periods*. (p. 249)

___F___  10. It is a good control to have just one person open the checks and
          deposit them in the bank.

   False—*Separate* individuals should be assigned custody, approval,
   and accounting tasks. (pp. 239–240)

# Multiple Choice

1. **Which of the following is not an objective of internal control? (p. 236)**
   a. Help safeguard the assets a business uses in its operations
   b. Guarantee a company will not go bankrupt
   c. Encourage adherence to company policies
   d. Promote operational efficiency

2. **Which of the following items used to reconcile cash requires an adjusting entry? (p. 251)**
   a. Bank service charge
   b. Outstanding checks
   c. Bank error
   d. Deposits in transit

3. **Which of the following statements about bank reconciliations is correct? (pp. 239–240, 248)**
   a. Should not be prepared by an employee who handles cash transactions
   b. Is required by Sarbanes-Oxley
   c. Is a formal financial statement
   d. Both (a) and (b) are correct

4. **Which of the following items does not cause a difference between the cash balance per bank and book? (p. 249)**
   a. NSF checks
   b. Deposits in transit
   c. Outstanding checks
   d. Canceled checks

5. **The following data are available for Wonder Boutique for October:**

| | |
|---|---|
| Book balance, October 31 | $5,575 |
| Outstanding checks | 584 |
| Deposits in transit | 2,500 |
| Service charges | 75 |
| Interest revenue | 25 |

   **What is the adjusted book balance on October 31 for Wonder Boutique based on the preceding data? (p. 250)**
   a. $5,500
   b. $5,525
   c. $5,550
   d. $7,466

6. **The bank statement lists a $70 deposit as $700. On a bank reconciliation, this will appear as which of the following? (p. 249)**
   a. Addition to the book balance
   b. Deduction from the book balance
   c. Addition to the bank balance
   d. Deduction from the bank balance

7. **Which of the following is the first step in preparing a cash budget? (p. 260)**
   a. Add budgeted cash receipts and subtract budgeted cash payments.
   b. Compare the ending cash balance to the budgeted cash balance at the end of the period.
   c. Determine the company's cash balance at the beginning of the period.
   d. Take the beginning balance, add receipts, and subtract payments to give the expected cash balance at the end of the period.

8. **For which items must journal entries be prepared? (p. 251)**
   a. Any errors made on the books revealed by the bank reconciliation
   b. Any errors made by the bank revealed by the bank reconciliation
   c. All items on the bank's side
   d. Only outstanding checks

9. **Which of the following is *not* a control over petty cash? (pp. 259–260)**
   a. Keeping an unlimited amount of cash on hand
   b. Supporting all fund disbursements with a petty cash ticket
   c. Replenishing the fund through normal cash disbursement procedures
   d. Designating one employee to administer the fund

10. **What are the most common reconciling items that will be on the bank's side of the reconciliation? (p. 249)**
    a. Interest earned, deposits in transit, and outstanding checks
    b. Deposits in transit, outstanding checks, and electronic fund transfers
    c. NSF checks, outstanding checks, and deposits in transit
    d. Outstanding checks, bank errors, and deposits in transit

11. **Which of the following is *not* an objective of internal control? (p. 238)**
    a. Encourage employees to follow company policy
    b. Encourage employees to come to work on time each day
    c. Safeguard assets
    d. Encourage employees to comply with legal requirements

12. **If a manager is convicted of fraud, he or she could be subject to which of the following? (p. 238)**
    a. Fines
    b. Payment of monetary damages
    c. Imprisonment
    d. All of the above

# Quick Exercises

**4-1.** **Classify each of the following reconciling items of the Bread and Butter Company as one of the following: (pp. 249–250)**

a. An addition to the bank balance
b. A deduction from the bank balance
c. An addition to the book balance
d. A deduction from the book balance
e. Not a reconciling item

| | |
|---|---|
| ___c___ | **1.** Collection of note receivable plus interest revenue by bank |
| ___d___ | **2.** Bookkeeper recorded check #849 as $557 instead of the correct amount of $755 |
| ___d___ | **3.** Bank service charges |
| ___c___ | **4.** Bank credited the account for interest revenue |
| ___b___ | **5.** Bank added deposit to Bread and Butter's account in error |
| ___a___ | **6.** Deposits in transit |
| ___b___ | **7.** Bank withdrew $1,270 from Bread and Butter's account for a check written for $12,700 |
| ___d___ | **8.** Bookkeeper failed to record a check that was returned with the bank statement |
| ___d___ | **9.** Check deposited and returned by the bank marked NSF |
| ___b___ | **10.** Outstanding checks |

**4-2.** **Using the following information, record the journal entries that would be necessary after preparing the bank reconciliation for Storm, Inc., on May 31, 2011. Some items may not require an entry. (p. 251)**

a. Outstanding checks total $2,600.

| Journal | | | | |
|---|---|---|---|---|
| | Date | Accounts and Explanation | Debit | Credit |
| a. | | No entry required | | |
| | | | | |

b. The bookkeeper recorded a $12,300 check as $1,230 in payment of the current month's rent.

| Journal | | | | |
|---|---|---|---|---|
| | Date | Accounts and Explanation | Debit | Credit |
| b. | May 31 | Rent Expense | 11,070 | |
| | | Cash | | 11,070 |

**c.** A deposit of $300 from a customer was credited to Storm, Inc., for $3,000 by the bank.

| Journal | | | | |
|---|---|---|---|---|
| | Date | Accounts and Explanation | Debit | Credit |
| c. | | No entry required | | |

**d.** A customer's check for $1,380 was returned for nonsufficient funds.

| Journal | | | | |
|---|---|---|---|---|
| | Date | Accounts and Explanation | Debit | Credit |
| d. | May 31 | Accounts Receivable | 1,380 | |
| | | Cash | | 1,380 |

**e.** The bank service charge based on the bank statement is $50.

| Journal | | | | |
|---|---|---|---|---|
| | Date | Accounts and Explanation | Debit | Credit |
| e. | May 31 | Miscellaneous Expense | 50 | |
| | | Cash | | 50 |

**4-3.** **The following data have been gathered for Batter Company to assist you in preparing the September 30, 2011, bank reconciliation: (pp. 250–251)**

**a.** The September 30 bank balance was $5,460.

**b.** The bank statement included $30 of service charges.

**c.** There was an EFT deposit of $1,800 on the bank statement for the monthly rent due from a tenant.

**d.** Checks #541 and #543, for $205 and $420, respectively, were not among the canceled checks returned with the statement.

**e.** The September 30 deposit of $3,800 did not appear on the bank statement.

**f.** The bookkeeper had erroneously recorded a $500 check as $5,000. The check was payment for an amount due on account.

**g.** Included with the canceled checks was a check written by Bitter Company for $200, which was deducted from Batter Company's account.

**h.** The bank statement included an NSF check written by Tate Company for a $360 payment on account.

**i.** The Cash account showed a balance of $2,925 on September 30.

**1. Prepare the September 30, 2011, bank reconciliation for Batter Company.**

### Batter Company
### Bank Reconciliation
### September 30, 2011

**Bank:**

| | | |
|---|---:|---:|
| Balance, September 30, 2011 ........................................ | | $5,460 |
| Add: Deposit in transit.................................................. | $3,800 | |
|     Bank error—Bitter Co. check .................................. | 200 | |
| | | 4,000 |
| | | |
| Less: Outstanding checks | | |
|     Check #541............................................................. | 205 | |
|     Check #543............................................................. | 420 | |
| | | (625) |
| Adjusted bank balance, September 30, 2011 ............... | | $8,835 |
| | | |
| **Books:** | | |
| Balance, September 30, 2011 ........................................ | | $2,925 |
| Add: | | |
| EFT—Rent deposit........................................................ | $1,800 | |
| Bookkeeper error ($5,000 – $500) ............................... | 4,500 | |
| | | 6,300 |
| | | |
| Less: | | |
| Bank service charge ...................................................... | 30 | |
| NSF check ..................................................................... | 360 | |
| | | (390) |
| Adjusted book balance, September 30, 2011 ............... | | $8,835 |

**4-4.** The following data have been gathered for Ragpicker Company. Calculate the correct cash balance on February 29, 2012, by performing the part of the bank reconciliation beginning with the balance per bank as shown. NOTE: Not all of the following information may be needed. (pp. 250–251)

**a.** The service charges for February amount to $90.

**b.** Outstanding checks amount to $650.

**c.** The bank erroneously credited Ragpicker Company's account for $300 for a deposit made by another company.

**d.** Check #665 for $3,000 for the cash purchase of office equipment was erroneously recorded by the bookkeeper as $2,080.

**e.** A deposit ticket correctly prepared for $975 appeared on the bank statement as a deposit for $795.

**f.** A customer's check for $560 was returned with the bank statement and stamped NSF.

**g.** Check #650 for $125 for utilities expense was erroneously recorded by the bookkeeper as $1,250.

**Ragpicker Company**
**Bank Reconciliation**
**February 29, 2012**

| | | |
|---|---|---|
| Bank: | | |
| Balance, February 29, 2012 | | $7,975 |
| Add: | | |
| Bank error—Deposit of $975 recorded as $795 | $180 | |
| | | 180 |
| Less: | | |
| Outstanding checks | 650 | |
| Bank error | 300 | |
| | | (950) |
| Adjusted bank balance, February 29, 2012 | | $7,205 |

NOTE: Remember that the adjusted bank balance is the correct book balance.

# Do It Yourself! Question 1 Solutions

1. Prepare Quint's bank reconciliation at May 31, 2011.

| Quint | Reconciling Items | Bank |
|---|---|---|
| 1,600 | May 31 Balance | 850 |
| | Deposits in Transit | 700 |
| | Outstanding Checks | (500) |
| (1,300) | Mortgage Payment | |
| (400) | NSF Check | |
| (100) | Service Charges | |
| 1,200 | Rent Collection | |
| 50 | Interest Earned | |
| 1,050 | Total | 1,050 |

## Quint, Inc.
## Bank Reconciliation
## May 31, 2011

**Bank:**

| | | |
|---|---|---|
| Balance, May 31, 2011 ................................................. | | 850 |
| Add: May 28 deposit in transit...................................... | | 700 |
| | | 1,550 |
| | | |
| Less: May 30 outstanding check | | (500) |
| | | |
| Adjusted bank balance, May 31, 2011 ........................ | | 1,050 |

**Books:**

| | | |
|---|---|---|
| Balance, May 31, 2011 ................................................. | | 1,600 |
| Add: Bank collection of rent......................................... | | 1,200 |
| Interest earned on account ...................................... | | 50 |
| | | 2,850 |
| Less: Mortgage payment ............................................. | 1,300 | |
| NSF check—B. Smith............................................. | 400 | |
| Service charges........................................................ | 100 | (1,800) |
| | | |
| Adjusted book balance, May 31, 2011........................ | | 1,050 |

**2. Journalize any entries required by Quint and update Quint's Cash T-account. Explanations are not required.**

| | | | |
|---|---|---|---|
| May 31 | Cash | 1,200 | |
| | Rent Revenue | | 1,200 |

| | | | |
|---|---|---|---|
| May 31 | Cash | 50 | |
| | Interest Revenue | | 50 |

| | | | |
|---|---|---|---|
| May 31 | Mortgage Payable | 950 | |
| | Interest Expense | 350 | |
| | Cash | | 1,300 |

| | | | |
|---|---|---|---|
| May 31 | Accounts Receivable—Bennet Smith | 400 | |
| | Cash | | 400 |

| | | | |
|---|---|---|---|
| May 31 | Miscellaneous Expense | 100 | |
| | Cash | | 100 |

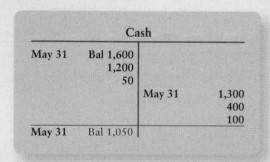

Cash

| May 31 | Bal 1,600 | | |
| | 1,200 | | |
| | 50 | | |
| | | May 31 | 1,300 |
| | | | 400 |
| | | | 100 |
| May 31 | Bal 1,050 | | |

# The Power of Practice

For more practice using the skills learned in this chapter, visit MyAccountingLab. There you will find algorithmically generated questions that are based on these Demo Docs and your main textbook's Review and Assess Your Progress sections.

Go to MyAccountingLab and follow these steps:

1. Direct your URL to www.myaccountinglab.com.
2. Log in using your name and password.
3. Click the MyAccountingLab link.
4. Click Study Plan in the left navigation bar.
5. From the table of contents, select Chapter 4, Internal Control & Cash.
6. Click a link to work tutorial exercises.

# 5 Short-Term Investments & Receivables

## WHAT YOU PROBABLY ALREADY KNOW

You probably already know that if a friend borrows money from you, there is a *chance* you may not be repaid. You would not loan money to a friend if you didn't believe that he or she is creditworthy and will likely repay the debt. However, until the money is received, there is no guarantee. If the friend asks to borrow more money before repaying the original loan, you may be more likely to refuse your friend because your risk of nonpayment is increased. There has been no history of successful repayment yet. If the friend never pays, you have incurred a loss equal to the amount of the loan.

The same concerns exist for a business. Sales on account are made only after a company has been approved by the credit department. Despite the most thorough investigation, there will always be some customers who may not pay the amount due. The uncollectible accounts receivable results in a reduction to the asset and to net income.

## Learning Objectives

 **Account for short-term investments**

Short-term investments, also known as *marketable securities*, are investments that a company plans to sell within one year. Trading investments are a type of short-term investment whose purpose is to sell the investment for more than its cost. Increases and decreases in the value of these investments, while they are being held, are called unrealized gains and losses. *Review the financial statement presentation of these investments and unrealized gains and losses in Exhibit 5-1 (p. 293).*

 **Account for, and control, accounts receivable**

In Chapter 4, we learned that an important feature of a strong system of internal control is to separate responsibility for custody of assets from the accounting and operating departments. The individual handling cash should not be granting credit, nor should he or she be accounting for receivables.

 **Use the allowance method for uncollectible receivables**

The **allowance method** matches the sales revenues with the uncollectible accounts expense. An *estimate* of the uncollectible accounts expense must be made in the period of sale using either the aging of receivables or the percent-of-sales methods. The entry required at the end of the period is

| | | | |
|---|---|---|---|
| | Uncollectible-Account Expense | X | |
| | Allowance for Doubtful Accounts | | X |

The **Allowance for Uncollectible Accounts** is a contra asset account. This account is credited, rather than Accounts Receivable, because it is unknown on the entry date which specific customers will eventually not pay. When it is determined which customer's receivable is uncollectible, the Allowance account is reduced (debited) and the specific customer Accounts Receivable is reduced (credited). *Carefully review "Accounting for Uncollectible Receivables" in the text. This can be a challenging concept.*

 **Account for notes receivable**

A **note receivable** is a formal written promise to pay the amount borrowed by the debtor plus interest. Interest must be recorded for the period of indebtedness. *Study the key components of a note in Exhibit 5-4 (p. 307). Review the journal entries that follow.*

 **Use two new ratios to evaluate a business**

A measure of liquidity is the **acid-test ratio**. The current assets most quickly converted into cash are compared to the total current liabilities. A higher result is usually more favorable. The ratio is calculated as follows:

$$\text{Acid-test ratio} = \frac{\text{Cash} + \text{Short-term investments} + \text{Net current receivables}}{\text{Total current liabilities}}$$

The **days' sales in receivables** indicates the number of days it takes on average to collect from customers. The objective is to minimize the collection period.

*Review the ratio computations in "Using Two Key Ratios to Make Decisions" in the text.*

# Demo Doc 1

## Trading Investments

*Learning Objective*     *1*

On January 1, 2009, Swan Corp. purchased 1,000 shares of Eagle, Inc., for $2 cash per share. This stock is considered by Swan to be a trading investment.

On November 30, 2009, Eagle paid cash dividends of $0.40 per share to all shareholders. The market price of Eagle's stock on December 31, 2009, was $2.30 per share.

### Requirements

1. For Swan Corp., journalize all transactions relating to the Eagle investment in 2009.

2. What is the impact of the Eagle investment on Swan's income statement and balance sheet for 2009?

# Demo Doc 1 Solutions

## Requirement 1

**For Swan Corp., journalize all transactions relating to the Eagle investment in 2009.**

① Account for short-term investments

### Purchase of investment

Cash is being paid to purchase the investment, so Cash (an asset) is decreased (a credit) by 1,000 shares × $2 per share = $2,000.

The Eagle shares purchased are a trading investment, which is an asset. Short-Term Investments (an asset) is increased (a debit) by $2,000.

| | | | |
|---|---|---|---|
| Short-Term Investments | | 2,000 | |
| Cash ($2 × 1,000) | | | 2,000 |

### Cash dividends received

Cash (an asset) is received, so it is increased (a debit) by

$$\$0.40 \text{ per share} \times 1,000 \text{ shares} = \$400$$

*Dividend Revenue* (revenue) is also increased (a credit) by $400.

| | | | |
|---|---|---|---|
| Cash ($0.40 × 1,000) | | 400 | |
| Dividend Revenue | | | 400 |

Notice the difference between this treatment for dividends *received* and the treatment for dividends *paid* (introduced in Chapter 2). Dividends *paid* result in a *decrease* in Cash. This cash goes to the company's own shareholders, and is considered an equity transaction. Dividends *received* result in an *increase* in Cash. This cash goes into the company's pocket. It is *earned* by the company, as a result of owning the investment, and so is called Dividend Revenue.

Remember: Dividends *paid* result in an increase to the Dividends account. Dividends *received* result in an increase to the Dividend Revenue account.

Dividend Revenue is reported on the income statement, just like other revenues you have encountered (such as Service Revenue and Interest Revenue).

### Year-end adjustment

We are required to adjust the value of trading investments to market price at year-end (for presentation on the balance sheet).

This means that we must adjust the Eagle investment from its original balance/value of $2,000 to its new market value of

$$\$2.30 \text{ market price per share} \times 1,000 \text{ shares} = \$2,300$$

The Eagle investment has increased in value by

$$\$2,300 - \$2,000 = \$300$$

So the Short-Term Investments account (an asset) is increased (a debit) by $300.

This increase is an *unrealized* gain (a credit) of $300. We know that the gain is unrealized because there is no cash involved in the transaction to ensure that the gain is "real." In the case of trading investments, we are uncertain because the stock was not actually sold. Market prices change constantly and today's gain could be tomorrow's loss. We emphasize this uncertainty on the income statement by highlighting this gain as an *unrealized* (paper) gain.

| | | | | |
|---|---|---|---|---|
| | Short-Term Investments ($2,300 - $2,000) | 300 | | |
| | Unrealized Gain on Investments | | | 300 |

## Requirement 2

**What is the impact of the Eagle investment on Swan's income statement and balance sheet for 2009?**

①  Account for short-term investments

Short-Term Investments have been adjusted to their market value of $2,300 at December 31, 2009. So, we would see Short-Term Investments of $2,300 reported on the balance sheet, under current assets.

There are two impacts of the Eagle investment on the income statement. First, there is Dividend Revenue of $400, and second, there is Unrealized Gain on Investments of $300. Both of these are reported on the income statement as positive/credit amounts.

*DEMO DOC COMPLETE*

# Demo Doc 2

## Uncollectible Receivables

*Learning Objectives*   2, 3, 5

Hart, Inc.'s, December 31, 2010, balance sheet reported:

| | |
|---|---|
| Accounts Receivable............................................ | $800 |
| Allowance for Uncollectible Accounts................ | (40) |
| Accounts Receivable (net) ................................. | $760 |

## Requirements

1. **Is Hart using the allowance method or the direct write-off method to account for uncollectible receivables? How much of the December 31, 2010, balance of accounts receivable did Hart expect to collect?**

2. **During 2011, Hart wrote off accounts receivable totaling $35 from Amanda Blake. Journalize these write-offs as one transaction. How does this transaction affect the net accounts receivable balance? How would this transaction have been recorded if the direct write-off method were being used?**

3. **During 2011, Hart earned $2,800 of service revenues, all on account. Journalize these revenues as one transaction.**

4. **During 2011, Hart collected $2,745 cash from customers. Journalize this transaction and calculate the gross accounts receivable balance at December 31, 2011.**

5. **Assume that Hart estimates uncollectible account expense to be 1.5% of revenues. Journalize the entry to adjust the allowance at December 31, 2011. What is the December 31, 2011, balance in the allowance?**

6. **Ignoring Requirement 5, assume that Hart has the following information at December 31, 2011:**

| Age | Gross Accounts Receivable | Percentage Estimated Uncollectible |
|---|---|---|
| < 30 days................ | $100 | 2% |
| 30–60 days............. | 500 | 4% |
| > 60 days................ | 220 | 10% |
| Total...................... | $820 | |

**Journalize the entry to adjust the allowance at December 31, 2011. What is the December 31, 2011, balance in the allowance? Show how accounts receivable would be reported on the balance sheet at December 31, 2011.**

7. In 2012, Hart wrote off $48 of accounts receivable. On June 30, 2012, Hart estimated uncollectible accounts expense was $10 for the first six months of the year, based on the percent-of-sales method. Journalize these transactions.

8. At December 31, 2012, based on the aging-of-receivables method, Hart estimated the allowance balance to be $35. Journalize Hart's entry to adjust the allowance for the year-end financial statements. (Assume the December 31, 2011, balance in the allowance was $30.) What is total uncollectible-account expense for 2012?

9. Calculate Hart's days' sales in accounts receivable for 2011. (Assume Hart uses the aging-of-receivables method in Requirement 6.) What does this ratio mean?

10. The employee at Hart who opens the mail and physically collects the cash is the same person who updates the cash receipts journal and accounts receivable ledger. Is this a good internal control system?

# Demo Doc 2 Solutions

## Requirement 1

③ Use the allowance method for uncollectible receivables

**Is Hart using the allowance method or the direct write-off method to account for uncollectible receivables? How much of the December 31, 2010, balance of accounts receivable did Hart expect to collect?**

Hart is using the allowance method. We know this because an allowance for uncollectible accounts has been set up. If Hart were using the direct write-off method, there would be no allowance for uncollectible accounts.

Gross accounts receivable is the total amount of receivables that exist. For Hart, this is $800. The allowance is (by definition) the amount of receivables we do *not* expect to collect.

The total receivables minus the amount we do not expect to collect (that is, the gross accounts receivable minus the allowance) is the amount we *do* expect to collect (that is, the *net* accounts receivable).

Hart expects to collect $760 of the accounts receivable.

## Requirement 2

③ Use the allowance method for uncollectible receivables

**During 2011, Hart wrote off accounts receivable totaling $35 from Amanda Blake. Journalize these write-offs as one transaction. How does this transaction affect the net accounts receivable balance? How would this transaction have been recorded if the direct write-off method were being used?**

Writing off an account receivable means removing it from the accounting books/records because it has been determined that this specific amount will *not* be collected. This means that we have to reduce (credit) the Accounts Receivable. Additionally, now that we have found one of the accounts that will not be collected, we can take it out of our estimate of uncollectible accounts (the Allowance for Uncollectible Accounts). This results in a decrease to this account (a debit).

| | | |
|---|---|---|
| Allowance for Uncollectible Accounts | 35 | |
| Accounts Receivable—Amanda Blake | | 35 |

This is the standard format to write off Accounts Receivable when using the allowance method. The entry structure is always the same; only the amount changes.

Note that this entry does *not* change the *net* accounts receivable. Gross accounts receivable decreases, but so does the allowance. Overall the change is zero:

| | |
|---|---|
| Gross Accounts Receivable................................... | change of –$35 |
| – Allowance for Uncollectible Accounts................ | (change of –$35) |
| Net Accounts Receivable..................................... | no change |

The impact of this transaction is:

| | |
|---|---|
| Gross Accounts Receivable................. | $800 – $35 = $765 |
| – Allowance .......................................... | ($ 40 – $35 = $ 5) |
| Net Accounts Receivable.................... | $760 – $ 0 = $760 |

There is no allowance under the direct write-off method, so the debit in the write-off entry is an increase to Uncollectible-Account Expense.

| | | |
|---|---|---|
| Uncollectible-Account Expense | 35 | |
| Accounts Receivable—Amanda Blake | | 35 |

## Requirement 3

**During 2011, Hart earned $2,800 of service revenues, all on account. Journalize these revenues as one transaction.**

When revenues are earned, we increase the Revenues account (a credit). In this case, we are not receiving cash, so instead we increase Accounts Receivable (a debit) to show that we intend to collect this amount later from our customer(s).

| | | |
|---|---|---|
| Accounts Receivable | 2,800 | |
| Service Revenue | | 2,800 |

## Requirement 4

**During 2011, Hart collected $2,745 cash from customers. Journalize this transaction and calculate the gross accounts receivable balance at December 31, 2011.**

When cash is collected, we increase the Cash account (a debit) and decrease Accounts Receivable (a credit).

| | | |
|---|---|---|
| Cash | 2,745 | |
| Accounts Receivable | | 2,745 |

③ Use the allowance method for uncollectible receivables

From the initial data given in the question, we can see that *gross* accounts receivable had a balance of $800 at the beginning of the year ($760 is the *net* balance). Accounts Receivable increased in the year as revenues were earned. Accounts Receivable decreased when uncollectible accounts were written off and when cash was collected. Using this information, we can calculate the ending balance in (gross) Accounts Receivable:

| Accounts Receivable | | | |
|---|---|---|---|
| Dec 31, 2010 Bal | 800 | | |
| 2011 Revenues | 2,800 | | |
| | | 2011 Write-Offs | 35 |
| | | 2011 Cash Collections | 2,745 |
| Dec 31, 2011 Bal | 820 | | |

## Requirement 5

Use the allowance method for uncollectible receivables

**Assume that Hart estimates uncollectible account expense to be 1.5% of revenues. Journalize the entry to adjust the allowance at December 31, 2011. What is the December 31, 2011, balance in the allowance?**

The problem states, "*Hart estimates uncollectible account expense to be 1.5% of revenues.*" The key phrase here is "*1.5% of revenues.*" This informs us that Hart is using the percent-of-sales method to calculate the expense and allowance.

Under the percent-of-sales method, the percent of sales equals the uncollectible-account expense. Therefore, we can calculate that 1.5% of $2,800 = $42 = the uncollectible-account expense. This means that we record $42 of expense in our journal entry.

Recording the Uncollectible-Account Expense increases that account (a debit) and also increases the total estimate of uncollectible accounts: the Allowance (a credit).

| | | |
|---|---|---|
| Uncollectible-Account Expense ($2,800 3 1.5%) | 42 | |
| Allowance for Uncollectible Accounts | | 42 |

This is the standard journal entry format to record Uncollectible-Account Expense and adjust the Allowance. The entry structure is always the same; only the amount changes.

The balance in the Allowance account must be calculated. The beginning balance in the allowance for 2011 is the ending balance for 2010 (the $40 shown at the beginning of the question). During the year, write-offs will decrease the allowance ($35, as in Requirement 2) and the year-end adjustment will increase it ($42, as in this Requirement). We can fill in this information to calculate an ending balance of $47 in the Allowance account.

| Allowance for Uncollectible Accounts | | | |
|---|---|---|---|
| | | Dec 31, 2010 Bal | 40 |
| 2011 Write-Offs | 35 | | |
| | | 2011 Uncollectible- Account Expense Adjustment | 42 |
| | | Dec 31, 2011 Bal | 47 |

## Requirement 6

Ignoring Requirement 5, assume that Hart has the following information at December 31, 2011:

| Age | Gross Accounts Receivable | Percentage Estimated Uncollectible |
|---|---|---|
| < 30 days............... | $100 | 2% |
| 3–60 days............... | 500 | 4% |
| > 60 days............... | 220 | 10% |
| Total ...................... | $820 | |

**Journalize the entry to adjust the allowance at December 31, 2011. What is the December 31, 2011, balance in the allowance? Show how accounts receivable would be reported on the balance sheet at December 31, 2011.**

③ Use the allowance method for uncollectible receivables

The problem does not explicitly state which method is being used; however, the table clearly shows estimated uncollectible percentages of *accounts receivable*. This informs us that Hart is using the aging-of-receivables method to calculate the allowance and *then* the expense.

Under the aging-of-receivables method, the percentage of receivables equals the ending balance in the allowance. Therefore, we can calculate that (2% of $100) + (4% of $500) + (10% of $220) = $44 = the required (or target) ending balance in the allowance.

| Age | Gross Accounts Receivable | | Percentage Estimated Uncollectible | | Amount Estimated Uncollectible |
|---|---|---|---|---|---|
| < 30 days............... | $100 | × | 2% | = | $ 2 |
| 30–60 days............ | 500 | × | 4% | = | 20 |
| > 60 days............... | 220 | × | 10% | = | 22 |
| Total ...................... | $820 | | | | $44 |
| | | | | | Ending Allowance Balance |

We need an additional credit in the T-account to make it balance (to make the total correct).

We can use the $44 ending balance in the T-account (along with the beginning balance of $40 and the write-offs of $35) to calculate the Uncollectible-Account Expense of $39. This is the amount that must be used in the journal entry ($44 required balance − $5 credit balance = $39 amount for journal entry).

| Allowance for Uncollectible Accounts | | | |
|---|---|---|---|
| | | Dec 31, 2010 Bal | 40 |
| 2011 Write-Offs | 35 | | |
| | | 2011 Uncollectible-Account Expense Adjustments | X |
| | | Dec 31, 2011 Bal | 44 |

So $40 - 35 + X = 44$

$X = 44 - 40 + 35 = 39$

| | | | |
|---|---|---|---|
| Uncollectible-Account Expense | | 39 | |
| Allowance for Uncollectible Accounts | | | 39 |

This is the standard journal entry format to record Uncollectible-Account Expense and adjust the Allowance. The entry structure is always the same; only the amount changes.

On the balance sheet, we would see the gross accounts receivable combined with the Allowance contra account:

| | |
|---|---|
| Accounts Receivable.................................................. | $820 |
| Less Allowance for Uncollectible Accounts .............. | (44) |
| Accounts Receivable (net) ........................................ | $776 |

## Requirement 7

In 2012, Hart wrote off $48 of accounts receivable. On June 30, 2012, Hart estimated uncollectible-account expense was $10 for the first six months of the year, based on the percent-of-sales method. Journalize these transactions.

As in Requirement 2, we use the standard format to write off Accounts Receivable:

| | | | |
|---|---|---|---|
| Allowance for Uncollectible Accounts | | 48 | |
| Accounts Receivable | | | 48 |

We also use the standard format to record the Uncollectible-Account Expense:

| | | | |
|---|---|---|---|
| Uncollectible-Account Expense | | 10 | |
| Allowance for Uncollectible Accounts | | | 10 |

## Requirement 8

At December 31, 2012, based on the aging-of-receivables method, Hart estimated the allowance balance to be $35. Journalize Hart's entry to adjust the allowance for the year-end financial statements. (Assume the December 31, 2011, balance in the allowance was $30.) What is total uncollectible-account expense for 2012?

Because we only have the target balance in the allowance, we need to analyze the Allowance T-account in order to determine how much Uncollectible-Account Expense to record for the remaining three months of the year.

3 Use the allowance method for uncollectible receivables

3 Use the allowance method for uncollectible receivables

So far, the Allowance has been affected in 2012 by write-offs and the Uncollectible-Account Expense recorded in June:

| Allowance for Uncollectible Accounts | | | |
|---|---|---|---|
| | | Dec 31, 2011 Bal | 30 |
| 2012 Write-Offs | 48 | | |
| | | Jun 2012 Expense Adjustment | 10 |
| Bal Before Adj | 8 | | |
| | | Dec 31, 2012 Expense Adj | X |
| | | Dec 31, 2012 Bal | 35 |

So $X - 8 = 35$

$X = 35 + 8 = 43$

So the additional expense recorded on December 31, 2012, is $43. Again, we use the standard format to record Uncollectible-Account Expense:

| Uncollectible-Account Expense | 43 | |
|---|---|---|
| Allowance for Uncollectible Accounts | | 43 |

## Requirement 9

**Calculate Hart's days' sales in accounts receivable for 2011. (Assume Hart uses the aging-of-receivables method in Requirement 6.) What does this ratio mean?**

(5) Use two new ratios to evaluate a business

The days' sales ratio is calculated as:

$$\text{Days' sales in average accounts receivable} = \frac{\text{Average net accounts receivable}}{\text{One day's sales}}$$

From Requirement 3, we know that service revenues for 2011 are $2,800. From Requirement 6, we know that net accounts receivable were $760 on December 31, 2010, and $776 on December 31, 2011.

So for Hart,

$$\text{Days' sales in average accounts receivable} = \frac{\frac{1}{2} \times [\$760 + \$776]}{\$2,800 \div 365}$$

$$\text{Days' sales in average accounts receivable} = 100.1 \text{ days}$$

The average amount of time that it takes Hart to collect an account receivable is 100.1 days (more than three months). This is a very high number for this ratio, indicating poor collection efforts by Hart's collection department.

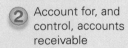

Account for, and
 control, accounts
 receivable

## Requirement 10

**The employee at Hart who opens the mail and physically collects the cash is the same person who updates the cash receipts journal and accounts receivable ledger. Is this a good internal control system?**

If an employee collects the cash *and* records the receipt of the cash *and* updates the accounts receivable ledger, there is an opportunity for fraud. The employee could steal the cash and delay recording the cash receipt or perhaps never record the cash receipt. The employee could hide his or her act for a long period of time by manipulating the accounts receivable ledger.

To avoid this problem, most internal control systems require <u>separation of duties</u>; that is, the employees who handle cash (both receipts and payments) are *not* the same employees who maintain the accounting records.

### *DEMO DOC COMPLETE*

# Demo Doc 3

## Notes Receivable

On November 1, 2009, Jordan, Inc., borrowed $1,800 cash from Donald Corp. Jordan signed a three-month, 10% note. Jordan paid the note plus interest in full on the due date. Both Jordan and Donald have December 31 year-ends.

### Requirements

1. When is the note due? What is the total interest that will be paid on this note? What is its maturity value?

2. Prepare all journal entries for this note for both companies from November 1, 2009, through the due date. Explanations are not required.

# Demo Doc 3 Solutions

## Requirement 1

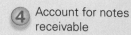

4   Account for notes receivable

**When is the note due? What is the total interest that will be paid on this note? What is its maturity value?**

The note was issued on November 1, 2009. Because it is a three-month note, it is due three months from that date on February 1, 2010.

The amount of interest incurred over the entire life of the note is calculated as:

$$\text{Interest incurred} = \text{Amount of debt} \times \text{Annual interest rate} \times \text{Time elapsed (in years)}$$

So in this case,

$$\text{Interest incurred} = \$1{,}800 \times 10\% \times \frac{3 \text{ months}}{12 \text{ months}}$$

$$\text{Interest incurred} = \$45$$

The maturity value is calculated as:

$$\text{Maturity value} = \text{Principal} + \text{Interest incurred over life of note}$$

So in this case,

$$\text{Maturity value} = \$1{,}800 + \$45 = \$1{,}845$$

## Requirement 2

**Prepare all journal entries for this note for both companies from November 1, 2009, through the due date. Explanations are not required.**

**November 1, 2009: Jordan borrows $1,800 from Donald.**
Jordan borrowed cash from Donald. This means that Donald has a decrease (a credit) to Cash of $1,800. Because Donald can expect to get this money back (that is, collect it) in the future, we can also set up a Note Receivable asset (a debit) for $1,800.

**Donald:**

| | | | |
|---|---|---|---|
| Nov 1 | Note Receivable | 1,800 | |
| | Cash | | 1,800 |

Jordan has an increase to Cash (a debit) and because the money must be paid back, we can set up a Note Payable liability (a credit) for $1,800.

**Jordan:**

| | | | |
|---|---|---|---|
| Nov 1 | Cash | 1,800 | |
| | Note Payable | | 1,800 |

## December 31, 2009: Accrue 10% interest on note.

Both companies have a December 31 year-end. This means that they need to adjust their accounting information on this date. By this time, the note has been outstanding for two months. This means that interest has been incurred on the note.

The amount of interest incurred is calculated as:

$$\text{Interest incurred} = \text{Amount of debt} \times \text{Annual interest rate} \times \text{Time elapsed (in years)}$$

So in this case,

$$\text{Interest incurred} = \$1,800 \times 10\% \times \frac{2 \text{ months}}{12 \text{ months}}$$

$$\text{Interest incurred} = \$30$$

Note that *all* interest rates that are given are assumed to be *annual* rates, unless specifically stated otherwise.

Donald has earned Interest Revenue (a credit) of $30. Because the cash has not yet been received, we must also set up an Interest Receivable account (a debit) of $30.

**Donald:**

| | | | |
|---|---|---|---|
| Dec 31 | Interest Receivable | 30 | |
| | Interest Revenue ($1,800 × 10% × 2/12) | | 30 |

Jordan has incurred Interest Expense (a debit) of $30. Because the cash has yet to be paid, we must also set up an Interest Payable account (a credit) of $30.

**Jordan:**

| | | | |
|---|---|---|---|
| Dec 31 | Interest Revenue | 30 | |
| | Interest Payable | | 30 |

## February 1, 2010: Note and interest are paid in full.

On this day, the note and interest are fully paid. For Donald, this causes a decrease to Notes Receivable (a credit) of $1,800. Additionally, Donald is receiving the interest that was accrued on December 31, so there will also be a decrease to Interest Receivable of $30 (a credit).

However, there is *more* interest than this! Donald has also earned interest between December 31 and February 1 (one month):

$$\text{Interest incurred} = \$1,800 \times 10\% \times \frac{1\ \text{month}}{12\ \text{months}}$$

$$\text{Interest incurred} = \$15$$

So Donald records Interest Revenue (a credit) of $15.

All of these amounts are being paid in cash, so Donald's Cash account will be increased (a debit) by $1,800 + $30 + $15 = $1,845 (the maturity value).

**Donald:**

| | | | | |
|---|---|---|---|---|
| Feb 1 | Cash (maturity value) | | 1,845 | |
| | Note Receivable | | | 1,800 |
| | Interest Receivable | | | 30 |
| | Interest Revenue ($1,800 × 10% × 1/12) | | | 15 |

With payment of the note and interest, Jordan will decrease Note Payable by $1,800 and Interest Payable by $30 (debits). Jordan will also record additional interest expense of $15 (a debit) and decrease Cash (a credit) by $1,845.

**Jordan:**

| | | | | |
|---|---|---|---|---|
| Feb 1 | Note Payable | | 1,800 | |
| | Interest Payable | | 30 | |
| | Interest Expense | | 15 | |
| | Cash | | | 1,845 |

*DEMO DOC COMPLETE*

# Quick Practice Questions

## True/False

_____ 1. The Allowance for Uncollectible Accounts is a contra account to Accounts Receivable.

_____ 2. Under the allowance method, the write-off of an account receivable has no effect on net income.

_____ 3. Under the allowance method, the entry to write off an account receivable that is determined to be uncollectible includes a debit to the Allowance for Uncollectible Accounts.

_____ 4. Under the allowance method, the entry to write off an account receivable that has been deemed uncollectible has no effect on the total assets of the firm.

_____ 5. The direct write-off method is the preferred way to apply the accrual basis for measuring uncollectible-account expense because it matches revenues and expenses on the income statement.

_____ 6. Under the direct write-off method, the entry to write off an account receivable that has been deemed uncollectible has no effect on the total assets of the firm.

_____ 7. A written promise to pay a specified amount of money at a particular future date is referred to as a promissory note.

_____ 8. The principal amount of a note is the amount borrowed by the debtor and lent by the creditor.

_____ 9. The acid-test ratio includes cash, inventory, and net accounts receivable in the numerator.

_____ 10. If a trading investment has increased in value, the year-end adjustment requires a debit to Loss on Trading Investment.

_____ 11. Factoring is the act of selling accounts receivable to a third party to generate cash quickly.

# Multiple Choice

1. **Chuck Battle's account of $5,000 must be written off. Which of the following would be journalized assuming that the allowance method is used?**
   a. A debit to Battle's Accounts Receivable and a credit to Allowance for Uncollectible Accounts
   b. A debit to Allowance for Uncollectible Accounts and a credit to Battle's Accounts Receivable
   c. A debit to Cash and a credit to Uncollectible-Account Expense
   d. A debit to Cash and a credit to Battle's Accounts Receivable

2. **The current credit balance in Allowance for Uncollectible Accounts before adjustment is $658. An aging schedule reveals $3,700 of uncollectible accounts. What is the ending balance in the Allowance for Uncollectible Accounts?**
   a. $3,042
   b. $3,700
   c. $4,029
   d. $4,358

3. **The current debit balance in Allowance for Uncollectible Accounts before adjustment is $742. An aging schedule reveals $3,500 of uncollectible accounts. What is the amount of the journal entry for Estimated Uncollectible Accounts?**
   a. $742
   b. $2,758
   c. $3,500
   d. $4,242

4. **What is the type of account and normal balance of Allowance for Uncollectible Accounts?**
   a. Asset, debit
   b. Contra asset, credit
   c. Liability, credit
   d. Contra liability, debit

5. **If the allowance method is used for uncollectible receivables, what account is credited when writing off a customer's account?**
   a. Accounts Receivable
   b. Allowance for Uncollectible Accounts
   c. Uncollectible-Account Expense
   d. Sales Returns and Allowances

6. **What is the effect on the financial statements of writing off an uncollectible account under the direct write-off method?**
   a. Increases expenses and decreases liabilities
   b. Decreases net income and decreases assets
   c. Decreases assets and increases stockholders' equity
   d. Increases expenses and increases assets

7. **How are trading securities reported on the balance sheet?**
   a. At market value as either current assets or long-term investments on the balance sheet
   b. At market value as current assets on the balance sheet
   c. At cost as current assets on the balance sheet
   d. At lower of cost or market as current assets on the balance sheet

8. **A 90-day, 12% note for $40,000, dated July 10, is received from a customer. What is the maturity value of the note?**
   a. $40,000
   b. $41,184
   c. $42,400
   d. $44,800

9. **Carolina Supply accepted an eight-month, $16,000 note receivable, with 8% interest, from Reading Corporation on August 1, 2011. Carolina Supply's year-end is December 31. What is the amount of interest to be accrued on December 31, 2011?**
   a. $320
   b. $533
   c. $853
   d. $1,280

10. **The entry to record dividends received from a trading investment includes which of the following?**
    a. A debit to Short-Term Investment
    b. A credit to Dividend Revenue
    c. A credit to Short-Term Investment
    d. A credit to Gain from Short-Term Investment

# Quick Exercises

**5-1. Prepare the adjusting journal entry on December 31, 2011, for the following independent situations:**

**a.** The Allowance for Uncollectible Accounts has a $700 credit balance prior to adjustment. Net credit sales during the year are $216,000 and 4% are estimated to be uncollectible.

| Journal | | | |
|---|---|---|---|
| Date | Accounts | Debit | Credit |
| | | | |
| | | | |
| | | | |

**b.** The Allowance for Uncollectible Accounts has a $500 credit balance prior to adjustment. An aging schedule prepared on December 31 reveals an estimated uncollectible accounts amount of $7,300.

| Journal | | | |
|---|---|---|---|
| Date | Accounts | Debit | Credit |
| | | | |
| | | | |
| | | | |

**c.** The Allowance for Uncollectible Accounts has a $525 debit balance prior to adjustment. An aging schedule prepared on December 31 reveals an estimated uncollectible accounts amount of $5,100.

| Journal | | | |
|---|---|---|---|
| Date | Accounts | Debit | Credit |
| | | | |
| | | | |
| | | | |

**d.** The Allowance for Uncollectible Accounts has an $800 credit balance prior to adjustment. Net credit sales during the year are $229,000 and 3.5% are estimated to be uncollectible.

| Journal | | | |
|---|---|---|---|
| Date | Accounts | Debit | Credit |
| | | | |
| | | | |
| | | | |

**5-2.** Compute the ending balance in the Allowance for Uncollectible Accounts after the adjusting entries in 5-1 have been prepared for the four independent situations, a–d.

a. _____

b. _____

c. _____

d. _____

**5-3.** Record the following independent transactions assuming the allowance method is used.

**a.** August 5, 2011—Wrote off Henderson Corp. account receivable for $3,100 as uncollectible.

| Date | Accounts | Debit | Credit |
|------|----------|-------|--------|
|      |          |       |        |
|      |          |       |        |
|      |          |       |        |

**b.** August 17, 2011—Collected the $3,100 from Henderson Corp. in full.

| Date | Accounts | Debit | Credit |
|------|----------|-------|--------|
|      |          |       |        |
|      |          |       |        |
|      |          |       |        |

| Date | Accounts | Debit | Credit |
|------|----------|-------|--------|
|      |          |       |        |
|      |          |       |        |
|      |          |       |        |

**c.** August 31, 2011—Recorded uncollectible-account expense of $18,000.

| Date | Accounts | Debit | Credit |
|------|----------|-------|--------|
|      |          |       |        |
|      |          |       |        |
|      |          |       |        |

**5-4. On December 31, 2011, Rainbow Appliances has $275,000 in accounts receivable and an Allowance account with a credit balance of $240. Current period net credit sales are $771,000, and cash sales are $68,000.**

**Rainbow Appliances performs an aging schedule; the results follow, along with the appropriate percentages that Rainbow applies to the categories shown:**

| Age | Gross Accounts Receivable | Estimated Uncollectible |
|---|---|---|
| Not yet due | $150,000 | 1% |
| 31–60 days past due | 50,000 | 5% |
| 61–90 days past due | 40,000 | 10% |
| 91–120 days past due | 25,000 | 25% |
| Over 120 days past due | 10,000 | 50% |
| Total | $275,000 | |

**a.** Assuming Rainbow uses the aging approach of accounting for uncollectible accounts, prepare the adjusting entry required at the end of the accounting period.

| Date | Accounts | Debit | Credit |
|---|---|---|---|
| | | | |
| | | | |

**b.** Assume now Rainbow uses the percent-of-sales method of accounting for uncollectible accounts. If historical data indicate that approximately 3% of net credit sales are uncollectible, what is the amount of uncollectible-account expense that should be recorded?

**What is the balance in the Allowance for Uncollectible Accounts after adjustment?**

**5-5. Peterson Company, which has a December 31 year-end, completed the following transactions during 2011 and 2012:**

| 2011 | |
|---|---|
| Oct 14 | Sold merchandise to Bruce Company, receiving a 60-day, 9% note for $10,000. |
| Nov 16 | Sold merchandise to Marine Company, receiving a 72-day, 8% note for $9,100. |
| Dec 13 | Received amount due from Bruce Company. |
| Dec 31 | Accrued interest on the Marine Company note. |
| 2012 | |
| Jan 27 | Collected in full from Marine Company. |

### 1. Prepare the necessary journal entries to record the preceding transactions.

| Date | Accounts | Debit | Credit |
|---|---|---|---|
| | | | |
| | | | |
| | | | |

| Date | Accounts | Debit | Credit |
|---|---|---|---|
| | | | |
| | | | |
| | | | |

| Date | Accounts | Debit | Credit |
|---|---|---|---|
| | | | |
| | | | |
| | | | |

| Date | Accounts | Debit | Credit |
|---|---|---|---|
| | | | |
| | | | |
| | | | |

| Date | Accounts | Debit | Credit |
|---|---|---|---|
| | | | |
| | | | |
| | | | |

# Do It Yourself! Question 1

## Short-Term Investments

In 2011, Rocket Corporation invested some idle cash in the stock of another business. Rocket had the following transactions in 2011 and 2012.

2011:

**Feb 1**    Rocket Corporation purchased 1,500 shares of stock in Missile Company for $15.50 per share. This investment was classified as a trading investment.

**Nov 15**    A dividend of $1.00 per share was received on the Missile Company stock.

**Dec 31**    Rocket Corporation prepared financial statements for the year ended December 31, 2011. On this date, the Missile Company stock was worth $16.25 per share.

2012:

**Jan 27**    Rocket Corporation sold 750 shares of Missile Company stock for $16.50 per share.

### Requirement

1. Journalize all of the transactions for Rocket Corporation.

| Date | Accounts | Debit | Credit |
|------|----------|-------|--------|
|      |          |       |        |
|      |          |       |        |
|      |          |       |        |

| Date | Accounts | Debit | Credit |
|------|----------|-------|--------|
|      |          |       |        |
|      |          |       |        |
|      |          |       |        |

| Date | Accounts | Debit | Credit |
|------|----------|-------|--------|
|      |          |       |        |
|      |          |       |        |
|      |          |       |        |

| Date | Accounts | Debit | Credit |
|------|----------|-------|--------|
|      |          |       |        |
|      |          |       |        |
|      |          |       |        |

# Do It Yourself! Question 2

## Uncollectible Accounts Receivable

Now Company's December 31, 2010, balance sheet reported the following:

| | |
|---|---|
| Accounts Receivable............................................. | $1,000 |
| Allowance for Uncollectible Accounts................ | (85) |
| Accounts Receivable (net) ................................. | $915 |

## Requirements

1. **How much of the December 31, 2010, balance of accounts receivable did Now expect to collect?**

2. **During 2011, Now wrote off accounts receivable totaling $110. Journalize these write-offs as one transaction.**

| Date | Accounts and Explanation | Debit | Credit |
|---|---|---|---|
| | | | |
| | | | |
| | | | |

3. **During 2011, Now earned $13,000 of service revenues, all on account. Journalize these revenues as one transaction.**

| Date | Accounts and Explanation | Debit | Credit |
|---|---|---|---|
| | | | |
| | | | |
| | | | |

4. During 2011, Now collected $12,840 cash from customers. Journalize this transaction and calculate the gross accounts receivable balance at December 31, 2011.

| Date | Accounts and Explanation | Debit | Credit |
|------|--------------------------|-------|--------|
|      |                          |       |        |
|      |                          |       |        |
|      |                          |       |        |

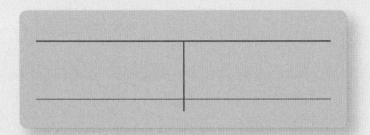

5. Assume that Now estimates uncollectible-account expense to be 0.75% of revenues. Journalize the entry to adjust the allowance at December 31, 2011. What is the December 31, 2011, balance in the allowance?

| Date | Accounts and Explanation | Debit | Credit |
|------|--------------------------|-------|--------|
|      |                          |       |        |
|      |                          |       |        |
|      |                          |       |        |

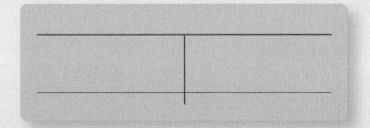

6. Ignoring Requirement 5, assume that Now has the following information at December 31, 2011:

| Age | Gross Accounts Receivable | Percentage Estimated Uncollectible |
|---|---|---|
| < 30 days.................. | $ 500 | 1% |
| 30–60 days.............. | 450 | 10% |
| > 60 days................. | 100 | 15% |
| Total....................... | $1,050 | |

Journalize the entry to adjust the allowance at December 31, 2011. What is the December 31, 2011, balance in the allowance? Show how accounts receivable would be reported on the balance sheet at December 31, 2011.

| Date | Accounts and Explanation | Debit | Credit |
|---|---|---|---|
| | | | |
| | | | |
| | | | |

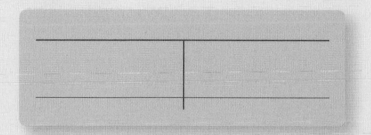

7. In 2012, Now wrote off $90 of accounts receivable. On September 30, 2012, Now estimated uncollectible-account expense was $55 for the first nine months of the year, based on the percent-of-sales method. Journalize these transactions.

| Date | Accounts and Explanation | Debit | Credit |
|---|---|---|---|
| | | | |
| | | | |

| Date | Accounts and Explanation | Debit | Credit |
|---|---|---|---|
| | | | |
| | | | |

8. At December 31, 2012, based on the aging-of-receivables method, Now estimated the allowance balance to be $78. Journalize Now's entry to adjust the allowance for the year-end financial statements. (Assume the December 31, 2011, balance in the allowance was $65.) What is total uncollectible-account expense for 2012?

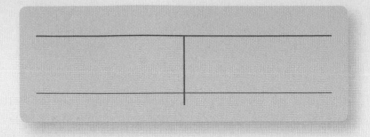

| Date | Accounts and Explanation | Debit | Credit |
|------|--------------------------|-------|--------|
|      |                          |       |        |
|      |                          |       |        |

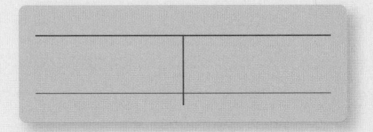

# Do It Yourself! Question 3

## Notes Receivable

On June 1, 2011, Anderson Corp. borrowed $6,000 cash from Neo Enterprises. Anderson signed a 10-month, 5% note. Anderson paid the note plus interest in full on the due date. Both Anderson and Neo have December 31 year-ends.

Requirements

1. When is the note due? What is the total interest incurred over the life of the note? What is the maturity value of the note?

2. Prepare all journal entries for this note for *both* companies from June 1, 2011, through the due date. Explanations are not required.

**Neo Enterprises:**

| Date | Accounts and Explanation | Debit | Credit |
|------|--------------------------|-------|--------|
|      |                          |       |        |
|      |                          |       |        |
|      |                          |       |        |
|      |                          |       |        |

**Anderson Corp.:**

| Date | Accounts and Explanation | Debit | Credit |
|------|--------------------------|-------|--------|
|      |                          |       |        |
|      |                          |       |        |
|      |                          |       |        |
|      |                          |       |        |

**Neo Enterprises:**

| Date | Accounts and Explanation | Debit | Credit |
|------|--------------------------|-------|--------|
|      |                          |       |        |
|      |                          |       |        |
|      |                          |       |        |
|      |                          |       |        |

**Anderson Corp.:**

| Date | Accounts and Explanation | Debit | Credit |
|------|--------------------------|-------|--------|
|      |                          |       |        |
|      |                          |       |        |
|      |                          |       |        |
|      |                          |       |        |

**Neo Enterprises:**

| Date | Accounts and Explanation | Debit | Credit |
|------|--------------------------|-------|--------|
|      |                          |       |        |
|      |                          |       |        |
|      |                          |       |        |
|      |                          |       |        |

**Anderson Corp.:**

| Date | Accounts and Explanation | Debit | Credit |
|------|--------------------------|-------|--------|
|      |                          |       |        |
|      |                          |       |        |
|      |                          |       |        |
|      |                          |       |        |

# Quick Practice Solutions

## True/False

<u>T</u>   1. The Allowance for Uncollectible Accounts is a contra account to Accounts Receivable. (pp. 299–300)

<u>T</u>   2. Under the allowance method, the write-off of an account receivable has no effect on net income. (p. 304)

<u>T</u>   3. Under the allowance method, the entry to write off an account receivable that is determined to be uncollectible includes a debit to the Allowance for Uncollectible Accounts. (p. 304)

<u>T</u>   4. Under the allowance method, the entry to write off an account receivable that has been deemed uncollectible has no effect on the total assets of the firm. (p. 304)

<u>F</u>   5. The direct write-off method is the preferred way to apply the accrual basis for measuring uncollectible-account expense because it matches revenues and expenses on the income statement.

      False—The *allowance method* is the preferred way to apply the accrual basis for measuring uncollectible-account expense because it matches revenues and expenses on the income statement. (p. 305)

<u>F</u>   6. Under the direct write-off method, the entry to write off an account receivable that has been deemed uncollectible has no effect on the total assets of the firm.

      False—The write-off of an account under the direct write-off method results in a credit to Accounts Receivable, which *reduces* total assets. (p. 305)

<u>T</u>   7. A written promise to pay a specified amount of money at a particular future date is referred to as a promissory note. (p. 307)

<u>T</u>   8. The principal amount of a note is the amount borrowed by the debtor and lent by the creditor. (p. 307)

<u>F</u>   9. The acid-test ratio includes cash, inventory, and net accounts receivable in the numerator.

      False—The acid-test ratio includes cash, *short-term investments*, and net accounts receivable in the numerator. (p. 311)

<u>F</u>  10. If a trading investment has increased in value, the year-end adjustment requires a debit to Loss on Trading Investment.

      False—If a trading investment increases in value, the year-end adjustment requires a *credit* to Gain on Trading Investment. (pp. 292–293)

<u>T</u>  11. Factoring is the act of selling accounts receivable to a third party to generate cash quickly. (p. 310)

# Multiple Choice

1. **Chuck Battle's account of $5,000 must be written off. Which of the following would be journalized assuming that the allowance method is used?** (p. 304)
   a. A debit to Battle's Accounts Receivable and a credit to Allowance for Uncollectible Accounts
   b. A debit to Allowance for Uncollectible Accounts and a credit to Battle's Accounts Receivable
   c. A debit to Cash and a credit to Uncollectible-Account Expense
   d. A debit to Cash and a credit to Battle's Accounts Receivable

2. **The current credit balance in Allowance for Uncollectible Accounts before adjustment is $658. An aging schedule reveals $3,700 of uncollectible accounts. What is the ending balance in the Allowance for Uncollectible Accounts?** (pp. 302–303)
   a. $3,042
   b. $3,700
   c. $4,029
   d. $4,358

3. **The current debit balance in Allowance for Uncollectible Accounts before adjustment is $742. An aging schedule reveals $3,500 of uncollectible accounts. What is the amount of the journal entry for Estimated Uncollectible Accounts?** (pp. 302–303)
   a. $742
   b. $2,758
   c. $3,500
   d. $4,242

4. **What is the type of account and normal balance of Allowance for Uncollectible Accounts?** (pp. 299–300)
   a. Asset, debit
   b. Contra asset, credit
   c. Liability, credit
   d. Contra liability, debit

5. **If the allowance method is used for uncollectible receivables, what account is credited when writing off a customer's account?** (p. 305)
   a. Accounts Receivable
   b. Allowance for Uncollectible Accounts
   c. Uncollectible-Account Expense
   d. Sales Returns and Allowances

6. **What is the effect on the financial statements of writing off an uncollectible account under the direct write-off method?** (p. 305)
   a. Increases expenses and decreases liabilities
   b. Decreases net income and decreases assets
   c. Decreases assets and increases stockholders' equity
   d. Increases expenses and increases assets

7. **How are trading securities reported on the balance sheet?
   (p. 292)**
   a. At market value as either current assets or long-term investments on
      the balance sheet
   b. At market value as current assets on the balance sheet
   c. At cost as current assets on the balance sheet
   d. At lower of cost or market as current assets on the balance sheet

8. **A 90-day, 12% note for $40,000, dated July 10, is received from a
   customer. What is the maturity value of the note? (p. 306)**
   a. $40,000
   b. $41,184
   c. $42,400
   d. $44,800

9. **Carolina Supply accepted an eight-month, $16,000 note receivable,
   with 8% interest, from Reading Corporation on August 1, 2011.
   Carolina Supply's year-end is December 31. What is the amount of
   interest to be accrued on December 31, 2011? (pp. 308–309)**
   a. $320
   b. $533
   c. $853
   d. $1,280

10. **The entry to record dividends received from a trading
    investment includes which of the following? (p. 291)**
    a. A debit to Short-Term Investment
    b. A credit to Dividend Revenue
    c. A credit to Short-Term Investment
    d. A credit to Gain from Short-Term Investment

# Quick Exercises

**5-1. Prepare the adjusting journal entry on December 31, 2011, for the following independent situations: (pp. 301–303)**

**a.** The Allowance for Uncollectible Accounts has a $700 credit balance prior to adjustment. Net credit sales during the year are $216,000 and 4% are estimated to be uncollectible.

| Journal | | | | |
|---|---|---|---|---|
| | Date | Accounts | Debit | Credit |
| a. | 12/31/11 | Uncollectible-Account Expense | 8,640 | |
| | | Allowance for Uncollectible Accounts | | 8,640 |
| | | ($216,000 × .04) = $8,640 | | |

**b.** The Allowance for Uncollectible Accounts has a $500 credit balance prior to adjustment. An aging schedule prepared on December 31 reveals an estimated uncollectible accounts amount of $7,300.

| Journal | | | | |
|---|---|---|---|---|
| | Date | Accounts | Debit | Credit |
| b. | 12/31/11 | Uncollectible-Account Expense | 6,800 | |
| | | Allowance for Uncollectible Accounts | | 6,800 |
| | | ($7,300 – $500 = $6,800) | | |

**c.** The Allowance for Uncollectible Accounts has a $525 debit balance prior to adjustment. An aging schedule prepared on December 31 reveals an estimated uncollectible accounts amount of $5,100.

| Journal | | | | |
|---|---|---|---|---|
| | Date | Accounts | Debit | Credit |
| c. | 12/31/11 | Uncollectible-Account Expense | 5,625 | |
| | | Allowance for Uncollectible Accounts | | 5,625 |
| | | ($5,100 + $525 = $5,625) | | |

**d.** The Allowance for Uncollectible Accounts has an $800 credit balance prior to adjustment. Net credit sales during the year are $229,000 and 3.5% are estimated to be uncollectible.

| Journal | | | | |
|---|---|---|---|---|
| | Date | Accounts | Debit | Credit |
| d. | 12/31/11 | Uncollectible-Account Expense | 8,015 | |
| | | Allowance for Uncollectible Accounts | | 8,015 |
| | | ($229,000 × 0.035 = $8,015) | | |

**5-2. Compute the ending balance in the Allowance for Uncollectible Accounts after the adjusting entries in 5-1 have been prepared for the four independent situations, a–d. (pp. 301–304)**

**a.** $9,340    ($700 + $8,640)

**b.** $7,300    ($500 + $6,800)

**c.** $5,100    ($5,625 − $525)

**d.** $8,815    ($800 + $8,015)

**5-3. Record the following independent transactions assuming the allowance method is used. (pp. 301–305)**

    **a.** August 5, 2011—Wrote off Henderson Corp. account receivable for $3,100 as uncollectible.

|    | Date | Accounts | Debit | Credit |
|----|------|----------|-------|--------|
| a. | 8/5/11 | Allowance for Uncollectible Accounts | 3,100 | |
|    |      | Accounts Receivable—Henderson Corp. | | 3,100 |
|    |      | *To write off Henderson Corp. account receivable.* | | |

    **b.** August 17, 2011—Collected the $3,100 from Henderson Corp. in full.

|    | Date | Accounts | Debit | Credit |
|----|------|----------|-------|--------|
| b. | 8/17/11 | Accounts Receivable—Henderson Corp. | 3,100 | |
|    |      | Allowance for Uncollectible Accounts | | 3,100 |
|    |      | *To reinstate Henderson Corp. account receivable.* | | |

| Date | Accounts | Debit | Credit |
|------|----------|-------|--------|
| 8/17/11 | Cash | 3,100 | |
|      | Accounts Receivable—Henderson Corp. | | 3,100 |
|      | *To record cash collected from Henderson Corp.* | | |

    **c.** August 31, 2011—Recorded uncollectible-account expense of $18,000.

|    | Date | Accounts | Debit | Credit |
|----|------|----------|-------|--------|
| c. | 8/31/11 | Uncollectible-Account Expense | 18,000 | |
|    |      | Allowance for Uncollectible Accounts | | 18,000 |
|    |      | *To record estimated uncollectible accounts.* | | |

**5-4.** On December 31, 2011, Rainbow Appliances has $275,000 in accounts receivable and an Allowance account with a credit balance of $240. Current period net credit sales are $771,000, and cash sales are $68,000.

Rainbow Appliances performs an aging schedule; the results follow, along with the appropriate percentages that Rainbow applies to the categories shown.
(pp. 301–303)

| Age | Gross Accounts Receivable | Estimated Uncollectible |
|---|---|---|
| Not yet due .................................. | $150,000 | 1% |
| 31–60 days past due...................... | 50,000 | 5% |
| 61–90 days past due...................... | 40,000 | 10% |
| 91–120 days past due.................... | 25,000 | 25% |
| Over 120 days past due................ | 10,000 | 50% |
| Total ............................................ | $275,000 | |

**a.** Assuming Rainbow uses the aging approach of accounting for uncollectible accounts, prepare the adjusting entry required at the end of the accounting period.

| Date | Accounts | Debit | Credit |
|---|---|---|---|
| 12/31/11 | Uncollectible-Account Expense | 19,010 | |
| | Allowance for Doubtful Accounts | | 19,010 |
| | ($150,000 × 0.01) + ($50,000 × 0.05) + ($40,000 × 0.10) + | | |
| | ($25,000 × 0.25) + ($10,000 × 0.5) = $19,250 – $240 | | |

**b.** Assume now Rainbow uses the percent-of-sales method of accounting for uncollectible accounts. If historical data indicate that approximately 3% of net credit sales are uncollectible, what is the amount of uncollectible-account expense that should be recorded? $23,130

**What is the balance in the Allowance for Uncollectible Accounts after adjustment?**

$23,370    ($240 + $23,130)

### 5-5. Peterson Company, which has a December 31 year-end, completed the following transactions during 2011 and 2012:

| 2011 | |
|---|---|
| Oct 14 | Sold merchandise to Bruce Company, receiving a 60-day, 9% note for $10,000. |
| Nov 16 | Sold merchandise to Marine Company, receiving a 72-day, 8% note for $9,100. |
| Dec 13 | Received amount due from Bruce Company. |
| Dec 31 | Accrued interest on the Marine Company note. |
| **2012** | |
| Jan 27 | Collected in full from Marine Company. |

### 1. Prepare the necessary journal entries to record the preceding transactions. (pp. 307–309)

| Date | Accounts | Debit | Credit |
|---|---|---|---|
| 10/14/11 | Note Receivable | 10,000 | |
| | Sales | | 10,000 |
| | | | |

| Date | Accounts | Debit | Credit |
|---|---|---|---|
| 11/16/11 | Note Receivable | 9,100 | |
| | Sales | | 9,100 |
| | | | |

| Date | Accounts | Debit | Credit |
|---|---|---|---|
| 12/13/11 | Cash | 10,148 | |
| | Note Receivable | | 10,000 |
| | Interest Revenue | | |
| | ($10,000 × .09 × 60/365) | | 148 |

| Date | Accounts | Debit | Credit |
|---|---|---|---|
| 12/31/11 | Interest Receivable | 90 | |
| | Interest Revenue | | |
| | ($9,100 × .08 × 45/365) | | 90 |
| | | | |

| Date | Accounts | Debit | Credit |
|---|---|---|---|
| 1/27/12 | Cash | 9,244 | |
| | Note Receivable | | 9,100 |
| | Interest Revenue | | 54 |
| | Interest Receivable | | 90 |

# Do It Yourself! Question 1 Solutions

1. Journalize all of the transactions for Rocket Corporation.

## 2011:

**Feb 1** Rocket Corporation purchased 1,500 shares of stock in Missile Company for $15.50 per share. This investment was classified as a trading investment.

| 2/1/11 | Short-Term Investment | 23,250 | |
|--------|------------------------|--------|--------|
| | Cash ($15.50 × 1,500) | | 23,250 |

**Nov 15** A dividend of $1.00 per share was received on the Missile Company stock.

| 11/15/11 | Cash ($1 × 1,500) | 1,500 | |
|----------|---------------------|-------|-------|
| | Dividend Revenue | | 1,500 |

**Dec 31** Rocket Corporation prepared financial statements for the year ended December 31, 2011. On this date, the Missile Company stock was worth $16.25 per share.

| 12/31/11 | Short-Term Investment ([$16.25 – $15.50] × 1,500) | 1,125 | |
|----------|---------------------------------------------------|-------|-------|
| | Unrealized Gain on Investment | | 1,125 |

## 2012:

**Jan 27** Rocket Corporation sold 750 shares of Missile Company stock for $16.50 per share.

| 1/27/12 | Cash ($16.50 × 750) | 12,375 | |
|---------|----------------------|--------|-----------|
| | Gain on Sale of Investment (to balance) | | 187.50 |
| | Short-Term Investment ($16.25 × 750) | | 12,187.50 |

# Do It Yourself! Question 2 Solutions

## Requirements

1. **How much of the December 31, 2010, balance of accounts receivable did Now expect to collect?**

   Now expected to collect $915 of the accounts receivable balance.

2. **During 2011, Now wrote off accounts receivable totaling $110. Journalize these write-offs as one transaction.**

   | | | | |
   |---|---|---|---|
   | Allowance for Uncollectible Accounts | | 110 | |
   | Accounts Receivable | | | 110 |

3. **During 2011, Now earned $13,000 of service revenues, all on account. Journalize these revenues as one transaction.**

   | | | | |
   |---|---|---|---|
   | Accounts Receivable | | 13,000 | |
   | Service Revenue | | | 13,000 |

4. **During 2011, Now collected $12,840 cash from customers. Journalize this transaction and calculate the gross accounts receivable balance at December 31, 2011.**

   | | | | |
   |---|---|---|---|
   | Cash | | 12,840 | |
   | Accounts Receivable | | | 12,840 |

   | Accounts Receivable | | | |
   |---|---|---|---|
   | Dec 31, 2010 Bal | 1,000 | | |
   | 2011 Revenues | 13,000 | | |
   | | | 2011 Write-Offs | 110 |
   | | | 2011 Cash Collections | 12,840 |
   | Dec 31, 2011 Bal | 1,050 | | |

5. **Assume that Now estimates uncollectible-account expense to be 0.75% of revenues. Journalize the entry to adjust the allowance at December 31, 2011. What is the December 31, 2011, balance in the allowance?**

$$0.75\% \times \$13,000 = \$97.50$$

| Uncollectible-Account Expense | 97.50 | |
|---|---|---|
| Allowance for Uncollectible Accounts | | 97.50 |

**Allowance for Uncollectible Accounts**

| | | | |
|---|---|---|---|
| | | Dec 31, 2010 Bal | 85.00 |
| 2011 Write-Offs | 110.00 | 2011 Uncollectible- Account Expense | 97.50 |
| | | Dec 31, 2011 Bal | 72.50 |

6. **Ignoring Requirement 5, assume that Now has the following information at December 31, 2011:**

| Age | Gross Accounts Receivable | Percentage Estimated Uncollectible |
|---|---|---|
| < 30 days................. | $ 500 | 1% |
| 30–60 days.............. | 450 | 10% |
| > 60 days................. | 100 | 15% |
| Total....................... | $1,050 | |

**Journalize the entry to adjust the allowance at December 31, 2011. What is the December 31, 2011, balance in the allowance? Show how accounts receivable would be reported on the balance sheet at December 31, 2011.**

| Age | Gross Accounts Receivable | | Percentage Estimated Uncollectible | | Amount Estimated Uncollectible |
|---|---|---|---|---|---|
| < 30 days................ | $   500 | × | 1% | = | $   5 |
| 30–60 days.............. | 450 | × | 10% | = | 45 |
| > 60 days................ | 100 | × | 15% | = | 15 |
| Total ...................... | $1,050 | | | | $65 |

| | | Uncollectible-Account Expense | | 90 | |
|---|---|---|---|---|---|
| | | Allowance for Uncollectible Accounts | | | 90 |

**Allowance for Uncollectible Accounts**

| | | | |
|---|---|---|---|
| | | Dec 31, 2010 Bal | 85 |
| 2011 Write-Offs | 110 | | |
| | | 2011 Uncollectible-Account Expense | $X$ |
| | | Dec 31, 2011 Bal | 65 |

$$\text{So } 85 - 110 + X = 65$$
$$X = 65 - 85 + 110 = 90$$

**On the balance sheet:**

| | |
|---|---|
| Accounts Receivable................................................. | $1,050 |
| Less Allowance for Uncollectible Accounts .............. | (65) |
| Accounts Receivable (net) ........................................ | $   985 |

7. In 2012, Now wrote off $90 of accounts receivable. On September 30, 2012, Now estimated uncollectible-account expense was $55 for the first nine months of the year, based on the percent-of-sales method. Journalize these transactions.

| Allowance for Uncollectible Accounts | 90 | |
|---|---|---|
| Accounts Receivable | | 90 |

| Uncollectible-Account Expense | 55 | |
|---|---|---|
| Allowance for Uncollectible Accounts | | 55 |

8. At December 31, 2012, based on the aging-of-receivables method, Now estimated the allowance balance to be $78. Journalize Now's entry to adjust the allowance for the year-end financial statements. (Assume the December 31, 2011, balance in the allowance was $65.) What is total uncollectible-account expense for 2012?

### Allowance for Uncollectible Accounts

| | | Dec 31, 2011 Bal | 65 |
|---|---|---|---|
| 2012 Write-Offs | 90 | | |
| | | Sep 2012 Expense | 55 |
| | | Bal Before Adj | 30 |
| | | Dec 31, 2012 Adj | $X$ |
| | | Dec 31, 2012 Bal | 78 |

So $65 - 90 + 55 + X = 78$
$X = 78 - 65 + 90 - 55 = 48$

| Uncollectible-Account Expense | 48 | |
|---|---|---|
| Allowance for Uncollectible Accounts | | 48 |

Total Uncollectible-Account Expense for 2012
= Expense recorded in September 2012 + Expense recorded in December 2012
= $55 + $48 = $103

### Uncollectible-Account Expense

| Jan 1, 2012 Bal | 0 | |
|---|---|---|
| Sep 2012 Expense Adjustment | 55 | |
| Dec 2012 Expense Adjustment | 48 | |
| Dec 31, 2012 Bal | 103 | |

# Do It Yourself! Question 3 Solutions

1. **When is the note due? What is the total interest incurred over the life of the note? What is the maturity value of the note?**

   The note is due 10 months from June 1, 2011, on April 1, 2012. The amount of interest incurred over the entire life of the note is calculated as follows:

$$\text{Interest incurred} = \$6{,}000 \times 5\% \times \frac{10 \text{ months}}{12 \text{ months}}$$

$$\text{Interest incurred} = \$250$$

$$\text{Maturity value} = \$6{,}000 + \$250 = \$6{,}250$$

2. **Prepare all journal entries for this note for *both* companies from June 1, 2011, through the due date. Explanations are not required.**

**June 1, 2011: Anderson borrowed $6,000 from Neo.**

**Neo Enterprises:**

| | | | |
|---|---|---|---|
| Jun 1 | Note-Receivable | 6,000 | |
| | Cash | | 6,000 |

**Anderson Corp.:**

| | | | |
|---|---|---|---|
| Jun 1 | Cash | 6,000 | |
| | Note Payable | | 6,000 |

**December 31, 2011: accrue 5% interest on note.**

**Neo Enterprises:**

| | | | |
|---|---|---|---|
| Dec 31 | Interest Receivable | 175 | |
| | Interest Revenue ($6,000 × 5% × 7/12) | | 175 |

**Anderson Corp.:**

| | | | |
|---|---|---|---|
| Dec 31 | Interest Expense | 175 | |
| | Interest Payable | | 175 |

**April 1, 2012: Note and interest are paid in full.**

### Neo Enterprises:

| | Apr 1 | Cash (maturity value) | 6,250 | |
|---|---|---|---|---|
| | | Note Receivable | | 6,000 |
| | | Interest Receivable | | 175 |
| | | Interest Revenue ($6,000 × 5% × 3/12) | | 75 |

### Anderson Corp.:

| | Apr 1 | Note Payable | 6,000 | |
|---|---|---|---|---|
| | | Interest Payable | 175 | |
| | | Interest Expense | 75 | |
| | | Cash | | 6,250 |

# The Power of Practice

For more practice using the skills learned in this chapter, visit MyAccountingLab. There you will find algorithmically generated questions that are based on these Demo Docs and your main textbook's Review and Assess Your Progress sections.

Go to MyAccountingLab and follow these steps:

1. Direct your URL to www.myaccountinglab.com.
2. Log in using your name and password.
3. Click the MyAccountingLab link.
4. Click Study Plan in the left navigation bar.
5. From the table of contents, select Chapter 5, Short-Term Investments & Receivables.
6. Click a link to work tutorial exercises.

# 6 Inventory & Cost of Goods Sold

## WHAT YOU PROBABLY ALREADY KNOW

Assume that you want to invest in the stock market. You purchase 100 shares of a stock mutual fund in January at $24/share, another 100 shares in February at $27/share, and another 100 shares in April at $30/share. In December, you decide to sell 200 shares of stock to purchase a used car. The market value of the stock at the date of sale is $35/share. You know that you will receive $7,000 (200 shares × $35/share) and that the market price of the shares is higher than what you paid, so you have a gain. To compute the amount of the gain you will have to report on your tax return, you must determine the cost of the shares. Because there were purchases over a period of time at several different prices, how is the cost computed for the 200 shares sold? Can we assume that the shares sold were the first 100 shares purchased at $24/share plus the next 100 shares purchased at $27/share for a total cost of $5,100, that is (100 shares × $24) + (100 shares × $27)? Can we calculate the cost using an average? Yes, either of these methods is allowed by the Internal Revenue Service. The same problem exists for businesses to determine the cost of the inventory units sold when the unit cost varies. Generally Accepted Accounting Principles (GAAP) also allow a choice from several methods to calculate the cost of goods sold (COGS).

## Learning Objectives

 **Account for inventory**

There are **two inventory accounting systems** that a business may use:

- **Periodic system**—Periodically, a physical inventory count is taken to determine the amount of inventory on hand. The inventory (asset) balance is not continually updated for the increase in inventory owing to purchases or the decrease in inventory owing to sales. The Purchases (expense) account is debited when inventory is purchased. This system has become increasingly less popular as the cost of technology and optical-scanning cash registers has decreased.
- **Perpetual system**—Continuously updates the Inventory account and Cost of Goods Sold for purchases and sales. The Inventory (asset) account is debited to record the purchase of inventory. A physical inventory count is still performed to verify the accuracy of the inventory balance.

Two entries must be recorded when inventory is sold under a perpetual system. One entry records the revenue amount charged to the customer and the cash or accounts receivable. The other records the cost of goods sold expense and the decrease in the cost of inventory. Sales Discounts and Sales Returns and Allowances are contra revenue, debit balance accounts. *Review the "Accounting for Inventory" section of the text.*

 **Understand the various inventory methods**

The inventory cost method selected for use is an *assumed* outflow of goods to determine the cost of goods sold expense and ending inventory; the actual physical outflow of goods sold may differ. **First In First Out (FIFO)** is a popular method that *assumes the oldest goods are sold first, leaving the newest goods in ending inventory.* **Last In First Out (LIFO)** is the opposite assumption; it *assumes that the newest goods are sold first, leaving the oldest goods in ending inventory.* **Average cost** assumes that the goods sold as well as those in ending inventory have the same cost.

$$\frac{\overbrace{\text{(Beginning inventory + Purchases)}}^{\text{Total cost of goods available for sale}}}{\text{Total quantity of goods available for sales}} = \text{Average cost per unit of inventory}$$

*Review the inventory records and journal entries for these methods in the "Inventory Costing" section of the text.*

 **Use gross profit percentage and inventory turnover to evaluate operations**

Two ratios that provide important information for a merchandiser are the gross profit percentage and inventory turnover. *Review the "Analyzing Financial Statements" section in the text.*

 **Estimate inventory by the gross profit method**

Sometimes a business may need to estimate its ending inventory. If there is a natural disaster and the inventory is destroyed, an estimate must be determined for insurance purposes.

**To calculate the estimate of inventory**

a. determine the cost of goods available for sale (Beginning inventory + Purchases).
b. estimate the cost of goods sold: Net sales − (Normal gross profit rate × Net sales).
c. subtract the estimate of cost of goods sold (b) from the cost of goods available for sale (a) to determine the estimated cost of ending inventory.

*Review the gross profit method of estimating inventory in Exhibit 6-15 (p. 365).*

 **Show how inventory errors affect the financial statements**

When measuring the effects of inventory errors, it is helpful to remember that

> Cost of goods sold + Cost of ending inventory = Cost of goods available

The cost of goods available is a defined amount. Therefore, if the cost of ending inventory is understated, the cost of goods sold must be overstated by the same amount to compensate for the error. **Understating ending inventory results in an understatement of net income.** The reverse is also true: **Overstating ending inventory results in an overstatement of net income.**

The ending inventory for one period becomes the beginning inventory for the next. An error in ending inventory is carried over into the succeeding period. **Whatever effect the ending inventory error had on the income statement in the initial period causes the opposite effect on net income in the next period.** *Review the impact of inventory errors in Exhibits 6-16 and 6-17 (p. 366).*

# Demo Doc 1

## Inventory Transaction Analysis (perpetual system)

*Learning Objectives    1, 3, 4*

Danner, Inc., began operations on January 1, 2009. Danner had the following transactions during the year:

**Jan 1**    Purchased inventory for $400 on account.

**Jan 12**   Paid for the January 1 purchase in full.

**Feb 1**    Sold 10 units costing $21 each to a customer for $360 on account.

**Feb 9**    Customer returned three units from his February 1 order because he did not like the color of the goods.

**Feb 18**   Customer paid for the February 1 order (less returns) in full.

**May 5**    Purchased inventory for $250 on account.

**May 6**    Paid special freight costs of $30 on the May 5 inventory purchase in cash.

**May 14**   Found that $48 worth of the goods purchased on May 5 were defective. Danner returned these goods.

**Jun 1**    Paid for the May 5 purchase (less returns) in full.

**Oct 1**    Sold $160 of goods to a customer for $220 on account.

**Oct 19**   Received cash payment in full for the October 1 sale.

### Requirements

1. Journalize these transactions using the perpetual method. Explanations are not required.

2. Show the Inventory and COGS T-accounts for the year.

3. Use the COGS formula to calculate COGS for the year.

4. Prepare the top portion of Danner's 2009 income statement (ending with gross profit).

5. Calculate Danner's inventory turnover for 2009.

# Demo Doc 1 Solutions

## Requirement 1

Journalize these transactions using the perpetual method. Explanations are not required.

**Jan 1      Purchased inventory for $400 on account.**

The Inventory account is involved here because inventory was purchased. Inventory is increased by $400 (a debit). Because the inventory was not paid for in cash (it was purchased on account), Accounts Payable must also be increased by $400 (a credit).

**① Account for inventory**

| Jan 1 | Inventory | 400 | |
|---|---|---|---|
| | Accounts Payable | | 400 |

**Jan 12     Paid for the January 1 purchase in full.**

We are paying the supplier, so we can decrease our Accounts Payable by $400 (a debit). Cash also decreases (a credit) by $400.

| Jan 12 | Accounts Payable | 400 | |
|---|---|---|---|
| | Cash | | 400 |

**Feb 1     Sold 10 units costing $21 each to a customer for $360 on account.**

There are two parts to this transaction. First, Danner is earning sales revenue of $360. This will cause an increase to Sales Revenue (a credit) and (because it is not paid for in cash but rather sold on account) an increase to Accounts Receivable (a debit).

    Second, Danner is also selling inventory. This means that Inventory will decrease (a credit) and COGS will increase (a debit) by:

$$10 \times \$21 = \$210$$

| Feb 1 | Accounts Receivable | 360 | |
|---|---|---|---|
| | Sales Revenue | | 360 |
| | COGS (10 units × $21) | 210 | |
| | Inventory | | 210 |

**Feb 9**    **Customer returned three units from his February 1 order because he did not like the color of the goods.**

Because the customer is returning goods to the company (and the goods are not defective), Danner's Inventory will increase (a debit) by $3 \times \$21 = \$63$. This then causes the COGS to decrease (a credit) by $63.

The customer has not yet paid, so this will decrease the amount of Accounts Receivable Danner can collect from the customer (a credit) by $(3/10) \times \$360 = \$108$. Instead of decreasing Sales Revenue, we will increase Sales Returns and Allowances (a debit) by $108. This allows Danner to keep track of sales returns and make better business decisions.

| Feb 9 | Inventory (3 × $21) | 63 | |
| | COGS | | 63 |
| | | | |
| | Sales Returns and Allowances ([3/10] × $360) | 108 | |
| | Accounts Receivable | | 108 |

**Feb 18**    **Customer paid for the February 1 order (less returns) in full.**

Cash is increased (a debit) by $\$360 - \$108 = \$252$ (original sale of $360 less the sales return of $108). Because the customer is paying Danner, Accounts Receivable is also decreased (a credit) by $252.

| Feb 18 | Cash ($360 − $108) | 252 | |
| | Accounts Receivable | | 252 |

**May 5**    **Purchased inventory for $250 on account.**

Inventory is increasing by $250 (a debit). Because the inventory was not paid for in cash but rather on account, Accounts Payable must also be increased by $250 (a credit).

| May 5 | Inventory | 250 | |
| | Accounts Payable | | 250 |

**May 6**    **Paid special freight costs of $30 on the May 5 inventory purchase in cash.**

The *total cost* of the inventory is the purchase price *plus* any additional purchasing costs (such as shipping or taxes). Therefore, we include the extra $30 of freight as part of the cost of the inventory.

Inventory is increased by $30 (a debit). Because these costs are being paid in cash, the Cash account is decreased (a credit) by $30.

| May 6 | Inventory | 30 | |
| | Cash | | 30 |

**May 14** **Found that $48 worth of the goods purchased on May 5 were defective. Danner returned these goods.**

When the goods are returned to the supplier, they are taken out of inventory. This decreases Inventory (a credit) by $48. Because Danner has not yet paid for the goods, Accounts Payable is decreased for the related amount (a debit).

| May 14 | Accounts Payable | 48 | |
|---|---|---|---|
| | Inventory | | 48 |

**Jun 1** **Paid for the May 5 purchase (less returns) in full.**

Accounts Payable decreases by the original payable less returns made: $250 − $48 = $202 (a debit). Cash also decreases (a credit).

| Jun 1 | Accounts Payable | 202 | |
|---|---|---|---|
| | Cash | | 202 |

**Oct 1** **Sold $160 of goods to a customer for $220 on account.**

The company is earning sales revenue of $220. This will cause an increase to Sales Revenue (a credit) and (because it is not paid for in cash) an increase to Accounts Receivable (a debit).

The company is also selling inventory. This means that Inventory will decrease (a credit) and COGS will increase (a debit) by $160.

Even though the sale was on account, the actual sale must be recorded at this time.

| Oct 1 | Accounts Receivable | 220 | |
|---|---|---|---|
| | Sales Revenue | | 220 |
| | COGS | 160 | |
| | Inventory | | 160 |

**Oct 19** **Received cash for payment in full for the October 1 sale.**

Accounts Receivable will be decreased by the $220 (a credit). Cash will increase by $220 (a debit).

| Oct 19 | Cash | 220 | |
|---|---|---|---|
| | Accounts Receivable | | 220 |

## Requirement 2

**Show the Inventory and COGS T-accounts for the year.**

The entries are posted into the T-accounts (just as in previous chapters). However, for this question, we only want to see the Inventory and COGS T-accounts in detail:

| Inventory | | | | | COGS | | | |
|-----------|-----|--------|-----|---|-------|-----|--------|----|
| Jan 1 | 400 | | | | Feb 1 | 210 | | |
| | | Feb 1 | 210 | | | | Feb 9 | 63 |
| Feb 9 | 63 | | | | Oct 1 | 160 | | |
| May 5 | 250 | | | | Bal | 307 | | |
| May 6 | 30 | | | | | | | |
| | | May 14 | 48 | | | | | |
| | | Oct 1 | 160 | | | | | |
| Bal | 325 | | | | | | | |

## Requirement 3

**Use the COGS formula to calculate COGS for the year.**

We can use the COGS formula to calculate COGS:

$$COGS = \text{Beginning inventory} + \text{Inventory purchases} - \text{Ending inventory}$$
$$COGS = 0 + (400 + [250 + 30 - 48]) - 325$$
$$COGS = 0 + (400 + 232) - 325$$
$$COGS = 0 + 632 - 325 = 307$$

## Requirement 4

**Prepare the top portion of Danner's 2009 income statement (ending with gross profit).**

Sales Returns and Allowances is a *contra account* to Sales Revenue. As we did with Accumulated Depreciation, this contra account must be shown on the financial statements, then combined with its associated account to create the *net* value (in this case, net sales revenue).

**Danner, Inc.**
**Income Statement**
**Year Ended December 31, 2009**

| | |
|---|---|
| Sales revenue............................ | $ 580 |
| Less: Sales returns ............... | (108) |
| Net sales revenue ................ | $ 472 |
| Cost of goods sold................... | (307) |
| Gross profit............................. | $ 165 |

## Requirement 5

**Calculate Danner's inventory turnover for 2009.**

④ Estimate inventory by the gross profit method

> Inventory turnover = COGS/Average inventory

*Average* (when used in a financial ratio) generally means the beginning balance plus the ending balance divided by two.

> 2009 Inventory turnover
> = $307/[($0 + $325)/2]$
> = $307/$162.50$
> = 1.9 times

## DEMO DOC COMPLETE

# Demo Doc 2

## Inventory Costing Methods and Lower of Cost or Market

*Learning Objective 2*

Collins Industries' inventory records show the following data for 2009:

| | | | |
|---|---|---|---|
| Inventory at January 1 | 400 units | @ | $2 each |
| Inventory Purchases, March | 200 units | @ | $3 each |
| Sales, May | 160 units | | |
| Inventory Purchases, July | 100 units | @ | $4 each |
| Sales, September | 460 units | | |
| Inventory Purchases, November | 250 units | @ | $5 each |

### Requirements

1. Calculate COGS for the year ended December 31, 2009, and inventory at December 31, 2009, under each of the following assumptions:

   - FIFO

   - LIFO

   - Average Cost

2. Sales revenues were $4,000 for 2009. Calculate gross profit under each method.

3. Which method would maximize net income? Which method would minimize income taxes?

4. Assume that Collins is using FIFO. The ending inventory has a market price of $4.50 per unit. Calculate the lower of cost or market and make any necessary adjustment.

# Demo Doc 2 Solutions

## Requirement 1

Calculate COGS for the year ended December 31, 2009, and inventory at December 31, 2009, under each of the following assumptions:

- FIFO
- LIFO
- Average Cost

Before doing any costing calculations, it is important to determine the goods available for sale (both in units and dollars). We must also determine the number of units that were sold and the number of units in ending inventory.

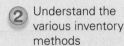

2 Understand the various inventory methods

> Goods available for sale = Beginning inventory + Purchases

> Beginning Inventory
>     400 units @ $2 = $  800
> Inventory Purchases
>     200 units @ $3 =    600
>     100 units @ $4 =    400
>     250 units @ $5 =  1,250
>     950 units      $3,050
>     = Goods Available for Sale

> Number of units sold = 160 in May + 460 in September
>     = 620 units for the year

> COGS = Beginning inventory + Inventory purchases – Ending inventory
>                       OR
> COGS = Goods available for sale – Ending inventory

This formula is expressed in *dollars,* but it also works in *units:*

Units sold = Units in beginning inventory + Units purchased − Units in ending inventory

OR

Units sold = Units available for sale − Units in ending inventory

620 units = 950 units − Units in ending inventory

Units in ending inventory = 330

### FIFO

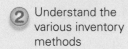

**2** Understand the various inventory methods

We are using the FIFO method. This means *first in, first out.* In other words, we always sell the *oldest* item we have. So what is left in inventory? The *newest* units.

There were 620 units sold. Under FIFO, these are the *oldest* inventory items. The oldest inventory is the beginning inventory of 400 units @ $2/unit. They must be part of COGS.

There are 620 − 400 = 220 other units that were sold. Some of these must be from the next oldest inventory: the March purchase of 200 units @ $3/unit.

There are 220 − 200 = 20 other units that were also sold (that were not part of beginning inventory or the March purchase).

These other units must have come from the July purchase of 100 units @ $4/unit (the next oldest units).

So we can calculate COGS as:

*From beginning inventory:*
400 units × $2 per unit = $   800
*From March purchase:*
200 units × $3 per unit =      600
*From July purchase:*
  20 units × $4 per unit =       80
COGS                          $1,480

There are 330 units in ending inventory. These are the 330 *newest* units the company has.

The newest units are the ones purchased in November of 250 units @ $5 per unit. They must be part of the ending inventory.

There are 330 − 250 = 80 other units that are also part of ending inventory (that were not from the November purchase). These other units must have come from the July purchase of 100 units @ $4 per unit (the next newest units). So we can calculate ending inventory as:

*From November purchase:*
250 units × $5 per unit = $1,250
*From July purchase:*
  80 units × $4 per unit =     320
**Ending Inventory**          $1,570

We can use the inventory formula to check our calculation:

$$COGS = \$800 + [\$600 + \$400 + \$1{,}250] - \$1{,}570 = \$1{,}480$$
$$COGS = \$800 + \$2{,}250 - \$1{,}570 = \$1{,}480$$
OR
$$COGS = \$3{,}050 - \$1{,}570 = \$1{,}480$$

So under FIFO, COGS = $1,480 and inventory at December 31, 2009 = $1,570.

## LIFO

What differs under LIFO is the *dollar* amount of ending inventory and COGS. Notice that the number of *units* sold and the number of *units* in ending inventory are still the same at 620 and 330 units, respectively.

② Understand the various inventory methods

    We are using the LIFO method. This means last-in-first-out. In other words, we always sell the *newest* item we have. So what is left in inventory? The *oldest* items.

    There were 620 units sold. Under LIFO, COGS is made up of the *newest* inventory items.

    The newest inventory is the November purchase of 250 units @ $5 per unit. These units must be part of COGS.

    There are 620 − 250 = 370 other units that were sold. Some of these must be from the next newest inventory: the July purchase of 100 units @ $4 per unit.

    There are 370 − 100 = 270 other units that were also sold (that were not part of the November or July purchases). Some of these must be from the next newest inventory: the March purchase of 200 units @ $3 per unit.

    There are 270 − 200 = 70 other units that were also sold (that were not part of the November, July, or March purchases). These other units must have come from the beginning inventory of 400 units @ $2 per unit (the next newest units).

    So we can calculate COGS as:

| | |
|---|---:|
| *From November purchase:* | |
| 250 units × $5 per unit = | $1,250 |
| *From July purchase:* | |
| 100 units × $4 per unit = | 400 |
| *From March purchase:* | |
| 200 units × $3 per unit = | 600 |
| *From beginning inventory:* | |
| 70 units × $2 per unit = | 140 |
| COGS | $2,390 |

    Under the LIFO method, we always sell the *newest* items we have. So what is left in inventory? The *oldest* units. Ending inventory must be the 330 oldest units the company has.

    The oldest units are the ones in beginning inventory: 400 units @ $2 per unit. All 330 units in ending inventory must have come from the beginning inventory.

    So we can calculate ending inventory as 330 units × $2 per unit = $660.

We can use the inventory formula to check our calculations:

$$COGS = \$800 + [\$600 + \$400 + \$1{,}250] - \$660 = \$2{,}390$$
$$COGS = \$800 + \$2{,}250 - \$660 = \$2{,}390$$
$$OR$$
$$COGS = \$3{,}050 - \$660 = \$2{,}390$$

## Average Cost

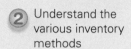

Under the average-cost method, we must calculate the average cost per unit of inventory. We only need to calculate this once for the entire period. Using the data calculated for the FIFO part of this problem,

$$\text{Average cost per unit} = \frac{\text{Goods available for sale}}{\text{Units available for sale}}$$

We know goods available for sale are the $800 (400 units) in beginning inventory + $2,250 (550 units) in inventory purchases = $3,050 (950 units). So the average cost per unit is:

$$\text{Average cost per unit} = \frac{\$3{,}050}{950 \text{ units}} = \$3.21 \text{ per unit}$$

We know that there are 330 units left in ending inventory, so inventory at December 31 is

$$330 \text{ units} \times \$3.21 = \$1{,}060 \text{ (rounded up)}$$

We know that there were 620 units sold during the period, so

$$COGS = 620 \text{ units} \times \$3.21 \text{ per unit} = \$1{,}990$$

We can check our calculations using the inventory formula:

$$COGS = \$800 + \$2{,}250 - \$1{,}060 = \$1{,}990$$
$$COGS = \$3{,}050 - \$1{,}060 = \$1{,}990$$

## Requirement 2

**Sales revenues were $4,000 for 2009. Calculate gross profit under each method.**

Gross profit = Sales revenue – COGS

|  | FIFO | LIFO | Average Cost |
|---|---|---|---|
| Sales Revenue | $4,000 | $4,000 | $4,000 |
| – COGS | 1,480 | 2,390 | 1,990 |
| Gross Profit | $2,520 | $1,610 | $2,010 |

## Requirement 3

**Which method would maximize net income? Which method would minimize income taxes?**

For the different methods, we have the following COGS:

| | |
|---|---|
| FIFO ............................ | $1,480 |
| LIFO ............................ | 2,390 |
| Average Cost ............... | 1,990 |

Of these, FIFO is the lowest and LIFO is the highest. Note that FIFO and LIFO will usually be the extremes with average cost being somewhere in the middle.

FIFO gives the lowest COGS, which means that it gives the highest gross profit. You can see this result in Requirement 2 of this question. This means that FIFO would maximize net income.

LIFO gives the highest COGS, which means that it gives the lowest gross profit. You can also see this result in Requirement 2 of this question. This means that LIFO would minimize net income, which in turn would minimize income taxes.

Note that if prices are decreasing over time (such as for high-tech items that quickly become obsolete), then the reverse of this analysis is true (FIFO gives highest COGS).

## Requirement 4

**Assume that Collins is using FIFO. The ending inventory has a market price of $4.50 per unit. Calculate the lower of cost or market and make any necessary adjustment.**

We have already determined that there are 330 units in ending inventory. Under FIFO, the cost of these units is $1,570. The market price of these units is:

$$330 \text{ units} \times \$4.50 \text{ per unit} = \$1,485$$

If cost is $1,570 and market price is $1,485, the lower of cost or market is $1,485 (the market value of the inventory).

The balance in the inventory T-account is currently the cost of $1,570. Therefore, Inventory must be decreased to the market value of $1,485. So Inventory is decreased (a credit) by $1,570 – $1,485 = $85. The other side of the journal entry is an adjustment to COGS. This will have to be a debit to balance out the credit to Inventory.

| | COGS | 85 | |
|---|---|---|---|
| | Inventory ($1,570 – $1,485) | | 85 |

### DEMO DOC COMPLETE

# Demo Doc 3

## Gross Profit Method and Inventory Errors

*Learning Objectives*    4, 5

On December 31, 2011, Talon Corp.'s warehouse and accounting records were destroyed in a flood. For insurance purposes, Talon must estimate the value of the inventory lost.

Through records from its bank and suppliers, Talon has been able to compile the following information:

| | |
|---|---:|
| Sales Revenue for 2011 ............................... | $20,000 |
| Inventory at December 31, 2010 ............... | 6,000 |
| Inventory Purchases for 2011 .................... | 23,000 |

Talon has historically had gross profit of 10%.

## Requirements

1. Estimate Talon's ending inventory value for 2011 using the gross profit method.

2. Assume that the actual value of inventory lost was $12,000. What is Talon's true COGS? Is COGS overstated or understated? How will this impact Talon's estimate of net income for 2011?

# Demo Doc 3 Solutions

## Requirement 1

 Estimate inventory by the gross profit method

**Estimate Talon's ending inventory value for 2011 using the gross profit method.**

The gross profit method uses the COGS formula:

COGS = Beginning inventory + Inventory purchases − Ending inventory

We are given information about purchases and beginning inventory, but to calculate ending inventory, we will need an estimate for COGS.

The formula for the gross profit percentage is:

$$\text{Gross profit percentage} = \frac{\text{Gross profit}}{\text{Sales revenue}} = \frac{\text{Sales} - \text{COGS}}{\text{Sales}}$$

So we know that 10% = ($20,000 − COGS)/$20,000.
From this, we can calculate COGS = $18,000. Using this in the COGS formula,

$18,000 = $6,000 + $23,000 − Ending inventory

From this, we can calculate ending inventory = $11,000.

## Requirement 2

(5) Show how inventory errors affect the financial statements

**Assume that the actual value of inventory lost was $12,000. What is Talon's true COGS? Is COGS overstated or understated? How will this impact Talon's estimate of net income for 2011?**

Using the actual value of $12,000 for ending inventory, we can recalculate COGS.

COGS = $6,000 + $23,000 − $12,000 = $17,000

Because Talon is estimating COGS of $18,000, COGS is overstated by $18,000 − $17,000 = $1,000. If Talon uses the wrong COGS number of $18,000 to calculate net income, then net income will be understated by $1,000.

***DEMO DOC COMPLETE***

# Quick Practice Questions

## True/False

_____  1. Under LIFO, the ending inventory cost comes from the oldest purchases.

_____  2. FIFO is the opposite of LIFO.

_____  3. The FIFO method can result in misleading inventory costs on the balance sheet because the oldest prices are left in ending inventory.

_____  4. When inventory costs are rising, LIFO will result in the lowest gross profit.

_____  5. When using a perpetual inventory system, a business will debit Inventory and credit Cost of Goods Sold each time a sale is recorded.

_____  6. If a company had 10 units of beginning inventory with a unit cost of $10 and a subsequent purchase of 15 units with a unit cost of $12, the average cost of one unit sold would be $11.

_____  7. When applying lower-of-cost-or-market rules to ending inventory valuation, market value generally refers to the company's current selling price for its inventory.

_____  8. Understating beginning inventory in the current year will overstate cost of goods sold in the current year.

_____  9. Overstating ending inventory in 2010 will overstate net income for 2011.

_____  10. The gross profit method is an estimate of inventory that can be used to estimate losses for insurance claims due to a fire or natural disaster.

_____  11. A higher inventory turnover is preferable to a lower turnover.

_____  12. A company with a gross profit percentage of 40% must have a higher net income than one with a gross profit percentage of 30%.

_____  13. IFRS do not permit the use of FIFO inventory costing.

# Multiple Choice

1. **Anticipating no gains but providing for all probable losses can be most closely associated with which of the following?**
   a. Conservatism
   b. Disclosure principle
   c. Consistency principle
   d. Materiality concept

2. **Which of the following are required to record the sale of merchandise on credit under a perpetual inventory system?**
   a. Debit Accounts Receivable; credit Sales Revenue
   b. Debit Cost of Goods Sold; credit Purchases
   c. Debit Cost of Goods Sold; credit Inventory
   d. Both (a) and (c) are necessary entries.

3. **What is the effect of using FIFO during a period of rising prices under a perpetual inventory system?**
   a. Less net income than LIFO
   b. Less operating expenses than LIFO
   c. Higher gross profit than LIFO
   d. Higher cost of goods sold than average costing

4. **Which of the following is NOT a reason for choosing the LIFO method?**
   a. LIFO reports the most up-to-date inventory values on the balance sheet.
   b. LIFO uses more current costs in calculating cost of goods sold.
   c. LIFO allows owners and managers to manage reported income.
   d. LIFO generally results in lower income taxes paid.

5. **Which of the following is true for ending inventory when prices are rising and the LIFO inventory system is used?**
   a. LIFO ending inventory is less than FIFO.
   b. LIFO ending inventory is greater than FIFO.
   c. LIFO ending inventory is equal to FIFO.
   d. LIFO ending inventory is equally likely to be higher or lower than FIFO.

6. **The following data are for Daisy's Florist Shop for the first seven months of its fiscal year:**

| | |
|---|---|
| Beginning inventory | $53,500 |
| Purchases | 75,500 |
| Net sales revenue | 93,700 |
| Normal gross profit percent | 30% |

   **What is the estimated inventory on hand as determined by the gross profit method?**
   a. $28,110
   b. $63,410
   c. $65,590
   d. $100,890

7. **Ending inventory for Commodity X consists of 20 units. Under the FIFO method, the cost of the 20 units is $5 each. Current replacement cost is $4.50 per unit. Using the lower-of-cost-or-market rule to value inventory, the balance sheet would show ending inventory at what amount?**
   a. $4.75
   b. $5.00
   c. $90.00
   d. $100.00

8. **Inventory at the end of the current year is understated by $20,000. What effect will this error have on the following year's net income?**
   a. Net income will be overstated $20,000.
   b. Net income will be understated $20,000.
   c. Net income will be correctly stated.
   d. Net income will be understated $40,000.

9. **Which of the following is necessary to journalize the purchase of merchandise on account under a perpetual inventory system?**
   a. A credit to Cash
   b. A debit to Accounts Payable
   c. A credit to Inventory
   d. A debit to Inventory

10. **What does inventory turnover indicate?**
   a. How quickly inventory is received from the supplier after the order is placed
   b. How many days it takes the inventory to travel between the seller's warehouse and the buyer's warehouse
   c. How rapidly inventory is sold
   d. How many days it takes from the time an order is received until the day it is shipped

# Quick Exercises

**6-1. Compute the missing income statement amounts for each of the following independent companies:**

| Company | Net Sales | Beginning Inventory | Purchases | Ending Inventory | Cost of Goods Sold | Gross Profit |
|---|---|---|---|---|---|---|
| A............... | $ 93,000 | $14,600 | $65,000 | (a) | $58,300 | (b) |
| B............... | (c) | $31,600 | (d) | $23,600 | $96,200 | $52,500 |
| C............... | $ 89,300 | $23,600 | $54,000 | (f) | (e) | $23,900 |
| D............... | $105,000 | $11,200 | (h) | $ 9,400 | (g) | $48,200 |

**6-2. Which inventory method would best meet the specific goals of management stated below? Show your answer by inserting the proper letter beside each statement.**

**a.** Specific unit cost
**b.** LIFO
**c.** FIFO
**d.** Average cost

_____ 1. Management desires to properly match net sales revenue with the most recent cost of goods.

_____ 2. Management desires to minimize the company's ending inventory balance during a period of falling prices.

_____ 3. The company sells rare antique items.

_____ 4. Management desires to show the current value of inventory on the balance sheet.

_____ 5. Management desires to minimize the company's tax liability during a period of rising prices.

**6-3. The following data are available for the month of March:**

| | | | |
|---|---|---|---|
| Inventory at March 1 .............................. | 25 units | @ | $16 each |
| Inventory Purchases, March 10 ................ | 40 units | @ | $18 each |
| Inventory Purchases, March 17 ................ | 30 units | @ | $20 each |
| Inventory Purchases, March 30 ................ | 10 units | @ | $21 each |
| Inventory on Hand, March 31 ................. | 35 units | | |

**1. Calculate cost of goods sold under the following methods:**

a. FIFO

b. LIFO

c. Average cost (Round the per-unit cost to the nearest cent; round the final answer to the nearest dollar.)

**6-4. Plastic Products Company lost some of its inventory due to a flood and needs to determine the amount of the inventory lost. The following data are available for 2011:**

| | |
|---|---|
| Sales revenue ........................................... | $400,000 |
| Estimated gross profit rate ...................... | 35% |
| January 1, beginning inventory .............. | 11,600 |
| Net purchases .......................................... | 275,000 |
| Inventory on hand, after flood ............... | 6,500 |

**1. Compute what the estimated ending inventory should be using the gross profit method.**

**2. Calculate the amount of the inventory loss.**

**6-5.** Determine the effect on cost of goods sold and net income for the current year of the following inventory errors. Indicate your answer with either a + (overstated) or a − (understated).

| Item | Error | Effect on Cost of Goods Sold | Effect on Net Income |
|---|---|---|---|
| 1 | Beginning inventory is understated. | | |
| 2 | Ending inventory is understated. | | |
| 3 | Beginning inventory is overstated. | | |
| 4 | Ending inventory is overstated. | | |

**6-6.** The following data are for the Griswold Corporation, which uses the periodic inventory system.

| | |
|---|---|
| Sales revenue................................................. | $600,000 |
| Freight-in ...................................................... | 42,000 |
| Beginning inventory ...................................... | 77,000 |
| Purchase discounts ........................................ | 19,000 |
| Sales returns and allowances ....................... | 33,000 |
| Ending inventory........................................... | 81,000 |
| Inventory purchases ...................................... | 415,000 |
| Sales discounts ............................................. | 35,000 |
| Purchase returns and allowances................. | 39,000 |

**1. Calculate Net Sales Revenue.**

**2. Calculate the Cost of Goods Available.**

**3. Calculate the Cost of Goods Sold.**

# Do It Yourself! Question 1

Franco Bros. began operations on January 1, 2011. Franco had the following transactions during the year:

**Jan 1**     Purchased inventory for $150 on account.

**Jan 8**     Paid for the January 1 purchase in full.

**Mar 1**     Purchased inventory for $240 on account.

**Apr 1**     Paid for the March 1 purchase in full.

**Jul 1**     Sold $80 worth of goods to a customer for $120 on account.

**Jul 12**     Received cash payment in full for the July 1 sale.

**Sep 1**     Found that $29 worth of the goods purchased on March 1 were defective. Franco Bros. returned these goods.

**Dec 1**     Sold $210 worth of goods to a customer for $320 on account.

**Dec 6**     Customer returned 20% of his December 1 order because he did not like the color of the goods.

**Dec 12**     Customer paid for the December 1 order (less returns) in full.

## Requirements

1. Journalize these transactions using the perpetual system. Explanations are not required.

| Date | Accounts | Debit | Credit |
|------|----------|-------|--------|
| Jan 1 |  |  |  |

| Date | Accounts | Debit | Credit |
|------|----------|-------|--------|
| Jan 8 |  |  |  |
|  |  |  |  |

| Date | Accounts | Debit | Credit |
|------|----------|-------|--------|
| Mar 1 |  |  |  |

| Date | Accounts | Debit | Credit |
|------|----------|-------|--------|
| Apr 1 |  |  |  |

| Date | Accounts | Debit | Credit |
|---|---|---|---|
| Jul 1 | | | |
| | | | |
| | | | |
| | | | |

| Date | Accounts | Debit | Credit |
|---|---|---|---|
| Jul 12 | | | |
| | | | |
| | | | |

| Date | Accounts | Debit | Credit |
|---|---|---|---|
| Sep 1 | | | |

| Date | Accounts | Debit | Credit |
|---|---|---|---|
| Dec 1 | | | |

| Date | Accounts | Debit | Credit |
|---|---|---|---|
| Dec 6 | | | |

| Date | Accounts | Debit | Credit |
|---|---|---|---|
| Dec 12 | | | |

**2. Show the Inventory and COGS T-accounts for the year.**

**3. Prepare the top portion of Franco's 2011 income statement (ending with gross profit).**

# Do It Yourself! Question 2

Sam, Inc.'s, inventory records show the following data for July 2011:

| | | | |
|---|---|---|---|
| Inventory at July 1 .............................. | 10 units | @ | $1 each |
| Inventory Purchases, July 5 ................. | 80 units | @ | $2 each |
| Sales, July 10 ....................................... | 50 units | | |
| Inventory Purchases, July 15 .............. | 20 units | @ | $3 each |
| Sales, July 20 ....................................... | 40 units | | |
| Inventory Purchases, July 25 .............. | 30 units | @ | $4 each |

## Requirements

1. Calculate COGS for the month ended July 31, 2011, and inventory at July 31, 2011, using the FIFO costing method.

2. Calculate COGS for the month ended July 31, 2011, and inventory at July 31, 2011, using the LIFO costing method.

3. Calculate COGS for the month ended July 31, 2011, and inventory at July 31, 2011, using the average cost method.

4. Sales revenues were $500 for July 2011. Calculate gross profit under each method.

5. The market value of ending inventory is $70. If Sam, Inc., uses LIFO, give any necessary adjustment for the lower-of-cost-or-market rule.

# Do It Yourself! Question 3

On December 31, 2011, Virga Brothers lost all of its inventory during a hurricane. Virga was able to gather the following information:

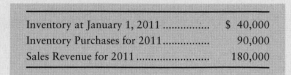

| | |
|---|---:|
| Inventory at January 1, 2011 ............... | $ 40,000 |
| Inventory Purchases for 2011............... | 90,000 |
| Sales Revenue for 2011 ........................ | 180,000 |

Historically, Virga has had gross profit of 40%.

## Requirement

1. Estimate the value of Virga's lost inventory.

# Quick Practice Solutions

## True/False

__T__  1. Under LIFO, the ending inventory cost comes from the oldest purchases. (p. 352)

__T__  2. FIFO is the opposite of LIFO. (p. 352)

__F__  3. The FIFO method can result in misleading inventory costs on the balance sheet because the oldest prices are left in ending inventory.

   False—It is the *LIFO* method that leaves the oldest prices in inventory. (p. 353)

__T__  4. When inventory costs are rising, LIFO will result in the lowest gross profit. (p. 353)

__F__  5. When using a perpetual inventory system, a business will debit Inventory and credit Cost of Goods Sold each time a sale is recorded.

   False—Using a perpetual inventory system, a business will *debit* Cost of Goods Sold and *credit* Inventory each time a sale is recorded. (p. 348)

__F__  6. If a company had 10 units of beginning inventory with a unit cost of $10 and a subsequent purchase of 15 units with a unit cost of $12, the average cost of one unit sold would be $11.

   False—Average cost is determined by dividing the cost of goods available (10 units × $10) + (15 units × $12) = $280, by the number of units available (10 + 15 = 25). $280/25 = $11.20. (p. 351)

__F__  7. When applying lower-of-cost-or-market rules to ending inventory valuation, market value generally refers to the company's current selling price for its inventory.

   False—Market value generally means current *replacement* cost. (p. 359)

__F__  8. Understating beginning inventory in the current year will overstate cost of goods sold in the current year.

   False—Understating beginning inventory in the current year will *understate* cost of goods sold in the current year. (p. 366)

  F      9. Overstating ending inventory in 2010 will overstate net income for 2011.

              False—Overstating ending inventory in 2010 will *understate* net income for 2011. (p. 366)

  T     10. The gross profit method is an estimate of inventory that can be used to estimate losses for insurance claims due to a fire or natural disaster. (pp. 364–365)

  T     11. A higher inventory turnover is preferable to a lower turnover. (p. 362)

  F     12. A company with a gross profit percentage of 40% must have a higher net income than one with a gross profit percentage of 30%.

              False—The gross profit percentage indicates the amount of gross profit per dollar of sales. It does not consider the operating expenses, which are deducted from gross profit to determine net income. (pp. 361–362)

  F     13. IFRS do not permit the use of FIFO inventory costing.

              False—IFRS does not allow *LIFO* inventory costing. (p. 356)

# Multiple Choice

1.  **Anticipating no gains but providing for all probable losses can be most closely associated with which of the following? (p. 359)**
    a. Conservatism
    b. Disclosure principle
    c. Consistency principle
    d. Materiality concept

2.  **Which of the following are required to record the sale of merchandise on credit under a perpetual inventory system? (p. 348)**
    a. Debit Accounts Receivable; credit Sales Revenue
    b. Debit Cost of Goods Sold; credit Purchases
    c. Debit Cost of Goods Sold; credit Inventory
    d. Both (a) and (c) are necessary entries.

3.  **What is the effect of using FIFO during a period of rising prices under a perpetual inventory system? (pp. 352–354)**
    a. Less net income than LIFO
    b. Less operating expenses than LIFO
    c. Higher gross profit than LIFO
    d. Higher cost of goods sold than average costing

4.  **Which of the following is NOT a reason for choosing the LIFO method? (pp. 353–354)**
    a. LIFO reports the most up-to-date inventory values on the balance sheet.
    b. LIFO uses more current costs in calculating cost of goods sold.
    c. LIFO allows owners and managers to manage reported income.
    d. LIFO generally results in lower income taxes paid.

5.  **Which of the following is true for ending inventory when prices are rising and the LIFO inventory system is used? (p. 353)**
    a. LIFO ending inventory is less than FIFO.
    b. LIFO ending inventory is greater than FIFO.
    c. LIFO ending inventory is equal to FIFO.
    d. LIFO ending inventory is equally likely to be higher or lower than FIFO.

6.  The following data are for Daisy's Florist Shop for the first
    seven months of its fiscal year:

    | | |
    |---|---:|
    | Beginning inventory | $53,500 |
    | Purchases | 75,500 |
    | Net sales revenue | 93,700 |
    | Normal gross profit percent | 30% |

    What is the estimated inventory on hand as determined by the
    gross profit method? (pp. 364–365)
    a. $28,110
    b. $63,410
    c. $65,590
    d. $100,890

7.  Ending inventory for Commodity X consists of 20 units. Under
    the FIFO method, the cost of the 20 units is $5 each. Current
    replacement cost is $4.50 per unit. Using the lower-of-cost-or-
    market rule to value inventory, the balance sheet would show
    ending inventory at what amount? (p. 359)
    a. $4.75
    b. $5.00
    c. $90.00
    d. $100.00

8.  Inventory at the end of the current year is understated by $20,000.
    What effect will this error have on the following year's net
    income? (p. 366)
    a. Net income will be overstated $20,000.
    b. Net income will be understated $20,000.
    c. Net income will be correctly stated.
    d. Net income will be understated $40,000.

9.  Which of the following is necessary to journalize the purchase of
    merchandise on account under a perpetual inventory system?
    (p. 348)
    a. A credit to Cash
    b. A debit to Accounts Payable
    c. A credit to Inventory
    d. A debit to Inventory

10. What does inventory turnover indicate? (p. 362)
    a. How quickly inventory is received from the supplier after the order
       is placed
    b. How many days it takes the inventory to travel between the seller's
       warehouse and the buyer's warehouse
    c. How rapidly inventory is sold
    d. How many days it takes from the time an order is received until the
       day it is shipped

# Quick Exercises

## 6-1. Compute the missing income statement amounts for each of the following independent companies: (pp. 344–349)

| Company | Net Sales | Beginning Inventory | Purchases | Ending Inventory | Cost of Goods Sold | Gross Profit |
|---------|-----------|---------------------|-----------|------------------|--------------------|--------------|
| A............. | $ 93,000 | $14,600 | $65,000 | (a) | $58,300 | (b) |
| B............. | (c) | $31,600 | (d) | $23,600 | $96,200 | $52,500 |
| C............. | $ 89,300 | $23,600 | $54,000 | (f) | (e) | $23,900 |
| D............. | $105,000 | $11,200 | (h) | $ 9,400 | (g) | $48,200 |

| | |
|---|---|
| (a) | $14,600 + $65,000 − $58,300 = $21,300 |
| (b) | $93,000 − $58,300 = $34,700 |
| (c) | $96,200 + $52,500 = $148,700 |
| (d) | $23,600 + $96,200 − $31,600 = $88,200 |
| (e) | $89,300 − $23,900 = $65,400 |
| (f) | $23,600 + $54,000 − $65,400 = $12,200 |
| (g) | $105,000 − $48,200 = $56,800 |
| (h) | $9,400 + $56,800 − $11,200 = $55,000 |

## 6-2. Which inventory method would best meet the specific goals of management stated below? Show your answer by inserting the proper letter beside each statement. (pp. 349–356)

**a.** Specific unit cost
**b.** LIFO
**c.** FIFO
**d.** Average cost

_____b_____ **1.** Management desires to properly match net sales revenue with the most recent cost of goods.

_____c_____ **2.** Management desires to minimize the company's ending inventory balance during a period of falling prices.

_____a_____ **3.** The company sells rare antique items.

_____c_____ **4.** Management desires to show the current value of inventory on the balance sheet.

_____b_____ **5.** Management desires to minimize the company's tax liability during a period of rising prices.

**6-3. The following data are available for the month of March:** (pp. 351–353)

| | | | |
|---|---|---|---|
| Inventory at March 1 ............................... | 25 units | @ | $16 each |
| Inventory Purchases, March 10................ | 40 units | @ | $18 each |
| Inventory Purchases, March 17................ | 30 units | @ | $20 each |
| Inventory Purchases, March 30................ | 10 units | @ | $21 each |
| Inventory on Hand, March 31 ................. | 35 units | | |

## 1. Calculate cost of goods sold under the following methods:

### a. FIFO

105 units available – 35 ending units = 70 units sold
Cost of goods sold:
$(25 \times \$16) + (40 \times \$18) + (5 \times \$20) = \$400 + \$720 + \$100 = \$1,220$

### b. LIFO

$(10 \times \$21) + (30 \times \$20) + (30 \times \$18) = \$210 + \$600 + \$540 = \$1,350$

### c. Average cost (Round the per-unit cost to the nearest cent; round the final answer to the nearest dollar.)

$(25 \times \$16) + (40 \times \$18) + (30 \times \$20) + (10 \times \$21) = \$400 + \$720 + \$600 + \$210 = \$1,930$
$\$1,930/105$ units $= \$18.38$
$\$18.38 \times 70 = \$1,287$

**6-4. Plastic Products Company lost some of its inventory due to a flood and needs to determine the amount of the inventory lost. The following data are available for 2011:** (pp. 364–365)

| | |
|---|---|
| Sales Revenue............................................. | $400,000 |
| Estimated gross profit rate ...................... | 35% |
| January 1, beginning inventory .............. | 11,600 |
| Net purchases............................................ | 275,000 |
| Inventory on hand, after flood ............... | 6,500 |

**1. Compute what the estimated ending inventory should be using the gross profit method.**

| | | |
|---|---|---|
| Beginning inventory ......................................... | | $ 11,600 |
| Net purchases.................................................... | | 275,000 |
| Cost of goods available .................................... | | 286,600 |
| Estimated cost of goods sold: | | |
| Sales Revenue.................................................. | 400,000 | |
| Less: Estimated gross profit of 35% .............. | (140,000) | |
| Estimated cost of goods sold ........................... | | 260,000 |
| Estimated cost of ending inventory................. | | $ 26,600 |

**2. Calculate the amount of the inventory loss.**

| | |
|---|---|
| Estimated cost of ending inventory.................. | $26,600 |
| Less: Inventory on hand, after flood............... | 6,500 |
| Amount of inventory loss................................ | $20,100 |

**6-5. Determine the effect on cost of goods sold and net income for the current year of the following inventory errors. Indicate your answer with either a + (overstated) or a – (understated).** (p. 366)

| Item | Error | Effect on Cost of Goods Sold | Effect on Net Income |
|---|---|---|---|
| 1 | Beginning inventory is understated. | – | + |
| 2 | Ending inventory is understated. | + | – |
| 3 | Beginning inventory is overstated. | + | – |
| 4 | Ending inventory is overstated. | – | + |

**6-6. The following data are for the Griswold Corporation, which uses the periodic inventory system.** (pp. 344–349)

| | |
|---|---:|
| Sales revenue | $600,000 |
| Freight-in | 42,000 |
| Beginning inventory | 77,000 |
| Purchase discounts | 19,000 |
| Sales returns and allowances | 33,000 |
| Ending inventory | 81,000 |
| Inventory purchases | 415,000 |
| Sales discounts | 35,000 |
| Purchase returns and allowances | 39,000 |

**1. Calculate Net Sales Revenue.**

$$\$600,000 - 33,000 - 35,000 = \$532,000$$

**2. Calculate the Cost of Goods Available.**

$$\$77,000 + 415,000 + 42,000 - 19,000 - 39,000 = \$476,000$$

**3. Calculate the Cost of Goods Sold.**

$$\$476,000 - 81,000 = \$395,000$$

# Do It Yourself! Question 1 Solutions

1. Journalize these transactions using the perpetual system. Explanations are not required.

| Date | Accounts | Debit | Credit |
|------|----------|-------|--------|
| Jan 1 | Inventory | 150 | |
| | Accounts Payable | | 150 |

| Date | Accounts | Debit | Credit |
|------|----------|-------|--------|
| Jan 8 | Accounts Payable | 150 | |
| | Cash | | 150 |

| Date | Accounts | Debit | Credit |
|------|----------|-------|--------|
| Mar 1 | Inventory | 240 | |
| | Accounts Payable | | 240 |

| Date | Accounts | Debit | Credit |
|------|----------|-------|--------|
| Apr 1 | Accounts Payable | 240 | |
| | Cash | | 240 |

| Date | Accounts | Debit | Credit |
|------|----------|-------|--------|
| Jul 1 | Accounts Receivable | 120 | |
| | Sales Revenue | | 120 |
| | | | |
| | COGS | 80 | |
| | Inventory | | 80 |

| Date | Accounts | Debit | Credit |
|------|----------|-------|--------|
| Jul 12 | Cash | 120 | |
| | Accounts Receivable | | 120 |

| Date | Accounts | Debit | Credit |
|------|----------|-------|--------|
| Sep 1 | Accounts Payable | 29 | |
| | Inventory | | 29 |

| Date | Accounts | Debit | Credit |
|---|---|---|---|
| Dec 1 | Accounts Receivable | 320 | |
| | Sales Revenue | | 320 |
| | | | |
| | COGS | 210 | |
| | Inventory | | 210 |

| Date | Accounts | Debit | Credit |
|---|---|---|---|
| Dec 6 | Inventory (20% × $210) | 42 | |
| | COGS | | 42 |
| | | | |
| | Sales Returns and Allowances (20% × $320) | 64 | |
| | Accounts Receivable | | 64 |

| Date | Accounts | Debit | Credit |
|---|---|---|---|
| Dec 12 | Cash ($320 – $64) | 256 | |
| | Accounts Receivable | | 256 |

**2. Show the Inventory and COGS T-accounts for the year.**

| Inventory | | | | COGS | | | |
|---|---|---|---|---|---|---|---|
| Jan 1 | 150 | | | Jul 1 | 80 | | |
| Mar 1 | 240 | | | Dec 1 | 210 | | |
| | | Jul 1 | 80 | | | Dec 6 | 42 |
| | | Sep 1 | 29 | Bal | 248 | | |
| | | Dec 1 | 210 | | | | |
| Dec 6 | 42 | | | | | | |
| Bal | 113 | | | | | | |

**3. Prepare the top portion of Franco's 2011 income statement (ending with gross profit).**

**Franco Bros.**
**Income Statement**
**Year Ended December 31, 2011**

| | | |
|---|---|---|
| Sales revenue............................ | $440 | |
| Less: Sales returns .............. | (64) | |
| Net sales revenue ................ | | $ 376 |
| Cost of goods sold................... | | (248) |
| Gross profit............................. | | $ 128 |

# Do It Yourself! Question 2 Solutions

1. Calculate COGS for the month ended July 31, 2011, and inventory at July 31, 2011, using the FIFO costing method.

| | | |
|---|---|---|
| Beginning Inventory | 10 units @ $1 per unit = | $ 10 |
| Inventory Purchases | | |
| July  5 ........................... | 80 units @ $2 per unit = | 160 |
| July 15 ........................... | 20 units @ $3 per unit = | 60 |
| July 25 ........................... | 30 units @ $4 per unit = | 120 |
| Goods Available for Sale | 140 units | $350 |

Number of units sold
= 50 on July 10 + 40 on July 20 = 90 units
90 units = 10 units + 130 units – Units in ending inventory
OR
90 units = 140 units – Units in ending inventory
Units in ending inventory = 50

*From beginning inventory:*
10 units × $1 per unit = $ 10
*From July 5 purchase:*
80 units × $2 per unit = 160
COGS $170

*From July 25 purchase:*
30 units × $4 per unit = $120
*From July 15 purchase:*
20 units × $3 per unit = 60
Ending Inventory $180

Check:

COGS = $10 + $340 – $180 = $170
OR
COGS = $350 – $180 = $170

2. **Calculate COGS for the month ended July 31, 2011, and inventory at July 31, 2011, using the LIFO costing method.**

*From July 25 purchase:*
30 units $\times$ \$4 per unit = \$120
*From July 15 purchase:*
20 units $\times$ \$3 per unit =     60
*From July 5 purchase:*
40 units $\times$ \$2 per unit =     80
COGS                                \$260

*From beginning inventory:*
10 units $\times$ \$1 per unit = \$ 10
*From July 5 purchase:*
40 units $\times$ \$2 per unit =     80
Ending Inventory                \$ 90

Check:

COGS = \$10 + \$340 − \$90 = \$260
OR
COGS = \$350 − \$90 = \$260

3. **Calculate COGS for the month ended July 31, 2011, and inventory at July 31, 2011, using the average cost method.**

$$\text{Average cost per unit} = \frac{\$10 + \$340}{10 \text{ units} + 130 \text{ units}} = \frac{\$350}{140 \text{ units}}$$

$$= \$2.50 \text{ per unit}$$

Ending inventory = 50 units $\times$ \$2.50 = \$125
COGS = 90 units $\times$ \$2.50 per unit = \$225

Check:

COGS = \$10 + \$340 − \$125 = \$225
OR
COGS = \$350 − \$125 = \$225

**4. Sales revenues were $500 for 2011. Calculate gross profit under each method.**

|  | FIFO | LIFO | Average Cost |
|---|---|---|---|
| Sales Revenue | $500 | $500 | $500 |
| – COGS | 170 | 260 | 225 |
| Gross Profit | $330 | $240 | $275 |

**5. The market value of ending inventory is $70. If Sam, Inc., uses LIFO, give any necessary adjustment for the lower-of-cost-or-market rule.**

Cost (under LIFO)   = $90   Market = $70
Lower of cost or market = $70

| | | | | |
|---|---|---|---|---|
| | | COGS | | 20 | |
| | | Inventory ($90 – $70) | | | 20 |

# Do It Yourself! Question 3 Solutions

## Requirement

1. **Estimate the value of Virga's lost inventory.**

$$\text{Gross profit percentage} = \frac{\text{Gross profit}}{\text{Sales revenue}} = \frac{\text{Sales} - \text{COGS}}{\text{Sales}}$$

$$40\% = (\$180,000 - \text{COGS})/\$180,000$$

$$\text{COGS} = \$108,000$$

$$\text{COGS} = \text{Beginning inventory} + \text{Inventory purchases} - \text{Ending inventory}$$

$$\$108,000 = \$40,000 + \$90,000 - \text{Ending inventory}$$

$$\text{Ending inventory} = \$22,000$$

# The Power of Practice

For more practice using the skills learned in this chapter, visit MyAccountingLab. There you will find algorithmically generated questions that are based on these Demo Docs and your main textbook's Review and Assess Your Progress sections.

Go to MyAccountingLab and follow these steps:

1. Direct your URL to www.myaccountinglab.com.
2. Log in using your name and password.
3. Click the MyAccountingLab link.
4. Click Study Plan in the left navigation bar.
5. From the table of contents, select Chapter 6, Inventory & Cost of Goods Sold.
6. Click a link to work tutorial exercises.

# 7 Plant Assets & Intangibles

## WHAT YOU PROBABLY ALREADY KNOW

You probably already know that when you decide to get a car, you must decide if you want to purchase or lease it. If you lease a car, you pay a monthly amount for the use of that vehicle, which is a benefit or expense to you. If you purchase a car for cash instead, there is still a monthly benefit to you, although there are no future payments. The benefit or cost incurred is called depreciation expense. The more a car is used, the less remaining future value to be derived from that asset. In business, the asset is reduced for the loss in usefulness or future benefit as the vehicle is used.

## Learning Objectives

 **Determine the cost of a plant asset**

The **cost of a plant asset** should include all of the necessary costs to acquire the asset and get it ready for use. In addition to the purchase price of the plant asset, other items that may be necessary and would increase the cost of the asset include the following:

- Taxes, commissions, shipping costs, and insurance on the asset while in transit
- Installation and testing costs
- Architectural fees, building permits, and costs to repair and renovate the asset for use
- Interest on money borrowed to construct the plant asset
- Brokerage fees, survey, title and legal fees, payment of back property taxes, and the cost of clearing land and razing unneeded structures

If discounts are available and taken advantage of, those amounts would reduce the cost of the plant asset. *Review the discussion of "Measuring the Cost of a Plant Asset" (pp. 411–413) to see examples of items that are considered to be a part of the cost of different assets. Review the section "Lump-Sum (or Basket) Purchase of Assets" in the text to see how the cost of individual plant assets is determined when a single price is charged for the group.*

 **Account for depreciation**

**Depreciation** is the allocation of cost over a plant asset's useful life. The expense of depreciation is matched against the revenue generated, as shown in *Exhibit 7-3 (p. 416)*. The three most popular methods of depreciation are the straight-line, units-of-production, and double-declining-balance methods. The adjusting entry to depreciate any plant asset is to debit Depreciation Expense and credit Accumulated Depreciation.

Three elements necessary to calculate depreciation are the following:

a. Asset cost—known amount on the books
b. Estimated useful life—period of asset usefulness
c. Estimated residual value—expected value at the end of the useful life

*Review "Depreciation Methods" in the text for examples of the various depreciation methods. See Exhibit 7-8 (p. 422) for a comparison of the three methods.*

### ③ Select the best depreciation method

The straight-line method is simple and intuitive. The units-of-production method is the most accurate representation of true depreciation—if the appropriate data is available. The accelerated-declining-balance methods permit more depreciation to be deducted in the early years, which conserves cash flow by lowering taxes in those years.

### ④ Analyze the effect of a plant asset disposal

When a plant asset is sold, it should be depreciated until the date of disposal. Then the following should be accounted for:

- Debit the cash or other proceeds received
- Debit the accumulated depreciation
- Credit the plant asset cost

The difference between the asset cost and accumulated depreciation is book value. If the book value is greater than the proceeds, a debit must also be recorded as a loss on disposal. If the book value is less than the proceeds, a credit must also be recorded as a gain on disposal.

A plant asset may also be exchanged for a new asset. The book value of the old asset is removed as described earlier. The cash paid on exchange is credited and the market value of the new asset is debited. Any difference between the market value of the new asset and the book value of the old plus cash paid is the gain or loss. *Review the related examples in "Accounting for Disposal of Plant Assets" in the text.*

### ⑤ Account for natural resources and depletion

**Natural resources** are long-term assets that include iron ore, natural gas, and timber. As the inventory of the iron, gas, or other natural resource is used up, it is considered to be depleted. The depletion entry is similar to depreciation (debit Depletion Expense and credit Accumulated Depletion). The depletion amount is determined using the units-of-production formula.

**Accumulated Depletion** is a contra asset account like Accumulated Depreciation. *Review "Accounting for Natural Resources" in the text.*

## 6   Account for intangible assets and amortization

**Intangible assets** are rights that provide future value or benefit to the organization. Patents, copyrights, franchises, and trademarks are examples of these assets. Those intangible assets with a defined useful life are amortized by the straight-line method. The entry to amortize the intangible asset is to debit Amortization Expense and to credit the intangible asset.

**Goodwill** represents the sum of the market values of the acquired company's net assets (assets minus liabilities). Goodwill is not amortized but may need to be written down due to a loss of value. *Review the description of the types of intangible assets and especially the treatment of goodwill included under the "Accounting for Intangible Assets" section of the text.*

## 7   Report plant asset transactions on the statement of cash flows

As long-term assets, plant assets impact the investing activities section of the statement of cash flows. Purchases of plant assets decrease cash, while disposals of plant assets increase cash. *Review Exhibit 7-12 (p. 439) to see the placement of plant asset transactions on the statement of cash flows.*

# Demo Doc 1

## Depreciation

*Learning Objectives 1–4, 7*

Peters Corp. purchased a truck for $13,800 cash on January 1, 2009. Peters also had to pay taxes of $1,200 cash. The truck had a residual value of $1,000 and a useful life of seven years or 100,000 miles driven. Peters has a December 31 year-end.

The truck was driven for 15,000 miles in 2009, 12,000 miles in 2010, and 17,000 miles in 2011.

### Requirements

1. Calculate the total cost of the truck.

2. Calculate the depreciation expense and accumulated depreciation balance at December 31 for 2009, 2010, and 2011 using the straight-line, units-of-production, and double-declining-balance methods.

3. Using the double-declining-balance method only, show how the Truck account would look on the December 31 balance sheets for 2009, 2010, and 2011.

4. Which of the three methods maximizes income for 2009? Which method minimizes income taxes for 2009?

5. Peters sold the truck on September 1, 2012, for $7,000 cash. Journalize the sale transaction using each method. (The truck was driven for 8,000 miles in 2012.)

6. What impact does the truck have on investing cash flows for 2012?

# Demo Doc 1 Solutions

## Requirement 1

**Calculate the total cost of the truck.**

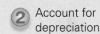

1  Determine the cost of a plant asset

The total cost of the truck is the total cost to make it ready for use. Any expenditure that *must be paid in order to use the asset* is part of the asset's total cost.

In this case, the truck cannot be used until the taxes are paid on the truck. Therefore, the taxes are added to the total cost of the truck.

| | |
|---|---|
| Purchase Price ........................ | $13,800 |
| Taxes ...................................... | 1,200 |
| Total Cost of Truck ................ | $15,000 |

## Requirement 2

**Calculate the depreciation expense and accumulated depreciation balance at December 31 for 2009, 2010, and 2011 using the straight-line, units-of-production, and double-declining-balance methods.**

2  Account for depreciation

### Straight-Line Method

The straight-line method allocates an equal amount of depreciation over the useful life.

Straight-line depreciation is calculated as:

$$\frac{\text{Cost} - \text{Residual value}}{\text{Years of useful life}} = \text{Annual depreciation expense}$$

Or, in this particular question:

$$\frac{\$15,000 - \$1,000}{7 \text{ years}} = \$2,000 \text{ Depreciation expense per year}$$

Remember that cost minus residual value is sometimes called *depreciable cost*, because this is the total depreciation that will be recorded over the asset's life. At the end of the asset's life, the book value equals the residual value.

Remember that the depreciation expense will be the same for *each* year. Depreciation expense does not change (unless there is a partial year, as demonstrated in Requirement 5 of this question). This is why the method is called "straight-line": because if the annual depreciation expense is charted on a graph, it is a straight line (see Exhibit 7-8, p. 422, in the main textbook).

So depreciation expense in 2009 is:

| |
|---|
| _____ |
| = depreciation expense in 2010 |
| = depreciation expense in 2011 |
| = $2,000. |

Accumulated depreciation is the total of *all* the depreciation expense that the company has accumulated up to a certain time. In other words, it is the sum of the depreciation expense in *every* year that has passed.

You can use a T-account to calculate accumulated depreciation each year:

| Accumulated Depreciation—Truck | | |
|---|---|---|
| | 12/31/09 | 2,000 |
| | 2009 Bal | 2,000 |
| | 12/31/10 | 2,000 |
| | 2010 Bal | 4,000 |
| | 12/31/11 | 2,000 |
| | 2011 Bal | 6,000 |

So in 2009, accumulated depreciation is the 2009 depreciation expense (because this is the only year of depreciation so far) = $2,000. In 2010, accumulated depreciation is the sum of the 2009 and 2010 depreciation expense = $2,000 + $2,000 = $4,000. In 2011, accumulated depreciation is the sum of the 2009, 2010, and 2011 depreciation expense = $2,000 + $2,000 + $2,000 = $6,000.

If you want to make things a little easier on yourself, instead of adding up all of the accumulated depreciation from scratch, you can instead add the current year's depreciation expense to the prior balance. In other words:

Accumulated depreciation this year = Accumulated depreciation last year + This year's depreciation expense

2010 accumulated depreciation of $4,000 + $2,000 depreciation expense for 2011 = $6,000 accumulated depreciation for 2011.

The truck's book value is its cost minus its accumulated depreciation. This is the net value shown for the truck on the balance sheet.

| | Straight-Line Method | | |
|---|---|---|---|
| Year | Annual Depreciation Expense | Accumulated Depreciation | Book Value |
| 2009 ............... | $2,000 | $2,000 | $13,000 |
| 2010 ............... | 2,000 | 4,000 | 11,000 |
| 2011 ............... | 2,000 | 6,000 | 9,000 |

## Units-of-Production Method

The unit method is similar to the straight-line method, but instead of calculating depreciation expense per *year*, we calculate it per *unit*. It allocates an equal amount of depreciation for each unit of production. Notice how the formula is similar to the straight-line method:

$$\frac{\text{Cost} - \text{Residual value}}{\text{Units of production in useful life}} = \text{Depreciation expense per unit}$$

Or, in this particular question:

$$\frac{\$15,000 - \$1,000}{100,000 \text{ miles}} = \$0.14 \text{ Depreciation expense per actual mile driven}$$

Because a different number of miles is driven every year, the *annual* depreciation expense will be different from year to year; however, the depreciation rate per *unit/mile* remains constant.

Units of production is another way of measuring an asset's life or productivity. For example, we could say that a machine will last for five years, or we might say that it will have 50,000 hours of operation. Both statements are reasonable ways to express how long the machine will last. The straight-line method focuses on the *years* (for example, five years of life) and the unit method focuses on the *production* (such as the 50,000 hours). It is obvious from reading the question whether there are any ways to measure an asset's life other than by years. In this question, the miles driven are highlighted and are the only other measure of asset life we can use.

Under the unit method, we calculate depreciation as:

Depreciation expense this year = Units used this year × Depreciation expense per unit

So, in this question we can calculate depreciation expense on the truck each year as:

|  | Actual |  | Rate |  | Annual Expense |
| --- | --- | --- | --- | --- | --- |
| 2009 ............... | 15,000 miles | × | $0.14 per mile | = | $2,100 |
| 2010 ............... | 12,000 miles | × | $0.14 per mile | = | $1,680 |
| 2011 ............... | 17,000 miles | × | $0.14 per mile | = | $2,380 |

We calculate accumulated depreciation the same way we did for the straight-line method (only the depreciation *expense* is calculated differently from method to method).

We can use a T-account to calculate accumulated depreciation each year:

| Accumulated Depreciation—Truck | |
| --- | --- |
| | 12/31/09 2,100 |
| | 2009 Bal 2,100 |
| | 12/31/10 1,680 |
| | 2010 Bal 3,780 |
| | 12/31/11 2,380 |
| | 2011 Bal 6,160 |

We can also calculate accumulated depreciation directly:

Accumulated depreciation this year = Accumulated depreciation last year + This year's depreciation expense

So, in this question we can calculate accumulated depreciation each year as:

| | | | | | | |
|---|---|---|---|---|---|---|
| 2009 ............... | $0 | + | $2,100 | = | $2,100 |
| 2010 ............... | $2,100 | + | $1,680 | = | $3,780 |
| 2011 ............... | $3,780 | + | $2,380 | = | $6,160 |

| | Units-of-Production Method | | |
|---|---|---|---|
| Year | Depreciation Expense | Accumulated Depreciation | Book Value (Cost − Accumulated Depreciation) |
| 2009 ............... | $2,100 | $2,100 | $12,900 |
| 2010 ............... | 1,680 | 3,780 | 11,220 |
| 2011 ............... | 2,380 | 6,160 | 8,840 |

## Double-Declining-Balance Method

This method is somewhat more complicated than straight-line or unit depreciation. It allocates more depreciation in the early years than in the later years.

Instead of a set depreciation amount, we use a depreciation *rate:*

Double-declining-balance (DDB) depreciation rate = 2/years of useful life

Or, in this particular question:

DDB rate = 2/7

You may notice that the years of useful life is the *same* denominator as we used in the straight-line method. This is why the method is called *double-declining-balance*: It is two times the amount used for straight-line (that is, $2 \times 1$/Years of useful life).

To get the depreciation expense each year, we need to use the following formula:

This year's depreciation expense = Book value ( = cost − last year's accumulated depreciation) × Depreciation rate

Sometimes the cost minus last year's accumulated depreciation is called the *net* value of the asset. You will see why in Requirement 3 of this question.

Because the accumulated depreciation is used in the depreciation expense formula, we need to calculate both together every year; however, the methods we can use to calculate accumulated depreciation are the same as before.

2009 depreciation expense = ($15,000 − $0) × 2/7 = $4,286
Accumulated depreciation = $0 + $4,286 = $4,286

2010 depreciation expense = ($15,000 − $4,286) × 2/7 = $3,061
Accumulated depreciation = $4,286 + $3,061 = $7,347

2011 depreciation expense = ($15,000 − $7,347) × 2/7 = $2,187
Accumulated depreciation = $7,347 + $2,187 = $9,534

We can also use a T-account to calculate accumulated depreciation each year:

| Accumulated Depreciation—Truck | | |
|---|---|---|
| | 12/31/09 | 4,286 |
| | 2009 Bal | 4,286 |
| | 12/31/10 | 3,061 |
| | 2010 Bal | 7,347 |
| | 12/31/11 | 2,187 |
| | 2011 Bal | 9,534 |

It is important to keep an eye on accumulated depreciation with the double-declining-balance method. Remember, we did *not* use the residual value to calculate depreciation expense.

However, we need to ensure that the *book value* of the asset does not go below the residual value. When the book value of the asset reaches the residual value, we *stop* taking depreciation expense (even if the asset is still being used).

| | Double-Declining-Balance Method | | |
|---|---|---|---|
| Year | Depreciation Expense | Accumulated Depreciation | Book Value (Cost − Accumulated Depreciation) |
| 2009 ............... | $4,286 | $4,286 | $10,714 |
| 2010 ............... | 3,061 | 7,347 | 7,653 |
| 2011 ............... | 2,187 | 9,534 | 5,466 |

## Requirement 3

**Using the double-declining-balance method only, show how the Truck account would look on the December 31 balance sheets for 2009, 2010, and 2011.**

Although the question only requires this to be done for the double-declining-balance method, keep in mind that the balance sheet presentation is the *same* for *all* depreciation methods:

② Account for depreciation

③ Select the best depreciation method

| Cost |
|---|
| − Accumulated depreciation |
| Net value of asset |

This *net* value of the asset is the *same* amount that is used in the double-declining-balance calculation for depreciation expense in the *following* year.

So on the balance sheet for each year (under the double-declining-balance method), you would see:

|  | 2009 | 2010 | 2011 |
|---|---|---|---|
| Truck | $15,000 | $15,000 | $15,000 |
| − Accumulated Depreciation | (4,286) | (7,347) | (9,534) |
| Truck (net) | $10,714 | $ 7,653 | $ 5,466 |

## Requirement 4

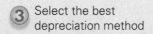
Select the best depreciation method

**Which of the three methods maximizes income for 2009? Which method minimizes income taxes for 2009?**

The depreciation expense for each method in 2009 is:

| | |
|---|---|
| Straight-Line | $2,000 |
| Units of Production | 2,100 |
| Double-Declining-Balance | 4,286 |

Revenues − Expenses = Net income, so higher expense (holding revenue constant) gives a lower net income.

In this example, the straight-line method has the lowest depreciation expense, which means that it has the highest net income.

The double-declining-balance method has the highest depreciation expense, which means that it has the lowest net income and, therefore, the lowest income taxes.

## Requirement 5

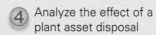
Analyze the effect of a plant asset disposal

**Peters sold the truck on September 1, 2012, for $7,000 cash. Journalize the sale transaction using each method. (The truck was driven for 8,000 miles in 2012.)**

### Straight-Line Method

When an asset is sold, we must journalize that sale. However, before we can do this, we must *update the depreciation* on the asset.

Depreciation represents the portion (the *benefit*) of the asset that has been used. The truck was sold on September 1, which means that Peters got to use it for eight months of 2012 before it was sold. We must represent that use as depreciation expense.

The depreciation expense that we record for eight months is *not* the same as the amount we would record for an entire year, because it is a shorter period of time (and, therefore, the asset was used less). Therefore, we must calculate a partial year's depreciation.

Under straight-line depreciation, the *annual* depreciation expense is $2,000 (that is, for 12 months). So for eight months:

$$2012 \text{ depreciation expense} = \$2,000 \times \frac{8 \text{ months}}{12 \text{ months}} = \$1,333$$

This depreciation would then be recorded as:

| Sep 1 | Depreciation Expense | 1,333 | |
|---|---|---|---|
| | Accumulated Depreciation—Truck | | 1,333 |

This brings the total accumulated depreciation to $6,000 + $1,333 = $7,333. Now we can record the sale of the truck.

Cash was received, so it increases (a debit) by $7,000.

The truck has been sold, so that account decreases to a zero balance (a credit) by $15,000. The Accumulated Depreciation goes along with it (contra accounts *always* go with their associated account), so that account decreases to a zero balance (a debit) as well by $7,333.

Putting these amounts into the journal entry:

| Sep 1 | Cash | 7,000 | |
|---|---|---|---|
| | Accumulated Depreciation—Truck | 7,333 | |
| | ??? | | |
| | Truck | | 15,000 |

Obviously, the entry is not complete because it *does not balance*. In order to get it to balance, we need equal debits and credits, which means that we need a $15,000 − $7,000 − $7,333 = $667 debit for the entry to balance.

The $667 is a balancing amount representing a loss, because the cash received ($7,000) is less than the net book value of the truck ($15,000 − $7,333 = $7,667).

So the completed entry is:

| Sep 1 | Cash | 7,000 | |
|---|---|---|---|
| | Accumulated Depreciation—Truck | 7,333 | |
| | Loss on Sale of Truck (to balance) | 667 | |
| | Truck | | 15,000 |

## Units-of-Production Method

We must record the depreciation expense for the first eight months of the year.

$$2012 \text{ depreciation expense} = 8,000 \text{ miles} \times \$0.14 = \$1,120$$

Notice that we did *not* need to multiply by 8/12 like we did in the straight-line method. This is because the short period of use is *already incorporated* into the 8,000 miles. If the truck had been used for a full year, the number of miles would have been bigger, and so depreciation expense would have been higher. With the unit method, all that matters is the *actual* number of miles the truck was driven.

Depreciation is recorded as:

| Sep 1 | Depreciation Expense | 1,120 | |
|---|---|---|---|
| | Accumulated Depreciation—Truck | | 1,120 |

Accumulated depreciation is now $6,160 + $1,120 = $7,280.

Cash was received, so it increases (a debit) by $7,000.

The truck has been sold, so that account decreases to a zero balance (a credit) by $15,000. Accumulated Depreciation decreases to a zero balance (a debit) as well by $7,280.

Putting these amounts into the journal entry:

| Sep 1 | Cash | 7,000 | |
|---|---|---|---|
| | Accumulated Depreciation—Truck | 7,280 | |
| | ??? | | |
| | Truck | | 15,000 |

In order to get it to balance, we need a $15,000 − $7,000 − $7,280 = $720 debit.

This amount represents a loss because the cash received ($7,000) is less than the book value of the truck ($15,000 − $7,280 = $7,720).

So the completed entry is:

| Sep 1 | Cash | 7,000 | |
|---|---|---|---|
| | Accumulated Depreciation—Truck | 7,280 | |
| | Loss on Sale of Truck (to balance) | 720 | |
| | Truck | | 15,000 |

## Double-Declining-Balance Method

$$2012 \text{ depreciation expense} = (\$15,000 - \$9,534) \times 2/7 = \$1,561.71 = 12 \text{ months of depreciation}$$

$$\$1,561.71 \times \frac{8 \text{ months}}{12 \text{ months}} = \$1,041 = 8 \text{ months of depreciation}$$

| Sep 1 | Depreciation Expense | 1,041 | |
|---|---|---|---|
| | Accumulated Depreciation—Truck | | 1,041 |

This brings the accumulated depreciation to:

$$\$9,534 + \$1,041 = \$10,575$$

Cash was received, so it increases (a debit) by $7,000.

The truck has been sold, so that account decreases to a zero balance (a credit) by $15,000. Accumulated Depreciation decreases to a zero balance (a debit) by $10,575.

Putting these amounts into the journal entry:

| Sep 1 | Cash | 7,000 | |
|---|---|---|---|
| | Accumulated Depreciation—Truck | 10,575 | |
| | ??? | | |
| | Truck | | 15,000 |

We need a $7,000 + $10,575 − $15,000 = $2,575 credit for the entry to work.

This amount represents a gain because the cash received ($7,000) is greater than the book value (net value) of the truck ($15,000 − $10,575 = $4,425).

So the completed entry is:

| Sep 1 | Cash | 7,000 | |
|---|---|---|---|
| | Accumulated Depreciation—Truck | 10,575 | |
| | Gain on Sale of Truck (to balance) | | 2,575 |
| | Truck | | 15,000 |

## Requirement 6

**What impact does the truck have on investing cash flows for 2012?**

7 Report plant asset transactions on the statement of cash flows

Purchases and sales of plant assets impact investing activities on the statement of cash flows. Because the truck was sold/disposed of for $7,000 cash, there would be a cash inflow of $7,000 to investing cash flows.

Note that depreciation expense does *not* impact investing cash flows. Depreciation is a *non-cash* transaction, and is therefore *not* included in investing activities.

**DEMO DOC COMPLETE**

# Demo Doc 2

## Natural Resource Assets

*Learning Objectives 1, 5*

Xander, Inc., purchased a coal mine for $900 million cash on January 1, 2009. After the purchase, an independent analyst determined that the value of the land was $200 million and that the value of the coal was $800 million (based on an estimate that there were 20 million tons of coal below the ground).

In 2009, Xander mined and sold one million tons of coal.

### Requirements

1. Journalize Xander's purchase of the mine.

2. Journalize Xander's depletion expense for 2009.

# Demo Doc 2 Solutions

## Requirement 1

### Journalize Xander's purchase of the mine.

Xander purchased two assets at one time *for one price*. This is called a *lump-sum purchase*. We need to determine how much of the purchase price to allocate to each asset.

① Determine the cost of a plant asset

This is important because it impacts depreciation and depletion calculations in the future (because the cost of the asset is an important number in these calculations).

We use the independent valuations to determine a *proportional* value for the assets. According to the analyst, the total value of the assets purchased = $200 million + $800 million = $1 billion.

This means that the land has a proportion of 200,000,000/1,000,000,000 = 20%.
The coal has a proportion of 800,000,000/1,000,000,000 = 80%.
The cost of each asset is assigned as this proportion of the total cost.
So the cost of the land = 20% × $900 million total cost = $180 million.
The cost of the coal = 80% × $900 million total cost = $720 million.
In the journal entry, Land and Coal Reserves are increased (debit) by these amounts and cash is decreased (credit).

| | | |
|---|---|---|
| Land (20% × $900,000,000) | 180,000,000 | |
| Coal Reserves (80% × $900,000,000) | 720,000,000 | |
| Cash | | 900,000,000 |

## Requirement 2

### Journalize Xander's depletion expense for 2009.

⑤ Account for natural resources and depletion

Depletion expense is *the same* as depreciation expense, except that this term is *only* used for natural resource assets. Depletion is always calculated using the *units-of-production* method (never the straight-line or declining-balance methods).

The units are the amount of natural resources purchased. In this case, the units are tons of coal.

$$\frac{\text{Cost}}{\text{Units of production}} = \text{Depletion expense per unit}$$

$$\frac{\$720,000,000}{20,000,000 \text{ tons}} = \$36 \text{ per ton}$$

Under the units-of-production method, we calculate depletion as:

Depletion expense this year = Actual units used this year × Depletion expense per unit
Depletion expense for 2009 = 1,000,000 tons × $36 per ton = $36,000,000

When we record depreciation, we increase (debit) Depreciation Expense and increase (credit) Accumulated Depreciation. The entry for depletion is *the same* except that we use Depletion Expense (debit) and Accumulated Depletion (credit).

| | Depletion Expense ($36 × 1,000,000) | 36,000,000 | |
|---|---|---|---|
| | Accumulated Depletion—Coal Reserves | | 36,000,000 |

## *DEMO DOC COMPLETE*

# Demo Doc 3

## Intangible Assets

*Learning Objective 6*

On July 1, 2009, Franco Co. acquired a patent from Juarez, Inc., for $5,000 cash and by signing a $10,000, 6% note payable. Franco believes that the patent will have a life of 10 years.

On the same date, Franco purchased all outstanding shares of Germano, Inc., for $50,000. The book value of Germano's net assets at this time was $35,000 and the market value was $40,000.

### Requirements

1. Journalize Franco's purchase of the patent. What kind of asset is the patent? Why do you think so?

2. Journalize Franco's amortization expense for the patent in 2009.

3. Franco did not make any interest payments on the note in 2009. Journalize Franco's interest expense for the year.

4. Calculate the amount of goodwill that will be recorded for Franco as a result of the Germano purchase.

5. Journalize any adjustment to the value of Franco's goodwill if it is determined to be worth $2,500 at the end of the year.

# Demo Doc 3 Solutions

## Requirement 1

**Journalize Franco's purchase of the patent. What kind of asset is the patent? Why do you think so?**

⑥ Account for intangible assets and amortization

Cash decreases (a credit) by $5,000 and Notes Payable increases (a credit) by $10,000.

There is also an increase to Patent (a debit) of $5,000 + $10,000 = $15,000.

| | | | |
|---|---|---|---|
| Jul 1 | Patent | 15,000 | |
| | Cash | | 5,000 |
| | Note Payable | | 10,000 |

The patent is an *intangible asset*. This is because the patent is a *right* to produce a certain product or use a certain technology. A right is not a physical asset: It cannot be touched. This means that it is *intangible*.

## Requirement 2

**Journalize Franco's amortization expense for the patent in 2009.**

⑥ Account for intangible assets and amortization

Intangible assets are amortized. This is essentially the same concept as depreciation for tangible assets, except that for intangible assets, we usually do not record an "accumulated amortization" account, but instead *directly* reduce the asset account.

Amortization expense is usually calculated using the straight-line method.

$$\text{Amortization expense (annual)} = \frac{\text{Cost of intangible asset}}{\text{Years of useful life}}$$

$$\frac{\$15,000}{10 \text{ years}} = \$1,500 \text{ per year}$$

Because the patent was purchased on July 1, only six months have been used. Therefore, we must calculate a partial year's amortization:

$$\$1,500 \times \frac{6 \text{ months}}{12 \text{ months}} = \$750 \text{ Amortization Expense for 6 months}$$

Amortization Expense increases (a debit) by $750.

Remember that for intangible assets, we do *not* have an accumulated account. This means that instead we must decrease the Patent account (a credit) *directly* for $750.

| | | | |
|---|---|---|---|
| Dec 31 | Amortization Expense—Patents | 750 | |
| | Patent | | 750 |

## Requirement 3

**Franco did not make any interest payments on the note in 2009. Journalize Franco's interest expense for the year.**

6 Account for intangible assets and amortization

Interest expense for the year is:

$$\$10,000 \times 6\% \times \frac{6 \text{ months}}{12 \text{ months}} = \$300$$

Interest Expense is increased (a debit) and Interest Payable is increased (a credit) by $300.

| Dec 31 | Interest Expense | 300 | |
|---|---|---|---|
| | Interest Payable | | 300 |

## Requirement 4

**Calculate the amount of goodwill that will be recorded for Franco as a result of the Germano purchase.**

6 Account for intangible assets and amortization

$$\text{Goodwill} = \text{Purchase price} - \text{Market value of net assets}$$
$$= \$50,000 - \$40,000 = \$10,000$$

This could also be calculated by preparing the journal entry for Franco to purchase Germano.

Franco increases its Net Assets (debit) by the market value of $40,000. Cash is decreased (credit) for the purchase price paid.

The remaining amount in the entry is the amount of goodwill purchased. This is the balancing amount in the entry.

| Jul 1 | Net Assets | 40,000 | |
|---|---|---|---|
| | Goodwill (to balance) | 10,000 | |
| | Cash | | 50,000 |

## Requirement 5

**Journalize any adjustment to the value of Franco's goodwill if it is determined to be worth $2,500 at the end of the year.**

Account for intangible assets and amortization

Franco recorded the goodwill at $10,000. Because it is now worth only $2,500, it has a loss in value of $10,000 − $2,500 = $7,500. The loss is recorded (a debit) and the value of Goodwill is decreased (a credit).

| | | | | |
|---|---|---|---|---|
| | Loss on Goodwill | | 7,500 | |
| | Goodwill | | | 7,500 |

## *DEMO DOC COMPLETE*

# Quick Practice Questions

## True/False

_____ 1. The cost of land includes fencing, paving, sprinkler systems, and lighting.

_____ 2. Land improvements are not subject to annual depreciation.

_____ 3. Book value is equal to the cost of the asset less the depreciation expense.

_____ 4. The modified accelerated cost recovery system of depreciation is used for income tax purposes and segments assets into classes by asset life.

_____ 5. A loss on sale of an asset occurs when the book value is more than the cash received.

_____ 6. The depreciable cost of a plant asset is the original cost less the expected residual value.

_____ 7. Depletion expense is computed in the same manner as units-of-production.

_____ 8. Goodwill is recorded only by a company when it purchases another company and is not subject to amortization.

_____ 9. A characteristic of a plant asset is that it is used in the production of income for a business.

_____ 10. Routine repairs and maintenance are capital expenditures.

_____ 11. Under IFRS, all research and development costs are expensed.

# Multiple Choice

1. Which of the following is *not* a plant asset?
   a. Land
   b. Building
   c. Equipment
   d. Goodwill

2. The cost of a building would include all of the following *except*:
   a. Architectural fees
   b. Clearing and grading the land prior to construction of the building
   c. Cost of repairs made to an old building to get it ready for occupancy
   d. Costs of construction

3. Five hundred acres of land are purchased for $130,000. Additional costs include $5,000 brokerage commission, $10,000 for removal of an old building, $6,000 for paving, and an $800 survey fee. What is the cost of the land?
   a. $135,800
   b. $145,800
   c. $151,000
   d. $151,800

4. Westchester Company recently sold some used furniture for $3,800 cash. The furniture cost $19,600 and had accumulated depreciation through the date of sale totaling $17,300. What is the journal entry to record the sale of the furniture?

a.

| Cash | 3,800 | |
| Accumulated Depreciation—Furniture | 15,800 | |
| Furniture | | 19,600 |

b.

| Cash | 3,800 | |
| Furniture | | 3,800 |

c.

| Cash | 3,800 | |
| Gain on Sale of Furniture | | 3,800 |

d.

| Cash | 3,800 | |
| Accumulated Depreciation—Furniture | 17,300 | |
| Furniture | | 19,600 |
| Gain on Sale of Furniture | | 1,500 |

5. New equipment with a list price of $97,000 and transportation cost of $7,000 is acquired by a company. Insurance while in transit amounts to $200. Insurance on the equipment during its first year of use amounts to $800. What is the amount debited to Equipment?
   a. $97,000
   b. $104,200
   c. $104,000
   d. $97,200

6. Which of the following expenditures would be debited to an expense account?
   a. Oil change on a company car
   b. Research and development costs
   c. Replacement of tires
   d. All of the above

7. What is the effect of treating a current period expense as a capital expenditure?
   a. Understates expenses and understates net income
   b. Overstates assets and overstates net income
   c. Overstates expenses and understates net income
   d. Understates expenses and understates assets

8. Which of the following is true of Accumulated Depreciation?
   a. It is a contra liability account.
   b. It is an expense account.
   c. It is a contra asset account.
   d. It is a contra equity account.

9. When the amount of use of a plant asset varies from year to year, which method of determining depreciation best matches revenues and expenses?
   a. Straight-line method
   b. Double-declining-balance method
   c. Units-of-production method
   d. Either the straight-line method or the double-declining-balance method

10. Which depreciation method generally results in the greatest depreciation expense in the first full year of an asset's life?
    a. Double-declining-balance method
    b. Units-of-production method
    c. Straight-line method
    d. Either the straight-line or the double-declining-balance method

## Quick Exercises

**7-1.** Morgan Construction bought land, a building, and equipment for a lump sum of $600,000. Following are the appraised fair market values of the newly acquired assets:

Land, $400,000
Building, $250,000
Equipment, $150,000

1. Determine the cost of each asset.

   **a.** Land _____

   **b.** Building _____

   **c.** Equipment _____

**7-2.** Sue Glover purchased a tract of land and contracted with a builder to build an office building on the property. She also engaged other contractors for lighting, fencing, paving, and so forth. Based on the following transactions, determine the total costs allocated to the Land, Building, and Land Improvements accounts.

   **a.** Purchased land for $135,000.
   **b.** Paid a contractor $333,000 to design and build the office building.
   **c.** Paid a demolition company $40,000 to remove an old structure on the property.
   **d.** Paid $14,000 in delinquent taxes on the property.
   **e.** Paid $34,700 for fencing.
   **f.** Paid $39,500 for paving.
   **g.** Paid an electrical contractor $14,900 for outdoor lighting.

   Cost of land _____

   Cost of building _____

   Cost of land improvements _____

**7-3.** Venus Company acquired equipment on January 1, 2011, for $470,000. The equipment has an estimated useful life of five years and an estimated residual value of $30,000. Calculate depreciation expense for 2011 and 2012 under each of the following methods. The equipment is estimated to produce 150,000 units. During 2011 and 2012, the equipment produced 24,000 and 60,000 units, respectively. Round the answer to the nearest dollar where necessary.

|  | | 2011 | 2012 |
|---|---|---|---|
| **a.** | Straight-line method | _____ | _____ |
| **b.** | Double-declining-balance method | _____ | _____ |
| **c.** | Units-of-production method | _____ | _____ |

7-4. On April 1, 2011, Carter Craft & Company purchased a mineral deposit by paying $50,000 in cash and signing a $440,000 promissory note. A geological report estimated the mineral deposit contained 140,000 tons of ore. Carter Craft & Company expects the asset to have a zero residual value when fully depleted. During 2011, 40,000 tons of ore were mined.

1. Prepare the journal entry for December 31, 2011, to record the depletion of the mineral deposit.

| Date | Accounts | Debit | Credit |
|------|----------|-------|--------|
|      |          |       |        |
|      |          |       |        |
|      |          |       |        |

7-5. On July 31, 2011, Austin Manufacturing acquired an existing patent for $340,000. The remaining legal life of the patent is 13 years; however, management thinks the patent will hold economic benefit for the company for only seven more years.

1. Prepare journal entries for July 31, 2011, to acquire the patent and December 31, 2011, to amortize the patent.

| Date | Accounts | Debit | Credit |
|------|----------|-------|--------|
|      |          |       |        |
|      |          |       |        |
|      |          |       |        |

| Date | Accounts | Debit | Credit |
|------|----------|-------|--------|
|      |          |       |        |
|      |          |       |        |
|      |          |       |        |

# Do It Yourself! Question 1

## Depreciation

Winters Co. purchased equipment for $8,000 cash on January 1, 2010. The equipment had a residual value of $500 and a useful life of six years or 2,000 hours of operation. Winters has a December 31 year-end.

The equipment was used for 400 hours in 2010, 200 hours in 2011, and 300 hours in 2012.

### Requirements

1. Calculate the depreciation expense and accumulated depreciation balance at December 31 for 2010, 2011, and 2012 using the straight-line method.

| Year | Depreciation Expense | Accumulated Depreciation | Book Value (Cost – Accumulated Depreciation) |
|---|---|---|---|
| 2010 ............... | | | |
| 2011 ............... | | | |
| 2012 ............... | | | |

2. Calculate the depreciation expense and accumulated depreciation balance at December 31 for 2010, 2011, and 2012 using the units-of-production method.

| Year | Depreciation Expense | Accumulated Depreciation | Book Value (Cost – Accumulated Depreciation) |
|---|---|---|---|
| 2010 ............... | | | |
| 2011 ............... | | | |
| 2012 ............... | | | |

3. Calculate the depreciation expense and accumulated depreciation balance at December 31 for 2010, 2011, and 2012 using the double-declining-balance method.

| Year | Depreciation Expense | Accumulated Depreciation | Book Value (Cost – Accumulated Depreciation) |
|---|---|---|---|
| 2010 ............... | | | |
| 2011 ............... | | | |
| 2012 ............... | | | |

4. Using the units-of-production method only, show how the equipment would look on the December 31 balance sheets for 2010, 2011, and 2012.

| | 2010 | 2011 | 2012 |
|---|---|---|---|
| | | | |
| | | | |
| | | | |

5. Winters sold the machine on March 1, 2013, for $4,000 cash. Journalize the depreciation and the sale transaction using each method. (The equipment was used for 100 hours in 2013.)

### Straight-Line Method

| Date | Accounts | Debit | Credit |
|---|---|---|---|
| | | | |
| | | | |

| Date | Accounts | Debit | Credit |
|---|---|---|---|
| | | | |
| | | | |
| | | | |

### Units-of-Production Method

| Date | Accounts | Debit | Credit |
|---|---|---|---|
| | | | |
| | | | |

| Date | Accounts | Debit | Credit |
|---|---|---|---|
| | | | |
| | | | |
| | | | |

### Double-Declining-Balance Method

| Date | Accounts | Debit | Credit |
|---|---|---|---|
| | | | |
| | | | |

| Date | Accounts | Debit | Credit |
|---|---|---|---|
| | | | |
| | | | |
| | | | |

# Do It Yourself! Question 2

## Natural Resource Assets

Woody, Inc., purchased logging rights in a county forest for $800,000 cash. Woody estimates that there are 40,000 tons of lumber that can be harvested from the forest. Because Woody only purchased the right to log, it does not own the land.

### Requirement

1. Journalize Woody's depletion expense for the first year, assuming that 15,000 tons of lumber were cut and sold.

| Date | Accounts | Debit | Credit |
|------|----------|-------|--------|
|      |          |       |        |
|      |          |       |        |

# Do It Yourself! Question 3

## Intangible Assets

On October 1, 2011, Kevin, Inc., acquired a trademark from Daniel Co. for $10,000 cash. Kevin believes that the trademark will have a life of 20 years.

### Requirements

1. Journalize Kevin's purchase of the trademark.

| Date | Accounts | Debit | Credit |
|------|----------|-------|--------|
|      |          |       |        |
|      |          |       |        |

2. Journalize Kevin's amortization expense for the trademark in 2011.

| Date | Accounts | Debit | Credit |
|------|----------|-------|--------|
|      |          |       |        |
|      |          |       |        |

# Quick Practice Solutions

## True/False

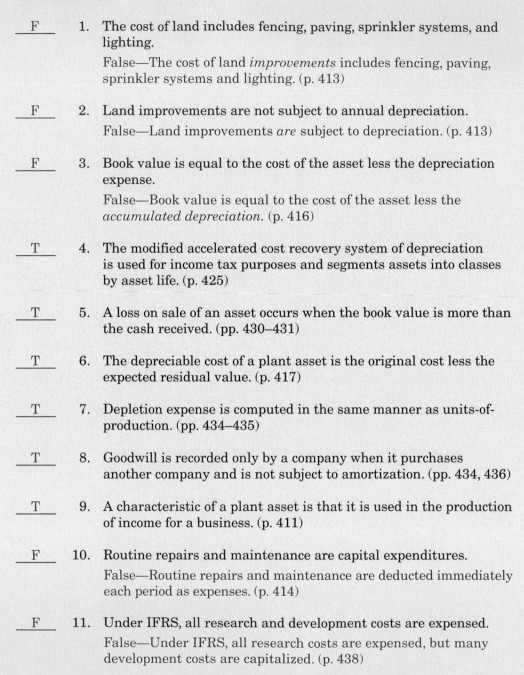

F    1. The cost of land includes fencing, paving, sprinkler systems, and lighting.

False—The cost of land *improvements* includes fencing, paving, sprinkler systems and lighting. (p. 413)

F    2. Land improvements are not subject to annual depreciation.

False—Land improvements *are* subject to depreciation. (p. 413)

F    3. Book value is equal to the cost of the asset less the depreciation expense.

False—Book value is equal to the cost of the asset less the *accumulated depreciation.* (p. 416)

T    4. The modified accelerated cost recovery system of depreciation is used for income tax purposes and segments assets into classes by asset life. (p. 425)

T    5. A loss on sale of an asset occurs when the book value is more than the cash received. (pp. 430–431)

T    6. The depreciable cost of a plant asset is the original cost less the expected residual value. (p. 417)

T    7. Depletion expense is computed in the same manner as units-of-production. (pp. 434–435)

T    8. Goodwill is recorded only by a company when it purchases another company and is not subject to amortization. (pp. 434, 436)

T    9. A characteristic of a plant asset is that it is used in the production of income for a business. (p. 411)

F    10. Routine repairs and maintenance are capital expenditures.

False—Routine repairs and maintenance are deducted immediately each period as expenses. (p. 414)

F    11. Under IFRS, all research and development costs are expensed.

False—Under IFRS, all research costs are expensed, but many development costs are capitalized. (p. 438)

# Multiple Choice

1.  **Which of the following is *not* a plant asset? (pp. 410–411)**
    a. Land
    b. Building
    c. Equipment
    d. Goodwill

2.  **The cost of a building would include all of the following *except*: (p. 412)**
    a. Architectural fees
    b. Clearing and grading the land prior to construction of the building
    c. Cost of repairs made to an old building to get it ready for occupancy
    d. Costs of construction

3.  **Five hundred acres of land are purchased for $130,000. Additional costs include $5,000 brokerage commission, $10,000 for removal of an old building, $6,000 for paving, and an $800 survey fee. What is the cost of the land? (pp. 411–412)**
    a. $135,800
    b. $145,800 (130,000 + 5,000 + 10,000 + 800)
    c. $151,000
    d. $151,800

4.  **Westchester Company recently sold some used furniture for $3,800 cash. The furniture cost $19,600 and had accumulated depreciation through the date of sale totaling $17,300. What is the journal entry to record the sale of the furniture? (pp. 430–431)**

    a.
    | | | |
    |---|---|---|
    | Cash | 3,800 | |
    | Accumulated Depreciation—Furniture | 15,800 | |
    | Furniture | | 19,600 |

    b.
    | | | |
    |---|---|---|
    | Cash | 3,800 | |
    | Furniture | | 3,800 |

    c.
    | | | |
    |---|---|---|
    | Cash | 3,800 | |
    | Gain on Sale of Furniture | | 3,800 |

    d.
    | | | |
    |---|---|---|
    | Cash | 3,800 | |
    | Accumulated Depreciation—Furniture | 17,300 | |
    | Furniture | | 19,600 |
    | Gain on Sale of Furniture | | 1,500 |

5. New equipment with a list price of $97,000, and transportation cost of $7,000 is acquired by a company. Insurance while in transit amounts to $200. Insurance on the equipment during its first year of use amounts to $800. What is the amount debited to Equipment? (pp. 412–413)
   a. $97,000
   b. $104,200 (97,000 + 7,000 + 200)
   c. $104,000
   d. $97,200

6. Which of the following expenditures would be debited to an expense account? (pp. 414, 437)
   a. Oil change on a company car
   b. Research and development costs
   c. Replacement of tires
   d. All of the above

7. What is the effect of treating a current period expense as a capital expenditure? (p. 415)
   a. Understates expenses and understates net income
   b. Overstates assets and overstates net income
   c. Overstates expenses and understates net income
   d. Understates expenses and understates assets

8. Which of the following is true of Accumulated Depreciation? (pp. 416–417)
   a. It is a contra liability account.
   b. It is an expense account.
   c. It is a contra asset account.
   d. It is a contra equity account.

9. When the amount of use of a plant asset varies from year to year, which method of determining depreciation best matches revenues and expenses? (p. 419)
   a. Straight-line method
   b. Double-declining-balance method
   c. Units-of-production method
   d. Either the straight-line method or the double-declining-balance method

10. Which depreciation method generally results in the greatest depreciation expense in the first full year of an asset's life? (pp. 420–421)
    a. Double-declining-balance method
    b. Units-of-production method
    c. Straight-line method
    d. Either the straight-line or the double-declining-balance method

# Quick Exercises

**7-1. Morgan Construction bought land, a building, and equipment for a lump sum of $600,000. Following are the appraised fair market values of the newly acquired assets:**

Land, $400,000

Building, $250,000

Equipment, $150,000

**1. Determine the cost of each asset.** (p. 413)

> a.  Land = ($400,000/$800,000) × $600,000 = $300,000
> b.  Building = ($250,000/$800,000) × $600,000 = $187,500
> c.  Equipment = ($150,000/$800,000) × $600,000 = $112,500

**7-2. Sue Glover purchased a tract of land and contracted with a builder to build an office building on the property. She also engaged other contractors for lighting, fencing, paving, and so forth. Based on the following transactions, determine the total costs allocated to the Land, Building, and Land Improvements accounts.** (pp. 411–413)

**a.** Purchased land for $135,000.
**b.** Paid a contractor $333,000 to design and build the office building.
**c.** Paid a demolition company $40,000 to remove an old structure on the property.
**d.** Paid $14,000 in delinquent taxes on the property.
**e.** Paid $34,700 for fencing.
**f.** Paid $39,500 for paving.
**g.** Paid an electrical contractor $14,900 for outdoor lighting.

| | |
|---|---|
| Cost of land | $189,000 ($135,000 + $40,000 + $14,000 = $189,000; transactions a, c, and d) |
| Cost of building | $333,000 (transaction b) |
| Cost of land improvements | $89,100 ($34,700 + $39,500 + $14,900 = $89,100; transactions e–g) |

**7-3.** Venus Company acquired equipment on January 1, 2011, for $470,000. The equipment has an estimated useful life of five years and an estimated residual value of $30,000. Calculate depreciation expense for 2011 and 2012 under each of the following methods. The equipment is estimated to produce 150,000 units. During 2011 and 2012, the equipment produced 24,000 and 60,000 units, respectively. Round the answer to the nearest dollar where necessary. (pp. 418–421)

|  |  | 2011 | 2012 |
|---|---|---|---|
| a. | Straight-line method | $ 88,000 | $ 88,000 |
| b. | Double-declining-balance method | $188,000 | $112,800 |
| c. | Units-of-production method | $ 70,400 | $176,000 |

$$a. \quad \frac{\$470,000 - \$30,000}{5 \text{ years}} = \$88,000/\text{year}$$

$$b. \quad \text{DDB rate} = 1/5 \text{ years} \times 2 = 40\% \ (0.40)$$
$$\$470,000 \times 0.40 = \$188,000$$
$$(\$470,000 - \$188,000) \times 0.40 = \$112,800$$

$$c. \quad \frac{\$470,000 - \$30,000}{150,000} = \$2.93/\text{unit}; \ \$2.93 \times 24,000 \text{ units} = \$70,320$$

$$\$2.93/\text{unit} \times 60,000 \text{ units} = \$175,800$$

**7-4.** On April 1, 2011, Carter Craft & Company purchased a mineral deposit by paying $50,000 in cash and signing a $440,000 promissory note. A geological report estimated the mineral deposit contained 140,000 tons of ore. Carter Craft & Company expects the asset to have a zero residual value when fully depleted. During 2011, 40,000 tons of ore were mined.

1. Prepare the journal entry for December 31, 2011, to record the depletion of the mineral deposit. (p. 434)

| Date | Accounts | Debit | Credit |
|---|---|---|---|
| 12/31/11 | Depletion Expense | 140,000 | |
| | Accumulated Depletion—Ore | | 140,000 |
| | *To record depletion of mineral deposits.* | | |
| | ($50,000 + $440,000)/140,000 tons = $3.50/ton × 40,000 tons = $140,000 | | |

**7-5.** On July 31, 2011, Austin Manufacturing acquired an existing patent for $340,000. The remaining legal life of the patent is 13 years; however, management thinks the patent will hold economic benefit for the company for only seven more years.

1. Prepare journal entries for July 31, 2011, to acquire the patent and December 31, 2011, to amortize the patent. (p. 435)

| Date | Accounts | Debit | Credit |
|------|----------|-------|--------|
| 7/31/11 | Patents | 340,000 | |
| | Cash | | 340,000 |
| | *To record purchase of patent.* | | |

| Date | Accounts | Debit | Credit |
|------|----------|-------|--------|
| 12/31/11 | Amortization Expense—Patents | 20,238 | |
| | Patents | | 20,238 |
| | *To amortize patents ($340,000 × 5/84 months = $20,238)* | | |

# Do It Yourself! Question 1 Solutions

## Requirements

1. Calculate the depreciation expense and accumulated depreciation balance at December 31 for 2010, 2011, and 2012 using the straight-line method.

$$\frac{\$8,000 - \$500}{6 \text{ years}} = \$1,250 \text{ depreciation expense per year}$$

2010 accumulated depreciation = $1,250

2011 accumulated depreciation = $2,500

2012 accumulated depreciation = $3,750

| Year | Depreciation Expense | Accumulated Depreciation | Book Value (Cost – Accumulated Depreciation) |
|------|---------------------|-------------------------|----------------------------------------------|
| 2010 ............... | $1,250 | $1,250 | $6,750 |
| 2011 ............... | 1,250 | 2,500 | 5,500 |
| 2012 ............... | 1,250 | 3,750 | 4,250 |

2. Calculate the depreciation expense and accumulated depreciation balance at December 31 for 2010, 2011, and 2012 using the units-of-production method.

$$\frac{\$8,000 - \$500}{2,000 \text{ hours of operation}} = \$3.75 \text{ depreciation expense per hour of actual operation}$$

Depreciation expense each year is

| | Actual | | Rate | | Expense |
|------|-----------|---|----------------|---|---------|
| 2010 ............... | 400 hours | × | $3.75 per mile | = | $1,500 |
| 2011 ............... | 200 hours | × | $3.75 per mile | = | $ 750 |
| 2012 ............... | 300 hours | × | $3.75 per mile | = | $1,125 |

Accumulated depreciation each year is

| | Accumulated Depreciation | | | | |
|------|--------|---|--------|---|--------|
| 2010 ............... | $0 | + | $1,500 | = | $1,500 |
| 2011 ............... | $1,500 | + | $ 750 | = | $2,250 |
| 2012 ............... | $2,250 | + | $1,125 | = | $3,375 |

| Year | Depreciation Expense | Accumulated Depreciation | Book Value (Cost – Accumulated Depreciation) |
|------|---------------------|--------------------------|----------------------------------------------|
| 2010 ............... | $1,500 | $1,500 | $6,500 |
| 2011 ............... | 750 | 2,250 | 5,750 |
| 2012 ............... | 1,125 | 3,375 | 4,625 |

3. **Calculate the depreciation expense and accumulated depreciation balance at December 31 for 2010, 2011, and 2012 using the double-declining-balance method.**

DDB Rate = 2/6 = 1/3
2010 depreciation expense = ($8,000 − $0) × 1/3 = $2,667
Accumulated depreciation = $0 + $2,667 = $2,667
2011 depreciation expense = ($8,000 − $2,667) × 1/3 = $1,778
Accumulated depreciation = $2,667 + $1,778 = $4,445
2012 depreciation expense = ($8,000 − $4,445) × 1/3 = $1,185
Accumulated depreciation = $4,445 + $1,185 = $5,630

| Year | Depreciation Expense | Accumulated Depreciation | Book Value (Cost – Accumulated Depreciation) |
|------|---------------------|--------------------------|----------------------------------------------|
| 2010 ............... | $2,667 | $2,667 | $5,333 |
| 2011 ............... | 1,778 | 4,445 | 3,555 |
| 2012 ............... | 1,185 | 5,630 | 2,370 |

4. **Using the units-of-production method only, show how the equipment would look on the December 31 balance sheets for 2010, 2011, and 2012.**

| | 2010 | 2011 | 2012 |
|------|------|------|------|
| Equipment......................................... | $ 8,000 | $ 8,000 | $ 8,000 |
| − Accumulated Depreciation ............... | (1,500) | (2,250) | (3,375) |
| Equipment (net) ............................... | $ 6,500 | $ 5,750 | $ 4,625 |

5. **Winters sold the machine on March 1, 2013, for $4,000 cash. Journalize the depreciation and the sale transaction using each method. (The equipment was used for 100 hours in 2013.)**

### Straight-Line Method

$$2013 \text{ depreciation expense} = \$1,250 \times \frac{2 \text{ months}}{12 \text{ months}} = \$208$$

| | | | |
|---|---|---|---|
| Mar 1 | Depreciation Expense | 208 | |
| | Accumulated Depreciation—Equipment | | 208 |

Total accumulated depreciation = $3,750 + $208 = $3,958.

| | | | |
|---|---|---|---|
| Mar 1 | Cash | 4,000 | |
| | Accumulated Depreciation—Equipment | 3,958 | |
| | Loss on Sale of Equipment (to balance) | 42 | |
| | Equipment | | 8,000 |

### Units-of-Production Method

$$2013 \text{ depreciation expense} = 100 \text{ hours} \times \$3.75 = \$375$$

| | | | |
|---|---|---|---|
| Mar 1 | Depreciation Expense | 375 | |
| | Accumulated Depreciation—Equipment | | 375 |

Total accumulated depreciation = $3,375 + $375 = $3,750.

| | | | |
|---|---|---|---|
| Mar 1 | Cash | 4,000 | |
| | Accumulated Depreciation—Equipment | 3,750 | |
| | Loss on Sale of Equipment (to balance) | 250 | |
| | Equipment | | 8,000 |

## Double-Declining-Balance Method

2013 depreciation expense = ($8,000 − $5,630) × 1/3 = $790 for 12 months

$$\$790 \times \frac{2 \text{ months}}{12 \text{ months}} = \$132 \text{ for 2 months}$$

| | | | | |
|---|---|---|---|---|
| Mar 1 | Depreciation Expense | | 132 | |
| | Accumulated Depreciation—Equipment | | | 132 |

Total accumulated depreciation = $5,630 + $132 = $5,762.

| | | | | |
|---|---|---|---|---|
| Mar 1 | Cash | | 4,000 | |
| | Accumulated Depreciation—Equipment | | 5,762 | |
| | Gain on Sale of Equipment (to balance) | | | 1,762 |
| | Equipment | | | 8,000 |

# Do it Yourself! Question 2 Solutions

1. Journalize Woody's depletion expense for the first year, assuming that 15,000 tons of lumber were cut and sold.

$$\text{Depletion per ton} = \frac{\$800,000}{40,000 \text{ tons}} = \$20 \text{ per ton}$$

$$15,000 \text{ tons} \times \$20 \text{ per ton} = \$300,000$$

| | | |
|---|---|---|
| Depletion Expense | 300,000 | |
| Accumulated Depletion—Lumber | | 300,000 |

# Do It Yourself! Question 3 Solutions

1. **Journalize Kevin's purchase of the trademark.**

| | | | | |
|---|---|---|---|---|
| Jan 1 | Trademark | | 10,000 | |
| | Cash | | | 10,000 |

2. **Journalize Kevin's amortization expense for the trademark in 2011.**

$$\text{Amortization expense} = \frac{\$10,000}{20 \text{ years}} = \$500 \text{ per year}$$

$$\$500 = \frac{3 \text{ months}}{12 \text{ months}} = \$125 \text{ for 3 months}$$

| | | | | |
|---|---|---|---|---|
| Dec 31 | Amortization Expense—Trademarks | | 125 | |
| | Trademark | | | 125 |

# The Power of Practice

For more practice using the skills learned in this chapter, visit MyAccountingLab. There you will find algorithmically generated questions that are based on these Demo Docs and your main textbook's Review and Assess Your Progress sections.

Go to MyAccountingLab and follow these steps:

1. Direct your URL to www.myaccountinglab.com.
2. Log in using your name and password.
3. Click the MyAccountingLab link.
4. Click Study Plan in the left navigation bar.
5. From the table of contents, select Chapter 7, Plant Assets & Intangibles.
6. Click a link to work tutorial exercises.

# 8 Liabilities

## WHAT YOU PROBABLY ALREADY KNOW

You may already be familiar with debt, such as debt incurred on a credit card balance, or student loans. Suppose you obtain a student loan with a fixed monthly payment, starting after graduation. As you pay off the loan in subsequent years, interest rates may increase or decrease, but they don't affect your fixed monthly payment. If the interest rates decrease significantly, you may choose to refinance your student loan to save on future interest costs. Refinancing means that your old loans are paid off by a new loan. The characteristics of a bond are similar to those of a loan. The issuer of a bond has incurred a long-term liability and is committed to pay interest at the fixed interest rate included in the bond agreement. Sometimes issuers will refinance their debt if the interest rate decreases by issuing new bonds at the lower interest rate and paying off the higher-rate bonds. In this chapter, we will learn about current and long-term liabilities and how to account for them.

## Learning Objectives

**Account for current liabilities and contingent liabilities**

Some current liabilities that are recorded at known amounts include accounts payable, short-term notes payable, sales tax payable, current portion of long-term notes payable, accrued expenses or liabilities, and unearned or deferred revenues. *Review the "Current Liabilities of Known Amount" section of the text, and be sure to take note of the presentation of current liabilities in the balance sheet as shown at the beginning of the chapter (p. 468).*

Sometimes a liability has been incurred but the amount is uncertain. Examples of this may include estimated warranty payable or estimated income taxes payable. A contingent liability is a potential liability that is sometimes listed in the footnotes or even on the balance sheet.

**Account for bonds payable**

A **bond** is a long-term liability that may be issued by corporations; local, state, or federal governments; and agencies. The **principal amount,** the amount on the bond certificate, is the amount that is to be paid to the investor on the maturity date. It is also the amount that is recorded in the Bond Payable account. Over the life of the bond, interest will be paid at the **stated rate,** the fixed interest rate for the bond.

### ③ Measure interest expense

A discount occurs when the bond is sold for less than the principal amount. When the stated rate of interest is less than the market rate of interest, a bond is sold at a discount. A premium occurs when the bond is sold for more than the principal amount. When the stated rate of interest is higher than the market rate of interest, a bond is sold at a premium. A Discount on Bonds Payable and a Premium on Bonds Payable need to be amortized into Interest Expense over the life of the bond. Amortization reduces the account balance and affects the amount of interest expense. A discount is a debit balance; a premium is a credit balance. To reduce a debit balance, a credit entry must be made and then Interest Expense is debited. To reduce a credit balance, a debit entry must be made and then Interest Expense is credited. *Review "The Straight-Line Amortization Method" and " Interest Expense on Bonds Issued at a Discount" in the text for illustrations on the calculation and accounting for amortization by both the straight-line and the effective-interest methods.*

### ④ Understand the advantages and disadvantages of borrowing

Borrowing may result in earning more money than the cost of the interest expense incurred. This concept of **leverage** is favorable because it serves to increase earnings per share. Borrowing has the disadvantage of creating a liability for the repayment of debt. Future interest payments will also be required. This increases the company's risk. *Review Exhibit 8-10 (p. 493) for an illustration of the earnings-per-share advantage of borrowing versus issuing stock.*

### ⑤ Report liabilities on the balance sheet

Similar to the handling of Notes Payable, the portion of the Bond Payable that is due within a year is classified as a current liability. Amounts due beyond one year are listed as long-term liabilities. *Review the illustration under "Reporting on the Balance Sheet" in the text. Review the presentation of both current and long-term liabilities in the balance sheet and footnotes as shown in Exhibit 8-11 (p. 499).*

# Demo Doc 1

## General Current Liabilities

*Learning Objective 1*

Freddie Enterprises sells products with warranties included in the selling price. During August 2009, Freddie sold goods for $250,000 cash. These goods cost $180,000 to manufacture. Freddie is required by law to collect 7% sales tax on all sales.

Freddie estimates warranty costs to be 1.5% of the selling price. During August 2009, Freddie made $3,000 of repairs under warranty (paid in cash to a repair service).

On August 31, 2009, Freddie remitted all sales tax collected in August to the state government.

### Requirements

1. Journalize all of Freddie's transactions in the month of August 2009.

2. Is sales tax payable a contingent liability? Why or why not?

3. Is estimated warranty payable a contingent liability? Why or why not?

# Demo Doc 1 Solutions

## Requirement 1

① Account for current liabilities and contingent liabilities

**Journalize all of Freddie's transactions in the month of August 2009.**

**During August 2009, Freddie sold goods for $250,000 cash. These goods cost $180,000 to manufacture. Freddie is required by law to collect 7% sales tax on all sales.**

Freddie sold $250,000 worth of products. This means that Sales Revenue increases (a credit) by $250,000.

However, the cash that Freddie collected was *more* than $250,000 because it included the sales tax.

Freddie collected $250,000 × (1 + 7%) = $267,500 cash from the customer.

The $250,000 × 7% = $17,500 that Freddie collected in sales tax is *not* revenue because it was *not earned* by Freddie and *does not belong* to Freddie. These taxes belong to the government and are owed/payable by Freddie to the government. Therefore, we must increase (a credit) the Sales Taxes Payable account by $17,500.

| | | |
|---|---|---|
| Cash ($250,000 × [1 + 7%]) | 267,500 | |
| Sales Revenue | | 250,000 |
| Sales Taxes Payable ($250,000 × 7%) | | 17,500 |

Freddie has sold these goods and so an adjustment to Inventory is necessary as well. COGS increases (a debit) and Inventory decreases (a credit) by $180,000, Freddie's cost of the products.

| | | |
|---|---|---|
| COGS | 180,000 | |
| Inventory | | 180,000 |

**Freddie estimates warranty costs to be 1.5% of the selling price.**

We must also account for the warranties included in the selling price of the goods. Once the products are sold, the warranty is in effect. This means that Freddie has an *obligation* (that is, a *liability*) to fix the products if they break down. We must record an Estimated Warranty Payable liability (a credit) of:

$$1.5\% \times \$250,000 = \$3,750$$

As the liability is recorded, so is the estimated Warranty Expense (a debit) of $3,750. There will be additional expense/cost to Freddie to make the repairs. This is good matching (as required by the matching principle under GAAP) because the expense is recorded *at the same time as the sales revenue,* not *when the actual cost is incurred (or warranty claim is made).*

| | | |
|---|---|---|
| Warranty Expense ($250,000 × 1.5%) | 3,750 | |
| Estimated Warranty Payable | | 3,750 |

**During August 2009, Freddie made $3,000 of repairs under warranty (paid in cash to a repair service).**

When Freddie Enterprises makes warranty repairs, it is *meeting its warranty obligation* (that is, it is reducing its warranty liability). This causes a decrease (a debit) to Estimated Warranty Payable of $3,000.

Because the repairs were paid for in cash, the Cash account also decreases (a credit) by $3,000.

Notice that the Warranty Expense account is *not* impacted by the repairs! The expense was *already recorded* at the time of sale. To debit it again now would be double-counting the expense.

| | | |
|---|---|---|
| Estimated Warranty Payable | 3,000 | |
| Cash | | 3,000 |

Note that there is $3,750 − $3,000 = $750 left in the Estimated Warranty Payable account. This remains to cover any future repairs that might be made under the warranty.

**On August 31, 2009, Freddie remitted all sales tax collected in August to the state government.**

The first transaction stated that during August, Freddie sold goods for $250,000 cash and collected 7% sales tax on all sales. At that time, Cash was increased by $267,500, Sales Revenue was increased by $250,000, and Sales Taxes Payable was increased by $250,000 × 7% = $17,500.

On August 31, Freddie remitted the sales taxes to the government. This means that the sales tax liability was paid in cash.

Cash is decreased (a credit) by $17,500 and Sales Taxes Payable is decreased (a debit) by $17,500.

| | | |
|---|---|---|
| Sales Taxes Payable | 17,500 | |
| Cash | | 17,500 |

## Requirement 2

**Is sales tax payable a contingent liability? Why or why not?**

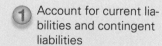
1 Account for current liabilities and contingent liabilities

Sales taxes *must* be collected and remitted to the government *by law*. Ethical companies have no choice but to meet the sales taxes payable obligation. Therefore, this amount *will* be paid and it is *not* a contingent liability, as it is *not* dependent upon any outside event. As described in the text, it is a current liability of known amount.

①  Account for current lia-
    bilities and contingent
    liabilities

**Is estimated warranty payable a contingent liability? Why or why not?**

Warranty payable is an *estimate*. It is not known *for sure* whether or not the products will break down or how much it might cost to repair them if they do. For this
reason, warranty payable is a contingent liability because it depends upon the
performance of the products after they leave Freddie's control.

Because payment for warranty repairs is probable and estimable, warranty
expense and estimated warranty payable are recorded in a journal entry, even
though they are contingent upon outside events.

*DEMO DOC COMPLETE*

# Demo Doc 2

## Bonds Payable (straight-line amortization)

*Learning Objectives 2, 3, 5*

Blue Co. issued $50,000 maturity value of bonds payable for $51,788 cash on January 1, 2009. The bonds had a stated rate of 12%, but the market rate was 10%. Interest is paid semiannually on June 30 and December 31 and the bonds are due in two years.

Blue uses the straight-line method of amortization.

### Requirements

1. Are these bonds issued at a discount or premium? How do you know?

2. Journalize Blue's issuance of the bonds on January 1, 2009.

3. Journalize Blue's first two interest payments on June 30, 2009, and December 31, 2009.

4. Show how the bonds would appear on Blue's December 31, 2009, balance sheet.

5. On January 2, 2010, 30% of the bonds were converted to 10,000 common shares with $1 par per share. Journalize this transaction.

6. On January 3, 2010, Blue purchased the remaining bonds from the marketplace for $36,000 cash. The bonds were immediately retired. Journalize this transaction.

# Demo Doc 2 Solutions

## Requirement 1

② Account for bonds payable

**Are these bonds issued at a discount or premium? How do you know?**

These bonds were issued at a **premium**. We know this because the cash received for the bonds is *more* than the maturity value and because the stated rate is *greater* than the market rate.

> 12% stated rate > 10% market rate

## Requirement 2

② Account for bonds payable

**Journalize Blue's issuance of the bonds on January 1, 2009.**

Cash is increased (a debit) by $51,788.

Bonds Payable is increased (a credit) by the bonds' *maturity* value of $50,000.

The difference between these two amounts is balanced to Premium on Bonds Payable. The amount of the premium is the difference between the cash received and the par or maturity value of the bond. In other words, it is a balancing credit of:

> $51,788 − $50,000 = $1,788

| | | |
|---|---|---|
| Cash | 51,788 | |
| Premium on Bonds Payable (to balance) | | 1,788 |
| Bonds Payable | | 50,000 |

## Requirement 3

② Account for bonds payable

③ Measure interest expense

**Journalize Blue's first two interest payments on June 30, 2009, and December 31, 2009.**

Under straight-line amortization, the premium will be amortized the *same amount* every interest period.

$$\text{Premium amortization each interest period} = \frac{\text{Premium}}{\text{Number of interest periods}}$$

The bonds are due in two years and have two interest payments per year. This results in $2 \times 2 = 4$ interest payment periods.

$$\text{Premium amortization each interest period} = \frac{\$1,788}{4}$$
$$= \$447$$

This means that *every* time interest expense is recorded, the premium will be amortized (that is, *decreased/debited*) by $447.

Cash will be decreased by the cash interest paid.

Cash interest paid = Maturity value × Stated rate × Frequency of interest payments (months/12)

Or, more simply,

$$\text{Cash interest paid} = \frac{\text{Maturity value} \times \text{Stated rate}}{\text{Number of interest payments per year}}$$

The question states that the bonds are semiannual; that is, they pay interest twice per year.

$$\text{Cash interest paid} = \frac{\$50{,}000 \times 12\%}{2}$$
$$= \$3{,}000$$

Interest Expense is increased (a debit) by the balancing amount of:

$$\$3{,}000 - \$447 = \$2{,}553$$

Because the cash interest paid and the premium amortization *do not change* from period to period, the entry to record the interest expense and payment is *always* the same. Notice that amortizing the premium reduces the interest cost (expense) for the corporation. So the entry for June 30, 2009, *and* December 31, 2009, is:

| | | | |
|---|---|---|---|
| | Interest Expense (to balance) | 2,553 | |
| | Premium on Bonds Payable ($1,788/4) | 447 | |
| | Cash ($50,000 × 12%/2) | | 3,000 |

## Requirement 4

**Show how the bonds would appear on Blue's December 31, 2009, balance sheet.**

⑤ Report liabilities on the balance sheet

The bonds are reported in the liabilities section of the balance sheet. The premium is added to the bonds payable to create a net value.

| | |
|---|---|
| Bonds payable.................................... | $50,000 |
| Plus Premium..................................... | 894* |
| Bonds payable (net)............................ | $50,894 |

*$1,788 − $447 (June amortization) − $447 (December amortization)

## Requirement 5

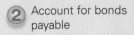
Account for bonds
payable

**On January 2, 2010, 30% of the bonds were converted to 10,000 common shares with $1 par per share. Journalize this transaction.**

Immediately before this transaction, the premium had a balance of $894:

| Premium on Bonds Payable | | | |
|---|---|---|---|
| | | Bal | 0 |
| | | Jan 1 | 1,788 |
| Jun 30 | 447 | | |
| Dec 31 | 447 | | |
| | | Bal | 894 |

If 30% of the bonds are converted, then 30% of the maturity value is converted:

$$30\% \times \$50,000 = \$15,000$$

Also 30% of the premium is converted:

$$30\% \times \$894 = \$268 \text{ (rounded)}$$

These bonds *will not exist* after the conversion, so the Bonds Payable account is decreased (a debit) by $15,000. The Premium is also decreased (a debit) by $268. New common stock is issued for the conversion, so Common Stock is increased (a credit) by the par value of the new shares:

$$10,000 \times \$1 = \$10,000$$

The remainder is balanced to Paid-In Capital in Excess of Par. This balancing amount is:

$$\$15,000 + \$268 - \$10,000 = \$5,268$$

| | | | |
|---|---|---|---|
| Bonds Payable ($50,000 × 30%) | | 15,000 | |
| Premium on Bonds Payable ($894 × 30%) | | 268 | |
| Paid-In Capital in Excess of Par (to balance) | | | 5,268 |
| Common Stock ($10,000 × $1) | | | 10,000 |

| Premium on Bonds Payable | | | | Bonds Payable | | |
|---|---|---|---|---|---|---|
| | Bal | 0 | | | Bal | 0 |
| | Jan 1 | 1,788 | | | Jan 1 | 50,000 |
| Jun 30 | 447 | | | Jan 2 | 15,000 | |
| Dec 31 | 447 | | | | Bal | 35,000 |
| Jan 2 | 268 | | | | | |
| | Bal | 626 | | | | |

## Requirement 6

**On January 3, 2010, Blue purchased the remaining bonds from the marketplace for $36,000 cash. The bonds were immediately retired. Journalize this transaction.**

② Account for bonds payable

Because 30% of the bonds were converted to common stock, 100% − 30% = 70% remained. These bonds will be retired.

If 70% of the bonds are retired, then 70% of the maturity value is retired:

$$70\% \times \$50,000 = \$35,000$$

Also 70% of the premium is retired:

$$70\% \times \$894 = \$626$$

The bonds *will not exist* after retirement, so the Bonds Payable account is decreased (a debit) by $35,000. The Premium is also decreased (a debit) by $626.
Cash is decreased (a credit) by $36,000.
The remainder is balanced to a gain or loss. In this case, the balancing amount is a debit, so there is a *loss* of:

$$\$36,000 - \$626 - \$35,000 = \$374$$

| | | | |
|---|---|---|---|
| Bonds Payable ($50,000 × 70%) | 35,000 | |
| Premium on Bonds Payable (70% × $894) | 626 | |
| Loss on Retirement (to balance) | 374 | |
| Cash | | 36,000 |

*DEMO DOC COMPLETE*

# Demo Doc 3

## Bonds Payable (effective-interest amortization)

*Learning Objectives 2, 3, 4*

Red Co. issued $2,000 maturity (face) value of bonds payable for $1,930 cash on January 1, 2009. The bonds had a stated rate of 8%, but the market rate was 10%. Interest is paid semiannually and the bonds are due in two years.
Red uses the effective-interest method of amortization.

### Requirements

1. Are these bonds issued at a discount or premium? How do you know?

2. Journalize Red's issuance of the bonds on January 1, 2009.

3. Prepare Red's effective-interest amortization table for the entire life of the bonds payable.

4. Journalize Red's first two interest payments on June 30, 2009, and December 31, 2009.

5. On January 2, 2010, 20% of the bonds were converted to 120 common shares with a $2 par value per share. Journalize this transaction.

6. On January 3, 2010, Red purchased the remaining bonds from the marketplace for $1,800 cash. The bonds were immediately retired. Journalize this transaction.

7. How do interest payments on bonds differ from dividend payments on stock?

# Demo Doc 3 Solutions

## Requirement 1

**Are these bonds issued at a discount or premium? How do you know?**

② Account for bonds payable

These bonds were issued at a **discount**. We know this because the cash received for the bonds is *less* than the maturity value and because the stated rate is *less* than the market rate.

> 8% stated rate < 10% market rate

## Requirement 2

**Journalize Red's issuance of the bonds on January 1, 2009.**

② Account for bonds payable

Cash is increased (a debit) by $1,930.

Bonds Payable is increased (a credit) by the bonds' *maturity* or face value of $2,000.

The difference between these two amounts is balanced to the Discount on Bonds Payable. The balancing amount is a debit of:

> $2,000 – $1,930 = $70

| | | |
|---|---|---|
| Cash | 1,930 | |
| Discount on Bonds Payable (to balance) | 70 | |
| Bonds Payable | | 2,000 |

## Requirement 3

**Prepare Red's effective-interest amortization table for the entire life of the bonds payable.**

② Account for bonds payable

③ Measure interest expense

### Interest Payment

The *cash interest payment is the same every interest period* and is calculated the same as under the straight-line method of amortization:

> Cash interest paid = Maturity value × Stated rate × Frequency of interest payments (months/12)

Or, more simply,

$$\text{Cash interest paid} = \frac{\text{Maturity value} \times \textbf{Stated rate}}{\text{Number of interest payments per year}}$$

The question states that the bonds are semiannual; that is, they pay interest twice per year.

$$\text{Cash interest paid} = \frac{\$2{,}000 \times 8\%}{2}$$
$$= \$80$$

So every line in the Interest Payment column will show $80.

## Interest Expense

Under the effective-interest method, the interest expense is calculated as:

$$\text{Interest expense} = \text{Carrying value} \times \text{Market rate} \times \text{Frequency of interest payments (months/12)}$$

Or, more simply,

$$\text{Interest expense} = \frac{\text{Carrying value} \times \textbf{Market rate}}{\text{Number of interest payments per year}}$$

The carrying value changes every time interest expense is recorded and the discount is amortized. This means that the *interest expense changes* as well.
The interest expense is calculated as:

| | |
|---|---|
| 06/30/09 | $1,930 × 10%/2 = $96* |
| 12/31/09 | $1,946 × 10%/2 = $97* |
| 06/30/10 | $1,963 × 10%/2 = $98* |
| 12/31/10 | $1,981 × 10%/2 = $99* |

*Adjusted for the effect of rounding

## Discount Amortization

Under the effective-interest method, the *discount (or premium) is the balancing amount.* It is the difference between the cash interest payment and the interest expense.
The discount amortization is calculated as:

| | |
|---|---|
| 06/30/09 | $96 − $80 = $16 |
| 12/31/09 | $97 − $80 = $17 |
| 06/30/10 | $98 − $80 = $18 |
| 12/31/10 | $99 − $80 = $19 |

## Discount Balance

The discount balance is the balance from the Discount T-account. By putting the discount amortization into the account, we can calculate the balance after each interest transaction.

| Discount on Bonds Payable | | | |
|---|---|---|---|
| 1/1/09 | 70 | | |
| | | 6/30/09 | 16 |
| Bal | 54 | | |
| | | 12/31/09 | 17 |
| Bal | 37 | | |
| | | 6/30/10 | 18 |
| Bal | 19 | | |
| | | 12/31/10 | 19 |
| Bal | 0 | | |

## Bond Carrying Value

The carrying value is the maturity value of the bonds combined with the discount (or premium).

The bonds' carrying value is calculated as the maturity value less the discount. After each interest period, this is:

| | |
|---|---|
| 01/01/09 | $2,000 − $70 = $1,930 |
| 06/30/09 | $2,000 − $54 = $1,946 |
| 12/31/09 | $2,000 − $37 = $1,963 |
| 06/30/10 | $2,000 − $19 = $1,981 |
| 12/31/10 | $2,000 − $ 0 = $2,000 |

Combining all of this information into the amortization table, we get:

| Date | Interest Payment | Interest Expense* | Discount Amortization | Discount Balance | Bonds' Carrying Value |
|---|---|---|---|---|---|
| 01/01/09 ............ | | | | 70 | 1,930 |
| 06/30/09 ............ | 80 | 96 | 16 | 54 | 1,946 |
| 12/31/09 ............ | 80 | 97 | 17 | 37 | 1,963 |
| 06/30/10 ............ | 80 | 98 | 18 | 19 | 1,981 |
| 12/31/10 ............ | 80 | 99 | 19 | 0 | 2,000 |

*Adjusted for the effect of rounding

## Requirement 4

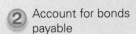

② Account for bonds payable

③ Measure interest expense

**Journalize Red's first two interest payments on June 30, 2009, and December 31, 2009.**

### June 30, 2009

Interest Expense is increased (a debit) by $96, as calculated in the table in Requirement 3.

Cash is decreased (a credit) by the cash interest paid of $80 (as calculated in Requirement 3).

The difference between these two amounts is balanced to Discount on Bonds Payable. The balancing amount is a credit of:

$$\$96 - \$80 = \$16$$

This is the discount amortization shown in Requirement 3.

| | | | | |
|---|---|---|---|---|
| | Interest Expense ($1,930 × 10%/2) | | 96 | |
| | Discount on Bonds Payable (to balance) | | | 16 |
| | Cash ($2,000 × 8%/2) | | | 80 |

### December 31, 2009

Interest Expense is increased (a debit) by $97, as calculated in the table in Requirement 3.

Cash is decreased (a credit) by the cash interest paid of $80 (as calculated in Requirement 3).

The difference between these two amounts is balanced to Discount on Bonds Payable. The balancing amount is a credit of:

$$\$97 - \$80 = \$17$$

This is the discount amortization shown in Requirement 3.

| | | | | |
|---|---|---|---|---|
| | Interest Expense ($1,946 × 10%/2) | | 97 | |
| | Discount on Bonds Payable (to balance) | | | 17 |
| | Cash ($2,000 × 8%/2) | | | 80 |

## Requirement 5

② Account for bonds payable

**On January 2, 2010, 20% of the bonds were converted to 120 common shares with a $2 par value per share. Journalize this transaction.**

If 20% of the bonds are converted, then 20% of the maturity value is converted:

$$20\% \times \$2,000 = \$400$$

Also 20% of the discount is converted:

$$20\% \times \$37 = \$7 \text{ (rounded)}$$

The bonds *will not exist* after the conversion, so the Bonds Payable account is decreased (a debit) by $400. The Discount on Bonds Payable is also decreased (a credit) by $7.

New common stock is issued for the conversion, so Common Stock is increased (a credit) by the par value of the new shares:

$$120 \times \$2 = \$240$$

The remainder is balanced to Additional Paid-In Capital. The balancing amount is:

$$\$400 - \$7 - \$240 = \$153$$

| | | |
|---|---|---|
| Bonds Payable ($2,000 × 20%) | 400 | |
| Discount on Bonds Payable ($37 × 20%) | | 7 |
| Paid-In Capital in Excess of Par (to balance) | | 153 |
| Common Stock (120 × $2) | | 240 |

| Discount on Bonds Payable | | | | Bonds Payable | | |
|---|---|---|---|---|---|---|
| Bal | 0 | | | | Bal | 0 |
| Jan 1, 2009 | 70 | | | | Jan 1, 2009 | 2,000 |
| | | Jun 30, 2009 | 16 | Jan 2, 2010    400 | | |
| | | Dec 31, 2009 | 17 | | Bal | 1,600 |
| | | Jan  2, 2010 | 7 | | | |
| Bal | 30 | | | | | |

## Requirement 6

**On January 3, 2010, Red purchased the remaining bonds from the marketplace for $1,800 cash. The bonds were immediately retired. Journalize this transaction.**

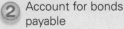 ② Account for bonds payable

Because 20% of the bonds were converted to common stock, 100% − 20% = 80% remained. These bonds will be retired.

If 80% of the bonds are retired, then 80% of the maturity value is retired:

$$80\% \times \$2,000 = \$1,600$$

Also 80% of the discount is retired:

$$80\% \times \$37 = \$30 \text{ (rounded)}$$

The bonds *will not exist* after retirement, so the Bonds Payable account is decreased (a debit) by $1,600. The Discount is also decreased (a credit) by $30.

Cash is decreased (a credit) by $1,800.

The remainder is balanced to a gain or loss. In this case, the balancing amount is a debit, so there is a *loss* of:

$$\$1,800 + \$30 - \$1,600 = \$230$$

| | | | |
|---|---|---|---|
| Bonds Payable ($2,000 × 80%) | | 1,600 | |
| Loss on Retirement (to balance) | | 230 | |
|     Discount on Bonds Payable (80% × $37) | | | 30 |
|     Cash | | | 1,800 |

## Requirement 7

④ Understand the advantages and disadvantages of borrowing

**How do interest payments on bonds differ from dividend payments on stock?**

If a company chooses to issue bonds instead of stock, it will have a higher earnings-per-share ratio as a result. (The earnings-per-share ratio is discussed more fully in Chapter 11.)

However, large interest payments (and principal payments when the bonds mature) can lead to bankruptcy if the company is unable to pay off the debt.

*DEMO DOC COMPLETE*

# Quick Practice Questions

## True/False

_____ 1. Sales tax payable is shown as a current liability on the balance sheet.

_____ 2. An accrued expense is an expense that has already been paid.

_____ 3. A contingent liability is not an actual liability.

_____ 4. The journal entry to record selling $200,000 face value bonds at 98 will involve a credit to Bonds Payable for $196,000.

_____ 5. When a bond is issued at a discount, the discount has the effect of raising the interest expense on the bonds to the market rate of interest.

_____ 6. The carrying value of bonds will increase each interest period if the bonds were sold at a discount.

_____ 7. The amount of discount amortized under the effective-interest method is the same amount each period.

_____ 8. Callable bonds give the issuer the benefit of being able to take advantage of low interest rates by paying off bonds whenever it is favorable to do so.

_____ 9. If convertible bonds were issued at a discount, the Discount on Bonds Payable must be credited when converting the bonds into common stock.

_____ 10. Bondholders are creditors of a corporation.

_____ 11. An operating lease is a long-term, noncancelable lease.

## Multiple Choice

1. **Which of the following is true about current liabilities?**
   a. Are due within one year or one operating cycle, whichever is longer
   b. Must be of a known amount
   c. Must be of an estimated amount
   d. Are subtracted from long-term liabilities on the balance sheet

2. **Which of the following best describes unearned revenue?**
   a. Revenue that has been earned and collected
   b. Revenue that has been earned but not yet collected
   c. Revenue that has been collected but not yet earned
   d. Revenue that has not been collected nor earned

3. **When is Estimated Warranty Payable credited?**
   a. In the period the product under warranty is repaired or replaced
   b. In the period after the product is sold
   c. In the period after the product is repaired or replaced
   d. In the period the revenue from selling the product was earned

4. **When a product is repaired under warranty, the entry includes which of the following?**
   a. A debit to Warranty Expense
   b. A credit to Warranty Expense
   c. A debit to Estimated Warranty Payable
   d. A credit to Estimated Warranty Payable

5. **Under what condition is a contingent liability recorded as an expense and a liability?**
   a. Under no condition
   b. When the likelihood of an actual loss is remote
   c. When the likelihood of an actual loss is reasonably possible
   d. When the likelihood of an actual loss is probable and the amount can be estimated

6. **On January 2, 2011, Lot Corporation issues $200,000 face value, 6% bonds for $196,000. What can be concluded about the effective (market) rate of interest?**
   a. It is less than 6%.
   b. It is more than 6%.
   c. It is equal to 6%.
   d. It is impossible to determine from the given data.

7. **Dalton Corporation issues 50, $1,000 face value, 10% bonds at 102.5. The journal entry includes which of the following?**
   a. A debit to Cash for $50,000
   b. A credit to Premium on Bonds Payable for $1,250
   c. A debit to Discount on Bonds Payable for $1,250
   d. A credit to Bonds Payable for $51,250

8. **What is the interest rate specified in the bond indenture called?**
   a. Stated rate
   b. Discount rate
   c. Yield rate
   d. Effective rate

9. **Which of the following statements about the discount on bonds payable is correct?**
   a. It is added to bonds payable on the balance sheet.
   b. It is a contra liability.
   c. It is amortized over the life of the bonds.
   d. Both (b) and (c) are correct.

10. **How is interest expense calculated under the effective-interest method of amortization?**
   a. The market rate times the carrying value of the bonds
   b. The market rate times the face value of the bonds
   c. The stated rate times the carrying value of the bonds
   d. The stated rate times the face value of the bonds

11. **A bond issued with a face value of $400,000 and a carrying amount of $391,000 is paid off at 98 1/2 and retired. What is the gain or loss on this transaction?**
   a. $3,000 loss
   b. $3,000 gain
   c. $6,000 loss
   d. $6,000 gain

12. **Which of the following is an advantage of issuing stock over bonds?**
   a. It is less risky to the issuing corporation.
   b. It creates assets.
   c. It generally results in higher earnings per share.
   d. It creates dividends that must be paid.

## Quick Exercises

**8-1.** Ideal Food Services had cash sales of $787,000 during the month of August 2011 and collected the 7% sales tax on these sales required by the state in which Ideal Food Services operates.

**1.** Journalize the cash sale and the sales tax collected on August 31.

| | General Journal | | | |
|---|---|---|---|---|
| Date | Accounts | | Debit | Credit |
| | | | | |
| | | | | |
| | | | | |
| | | | | |

**2.** Journalize the September 15 transaction when the sales tax is remitted to the proper agency.

| | General Journal | | | |
|---|---|---|---|---|
| Date | Accounts | | Debit | Credit |
| | | | | |
| | | | | |
| | | | | |

**8-2.** Freedom Vacuums warrants all of its products for one full year against any defect in manufacturing. Sales for 2011 and 2012 were $731,000 and $854,000, respectively. Freedom Vacuums expects warranty claims to run 4.5% of annual sales. Freedom paid $30,150 and $38,290, respectively, in 2011 and 2012 in warranty claims.

**a.** Compute Freedom's Warranty Expense for 2011 and 2012.

**b.** Compute the balance in Estimated Warranty Payable on December 31, 2012, assuming the January 1, 2011, balance in the account was $2,980.

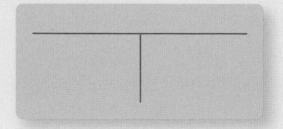

**8-3.** For each of the following independent situations, state whether the bonds were issued at a premium, at a discount, or at par.

**a.** Bonds with a face value of $60,000 were issued for $53,000.

_____

**b.** Bonds with a contract rate of 8% were issued to yield 7.5%.

_____

**c.** Bonds with a face value of $75,000 were issued for $75,000.

_____

**d.** Bonds with a contract rate of 9.25% were issued to yield 8.75%.

_____

**e.** Bonds with a face value of $110,000 were issued for $106,000.

_____

**8-4.** Fox Corporation issued 10-year, 10%, $1,000,000 bonds on January 1, 2011. The bonds pay interest every June 30 and December 31. The bonds were issued for $1,065,000. Fox Corporation uses straight-line amortization for any discount or premium amortization.

**1. Journalize the following:**

**a.** Issuance of the bonds on January 1, 2011.

| General Journal | | | | |
|---|---|---|---|---|
| Date | Accounts | | Debit | Credit |
| | | | | |
| | | | | |
| | | | | |
| | | | | |

**b.** Recording of the interest payment and amortization of the premium or discount on June 30, 2011.

| General Journal | | | | |
|---|---|---|---|---|
| Date | Accounts | | Debit | Credit |
| | | | | |
| | | | | |
| | | | | |
| | | | | |

**2. What is the carrying value of the bonds on June 30, 2011?**

**8-5.** On April 1, 2011, Needy Corporation issued $3,000,000 of 8%, 10-year bonds dated April 1, 2011, with interest payments made each October 1 and April 1. The bonds are issued at 95. Needy Corporation amortizes any premium or discount using the straight-line method.

**1. Journalize the following transactions:**

**a.** April 1, 2011, issuance of the bonds.

| General Journal | | | | |
|---|---|---|---|---|
| Date | Accounts | | Debit | Credit |
| | | | | |
| | | | | |
| | | | | |
| | | | | |

**b.** October 1, 2011, recording the payment of interest and the amortization of any discount or premium.

| General Journal | | | | |
|---|---|---|---|---|
| Date | Accounts | | Debit | Credit |
| | | | | |
| | | | | |
| | | | | |
| | | | | |

**c.** December 31, 2011, recording accrued interest and the amortization of any premium or discount.

| General Journal | | | | |
|---|---|---|---|---|
| Date | Accounts | | Debit | Credit |
| | | | | |
| | | | | |
| | | | | |

**8-6.** Cary Corporation issued $800,000 of 9.5%, eight-year bonds on June 1, 2011. Interest is paid semiannually on December 1 and June 1 of each year. On the issuance date, the market rate of interest was 8.5%, resulting in a price of 103 1/2 for these bonds. The effective-interest method of amortizing the premium or discount is used.

1. Journalize the following transactions:

   **a.** June 1, 2011, issuance of the bonds.

| General Journal | | | | |
|---|---|---|---|---|
| Date | Accounts | | Debit | Credit |
| | | | | |
| | | | | |
| | | | | |
| | | | | |

   **b.** December 1, 2011, recording of the first interest payment and the amortization of the premium.

| General Journal | | | | |
|---|---|---|---|---|
| Date | Accounts | | Debit | Credit |
| | | | | |
| | | | | |
| | | | | |

   **c.** Prepare the adjusting entry on December 31, 2011.

| General Journal | | | | |
|---|---|---|---|---|
| Date | Accounts | | Debit | Credit |
| | | | | |
| | | | | |
| | | | | |

8-7. Apex Corporation issued $500,000, callable, 10%, 10-year bonds at 93 on January 2, 2009. The bonds are callable at 102 anytime after January 2, 2011. On December 31, 2012, Apex Corporation calls the entire issuance.

1. Compute the balance in the Premium or Discount account on December 31, 2012. Apex Corporation uses the straight-line method of amortization.

2. Prepare the entry to call the bonds on December 31, 2012.

| General Journal | | | | |
|---|---|---|---|---|
| Date | Accounts | | Debit | Credit |
| | | | | |
| | | | | |
| | | | | |
| | | | | |
| | | | | |

# Do It Yourself! Question 1

## General Current Liabilities

Nitro Brothers sells products with warranties included in the selling price. During October 2011, Nitro sold goods for $10,000 cash. These goods cost $8,000 to manufacture. Nitro is required by law to collect 8% sales tax on all sales.

Nitro estimates warranty costs to be 1% of selling price. During October 2011, Nitro made $60 of repairs under warranty (paid in cash to a repair service).

On October 31, 2011, Nitro remitted all sales tax collected in October to the state government.

## Requirement

1. Journalize all of Nitro's transactions in the month of October, 2011.

| Date | Accounts | Debit | Credit |
|------|----------|-------|--------|
|      |          |       |        |
|      |          |       |        |
|      |          |       |        |

| Date | Accounts | Debit | Credit |
|------|----------|-------|--------|
|      |          |       |        |
|      |          |       |        |
|      |          |       |        |

| Date | Accounts | Debit | Credit |
|------|----------|-------|--------|
|      |          |       |        |
|      |          |       |        |
|      |          |       |        |

| Date | Accounts | Debit | Credit |
|------|----------|-------|--------|
|      |          |       |        |
|      |          |       |        |
|      |          |       |        |

| Date | Accounts | Debit | Credit |
|------|----------|-------|--------|
|      |          |       |        |
|      |          |       |        |
|      |          |       |        |

# Do It Yourself! Question 2

## Bonds Payable (straight-line amortization)

Circle, Inc., issued $20,000 maturity value of bonds payable for $19,337 cash on January 1, 2011. The bonds had a stated rate of 14%, but the market rate was 16%. Interest is paid semiannually on June 30 and December 31 and the bonds are due in two years.

     Circle uses the straight-line method of amortization.

### Requirements

1. Are these bonds issued at a discount or premium?

2. Journalize Circle's issuance of the bonds on January 1, 2011.

| General Journal | | | | |
|---|---|---|---|---|
| Date | Accounts | | Debit | Credit |
| | | | | |
| | | | | |
| | | | | |
| | | | | |

3. Journalize Circle's first two interest payments on June 30, 2011, and December 31, 2011.

| General Journal | | | | |
|---|---|---|---|---|
| Date | Accounts | | Debit | Credit |
| | | | | |
| | | | | |
| | | | | |
| | | | | |

| General Journal | | | | |
|---|---|---|---|---|
| Date | Accounts | | Debit | Credit |
| | | | | |
| | | | | |
| | | | | |
| | | | | |

4. Show how the bonds would appear on Circle's December 31, 2011, balance sheet.

_____

_____
_____
_____
_____

5. On January 2, 2012, 25% of the bonds were converted to 9,000 common shares with a $0.50 par value per share. Journalize this transaction.

| | General Journal | | |
|------|------|-------|--------|
| Date | Accounts | Debit | Credit |
| | | | |
| | | | |
| | | | |
| | | | |
| | | | |

6. On January 3, 2012, Circle purchased the remaining bonds from the marketplace for $14,000 cash. The bonds were immediately retired. Journalize this transaction.

| | General Journal | | |
|------|------|-------|--------|
| Date | Accounts | Debit | Credit |
| | | | |
| | | | |
| | | | |
| | | | |

# Do It Yourself! Question 3

## Bonds Payable (effective-interest amortization)

Square Corp. issued $10,000 maturity value of bonds payable for $10,346 cash on January 1, 2011. The bonds had a stated rate of 14% but the market rate was 12%. Interest is paid semiannually on June 30 and December 31 and the bonds are due in two years.

Square, Corp., uses the effective-interest method of amortization.

### Requirements

1. Are these bonds issued at a discount or premium?

2. Journalize Square's issuance of the bonds on January 1, 2011.

| | General Journal | | |
|---|---|---|---|
| Date | Accounts | Debit | Credit |
| | | | |
| | | | |
| | | | |
| | | | |

3. Prepare Square's effective-interest amortization table for the entire life of the bonds payable.

| | | | | |
|---|---|---|---|---|
| | | | | |
| | | | | |
| | | | | |
| | | | | |

4. Journalize Square's first two interest payments on June 30, 2011, and December 31, 2011.

| | General Journal | | | |
|---|---|---|---|---|
| Date | Accounts | | Debit | Credit |
| | | | | |
| | | | | |
| | | | | |
| | | | | |

| | General Journal | | | |
|---|---|---|---|---|
| Date | Accounts | | Debit | Credit |
| | | | | |
| | | | | |
| | | | | |
| | | | | |

5. On January 2, 2012, 50% of the bonds were converted to 3,000 common shares with a $1.50 par value per share. Journalize this transaction.

| | General Journal | | | |
|---|---|---|---|---|
| Date | Accounts | | Debit | Credit |
| | | | | |
| | | | | |
| | | | | |

6. On January 3, 2012, Square purchased the remaining bonds from the marketplace for $6,000 cash. The bonds were immediately retired. Journalize this transaction.

| | General Journal | | | |
|---|---|---|---|---|
| Date | Accounts | | Debit | Credit |
| | | | | |
| | | | | |
| | | | | |

# Quick Practice Solutions

## True/False

T     1. Sales tax payable is shown as a current liability on the balance sheet. (p. 470)

F     2. An accrued expense is an expense that has already been paid.
> False—An accrued expense is an expense that has *not yet* been paid. (p. 470)

T     3. A contingent liability is not an actual liability. (p. 474)

F     4. The journal entry to record selling $200,000 face value bonds at 98 will involve a credit to Bonds Payable for $196,000.
> False—The journal entry to record selling $200,000 face value bonds at 98 will involve a credit to Bonds Payable for *$200,000*. (pp. 479, 482)

T     5. When a bond is issued at a discount, the discount has the effect of raising the interest expense on the bonds to the market rate of interest. (pp. 482–483)

T     6. The carrying value of bonds will increase each interest period if the bonds were sold at a discount. (p. 484)

F     7. The amount of discount amortized under the effective-interest method is the same amount each period.
> False—The amount of discount amortized under the effective-interest method is a *different amount* each period. The *rate* of interest to calculate the amount of discount amortized each period is the same. (p. 484)

T     8. Callable bonds give the issuer the benefit of being able to take advantage of low interest rates by paying off bonds whenever it is favorable to do so. (p. 491)

T     9. If convertible bonds were issued at a discount, the Discount on Bonds Payable must be credited when converting the bonds into common stock. (pp. 491–492)

T     10. Bondholders are creditors of a corporation. (pp. 478–479)

F     11. An operating lease is a long-term, noncancelable lease.
> False—A *capital* lease is a long-term, noncancelable lease. (p. 496)

# Multiple Choice

1. **Which of the following is true about current liabilities? (p. 468)**
   a. Are due within one year or one operating cycle, whichever is longer
   b. Must be of a known amount
   c. Must be of an estimated amount
   d. Are subtracted from long-term liabilities on the balance sheet

2. **Which of the following best describes unearned revenue? (pp. 471–472)**
   a. Revenue that has been earned and collected
   b. Revenue that has been earned but not yet collected
   c. Revenue that has been collected but not yet earned
   d. Revenue that has not been collected nor earned

3. **When is Estimated Warranty Payable credited? (pp. 473–474)**
   a. In the period the product under warranty is repaired or replaced
   b. In the period after the product is sold
   c. In the period after the product is repaired or replaced
   d. In the period the revenue from selling the product was earned

4. **When a product is repaired under warranty, the entry includes which of the following? (p. 474)**
   a. A debit to Warranty Expense
   b. A credit to Warranty Expense
   c. A debit to Estimated Warranty Payable
   d. A credit to Estimated Warranty Payable

5. **Under what condition is a contingent liability recorded as an expense and a liability? (p. 474)**
   a. Under no condition
   b. When the likelihood of an actual loss is remote
   c. When the likelihood of an actual loss is reasonably possible
   d. When the likelihood of an actual loss is probable and the amount can be estimated

6. **On January 2, 2011, Lot Corporation issues $200,000 face value, 6% bonds for $196,000. What can be concluded about the effective (market) rate of interest? (p. 480)**
   a. It is less than 6%.
   b. It is more than 6%.
   c. It is equal to 6%.
   d. It is impossible to determine from the given data.

7. **Dalton Corporation issues 50, $1,000 face value, 10% bonds at 102.5. The journal entry includes which of the following? (p. 487)**
   a. A debit to Cash for $50,000
   b. A credit to Premium on Bonds Payable for $1,250
   c. A debit to Discount on Bonds Payable for $1,250
   d. A credit to Bonds Payable for $51,250

8. **What is the interest rate specified in the bond indenture called? (p. 480)**
   a. Stated rate
   b. Discount rate
   c. Yield rate
   d. Effective rate

9. **Which of the following statements about the discount on bonds payable is correct? (pp. 482–483)**
   a. It is added to bonds payable on the balance sheet.
   b. It is a contra liability.
   c. It is amortized over the life of the bonds.
   d. Both (b) and (c) are correct.

10. **How is interest expense calculated under the effective-interest method of amortization? (pp. 483–484)**
    a. The market rate times the carrying value of the bonds
    b. The market rate times the face value of the bonds
    c. The stated rate times the carrying value of the bonds
    d. The stated rate times the face value of the bonds

11. **A bond issued with a face value of $400,000 and a carrying amount of $391,000 is paid off at 98 1/2 and retired. What is the gain or loss on this transaction? (p. 491)**
    a. $3,000 loss
    b. $3,000 gain
    c. $6,000 loss
    d. $6,000 gain

12. **Which of the following is an advantage of issuing stock over bonds? (pp. 492–493)**
    a. It is less risky to the issuing corporation.
    b. It creates assets.
    c. It generally results in higher earnings per share.
    d. It creates dividends that must be paid.

# Quick Exercises

**8-1.** Ideal Food Services had cash sales of $787,000 during the month of August 2011 and collected the 7% sales tax on these sales required by the state in which Ideal Food Services operates. (p. 470)

1. Journalize the cash sale and the sales tax collected on August 31.

| General Journal | | | |
|---|---|---|---|
| Date | Accounts | Debit | Credit |
| Aug 31 | Cash | 842,090 | |
| | Sales | | 787,000 |
| | Sales Taxes Payable | | 55,090 |
| | *To record cash sales including 7% sales tax.* | | |

2. Journalize the September 15 transaction when the sales tax is remitted to the proper agency.

| General Journal | | | |
|---|---|---|---|
| Date | Accounts | Debit | Credit |
| Sep 15 | Sales Taxes Payable | 55,090 | |
| | Cash | | 55,090 |
| | *To record sales tax remittance.* | | |

**8-2.** Freedom Vacuums warrants all of its products for one full year against any defect in manufacturing. Sales for 2011 and 2012 were $731,000 and $854,000, respectively. Freedom Vacuums expects warranty claims to run 4.5% of annual sales. Freedom paid $30,150 and $38,290, respectively, in 2011 and 2012 in warranty claims. (pp. 473–474)

a. Compute Freedom's warranty expense for 2011 and 2012.

2011: $32,895 ($731,000 × 0.045)
2012: $38,430 ($854,000 × 0.045)

**b.** Compute the balance in Estimated Warranty Payable on December 31, 2012, assuming the January 1, 2011, balance in the account was $2,980.

$5,865 ($2,980 + $32,895 + $38,430 − $30,150 − $38,290)

| Estimated Warranty Payable | | | |
|---|---|---|---|
| | | Bal | 2,980 |
| | | 2011 Expense | 32,895 |
| 2011 Repairs | 30,150 | | |
| | | 2012 Expense | 38,430 |
| 2012 Repairs | 38,290 | | |
| | | Bal | 5,865 |

**8-3.** **For each of the following independent situations, state whether the bonds were issued at a premium, at a discount, or at par.** (p. 480)

**a. Bonds with a face value of $60,000 were issued for $53,000.**
Discount

**b. Bonds with a contract rate of 8% were issued to yield 7.5%.**
Premium

**c. Bonds with a face value of $75,000 were issued for $75,000.**
Par

**d. Bonds with a contract rate of 9.25% were issued to yield 8.75%.**
Premium

**e. Bonds with a face value of $110,000 were issued for $106,000.**
Discount

**8-4.** **Fox Corporation issued 10-year, 10%, $1,000,000 bonds on January 1, 2011. The bonds pay interest every June 30 and December 31. The bonds were issued for $1,065,000. Fox Corporation uses straight-line amortization for any discount or premium amortization.** (p. 490)

**1. Journalize the following:**

**a.** Issuance of the bonds on January 1, 2011.

| General Journal | | | |
|---|---|---|---|
| Date | Accounts | Debit | Credit |
| Jan 1 | Cash | 1,065,000 | |
| | Bonds Payable | | 1,000,000 |
| | Premium on Bonds Payable | | 65,000 |

**b.** Recording the interest payment and amortization of the premium or discount on June 30, 2011.

| General Journal | | | |
|---|---|---|---|
| Date | Accounts | Debit | Credit |
| Jun 30 | Interest Expense | 46,750 | |
| | Premium on Bonds Payable | 3,250 | |
| | Cash | | 50,000 |

**2. What is the carrying value of the bonds on June 30, 2011?**

Carrying value = $1,000,000 + ($65,000 − $3,250) = $1,061,750

**8-5.** **On April 1, 2011, Needy Corporation issued $3,000,000 of 8%, 10-year bonds dated April 1, 2011, with interest payments made each October 1 and April 1. The bonds are issued at 95. Needy Corporation amortizes any premium or discount using the straight-line method.** (p. 490)

**1. Journalize the following transactions:**

**a.** April 1, 2011, issuance of the bonds.

$3,000,000 × 0.95 = $2,850,000
$3,000,000 − $2,850,000 = $150,000

| General Journal | | | |
|---|---|---|---|
| Date | Accounts | Debit | Credit |
| Apr 1 | Cash | 2,850,000 | |
| | Discount on Bonds Payable | 150,000 | |
| | Bonds Payable | | 3,000,000 |

**b.** October 1, 2011, recording the payment of interest and the amortization of any discount or premium.

$3,000,000 × 0.08 × 6/12 = $120,000
($150,000/10) × 6/12 months = $7,500

| General Journal | | | |
| --- | --- | --- | --- |
| Date | Accounts | Debit | Credit |
| Oct 1 | Interest Expense | 127,500 | |
| | Discount on Bonds Payable | | 7,500 |
| | Cash | | 120,000 |

**c.** December 31, 2011, recording accrued interest and the amortization of any premium or discount.

$$\$3,000,000 \times 0.08 \times 3/12 = \$60,000$$
$$(\$150,000/10) \times 3/12 \text{ months} = \$3,750$$

| General Journal | | | |
| --- | --- | --- | --- |
| Date | Accounts | Debit | Credit |
| Dec 31 | Interest Expense | 63,750 | |
| | Discount on Bonds Payable | | 3,750 |
| | Interest Payable | | 60,000 |

**8-6. Cary Corporation issued $800,000 of 9.5%, eight-year bonds on June 1, 2011. Interest is paid semiannually on December 1 and June 1 of each year. On the issuance date, the market rate of interest was 8.5%, resulting in a price of 103 1/2 for these bonds. The effective-interest method of amortizing the premium or discount is used.** (pp. 487–489)

**1. Journalize the following transactions:**

**a.** June 1, 2011, issuance of the bonds.

$$\$800,000 \times 1.035 = \$828,000$$

| General Journal | | | |
| --- | --- | --- | --- |
| Date | Accounts | Debit | Credit |
| Jun 1 | Cash | 828,000 | |
| | Bonds Payable | | 800,000 |
| | Premium on Bonds Payable | | 28,000 |

**b.** December 1, 2011, recording the first interest payment and the amortization of the premium.

$$\$800,000 \times 0.095 \times 6/12 = \$38,000$$
$$\$800,000 + \$28,000 = \$828,000$$
$$\$828,000 \times 0.085 \times 6/12 = \$35,190$$

| | General Journal | | | |
|---|---|---|---|---|
| Date | Accounts | | Debit | Credit |
| Dec 1 | Interest Expense | | 35,190 | |
| | Premium on Bonds Payable | | 2,810 | |
| | Cash | | | 38,000 |

**c.** Prepare the adjusting entry on December 31, 2011.

$$\$800,000 \times 0.095 \times 1/12 = \$6,333$$
$$\$800,000 + \$28,000 - \$2,810 = \$825,190$$
$$\$825,190 \times 0.085 \times 1/12 = \$5,845$$

| | General Journal | | | |
|---|---|---|---|---|
| Date | Accounts | | Debit | Credit |
| Dec 31 | Interest Expense | | 5,845 | |
| | Premium on Bonds Payable | | 488 | |
| | Interest Payable | | | 6,333 |

**8-7.** Apex Corporation issued $500,000, callable, 10%, 10-year bonds at 93 on January 2, 2009. The bonds are callable at 102 anytime after January 2, 2011. On December 31, 2012, Apex Corporation calls the entire issuance. (p. 491)

1. Compute the balance in the Premium or Discount account on December 31, 2012. Apex Corporation uses the straight-line method of amortization.

$$\$500,000 \times 0.93 = \$465,000$$
$$\$500,000 - \$465,000 = \$35,000 \text{ discount}$$
$$\$35,000/10 \text{ years} = \$3,500 \text{ annual amortization of discount}$$
$$\$3,500 \times 4 \text{ years} = \$14,000 \text{ amortized discount as of December 31, 2012}$$
$$\$35,000 - \$14,000 = \$21,000 \text{ unamortized discount as of December 31, 2012}$$

**2. Prepare the entry to call the bonds on December 31, 2012.**

| Date | Accounts | Debit | Credit |
|---|---|---|---|
| | General Journal | | |
| 2012 | | | |
| Dec 31 | Bonds Payable | 500,000 | |
| | Loss on Retirement of Bonds Payable | 31,000 | |
| | ($500,000 + $21,000 − $510,000) | | |
| |     Discount on Bonds Payable | | 21,000 |
| |     Cash ($500,000 × 102%) | | 510,000 |

# Do It Yourself! Question 1 Solutions

## General Current Liabilities

### Requirement

1. Journalize all of Nitro's transactions in the month of October 2011.

During October 2011, Nitro sold goods for $10,000 cash. These goods cost $8,000 to manufacture. Nitro is required by law to collect 8% sales tax on all sales.

| | | | |
|---|---|---|---|
| Cash ($10,000 × [1 + 8%]) | | 10,800 | |
| Sales Revenue | | | 10,000 |
| Sales Tax Payable ($10,000 × 8%) | | | 800 |
| | | | |
| COGS | | 8,000 | |
| Inventory | | | 8,000 |

Nitro estimates warranty costs to be 1% of the selling price.

| | | | |
|---|---|---|---|
| Warranty Expense ($10,000 × 1%) | | 100 | |
| Estimated Warranty Payable | | | 100 |

During October 2011, Nitro made $60 of repairs under warranty (paid in cash to a repair service).

| | | | |
|---|---|---|---|
| Estimated Warranty Payable | | 60 | |
| Cash | | | 60 |

On October 31, 2011, Nitro remitted all sales tax collected in October to the state government.

| | | | |
|---|---|---|---|
| Sales Tax Payable ($10,000 × 8%) | | 800 | |
| Cash | | | 800 |

# Do It Yourself! Question 2 Solutions

## Bonds Payable (straight-line amortization)

### Requirements

1. **Are these bonds issued at a discount or premium?**

   These bonds were issued at a **discount**.

2. **Journalize Circle's issuance of the bonds on January 1, 2011.**

   | | | |
   |---|---|---|
   | Cash | 19,337 | |
   | Discount on Bonds Payable (to balance) | 663 | |
   | Bonds Payable | | 20,000 |

3. **Journalize Circle's first two interest payments on June 30, 2011, and December 31, 2011.**

   The entry for both June 30, 2011, and December 31, 2011, would be the same:

   | | | |
   |---|---|---|
   | Interest Expense | 1,566 | |
   | Discount on Bonds Payable ($663/4) | | 166 |
   | Cash ($20,000 × 14%/2) | | 1,400 |

4. **Show how the bonds would appear on Circle's December 31, 2011, balance sheet.**

   | | |
   |---|---|
   | Bonds payable....................... | $20,000 |
   | Less Discount....................... | (331) |
   | Bonds payable (net).............. | $19,669 |

5. **On January 2, 2012, 25% of the bonds were converted to 9,000 common shares with a $0.50 par value per share. Journalize this transaction.**

   Immediately before this transaction, the discount had a balance of $331:

   | Discount on Bonds Payable | | | |
   |---|---|---|---|
   | Bal | | | |
   | Jan 1 | 663 | | |
   | | | Jun 30 | 166 |
   | | | Dec 31 | 166 |
   | Bal | 331 | | |

| | | | | |
|---|---|---|---|---|
| Bonds Payable ($20,000 × 25%) | | | 5,000 | |
| Discount on Bonds Payable ($331 × 25%) | | | | 83 |
| Paid-In Capital in Excess of Par (to balance) | | | | 417 |
| Common Stock (9,000 × $0.50) | | | | 4,500 |

6. **On January 3, 2012, Circle purchased the remaining bonds from the marketplace for $14,000 cash. The bonds were immediately retired. Journalize this transaction.**

| | | | | |
|---|---|---|---|---|
| Bonds Payable ($20,000 × 75%) | | | 15,000 | |
| Gain on Retirement (to balance) | | | | 752 |
| Discount on Bonds Payable ($331 × 75%) | | | | 248 |
| Cash | | | | 14,000 |

# Do It Yourself! Question 3 Solutions

## Bonds Payable (effective-interest amortization)

### Requirements

1. **Are these bonds issued at a discount or premium?**

These bonds were issued at a **premium**.

2. **Journalize Square's issuance of the bonds on January 1, 2011.**

| | | |
|---|---|---|
| Cash | 10,346 | |
| Premium on Bonds Payable (to balance) | | 346 |
| Bonds Payable | | 10,000 |

3. **Prepare Square's effective-interest amortization table for the entire life of the bonds payable.**

| Date | Interest Payment | Interest Expense | Premium Amortization | Premium Balance | Bonds' Carrying Value |
|---|---|---|---|---|---|
| 01/01/11 ............. | | | | 346 | 10,346 |
| 06/30/11 ............. | 700 | 621 | 79 | 267 | 10,267 |
| 12/31/11 ............. | 700 | 617 | 83 | 184 | 10,184 |
| 06/30/12 ............. | 700 | 611 | 89 | 95 | 10,095 |
| 12/31/12 ............. | 700 | 605 | 95 | 0 | 10,000 |

4. **Journalize Square's first two interest payments on June 30, 2011, and December 31, 2011.**

**June 30, 2011**

| | | |
|---|---|---|
| Interest Expense ($10,346 × 12%/2) | 621 | |
| Premium on Bonds Payable (to balance) | 79 | |
| Cash ($10,000 × 14%/2) | | 700 |

**December 31, 2011**

| | | |
|---|---|---|
| Interest Expense ($10,267 × 12%/2) | 617 | |
| Premium on Bonds Payable (to balance) | 83 | |
| Cash ($10,000 × 14%/2) | | 700 |

5. **On January 2, 2012, 50% of the bonds were converted to 3,000 common shares with a $1.50 par value per share. Journalize this transaction.**

| | | |
|---|---|---|
| Bonds Payable ($10,000 × 50%) | 5,000 | |
| Premium on Bonds Payable ($184 × 50%) | 92 | |
| Paid-In Capital in Excess of Par (to balance) | | 592 |
| Common Stock (3,000 × $1.50) | | 4,500 |

6. **On January 3, 2012, Square purchased the remaining bonds from the marketplace for $6,000 cash. The bonds were immediately retired. Journalize this transaction.**

| | | |
|---|---|---|
| Bonds Payable ($10,000 × 50%) | 5,000 | |
| Premium on Bonds Payable ($184 × 50%) | 92 | |
| Loss on Retirement (to balance) | 908 | |
| Cash | | 6,000 |

# The Power of Practice

For more practice using the skills learned in this chapter, visit MyAccountingLab. There you will find algorithmically generated questions that are based on these Demo Docs and your main textbook's Review and Assess Your Progress sections.

Go to MyAccountingLab and follow these steps:

1. Direct your URL to www.myaccountinglab.com.
2. Log in using your name and password.
3. Click the MyAccountingLab link.
4. Click Study Plan in the left navigation bar.
5. From the table of contents, select Chapter 8, Liabilities.
6. Click a link to work tutorial exercises.

# 9 Stockholders' Equity

## WHAT YOU PROBABLY ALREADY KNOW

You probably already know that you can purchase shares of a company's stock as an investment. CNBC shows the trading price of various stocks as trades take place and the daily prices are reported in your financial newspapers. Much of the trading taking place is between investors rather than from the issuing corporation.

One way that a corporation issues its shares of stock is in an initial public offering (IPO). A recent popular IPO is Google (the featured company in Chapter 12). Google was doing business for six years before its founders took the company public in August 2004. The IPO provided investors an opportunity to purchase Google stock at a stated offer price of $85 a share. Nearly three years after Google's IPO, the stock traded at $515 per share. The cash received by the corporation from the initial sale of the Google stock and the shareholders' equity interest was recorded on the books of Google Corporation. In this chapter, we will see how to account for the equity transactions of a corporation.

## Learning Objectives

 **Explain the features of a corporation**

As a **separate legal entity,** a corporation can enter into contracts, own assets in its own name, and be sued. The owners of the corporation are the stockholders. Shares of stock can be transferred to others without affecting the operation of the business. *No mutual agency* means that the owners of a corporation (stockholders) cannot commit or obligate the corporation. Stockholders are not personally liable for the obligations of the corporation. The most that a stockholder can lose is the amount invested. This is known as *limited liability.* These are some of the characteristics of a corporation. *Review these and other characteristics in your text, and take note of Exhibit 9-1 (p. 536) for a list of advantages and disadvantages of the corporate form of business.*

## ② Account for the issuance of stock

When a company incorporates, the **par** or **stated value**, if any, will be indicated in the articles of incorporation. It is usually a nominal amount assigned to a share of stock that represents the minimum legal stated capital and does not indicate the value or worth of the stock. When the stock is sold by the corporation, the Common Stock account is credited for the par or stated value. Usually, the stock is sold above par, which is additional capital contributed by the shareholders. The excess of the stock sales price over the par or stated value is the amount credited to the **Paid-In Capital in Excess of Par** account. *Review the accounting for stock issuances under "Issuing Stock" in the text.*

## ③ Describe how treasury stock affects a company

**Treasury stock** is created when the company buys back its own shares from existing shareholders. The cost of the shares is debited to a contra equity account, Treasury Stock. If or when the treasury stock is subsequently sold, Cash is debited, Treasury Stock is credited for the cost of the shares, and Paid-In Capital from Treasury Stock Transactions is debited or credited for the difference, if any. *Review the impact of treasury stock on stockholders' equity, as shown in the financial statement excerpts on pp. 550–551.*

## ④ Account for dividends

If the board of directors declares dividends, Retained Earnings is debited and Dividends Payable is credited. On the date of payment, the Liability is debited (reduced); Cash is also credited (reduced). *Read "Retained Earnings, Dividends, and Splits" on pp. 552–559 to review the dividend dates and learn the difference between cumulative and noncumulative preferred stock.*

The board of directors may declare a stock dividend instead of a cash dividend. A **stock dividend** gives each shareholder more shares of stock based on the number of shares currently owned. Similar to a cash dividend, Retained Earnings is reduced (debited). However, unlike a cash dividend, a liability is not credited because there is no claim on assets; Common Stock is credited. *Review the journal entry in the "Stock Dividends" section of the text (p. 557) for the accounting of a stock dividend.*

### ⑤ Use stock values in decision making

**Market value** is the current price at which the stock is being offered for sale in the market. This value is of prime importance to investors. **Book value** indicates the amount of net assets that each common shareholder would receive if the assets were sold for the amount reported on the balance sheet. *Review the calculations of book value on p. 560 of the main text.*

### ⑥ Compute return on assets and return on equity

Ratios to assess profitability include the rate of return on total assets and return on common stockholders' equity. The rate of return on total assets indicates the amount of profitability per dollar of assets invested (Net income + Interest expense/Average total assets). The rate of return on common stockholders' equity indicates the amount of profitability per dollar of common equity (Net income – Preferred dividends/Average common stockholders' equity). Higher returns for both ratios are more favorable.

### ⑦ Report equity transactions on the statement of cash flows

Payment of cash dividends, stock, and treasury stock transactions impact the financing activities section of the statement of cash flows. Payment of cash dividends and purchases of treasury stock decrease cash, while issuance of new stock and sales of treasury stock increase cash. *Review Exhibit 9-9 (p. 563) to see the placement of stockholders' equity transactions on the statement of cash flows.*

# Demo Doc 1

## Common Stock

*Learning Objectives  1, 2, 4, 6, 7*

Jack, Inc., had the following information at December 31, 2010:

| Stockholders' Equity | |
| :--- | ---: |
| December 31, 2010 | |
| Common stock, 1,600,000 authorized, | |
| 350,000 issued and outstanding shares | $437,500 |
| Paid-in capital in excess of par | 787,500 |
| Total paid-in capital | 1,225,000 |
| Retained earnings | 4,200,000 |
| Total stockholder's equity | $5,425,000 |

## Requirements

1.  **What are Jack's two main sources of corporate capital?**

2.  **What is the par value per share of the common stock?**

3.  **On average, what was the original issue price per share of common stock?**

4.  **On February 12, 2011, Jack issued another 20,000 common shares for $5 cash per share. Journalize this transaction. What is the impact on Jack's cash flows as a result of this transaction?**

5.  **Jack earned net income of $150,000 and paid no dividends in 2011. There were no other equity transactions in 2011. Prepare the stockholders' equity section of Jack's balance sheet on December 31, 2011.**

6.  **Calculate Jack's return on equity and book value per share for 2011.**

# Demo Doc 1 Solutions

## Requirement 1

**What are Jack's two main sources of corporate capital?**

*Corporate capital* is another term for stockholders' equity.

Jack has paid-in capital. This is money that has been received from the stockholders. Jack also has retained earnings. This represents profits earned on the stockholders' behalf (that have not yet been distributed as dividends).

Every corporation has these two sources of capital.

① Explain the features of a corporation

## Requirement 2

**What is the par value per share of the common stock?**

Common Stock and Preferred Stock accounts hold *only* the par value of the *issued* shares. So the $437,500 in the Common Stock account represents the par value of *all* the issued shares.

② Account for the issuance of stock

$$\frac{\text{Par value}}{\text{per share}} = \frac{\text{Common stock balance}}{\text{Number of issued common shares}}$$

$$\frac{\text{Par value}}{\text{per share}} = \frac{\$437,500}{350,000 \text{ shares}}$$

$$= \$1.25 \text{ per share}$$

## Requirement 3

**On average, what was the original issue price per share of common stock?**

When stock is issued for cash, the Cash account increases (a debit) for cash received. The Common Stock account increases (a credit) for the par value and the excess is Paid-In Capital in Excess of Par—Common. Because the selling price per share is almost always more than the par value, this excess balancing amount to Paid-In Capital in Excess of Par—Common is usually an increase (a credit).

② Account for the issuance of stock

We know that total debits must equal total credits for any transaction. In this case, the debit is the cash received and the credits are the increases to Common Stock and Paid-In Capital in Excess of Par—Common. This means that

$$\frac{\text{Cash received from}}{\text{share issuance}} = \text{Common Stock} + \text{Paid-In Capital in Excess of Par}$$

So the total cash received from issuance of the common shares is

$$\$1.25 \text{ par} \times 350,000 \text{ shares} = \$437,500$$
$$\$437,500 + \$787,500 = \$1,225,000$$

This amount represents all 350,000 issued shares.

$$\$1,225,000/350,000 \text{ shares} = \$3.50 \text{ cash received per share}$$

The balancing credit to Paid-In Capital in Excess of Par—Common is ($3.50 received − $1.25 par) $2.25 × 350,000 shares = $787,500 additional cash paid.

## Requirement 4

Account for the issuance of stock

Report equity transactions on the statement of cash flows

**On February 12, 2011, Jack issued another 20,000 common shares for $5 cash per share. Journalize this transaction. What is the impact on Jack's cash flows as a result of this transaction?**

Cash increases (a debit) by $5 × 20,000 = $100,000.
Common Stock increases (a credit) by the par value of the new shares:

$$\$1.25 \times 20,000 = \$25,000$$

Paid-In Capital in Excess of Par—Common is the excess cash paid:

$$(\$5 - \$1.25) = \$3.75$$
$$\$3.75 \times 20,000 \text{ shares} = \$75,000$$

This is the balancing amount in the journal entry.

| | | |
|---|---|---|
| Cash ($5 × 20,000) | 100,000 | |
| Common Stock ($1.25 × 20,000) | | 25,000 |
| Paid-In Capital in Excess of Par—Common (to balance) | | 75,000 |

When Jack issued the shares, cash of $100,000 was received. This results in a $100,000 increase to cash flow. This would be shown in the financing activities section of the statement of cash flows.

## Requirement 5

Account for dividends

**Jack earned net income of $150,000 and paid no dividends in 2011. There were no other equity transactions in 2011. Prepare the stockholders' equity section of Jack's balance sheet on December 31, 2011.**

Because of the stock issuance in Requirement 4, the number of outstanding common shares has increased to

$$350,000 \text{ shares} + 20,000 \text{ shares} = 370,000 \text{ shares}$$

This must be shown for Common Stock as part of its descriptive line on the balance sheet.

The dollar amount in the Common Stock account has increased to

$$\$437,500 + \$25,000 = \$462,500$$

The other impact of this transaction on stockholder's equity was to increase Paid-In Capital in Excess of Par—Common to

$$\$787,500 + \$75,000 = \$862,500$$

The net income earned by Jack will increase Retained Earnings to

$$\$4,200,000 + \$150,000 = \$4,350,000$$

These new amounts create a new total stockholder's equity of $5,675,000.

### Stockholders' Equity
### December 31, 2011

| | |
|---|---:|
| Common stock, 1,600,000 issued, | |
| 370,000 issued and outstanding shares............................... | $462,500 |
| Paid-in capital in excess of par................................. | 862,500 |
| Total paid-in capital................................. | 1,325,000 |
| Retained earnings.................................................. | 4,350,000 |
| Total stockholders' equity ...................................... | $5,675,000 |

## Requirement 6

**Calculate Jack's return on equity and book value per share for 2011.**

⑥ Compute return on assets and return on equity

$$\frac{\text{Return on}}{\text{stockholders' equity}} = \frac{\text{Net income} - \text{Preferred dividends}}{\text{Average common stockholders' equity}}$$

*Common* stockholders' equity means the total stockholders' equity less the preferred equity (that is, less any preferred stock or any paid-in capital in excess of par relating to preferred stock).

*Average* common stockholders' equity is the *mathematical average* of the beginning and ending balances in Common Stockholders' Equity (that is, [Beginning balance + Ending balance]/2).

So using the data from this question,

$$\text{Return on stockholders' equity} = \frac{\$150,000 - \$0}{(\$5,425,000 + \$5,675,000)/2}$$

$$\text{Return on stockholders' equity} = 0.027 = 2.7\%$$

Using the data from this question,

$$\text{Book value per share} = \frac{\text{Common stockholders' equity}}{\text{Number of common shares outstanding}}$$

$$\text{Book value per share} = \frac{\$5,675,000}{370,000 \text{ shares}}$$

$$= \$15.34 \text{ per share}$$

***DEMO DOC COMPLETE***

# Demo Doc 2

## Preferred Stock

*Learning Objectives 2, 4*

Jill Co. issued 25,000, 6%, $100 par cumulative preferred shares on January 1, 2009, for $120 cash per share. Jill had never issued preferred shares before this date.
Jill paid the following cash dividends (in total, to *all* shares):

| | |
|---|---|
| 2009 ............... | $120,000 |
| 2010 ............... | $160,000 |
| 2011 ............... | $200,000 |

### Requirements

1. Journalize the issuance of the preferred shares on January 1, 2009, and the payment of the preferred share dividends in 2009 (assuming the dividends were declared and paid on the same day).

2. How much in dividends is Jill supposed to pay to the preferred shareholders each year?

3. Did Jill pay all of the required dividends in each year? If not, what happens to the amount not paid? How much in dividends did the preferred and common shareholders receive each year?

# Demo Doc 2 Solutions

## Requirement 1

**2** Account for the issuance of stock

**4** Account for dividends

**Journalize the issuance of the preferred shares on January 1, 2009, and the payment of the preferred share dividends in 2009 (assuming the dividends were declared and paid on the same day).**

The issuance of preferred shares is the same as the issuance of common shares, except for the account title.

Cash is increased (a debit) by

$$\$120 \times 25{,}000 = \$3{,}000{,}000$$

Preferred Stock is increased (a credit) by the par value of the new shares:

$$\$100 \times 25{,}000 = \$2{,}500{,}000$$

Paid-In Capital in Excess of Par—Preferred is the excess cash paid:

$$(\$120 - \$100 \text{ par}) = \$20 \times 25{,}000 \text{ shares} = \$500{,}000$$

This is the balancing amount in the journal entry.

| | | |
|---|---|---|
| Cash ($120 × 25,000) | 3,000,000 | |
| Paid-In Capital in Excess of Par—Preferred (to balance) | | 500,000 |
| Preferred Stock ($100 × 25,000) | | 2,500,000 |

When dividends are paid, Retained Earnings is decreased because the shareholders are removing some of their capital from the company. So Retained Earnings is decreased (a debit) by $120,000.

Cash is also decreased (a credit) by $120,000.

| | | |
|---|---|---|
| Retained Earnings | 120,000 | |
| Cash | | 120,000 |

## Requirement 2

**4** Account for dividends

**How much in dividends is Jill supposed to pay to the preferred shareholders each year?**

Each year, every preferred share is *supposed* to receive

$$\text{"Required" preferred share dividends} = \text{Par value per share} \times \text{Dividend percentage}$$

First, we should calculate the "required" annual dividends per share. In this case, it is

$$\$100 \times 6\% = \$6 \text{ per share}$$

Because there are 25,000 outstanding preferred shares, this works out to $6 × 25,000 = **$150,000** in dividends per year for all preferred shares.

## Requirement 3

**Did Jill pay all of the required dividends in each year? If not, what happens to the amount not paid? How much in dividends did the preferred and common shareholders receive each year?**

 Account for dividends

### 2009

Because $120,000 is less than the "required" $150,000, we know that Jill did *not* pay all of the required dividends in 2009.

The preferred shares only received

$$\$120,000/25,000 \text{ shares} = \$4.80 \text{ per share}$$

The difference of $150,000 − $120,000 = $30,000 is *dividends in arrears*. This amount is *not* recorded in a transaction because it has not yet been declared and, therefore, is not a liability. Dividends in arrears do *not* appear on the balance sheet. However, they are disclosed in a *note* to the financial statements.

Because the full $150,000 was not paid, the entire $120,000 goes to the preferred shareholders as dividends. The common shareholders get no dividends in 2009.

### 2010

For 2010, Jill must not only pay the $150,000 annual "requirement" but first must also "catch up" on the dividends in arrears of $30,000 from 2009.

So in order to completely fulfill her obligation to the preferred shareholders, Jill must pay $30,000 + $150,000 = $180,000 in dividends to the preferred shareholders.

Because $160,000 is less than $180,000, we know that Jill did *not* pay all of the required dividends in 2010.

The difference of $180,000 − $160,000 = $20,000 is *dividends in arrears*.

Because the full $180,000 was not paid, the entire $160,000 goes to the preferred shareholders as dividends. The common shareholders get no dividends in 2010.

### 2011

In 2011, Jill is *supposed* to pay the annual $150,000 of dividends *plus* the $20,000 dividends in arrears from 2010 for a total of $170,000.

Because $200,000 is greater than $170,000, we know that Jill did pay all of the required dividends in 2011.

The $170,000 shown above goes to the preferred shareholders, while the rest ($200,000 − $170,000 = $30,000) goes to the common shareholders.

## *DEMO DOC COMPLETE*

# Demo Doc 3

## Stock Splits and Dividends

*Learning Objectives 2, 4*

On December 31, 2010, Tinker Corp. had 25,000, $1.20 par common shares outstanding with a market price of $9 per share.

Retained Earnings had a balance of $60,000, but there was no balance in Paid-In Capital in Excess of Par.

### Requirements

1. On January 1, 2011, Tinker split its common stock 3 for 1. Journalize the split. What are the par and market values per share after the split? How does this split impact stockholders' equity?

2. On February 1, 2011, Tinker issued a 20% stock dividend. Journalize this dividend. What is the par value per share after the dividend? How does this dividend impact stockholders' equity?

3. On March 1, 2011, Tinker declared and paid a cash dividend of $0.60 per common share. Journalize this dividend. How does this dividend impact stockholders' equity?

# Demo Doc 3 Solutions

## Requirement 1

On January 1, 2011, Tinker split its common stock 3 for 1. Journalize the split. What are the par and market values per share after the split? How does this split impact stockholders' equity?

(2) Account for the issuance of stock

Before the split, Tinker has 25,000 common shares.
　With a 3-for-1 split, there will be **three** new shares for every **one** old share.

| Number of shares after stock split | = | Number of shares before stock split | × Split ratio |
|---|---|---|---|
| Number of shares after stock split | = | 25,000 | × $\frac{3}{1}$ |
| | = | 75,000 shares | |

Another result of the split is that the par value and the market price are also split.

| Par value per share after split | = | Par value per share before split | × $\frac{1}{\text{Split ratio}}$ |
|---|---|---|---|
| Par value per share after split | = | $1.20 | × $\frac{1}{3}$ |
| | = | $0.40 per share | |
| Market price per share after split | = | Market price per share before split | × $\frac{1}{\text{Split ratio}}$ |
| Market price per share after split | = | $9 | × $\frac{1}{3}$ |
| | = | $3 per share | |

There has been *no change* to the account balance of Common Stock. It remains the same, only it is now spread across more shares (resulting in a lower par value per share, as shown above).
　The net impact on Common Stock is *zero*. Essentially, this means that *there is no journal entry for a stock split*. However, a stock split is described in the notes to the financial statements.
　Because there is no journal entry, total equity is *not* impacted by the stock split.

## Requirement 2

On February 1, 2011, Tinker issued a 20% stock dividend. Journalize this dividend. What is the par value per share after the dividend? How does this dividend impact stockholders' equity?

(4) Account for dividends

This is a small stock dividend because the dividend percentage (20%) is less than 25%.
　Remember that after the stock split of January 1, Tinker has 75,000 common shares outstanding with a market price of $3 per share and a par value of $0.40 per share.

With a stock dividend, new shares are issued to existing shareholders.

| Number of new shares issued for stock dividend | = | Shares outstanding before dividend | × | Stock dividend % |
|---|---|---|---|---|
| Number of new shares issued for stock dividend | = | 75,000 | × | 20% |
| | = | 15,000 new shares | | |

Each of these new shares is *identical* to the shares that existed before the stock dividend. They have the same characteristics as the common shares that existed before the stock dividend. The par value of the new shares issued is $0.40 per share, as it is for the other common shares.

So Common Stock increases (a credit) by

$$15,000 \text{ new shares} \times \$0.40 \text{ par} = \$6,000$$

With *any* dividend, there is a decrease (a debit) to Retained Earnings because the shareholders are receiving some of their value/equity back from the company.

In the case of a small stock dividend, this value is the *market value* of the new shares issued.

So in this case, Retained Earnings decreases (a debit) by

$$15,000 \text{ new shares} \times \$3 \text{ market price per share} = \$45,000$$

The difference between these two amounts is balanced to Paid-In Capital in Excess of Par—Common—in this case, an increase (a credit) of

$$\$45,000 - \$6,000 = \$39,000$$

| | | | | |
|---|---|---|---|---|
| Feb 1 | Retained Earnings (15,000 × $3) | | 45,000 | |
| | Paid-In Capital in Excess of Par—Common (to balance) | | | 39,000 |
| | Common Stock (15,000 × $0.40) | | | 6,000 |

All of these accounts are part of the equity section. This means that there is an equal debit (decrease) and credit (increase) impact to the equity section. We are simply shifting value from Retained Earnings to Paid-In Capital.

This means that *total* equity *does not change* as a result of this transaction.

| | Before Stock Dividend | | After Stock Dividend |
|---|---|---|---|
| Common Stock | $30,000 | | $36,000 |
| Paid-In Capital in Excess of Par | 0 | | 39,000 |
| Retained Earnings | 60,000 | | 15,000 |
| Total Equity | $90,000 | (same) | $90,000 |

## Requirement 3

**On March 1, 2011, Tinker declared and paid a cash dividend of $0.60 per common share. Journalize this dividend. How does this dividend impact stockholders' equity?**

Cash will decrease (a credit) by the amount of dividends paid. After the stock dividend of February 1, there are 75,000 + 15,000 = 90,000 shares outstanding. Therefore, the cash paid is

90,000 shares × $0.60 per share = $54,000

With *any* dividend, there is a decrease to Retained Earnings (a debit). In this case, it is a decrease of the cash paid of $54,000.

| | | | |
|---|---|---|---|
| Mar 1 | Retained Earnings | 54,000 | |
| | Cash (90,000 × $0.60) | | 54,000 |

## *DEMO DOC COMPLETE*

# Demo Doc 4

## Treasury Stock

*Learning Objective 3*

On January 1, 2009, Unter, Inc., purchased 4,000 shares of treasury stock for $10 each. At this time, Paid-In Capital, Treasury Stock had a balance of $0.

Unter sold the treasury stock as follows:

| | |
|---|---|
| April 1, 2009................... | Sold 1,000 for $12.00 cash per share |
| July 1, 2009 ................... | Sold 2,500 for $9.50 cash per share |
| October 1, 2009............. | Sold 500 for $8.25 cash per share |

### Requirements

1. **Journalize all of Unter's treasury stock transactions.**

2. **Suppose instead of holding onto the common stock purchased as treasury stock, Unter retired the stock on January 2, 2009. Would it be possible for Unter to later reissue the stock?**

# Demo Doc 4 Solutions

## Requirement 1

### Journalize all of Unter's treasury stock transactions.

**3** Describe how treasury stock affects a company

On January 1, 2009, Unter, Inc., purchased 4,000 shares of treasury stock for $10 cash each. At this time, Paid-In Capital, Treasury Stock had a balance of $0.

The Common Stock account represents all *issued* common shares. When the company purchases treasury stock, these shares are still issued but are *no longer outstanding*. To represent this decrease in the number of outstanding shares, the Treasury Stock account has a debit balance. It is a *contra equity* account.

When treasury stock is purchased, the Treasury Stock account increases (a debit) by the cost of the treasury shares:

$$4,000 \times \$10 \text{ share} = \$40,000$$

Cash decreases (a credit) by $40,000.

| Jan 1 | Treasury Stock | 40,000 | |
|---|---|---|---|
| | Cash (4,000 × $10) | | 40,000 |

### April 1, 2009: Sold 1,000 shares for $12 cash each.

Cash increases (a debit) by

$$1,000 \text{ shares} \times \$12 = \$12,000$$

Treasury Stock decreases (a credit) by the *original cost* of the treasury shares:

$$1,000 \text{ shares} \times \$10 = \$10,000$$

The difference between these two amounts is a balancing amount to Paid-In Capital from Treasury Stock Transactions of ($12,000 − $10,000) = $2,000 credit (increase).

| Apr 1 | Cash (1,000 × $12) | 12,000 | |
|---|---|---|---|
| | Paid-In Capital from Treasury Stock Transactions (to balance) | | 2,000 |
| | Treasury Stock (1,000 × $10) | | 10,000 |

**July 1, 2009: Sold 2,500 shares for $9.50 cash each.**

Cash increases (a debit) by

$$2{,}500 \text{ shares} \times \$9.50 = \$23{,}750$$

Treasury Stock decreases (a credit) by the *original cost* of the treasury shares:

$$2{,}500 \text{ shares} \times \$10 = \$25{,}000$$

The difference between these two amounts is a balancing amount to Paid-In Capital from Treasury Stock Transactions. This is a debit (decrease) of

$$\$25{,}000 - \$23{,}750 = \$1{,}250$$

Note that we *cannot* have a *debit / negative balance* in Paid-In Capital from Treasury Stock Transactions. However, from the entry on April 1, we know that there is a balance of $2,000. This is more than enough to cover a $1,250 debit.

| | | | |
|---|---|---|---|
| Jul 1 | Cash (2,500 × $9.50) | 23,750 | |
| | Paid-In Capital from Treasury Stock Transactions (to balance) | 1,250 | |
| | Treasury Stock (2,500 × $10) | | 25,000 |

After this transaction, Paid-In Capital from Treasury Stock Transactions has a balance of $750 credit:

| Paid-In Capital from Treasury Stock Transactions | | | Treasury Stock | | |
|---|---|---|---|---|---|
| | Bal | 0 | Jan 1 | 40,000 | |
| | Apr 1 | 2,000 | | | Apr 1 10,000 |
| | | | | | Mar 1 25,000 |
| Jul 1 1,250 | | | | | |
| | Bal | 750 | Bal | 5,000 | |

**October 1, 2009: Sold 500 shares for $8.25 cash each.**

Cash increases (a debit) by

$$500 \text{ shares} \times \$8.25 = \$4{,}125$$

Treasury Stock decreases (a credit) by the *original cost* of the treasury shares:

$$500 \text{ shares} \times \$10 = \$5{,}000$$

The difference between these two amounts would normally be a balancing amount to Paid-In Capital from Treasury Stock Transactions, but in this case, the difference is a debit (a decrease) of

$$\$5,000 - \$4,125 = \$875$$

There is only $750 in the Paid-In Capital from Treasury Stock Transactions account. This is not enough to cover the debit that would normally be required.

Instead, we take *as much as possible* from the Paid-In Capital from Treasury Stock Transactions account. This means that we debit for the $750 left in the account. The remaining ($875 – $750) = $125 is balanced to Retained Earnings (debit/decrease).

| | | | | |
|---|---|---|---|---|
| Oct 1 | Cash (500 × $8.25) | | 4,125 | |
| | Paid-In Capital from Treasury Stock Transactions | | 750 | |
| | Retained Earnings (to balance) | | 125 | |
| | Treasury Stock (500 × $10) | | | 5,000 |

## Requirement 2

**Suppose instead of holding onto the common stock purchased as treasury stock, Unter retired the stock on January 2, 2009. Would it be possible for Unter to later reissue the stock?**

③ Describe how treasury stock affects a company

When stock is retired, the stock certificates are *canceled*. This means that the stock ceases to exist.

Retired/canceled stock can no longer be reissued.

## *DEMO DOC COMPLETE*

# Quick Practice Questions

## True/False

_____ 1. Stockholders in a corporation are not liable for the debts of the corporation.

_____ 2. Most corporations have continuous lives regardless of changes in the ownership of their stock.

_____ 3. Par value is an arbitrary amount assigned by a company to a share of its stock.

_____ 4. When a corporation sells par-value stock at an amount greater than par value, other income is reported on the income statement.

_____ 5. Dividends become a liability of the corporation on the payment date.

_____ 6. The owners of cumulative preferred stock must receive all dividends in arrears plus the current year's dividends or the common shareholders must pay a penalty fine.

_____ 7. A stock's par value is the price for which a person could buy or sell a share of the stock.

_____ 8. The book value of a stock is the amount of stockholders' equity on the company's books for each share of its stock.

_____ 9. The return on equity measures a company's success in using assets to earn income for those financing the business.

_____ 10. A stock dividend is a distribution by a corporation of its own stock to its stockholders.

_____ 11. Stock dividends have no effect on total stockholders' equity.

_____ 12. A stock split increases the number of outstanding shares of stock and decreases the par value of the stock.

_____ 13. When treasury stock is purchased, the balance in the Common Stock account remains unchanged.

_____ 14. A corporation purchases 200 shares of its $10 par common stock for $12 per share. Subsequently, all 200 shares are resold for $13 per share. The amount of revenue from these transactions is $200.

_____ 15. Only outstanding shares of stock receive cash and stock dividends.

_____ 16. Stock dividends may cause the price of the stock to increase.

# Multiple Choice

1. **What is the document called that is used by a state to grant permission to form a corporation?**
   a. Charter
   b. Proxy
   c. Stock certificate
   d. Bylaw agreement

2. **Which of the following statements describing a corporation is not true?**
   a. Stockholders are the owners of a corporation.
   b. A corporation is subject to greater governmental regulation than a proprietorship or a partnership.
   c. When ownership of a corporation changes, the corporation does not terminate.
   d. Stockholders own the business and manage its day-to-day operations.

3. **Which of the following best describes paid-in capital?**
   a. Investments by the stockholders of a corporation
   b. Investments by the creditors of a corporation
   c. Capital that the corporation has earned through profitable operations
   d. All of the above

4. **Which of the following best describes retained earnings?**
   a. It is classified as a liability on the corporate balance sheet.
   b. It does not appear on any financial statement.
   c. It represents capital that the corporation has earned through profitable operations.
   d. It represents investments by the stockholders of a corporation.

5. **What individual(s) has/have the authority to obligate the corporation to pay dividends?**
   a. Total stockholders
   b. The board of directors
   c. The president of the company
   d. The chief executive officer

6. **Which of the following would be recorded for the issuance of 55,000 shares of no-par common stock at $13.50 per share?**
   a. Debit to Common Stock for $742,500
   b. Credit to Common Stock for $742,500
   c. Credit to Cash for $742,500
   d. Debit to Paid-In Capital in Excess of No-Par—Common for $742,500

7. **Which of the following is true for dividends?**
   a. Dividends are a distribution of cash to the stockholders.
   b. Dividends decrease both the assets and the total stockholders' equity of the corporation.
   c. Dividends increase retained earnings.
   d. Both (a) and (b) are correct.

8.  Dividends on cumulative preferred stock of $2,500 are in arrears for 2010. During 2011, the total dividends declared amount to $10,000. There are 6,000 shares of $10 par, 10% cumulative preferred stock outstanding, and 10,000 shares of $5 par common stock outstanding. What is the total amount of dividends payable to each class of stock in 2011?
    a. $5,000 to preferred, $5,000 to common
    b. $6,000 to preferred, $4,000 to common
    c. $8,500 to preferred, $1,500 to common
    d. $10,000 to preferred, $0 to common

9.  Which of the following is true about dividends in arrears?
    a. They are a liability on the balance sheet.
    b. They are dividends passed on cumulative preferred stock.
    c. They are dividends passed on noncumulative preferred stock.
    d. They are dividends passed on common stock.

10. What is the effect of a stock split on a stockholder's ownership percentage?
    a. It increases.
    b. It decreases.
    c. It can increase or decrease depending on the type of stock dividend.
    d. It will stay the same.

11. What is the ownership percentage used as a cutoff point for distinguishing between a small and a large stock dividend?
    a. 15%
    b. 10%
    c. 25%
    d. 50%

12. What entry is made to record a 10% stock dividend?
    a. Debit to Common Stock
    b. Credit to Retained Earnings
    c. Debit to Retained Earnings
    d. There is no journal entry for stock dividends.

13. What effect does the purchase of treasury stock have on the number of a corporation's shares?
    a. It causes issued shares to exceed authorized shares.
    b. It causes outstanding shares to exceed issued shares.
    c. It causes outstanding shares to exceed authorized shares.
    d. It causes outstanding shares to be less than issued shares.

14. What type of account is Treasury Stock?
    a. Contra asset
    b. Liability
    c. Contra liability
    d. Contra Stockholders' Equity account

15. What is the effect of a common stock retirement?
    a. It decreases the number of shares of common stock outstanding.
    b. It increases the balance in the Common Stock account.
    c. It decreases the number of shares of common stock issued.
    d. Both (a) and (c) are correct.

# Quick Exercises

### 9-1. Journalize the following transactions:

**a.** Firm Body Corporation sells 12,000 shares of $10 par common stock for $13.00 per share.

| | Date | Accounts | Debit | Credit |
|---|---|---|---|---|
| | | | | |
| | | | | |
| | | | | |

*General Journal*

**b.** Firm Body Corporation sells 5,000 shares of $50 par, 10% cumulative preferred stock for $59 per share.

| | Date | Accounts | Debit | Credit |
|---|---|---|---|---|
| | | | | |
| | | | | |
| | | | | |

*General Journal*

**c.** Received a building with a market value of $115,000 and issued 6,400 shares of $10 par common stock in exchange.

| | Date | Accounts | Debit | Credit |
|---|---|---|---|---|
| | | | | |
| | | | | |
| | | | | |

*General Journal*

**d.** Firm Body Corporation reports net income of $66,000 at the end of its first year of operations.

| | Date | Accounts | Debit | Credit |
|---|---|---|---|---|
| | | | | |
| | | | | |
| | | | | |

*General Journal*

**9-2.** The following is a list of stockholders' equity accounts appearing on the balance sheet for O'Neil Corporation on December 31, 2011:

| | |
|---|---:|
| Common stock, $10 par value ................................. | $300,000 |
| Paid-in capital in excess of par—common ................ | 200,000 |
| Retained earnings..................................................... | 225,000 |
| Preferred stock, $50 par value................................. | 125,000 |
| Paid-in capital in excess of par—preferred .............. | 30,000 |

**1. Determine the following:**

**a.** How many shares of preferred stock have been issued?

**b.** What was the average issuance price of the preferred stock per share?

**c.** How many shares of common stock have been issued?

**d.** What is total paid-in capital?

**e.** What is total stockholders' equity?

**9-3.** Following is the stockholders' equity section of the balance sheet for Higher Corporation as of December 1, 2011:

**Higher Corporation**
**Stockholders' Equity**
**December 1, 2011**

| | |
|---|---:|
| Paid-in capital: | |
| Preferred stock, 10% cumulative, $100 par, 10,000 authorized, | |
| 7,500 shares issued......................................................... | $ 750,000 |
| Common stock, $10 par, 200,000 shares authorized, | |
| 130,000 shares issued...................................................... | 1,300,000 |
| Paid-in capital in excess of par—common......................... | 520,000 |
| Total paid-in capital.............................................................. | $2,570,000 |
| Retained earnings.................................................................. | 450,000 |
| Total stockholders' equity..................................................... | $3,020,000 |

**Higher Corporation reports the following transactions for December 2011:**

| | |
|---|---|
| Dec 10 | Declared the required cash dividend on the preferred stock and a $0.50 dividend on the common stock. |
| 30 | Paid the dividends declared on December 10. |

## 1. Journalize the transactions.

| General Journal | | | |
|---|---|---|---|
| Date | Accounts | Debit | Credit |
|  |  |  |  |
|  |  |  |  |
|  |  |  |  |

| General Journal | | | |
|---|---|---|---|
| Date | Accounts | Debit | Credit |
|  |  |  |  |
|  |  |  |  |
|  |  |  |  |

## 2. What is the total stockholders' equity after posting the entries?

## 9-4. Sparks Corporation has gathered the following data for the current year:

| | |
|---|---|
| Net Income | $40,000 |
| Interest Expense | 6,000 |
| Income Tax Expense | 12,500 |
| Preferred Dividends | 3,600 |

| Balance Sheet Data | Beginning of year | End of year |
|---|---|---|
| Current assets | $68,000 | $81,000 |
| Current liabilities | 41,000 | 39,000 |
| Plant assets | 340,000 | 365,000 |
| Long-term liabilities | 100,000 | 90,000 |
| Common stockholders' equity | 217,000 | 267,000 |
| Preferred stockholders' equity | 50,000 | 50,000 |

## 1. Calculate return on assets.

2. Calculate return on equity.

3. Comment on how these measures are used.

9-5. Jonathan Corporation reports the following transactions for 2011.

1. Journalize these transactions.

Jan 10   Sold 6,000 shares of 9%, noncumulative $50 par, preferred stock for $85 per share.

| General Journal | | | | |
|---|---|---|---|---|
| Date | Accounts | | Debit | Credit |
| | | | | |
| | | | | |
| | | | | |

Feb 19   Sold 3,000 shares of $10 par common stock for $15 per share.

| General Journal | | | | |
|---|---|---|---|---|
| Date | Accounts | | Debit | Credit |
| | | | | |
| | | | | |
| | | | | |

Oct 12   The board announced a 15% stock dividend on the common stock. The current market price of the common stock is $22 per share. Jonathan Corporation has 120,000 shares of common stock outstanding on October 12.

| General Journal | | | | |
|---|---|---|---|---|
| Date | Accounts | | Debit | Credit |
| | | | | |
| | | | | |
| | | | | |

**9-6. Following is the stockholders' equity section of the balance sheet of Standards, Inc., as of November 1, 2011:**

### Standards, Inc.
### Stockholders' Equity
### November 1, 2011

| | |
|---|---:|
| Paid-in capital: | |
| Preferred stock, 10%, noncumulative $50 par, 10,000 authorized, | |
| 6,500 shares issued.................................................................. | $ 325,000 |
| Common stock, $10 par, 300,000 shares authorized, | |
| 120,000 shares issued............................................................. | 1,200,000 |
| Paid-in capital in excess of par—common................................. | 420,000 |
| Total paid-in capital........................................................................ | $1,945,000 |
| Retained earnings........................................................................... | 467,200 |
| Total stockholders' equity............................................................... | $2,412,200 |

**Standards, Inc., reported the following transactions during November 2011:**

| | |
|---|---|
| Nov 1 | Declared the required annual cash dividend on the preferred stock and a $0.50 dividend on the common stock. |
| 15 | Paid the dividends declared on November 1. |
| 16 | Distributed a 5% common stock dividend. The market value of the common stock is $20 per share. |
| 30 | The board of directors announced a 2-for-1 stock split. |

**1. Show the dollar amount of the effect of each transaction on both total paid-in capital and total stockholders' equity.**

| Date | Total Paid-In Capital | Total Stockholders' Equity |
|---|---|---|
| | | |
| | | |
| | | |
| | | |
| | | |
| | | |

**9-7. Victory Corporation reported the following stockholders' equity items on December 31, 2011:**

| Victory Corporation Stockholders' Equity December 31, 2011 | |
|---|---:|
| Paid-in capital: | |
| Preferred stock, 5% cumulative, $100 par, 7,000 authorized, | |
| 1,000 shares issued...................................................... | $ 100,000 |
| Paid-in capital in excess of par—preferred......................... | 55,000 |
| Common stock, $50 par, 10,000 shares authorized, | |
| 5,000 shares issued...................................................... | 250,000 |
| Paid-in capital in excess of par—common......................... | 235,000 |
| Retained earnings................................................................ | 455,300 |
| Treasury common stock, at cost, 700 shares ......................... | 96,000 |

1. **Compute the following:**

   **a.** Number of shares of common stock outstanding

   **b.** Number of shares of preferred stock outstanding

   **c.** Average issue price of common stock

   **d.** Average issue price of preferred stock

2. **Assume that Victory Corporation declares a 4-for-1 stock split. Compute the following:**

   **a.** Number of shares of common outstanding

   **b.** Par value

**9-8. Clean Wash Corporation reported the following stockholders' equity on January 1, 2011:**

### Clean Wash Corporation
### Stockholders' Equity
### January 1, 2011

| | |
|---|---|
| Paid-in capital: | |
| Preferred stock, 5% cumulative, $50 par, 30,000 authorized, | |
| 7,500 shares issued...................................................... | $ 375,000 |
| Paid-in capital in excess of par—preferred........................ | 18,750 |
| Common stock, $1 par, 200,000 shares authorized, | |
| 135,000 shares issued................................................... | 135,000 |
| Paid-in capital in excess of par—common........................ | 472,500 |
| Total paid-in capital ............................................................. | $1,001,250 |
| Retained earnings.................................................................. | 218,500 |
| Total stockholders' equity ...................................................... | $1,219,750 |

**1. On June 15, 2011, the board of directors announced a 10% common stock dividend when the market price of the stock was $6 per share. Prepare the necessary journal entry to record the stock dividend.**

| General Journal | | | |
|---|---|---|---|
| Date | Accounts | Debit | Credit |
| | | | |
| | | | |
| | | | |
| | | | |

**2. What effect did the distribution of the common stock dividend have on the following?**

**a.** Total assets

**b.** Total liabilities

**c.** Total paid-in capital

**d.** Total stockholders' equity

**9-9.** On June 1, 2011, Hauser Corporation purchased 2,600 shares of its $10 par value common stock for $12.50 per share. The 2,600 shares had originally been issued for $11.25 per share. Hauser Corporation sold 1,700 of its treasury shares on August 4, 2011, for $14.75 per share.

**1. Journalize the transactions on June 1 and August 4, 2011.**

| | General Journal | | | |
|---|---|---|---|---|
| Date | Accounts | | Debit | Credit |
| | | | | |
| | | | | |
| | | | | |
| | | | | |
| | | | | |

| | General Journal | | | |
|---|---|---|---|---|
| Date | Accounts | | Debit | Credit |
| | | | | |
| | | | | |
| | | | | |
| | | | | |

# Do It Yourself! Question 1

## Common Stock

Dinner Co. had the following information at December 31, 2010:

| Stockholders' Equity December 31, 2010 | |
| --- | --- |
| Common stock, 500,000 authorized, 50,000 issued and outstanding shares | $100,000 |
| Paid-in capital in excess of par | 50,000 |
| Total paid-in capital | 150,000 |
| Retained earnings | 400,000 |
| Total stockholders' equity | $550,000 |

## Requirements

1. What is the par value per share of the common stock?

2. On average, what was the original issue price per share of the common stock?

3. On January 9, 2011, Dinner issued another 10,000 common shares for $4 cash per share. Journalize this transaction.

| General Journal | | | |
| --- | --- | --- | --- |
| Date | Accounts | Debit | Credit |
| | | | |
| | | | |
| | | | |

# Do It Yourself! Question 2

## Preferred Stock

Lunch Corp. issued 5,000, 8%, $20 par cumulative preferred shares on January 1, 2011, for $25 cash per share. Lunch had never had preferred shares before this date. On December 31, 2011, Lunch paid $5,000 in cash dividends to its shareholders. On December 31, 2012, Lunch paid $15,000 in cash dividends to its shareholders.

### Requirements

1. Journalize the issuance of the preferred shares on January 1, 2011.

| | General Journal | | | |
|---|---|---|---|---|
| Date | Accounts | | Debit | Credit |
| | | | | |
| | | | | |
| | | | | |

2. How much in dividends is Lunch supposed to pay to the preferred shareholders each year?

3. How much of the $5,000 paid as dividends in 2011 went to the preferred and common shareholders?

4. How much of the $15,000 paid as dividends in 2012 went to the preferred and common shareholders?

# Do It Yourself! Question 3

## Stock Splits and Dividends

On December 31, 2010, Garbage, Inc., had 12,000 common shares outstanding with a market price of $8 per share and a par value of $2 per share.

### Requirements

1. On January 1, 2011, Garbage issued a 15% stock dividend. Journalize this dividend.

| | General Journal | | |
|------|----------|-------|--------|
| Date | Accounts | Debit | Credit |
| | | | |
| | | | |
| | | | |
| | | | |

2. On January 2, 2011, Garbage split its common stock 2 for 1. Journalize the split. What are the par and market values per share after the split?

| | General Journal | | |
|------|----------|-------|--------|
| Date | Accounts | Debit | Credit |
| | | | |
| | | | |
| | | | |
| | | | |

3. On January 3, 2011, Garbage declared and paid a cash dividend of $0.30 per common share. Journalize this dividend.

| | General Journal | | |
|------|----------|-------|--------|
| Date | Accounts | Debit | Credit |
| | | | |
| | | | |
| | | | |
| | | | |

# Do It Yourself! Question 4

## Treasury Stock

On January 1, 2011, Hartnick Co. purchased 1,000 shares of treasury stock for $7 cash each. At this time, Paid-In Capital, Treasury Stock had a balance of $0. Hartnick sold the treasury stock as follows:

| | |
|---|---|
| February 1, 2011............ | Sold 200 shares for $10 cash per share |
| March 1, 2011 .............. | Sold 500 shares for $6 cash per share |
| April 1, 2011................. | Sold 300 shares for $6.50 cash per share |

## Requirement

1. **Journalize all of Hartnick's treasury stock transactions.**

### General Journal

| Date | Accounts | Debit | Credit |
|---|---|---|---|
| | | | |
| | | | |
| | | | |

### General Journal

| Date | Accounts | Debit | Credit |
|---|---|---|---|
| | | | |
| | | | |
| | | | |

### General Journal

| Date | Accounts | Debit | Credit |
|---|---|---|---|
| | | | |
| | | | |
| | | | |

### General Journal

| Date | Accounts | Debit | Credit |
|---|---|---|---|
| | | | |
| | | | |
| | | | |

# Quick Practice Solutions

## True/False

T    1. Stockholders in a corporation are not liable for the debts of the corporation. (p. 535)

T    2. Most corporations have continuous lives regardless of changes in the ownership of their stock. (p. 535)

T    3. Par value is an arbitrary amount assigned by a company to a share of its stock. (p. 540)

F    4. When a corporation sells par-value stock at an amount greater than par value, other income is reported on the income statement.

       False—When a corporation sells par value stock at an amount greater than par value, paid-in capital in excess of par value is recorded. There is no effect on the income statement from a company's stock transactions. (p. 542)

F    5. Dividends become a liability of the corporation on the payment date.

       False—Dividends become a liability of the corporation on the *declaration* date. (pp. 553–554)

F    6. The owners of cumulative preferred stock must receive all dividends in arrears plus the current year's dividends or the common shareholders must pay a penalty fine.

       False—Common shareholders do not pay a penalty for non-payment of preferred share dividends. However, common shareholders cannot receive common share dividends unless the preferred share dividends (including dividends in arrears, if any) are fully paid. (p. 556)

F    7. A stock's par value is the price for which a person could buy or sell a share of the stock.

       False—A stock's *market price* is the price for which a person could buy or sell a share of the stock. (p. 559)

T    8. The book value of a stock is the amount of stockholders' equity on the company's books for each share of its stock. (p. 560)

F    9. The return on equity measures a company's success in using assets to earn income for those financing the business.

       False—The *return on total assets* measures a company's success in using assets to earn income. (p. 561)

T    10. A stock dividend is a distribution by a corporation of its own stock to its stockholders. (p. 557)

  T   11. Stock dividends have no effect on total stockholders' equity. (pp. 557, 559)

  T   12. A stock split increases the number of outstanding shares of stock and decreases the par value of the stock. (p. 558)

  T   13. When treasury stock is purchased, the balance in the Common Stock account remains unchanged. (pp. 550–551)

  F   14. A corporation purchases 200 shares of its $10 par common stock for $12 per share. Subsequently, all 200 shares are resold for $13 per share. The amount of revenue from these transactions is $200.

              False—Revenue is not recorded from a company's stock transactions. Paid-In Capital from Treasury Stock Transactions is credited for $200. (p. 551)

  T   15. Only outstanding shares of stock receive cash and stock dividends. (pp. 552–553)

  F   16. Stock dividends may cause the price of the stock to increase.

              False—Stock dividends may cause the price of the stock to *decrease* because of the increased supply of the stock. (p. 557)

# Multiple Choice

1. **What is the document called that is used by a state to grant permission to form a corporation? (p. 536)**
   a. Charter
   b. Proxy
   c. Stock certificate
   d. Bylaw agreement

2. **Which of the following statements describing a corporation is not true? (pp. 535–538)**
   a. Stockholders are the owners of a corporation.
   b. A corporation is subject to greater governmental regulation than a proprietorship or a partnership.
   c. When ownership of a corporation changes, the corporation does not terminate.
   d. Stockholders own the business and manage its day-to-day operations.

3. **Which of the following best describes paid-in capital? (p. 538)**
   a. Investments by the stockholders of a corporation
   b. Investments by the creditors of a corporation
   c. Capital that the corporation has earned through profitable operations
   d. All of the above

4. **Which of the following best describes retained earnings? (p. 538)**
   a. It is classified as a liability on the corporate balance sheet.
   b. It does not appear on any financial statement.
   c. It represents capital that the corporation has earned through profitable operations.
   d. It represents investments by the stockholders of a corporation.

5. **What individual(s) has/have the authority to obligate the corporation to pay dividends? (p. 553)**
   a. Total stockholders
   b. The board of directors
   c. The president of the company
   d. The chief executive officer

6. **Which of the following would be recorded for the issuance of 55,000 shares of no-par common stock at $13.50 per share? (p. 544)**
   a. Debit to Common Stock for $742,500
   b. Credit to Common Stock for $742,500
   c. Credit to Cash for $742,500
   d. Debit Paid-In Capital in Excess of No-Par—Common for $742,500

7. **Which of the following is true for dividends? (p. 553)**
   a. Dividends are a distribution of cash to the stockholders.
   b. Dividends decrease both the assets and the total stockholders' equity of the corporation.
   c. Dividends increase retained earnings.
   d. Both (a) and (b) are correct.

8.  Dividends on cumulative preferred stock of $2,500 are in arrears for 2010. During 2011, the total dividends declared amount to $10,000. There are 6,000 shares of $10 par, 10% cumulative preferred stock outstanding and 10,000 shares of $5 par common stock outstanding. What is the total amount of dividends payable to each class of stock in 2011? (p. 556)
    a. $5,000 to preferred, $5,000 to common
    b. $6,000 to preferred, $4,000 to common
    c. $8,500 to preferred, $1,500 to common
    d. $10,000 to preferred, $0 to common

9.  Which of the following is true about dividends in arrears? (p. 556)
    a. They are a liability on the balance sheet.
    b. They are dividends passed on cumulative preferred stock.
    c. They are dividends passed on noncumulative preferred stock.
    d. They are dividends passed on common stock.

10. What is the effect of a stock split on a stockholder's ownership percentage? (p. 557)
    a. It increases.
    b. It decreases.
    c. It can increase or decrease depending on the type of stock dividend.
    d. It will stay the same.

11. What is the ownership percentage used as a cutoff point for distinguishing between a small and a large stock dividend? (p. 557)
    a. 15%
    b. 10%
    c. 25%
    d. 50%

12. What entry is made to record a 10% stock dividend? (p. 557)
    a. Debit to Common Stock
    b. Credit to Retained Earnings
    c. Debit to Retained Earnings
    d. There is no journal entry for stock dividends.

13. What effect does the purchase of treasury stock have on the number of a corporation's shares? (p. 550)
    a. It causes issued shares to exceed authorized shares.
    b. It causes outstanding shares to exceed issued shares.
    c. It causes outstanding shares to exceed authorized shares.
    d. It causes outstanding shares to be less than issued shares.

14. What type of account is Treasury Stock? (p. 550)
    a. Contra asset
    b. Liability
    c. Contra liability
    d. Contra Stockholders' Equity account

15. What is the effect of a common stock retirement? (p. 552)
    a. It decreases the number of shares of common stock outstanding.
    b. It increases the balance in the Common Stock account.
    c. It decreases the number of shares of common stock issued.
    d. Both (a) and (c) are correct.

# Quick Exercises

**9-1. Journalize the following transactions:** (pp. 542–547)

**a.** Firm Body Corporation sells 12,000 shares of $10 par common stock for $13.00 per share.

| | Date | Accounts | Debit | Credit |
|---|---|---|---|---|
| | | **General Journal** | | |
| a. | | Cash | 156,000 | |
| | | Common Stock | | 120,000 |
| | | Paid-In Capital in Excess of Par—Common | | 36,000 |

**b.** Firm Body Corporation sells 5,000 shares of $50 par, 10% cumulative preferred stock for $59 per share.

| | Date | Accounts | Debit | Credit |
|---|---|---|---|---|
| | | **General Journal** | | |
| b. | | Cash | 295,000 | |
| | | Preferred Stock | | 250,000 |
| | | Paid-In Capital in Excess of Par—Preferred | | 45,000 |

**c.** Received a building with a market value of $115,000 and issued 6,400 shares of $10 par common stock in exchange.

| | Date | Accounts | Debit | Credit |
|---|---|---|---|---|
| | | **General Journal** | | |
| c. | | Building | 115,000 | |
| | | Common Stock | | 64,000 |
| | | Paid-In Capital in Excess of Par—Common | | 51,000 |

**d.** Firm Body Corporation reports net income of $66,000 at the end of its first year of operations.

| | Date | Accounts | Debit | Credit |
|---|---|---|---|---|
| | | **General Journal** | | |
| d. | | Income Summary | 66,000 | |
| | | Retained Earnings | | 66,000 |

**9-2.** The following is a list of stockholders' equity accounts appearing on the balance sheet for O'Neil Corporation on December 31, 2011:

| | |
|---|---:|
| Common stock, $10 par value ............................ | $300,000 |
| Paid-in capital in excess of par—common ............ | 200,000 |
| Retained earnings.................................................. | 225,000 |
| Preferred stock, $50 par value............................. | 125,000 |
| Paid-in capital in excess of par—preferred ........... | 30,000 |

1. **Determine the following:** (pp. 542–547)

   **a.** How many shares of preferred stock have been issued?

   $125,000/$50 = 2,500

   **b.** What was the average issuance price of the preferred stock per share?

   ($125,000 + $30,000)/2,500 = $62

   **c.** How many shares of common stock have been issued?

   $300,000/$10 = 30,000

   **d.** What is total paid-in capital?

   $300,000 + $200,000 + $125,000 + $30,000 = $655,000

   **e.** What is total stockholders' equity?

   $655,000 + $225,000 = $880,000

**9-3. Following is the stockholders' equity section of the balance sheet for Higher Corporation as of December 1, 2011:**

**Higher Corporation**
**Stockholders' Equity**
**December 1, 2011**

| | |
|---|---:|
| Paid-in capital: | |
| Preferred stock, 10% cumulative, $100 par, 10,000 authorized, | |
| 7,500 shares issued...................................................... | $ 750,000 |
| Common stock, $10 par, 200,000 shares authorized, | |
| 130,000 shares issued.................................................. | 1,300,000 |
| Paid-in capital in excess of par—common......................... | 520,000 |
| Total paid-in capital................................................... | $2,570,000 |
| Retained earnings....................................................... | 450,000 |
| Total stockholders' equity............................................ | $3,020,000 |

**Higher Corporation reports the following transactions for December 2011:** (pp. 553–556)

| | |
|---|---|
| Dec 10 | Declared the required cash dividend on the preferred stock and a $0.50 dividend on the common stock. |
| 30 | Paid the dividends declared on December 10. |

**1. Journalize the transactions.**

Preferred Share Dividend = 10% × $750,000 = $ 75,000
Common Share Dividend = $0.50 × 130,000 = $ 65,000
$140,000

**General Journal**

| Date | Accounts | Debit | Credit |
|---|---|---|---|
| 12/10/11 | Retained Earnings | 140,000 | |
| | Dividends Payable | | 140,000 |

**General Journal**

| Date | Accounts | Debit | Credit |
|---|---|---|---|
| 12/30/11 | Dividends Payable | 140,000 | |
| | Cash | | 140,000 |

**2. What is the total stockholders' equity after posting the entries?**

$3,020,000 − $140,000 = $2,880,000

**9-4. Sparks Corporation has gathered the following data for the current year:** (pp. 561–562)

| | |
|---|---|
| Net Income ............................... | $40,000 |
| Interest Expense ....................... | 6,000 |
| Income Tax Expense ............... | 12,500 |
| Preferred Dividends................. | 3,600 |

| Balance Sheet Data | Begining of Year | End of Year |
|---|---|---|
| Current assets.................................... | $68,000 | $81,000 |
| Current liabilities .............................. | 41,000 | 39,000 |
| Plant assets....................................... | 340,000 | 365,000 |
| Long-term liabilities ......................... | 100,000 | 90,000 |
| Common stockholders' equity........... | 217,000 | 267,000 |
| Preferred stockholders' equity .......... | 50,000 | 50,000 |

## 1. Calculate return on assets.

$40,000 + $6,000 = $46,000
$46,000/$427,000* = 10.8%

*$68,000 + $340,000 = $408,000
$81,000 + $365,000 = $446,000
$408,000 + $446,000 = $854,000
$854,000/2 = $427,000

## 2. Calculate return on equity.

$40,000 − $3,600 = $36,400
$36,400/$242,000* = 15.0%

*$217,000 + $267,000 = $484,000
$484,000/2 = $242,000

## 3. Comment on how these measures are used.

The return on assets is used as a standard profitability measure that shows the company's success in using its assets to generate income. It helps investors compare one company to another, especially within the same industry.

The return on equity is used as a standard profitability measure that shows the relationship between net income and average common stockholders' equity. The higher the rate of return, the more successful the company.

## 9-5. Jonathan Corporation reports the following transactions for 2011. (pp. 542–547, 557)

### 1. Journalize these transactions.

**Jan 10  Sold 6,000 shares of 9%, noncumulative $50 par, preferred stock for $85 per share.**

| General Journal | | | |
|---|---|---|---|
| Date | Accounts | Debit | Credit |
| Jan 10 | Cash | 510,000 | |
| | Preferred Stock | | 300,000 |
| | Paid-In Capital in Excess of Par—Preferred | | 210,000 |

**Feb 19  Sold 3,000 shares of $10 par common stock for $15 per share.**

| General Journal | | | |
|---|---|---|---|
| Date | Accounts | Debit | Credit |
| Feb 19 | Cash | 45,000 | |
| | Common Stock | | 30,000 |
| | Paid-In Capital in Excess of Par—Common | | 15,000 |

**Oct 12  The board announced a 15% stock dividend on the common stock. The current market price of the common stock is $22 per share. Jonathan Corporation has 120,000 shares of common stock outstanding on October 12.**

| General Journal | | | |
|---|---|---|---|
| Date | Accounts | Debit | Credit |
| Oct 12 | Retained Earnings | 396,000 | |
| | Common Stock | | 180,000 |
| | Paid-In Capital in Excess of Par—Common | | 216,000 |

**9-6. Following is the stockholders' equity section of the balance sheet of Standards, Inc., as of November 1, 2011:**
(pp. 553–554, 557–558)

| Standards, Inc.<br>Stockholders' Equity<br>November 1, 2011 | |
|---|---|
| Paid-in capital: | |
| Preferred stock, 10% noncumulative $50 par, 10,000 authorized, 6,500 shares issued........................................... | $ 325,000 |
| Common stock, $10 par, 300,000 shares authorized, 120,000 shares issued.................................................... | 1,200,000 |
| Paid-in capital in excess of par—common.......................... | 420,000 |
| Total paid-in capital ................................................................ | $1,945,000 |
| Retained earnings..................................................................... | 467,200 |
| Total stockholders' equity ....................................................... | $2,412,200 |

**Standards, Inc., reported the following transactions during November 2011:**

| Nov | 1 | Declared the required cash dividend on the preferred stock and a $0.50 dividend on the common stock. |
|---|---|---|
| | 15 | Paid the dividends declared on November 1. |
| | 16 | Distributed a 5% common stock dividend. The market value of the common stock is $20 per share. |
| | 30 | The board of directors announced a 2-for-1 stock split. |

**1. Show the dollar amount of the effect of each transaction on both total paid-in capital and total stockholders' equity.**

| Date | Total Paid-In Capital | Total Stockholders' Equity |
|---|---|---|
| Nov 1 | No effect | Decrease of $92,500* |
| Nov 15 | No effect | No effect |
| Nov 16 | Increase of $120,000 | No effect |
| Nov 30 | No effect | No effect |

*Preferred Share Dividend = 10% × $325,000 = $32,500
Common Share Dividend = $0.50 × 120,000 = $60,000
$92,500

**9-7. Victory Corporation reported the following stockholders' equity items on December 31, 2011:** (pp. 543, 558)

|  |  |
|---|---|
| **Victory Corporation** | |
| **Stockholders' Equity** | |
| **December 31, 2011** | |
| Paid-in capital: | |
|    Preferred stock, 5% cumulative, $100 par, 7,000 | |
|      authorized, 1,000 shares issued................................... | $ 100,000 |
|    Paid-in capital in excess of par—preferred........................ | 55,000 |
|    Common stock, $50 par, 10,000 shares authorized, | |
|      5,000 shares issued....................................................... | 250,000 |
|    Paid-in capital in excess of par—common......................... | 235,000 |
| Retained earnings................................................................. | 455,300 |
| Treasury common stock, at cost, 700 shares.......................... | 96,000 |

## 1. Compute the following:

**a.** Number of shares of common stock outstanding

> $250,000/$50 per share = 5,000 shares issued
> $5,000 shares − 700 shares = 4,300 shares outstanding

**b.** Number of shares of preferred stock outstanding

> $100,000/$100 per share = 1,000 shares

**c.** Average issue price of common stock

> $250,000 + $235,000 = $485,000
> $485,000/5,000 shares = $97 per share

**d.** Average issue price of preferred stock

> $100,000 + $55,000 = $155,000
> $155,000/1,000 shares = $155 per share

**2. Assume that Victory Corporation declares a 4-for-1 stock split. Compute the following:**

**a.** Number of shares of common outstanding

4,300 shares × 4 = 17,200

**b.** Par value

$50/4 = $12.50

**9-8. Clean Wash Corporation reported the following stockholders' equity on January 1, 2011:** (p. 557)

|  |  |
|---|---|
| **Clean Wash Corporation** | |
| **Stockholders' Equity** | |
| **January 1, 2011** | |

| | |
|---|---:|
| Paid-in capital: | |
| Preferred stock, 5% cumulative, $50 par, 30,000 | |
|    authorized, 7,500 shares issued.................................... | $ 375,000 |
| Paid-in capital in excess of par—preferred........................ | 18,750 |
| Common stock, $1 par, 200,000 shares authorized, | |
|    135,000 shares issued.................................................... | 135,000 |
| Paid-in capital in excess of par—common......................... | 472,500 |
| Total paid-in capital............................................................... | $1,001,250 |
| Retained earnings.................................................................. | 218,500 |
| Total stockholders' equity..................................................... | $1,219,750 |

**1. On June 15, 2011, the board of directors announced a 10% common stock dividend when the market price of the stock was $6 per share. Prepare the necessary journal entry to record the stock dividend.**

| General Journal | | | | |
|---|---|---|---:|---:|
| Date | Accounts | | Debit | Credit |
| Jun 15 | Retained Earnings | | 81,000 | |
| | Common Stock | | | 13,500 |
| | Paid-In Capital in Excess of Par—Common | | | 67,500 |

2. **What effect did the distribution of the common stock dividend have on the following?**

   **a.** Total assets
   No effect
   **b.** Total liabilities
   No effect
   **c.** Total paid-in capital
   Increase of $81,000
   **d.** Total stockholders' equity
   No effect

**9-9.** On June 1, 2011, Hauser Corporation purchased 2,600 shares of its $10 par value common stock for $12.50 per share. The 2,600 shares had originally been issued for $11.25 per share. Hauser Corporation sold 1,700 of its treasury shares on August 4, 2011, for $14.75 per share. (pp. 550–552)

1. **Journalize the transactions on June 1 and August 4, 2011.**

| General Journal | | | |
|---|---|---|---|
| Date | Accounts | Debit | Credit |
| Jun 1 | Treasury Stock | 32,500 | |
| | Cash | | 32,500 |

| General Journal | | | |
|---|---|---|---|
| Date | Accounts | Debit | Credit |
| Aug 4 | Cash | 25,075 | |
| | Treasury Stock | | 21,250 |
| | Paid-In Capital from Treasury Stock Transactions | | 3,825 |

# Do It Yourself! Question 1 Solutions

## Common Stock

### Requirements

1. **What is the par value per share of the common stock?**

$$\text{Par value per share} = \frac{\$100,000}{50,000 \text{ shares}}$$

$$= \$2 \text{ per share}$$

2. **On average, what was the original issue price per share of the common stock?**

Total cash received from issuance of the common shares (par + paid-in capital in excess of par) is

$$\$100,000 + \$50,000 = \$150,000$$

$$\frac{\$150,000}{50,000 \text{ shares}} = \$3 \text{ cash received per share}$$

3. **On January 9, 2011, Dinner issued another 10,000 common shares for $4 cash per share. Journalize this transaction.**

| | | | | |
|---|---|---|---|---|
| Jan 9 | Cash ($4 × 10,000) | | 40,000 | |
| | Paid-In Capital in Excess of Par—Common (to balance) | | | 20,000 |
| | Common Stock ($2 × 10,000) | | | 20,000 |

$4 paid – $2 par = $2 excess cash
$2 excess cash × 10,000 shares = Paid-In Captial in Excess of Par, $20,000 balancing amount

# Do It Yourself! Question 2 Solutions

## Preferred Stock

**1. Journalize the issuance of the preferred shares on January 1, 2011.**

| | | | |
|---|---|---|---|
| Jan 1 | Cash ($25 × 5,000) | 125,000 | |
| | Paid-In Capital in Excess of Par—Preferred (to balance) | | 25,000 |
| | Preferred Stock ($20 × 5,000) | | 100,000 |

**2. How much in dividends is Lunch supposed to pay to the preferred shareholders each year?**

Preferred shareholders are *supposed* to receive the following:

$20 par × 8% = $1.60 per share annually
$1.60 × 5,000 = $8,000 dividends per year for all outstanding preferred shares

**3. How much of the $5,000 paid as dividends in 2011 went to the preferred and common shareholders?**

The full $8,000 was not paid; therefore, the entire $5,000 goes to the preferred shareholders. Common shareholders get nothing.

$8,000 − $5,000 = $3,000 of dividends in arrears

**4. How much of the $15,000 paid as dividends in 2012 went to the preferred and common shareholders?**

Preferred shareholders received the following:

$8,000 + $3,000 = $11,000

Common shareholders received the following:

$15,000 − $11,000 = $4,000

# Do It Yourself! Question 3 Solutions

## Stock Splits and Dividends

### Requirements

1. **On January 1, 2011, Garbage issued a 15% stock dividend. Journalize this dividend.**

   Number of new shares issued for stock dividend = 12,000 × 15% = 1,800 new shares

   | | | | | |
   |---|---|---|---|---|
   | Jan 1 | Retained Earnings (1,800 × $8) | | 14,400 | |
   | | Paid-In Capital in Excess of Par—Common (to balance) | | | 10,800 |
   | | Common Stock (1,800 × $2) | | | 3,600 |

2. **On January 2, 2011, Garbage split its common stock 2 for 1. Journalize the split. What are the par and market values per share after the split?**

   Common shares before split = 12,000 + 1,800 = 13,800
   Number of shares after stock split = 13,800 × 2/1 = 27,600 shares
   Par value per share after split = $2 × 1/2 = $1
   Market price per share after split = $8 × 1/2 = $4

There is no journal entry for a stock split.

3. **On January 3, 2011, Garbage declared and paid a cash dividend of $0.30 per common share. Journalize this dividend.**

   | | | | | |
   |---|---|---|---|---|
   | Jan 3 | Retained Earnings | | 8,280 | |
   | | Cash (27,600 × $0.30) | | | 8,280 |

# Do It Yourself! Question 4 Solutions

## Treasury Stock

### Requirement

1. **Journalize all of Hartnick's treasury stock transactions.**

On January 1, 2011, Hartnick Co. purchased 1,000 shares of treasury stock for $7 cash each. At this time, Paid-In Capital, Treasury Stock had a balance of $0.

| | | | |
|---|---|---|---|
| Jan 1 | Treasury Stock | 7,000 | |
| | Cash (1,000 × $7) | | 7,000 |

February 1, 2011: Sold 200 shares for $10 cash each.

| | | | |
|---|---|---|---|
| Feb 1 | Cash ($200 × $10) | 2,000 | |
| | Paid-In Capital from Treasury Stock Transactions (to balance) | | 600 |
| | Treasury Stock (200 × $7) | | 1,400 |

March 1, 2011: Sold 500 shares for $6 cash each.

| | | | |
|---|---|---|---|
| Mar 1 | Cash (500 × $6) | 3,000 | |
| | Paid-In Capital from Treasury Stock Transactions (to balance) | 500 | |
| | Treasury Stock (500 × $7) | | 3,500 |

After this transaction,

| Paid-In Capital from Treasury Stock Transactions | | | | Treasury Stock | | | |
|---|---|---|---|---|---|---|---|
| | | Bal | 0 | Jan 1 | 7,000 | | |
| | | Feb 1 | 600 | | | Feb 1 | 1,400 |
| | | | | | | Mar 1 | 3,500 |
| Mar 1 | 500 | | | | | | |
| | | Bal | 100 | Bal | 2,100 | | |

April 1, 2011: Sold 300 shares for $6.50 cash each.

| | | | |
|---|---|---|---|
| Apr 1 | Cash (300 × $6.50) | 1,950 | |
| | Paid-In Capital from Treasury Stock Transactions | 100 | |
| | Retained Earnings (to balance) | 50 | |
| | Treasury Stock (300 × $7) | | 2,100 |

# The Power of Practice

For more practice using the skills learned in this chapter, visit MyAccountingLab. There you will find algorithmically generated questions that are based on these Demo Docs and your main textbook's Review and Assess Your Progress sections.

Go to MyAccountingLab and follow these steps:

1. Direct your URL to www.myaccountinglab.com.
2. Log in using your name and password.
3. Click the MyAccountingLab link.
4. Click Study Plan in the left navigation bar.
5. From the table of contents, select Chapter 9, Stockholders' Equity.
6. Click a link to work tutorial exercises.

# 10 Long-Term Investments & International Operations

## WHAT YOU PROBABLY ALREADY KNOW

You probably already know that if you have excess cash, it is a good idea to invest this money. You could put this money into a bank account, or you could purchase an investment, such as some stocks or a bond.

Corporations face this same issue and the same potential types of investments. In this chapter, you will learn to account for these types of investments from a corporation's point of view.

Additional issues exist when a business purchases common shares of another business. Companies may buy each other's stock not for short-term gains, but to achieve long-term business goals, which could include outright ownership of other companies.

Perhaps you recently took a trip to a foreign country. Did you notice that the exchange rates for U.S. currency fluctuated between the date you planned the trip and the date you traveled, causing the trip to be more or less expensive than you planned? This chapter also discusses the impact on financial statements of doing business across international borders.

## Learning Objectives

 **Account for available-for-sale investments**

Stock investments where the company owns less than 20% of the invested business, and where the company may or may not intend to sell them quickly, are classified as available-for-sale investments. These investments can be short-term or long-term in nature.

Available-for-sale investments are adjusted to market value for reporting on the balance sheet; the unrealized gain or loss is either recognized on the income statement as part of other comprehensive income, or recognized directly in equity on the balance sheet. *Examine the financial statement impact of available-for-sale investments on pp. 606–610.*

 **Use the equity method for investments**

Stock investments where the company owns between 20% and 50% of the invested business are classified as equity-method investments. The company that owns such investments is not concerned about the stock price of the invested business, but rather the company's performance as a whole. The purpose of owning such large investments is to influence the operations of the invested business.

The value of equity-method investments is affected by the net income earned by the investee company, as well as any dividends the investee's business might pay out. Unlike available-for-sale investments, there is *no* adjustment to market value. *Review the T-account for entries affecting equity-method investments on p. 612.*

### 3 Understand consolidated financial statements

When a company owns more than 50% of another business, it *controls* the investee's business. This means that it has the final say on how the investee business operates. Because this investee business (the "subsidiary") is under the complete control of the owning company (the "parent"), its financial information is combined/consolidated with that of the parent company, so that all of the accounting information can be seen on one set of financial statements. *Examine the Consolidated Balance Sheet work sheet in Exhibit 10-8 (p. 615).*

### 4 Account for long-term investments in bonds

Some investments have a defined life, such as bonds. All bonds have maturity dates that signal the final payment of face value, and the time at which they stop accruing interest. If a company purchases such investments with the intention of keeping them until their life is over, they are called held-to-maturity investments.

Held-to-maturity investments are treated in a manner similar to that used for bonds payable. The difference is that investments are assets, so instead of having Bonds Payable and Interest Expense accounts, the company has Bond Investment and Interest Revenue accounts. *Review the journal entries for held-to-maturity investments on p. 618.*

### 5 Account for international operations

It is common for large companies to do business abroad. This can lead to revenues and expenses being incurred in foreign currencies, as well as foreign accounts receivable and payable. It is important to understand how such transactions impact the account data reported to U.S. stockholders. *Review foreign currency transactions on pp. 624–625.*

### 6 Report investing transactions on the statement of cash flows

Cash flows relating to long-term investments are reported on the statement of cash flows in the investing activities section. Purchases of investments are a decrease to cash flow, while sales of investments are an increase to cash flow. *Review the presentation of the investing activities section of the statement of cash flows in Exhibit 10-12 (p. 628).*

# Demo Doc 1

## Long-Term Investments

*Learning Objectives 1, 2, 3, 4, 6*

On January 1, 2009, Unity Corp. purchased the following long-term investments for cash:

| | |
|---|---|
| 20,000 shares Lake Corp. stock .............. | $60,000 |
| 4,000 shares Drop Corp. stock................. | $10,000 |

Both Lake and Drop have 50,000 common shares outstanding.
During 2009, Lake and Drop had the following information:

| | Net Income | Cash Dividends per Share | Market Price per Share at 12/31/09 |
|---|---|---|---|
| Lake Corp.................. | $120,000 | $0.70 | $2.50 |
| Drop Corp. ............... | $ 60,000 | $0.60 | $3.00 |

## Requirements

1. What kind of investments are these?

2. For each investment, journalize the following transactions for Unity Corp.:

   a. Purchase of investments on January 1, 2009
   b. Dividends received from the investments during 2009
   c. Any adjustment for net income earned by the investments
   d. Any adjustment for the investments' year-end market price

3. What impact does the Lake Corp. investment have on Unity's investing cash flows for 2009?

4. Suppose Unity purchased another 10,000 shares of Lake Corp. Would this still be the same kind of investment for Unity? Why or why not?

5. Unity purchased a bond issued by Drop Corp. and intended to hold it until it matured in 2015. The bond had a face value of $3,000 and was priced at 102. Give the journal entry for the purchase of the bond with cash. Does this purchase impact the investment in Drop stock?

# Demo Doc 1 Solutions

## Requirement 1

**1** Account for available-for-sale investments

**2** Use the equity method for investments

**What kind of investments are these?**

In order to determine the investment type, we need to know what percentage of the company Unity holds.

$$\% \text{ Ownership} = \frac{\# \text{ of shares held by investor company}}{\text{Total } \# \text{ of outstanding common shares of investee company}}$$

$$\% \text{ Ownership of Lake Corp.} = \frac{20{,}000 \text{ shares}}{50{,}000 \text{ shares}}$$

$$= 40\%$$

An investment between 20% and 50% ownership is an **equity method** investment. The Lake Corp. shares are an equity method investment.

$$\% \text{ Ownership of Drop Corp.} = \frac{4{,}000 \text{ shares}}{50{,}000 \text{ shares}}$$

$$= 8\%$$

An investment less than 20% ownership is an **available-for-sale** investment. The Drop Corp. shares are an available-for-sale investment.

## Requirement 2

**1** Account for available-for-sale investments

**2** Use the equity method for investments

**For each investment, journalize the following transactions for Unity Corp.:**

**a. Purchase of investments on January 1, 2009**
**Lake Corp.**

Cash is decreased (a credit) by $60,000.
    Equity-Method Investment—Lake Corp. is increased (a debit) by $60,000.

| | | |
|---|---|---|
| Equity-Method Investment—Lake Corp. | 60,000 | |
|     Cash | | 60,000 |

**Drop Corp.**

Cash is decreased (a credit) by $10,000.

| | | |
|---|---|---|
| Long-Term Available-for-Sale Investment—Drop Corp. | 10,000 | |
|     Cash | | 10,000 |

Long-Term Available-for-Sale Investment—Drop Corp. is increased (a debit) by $10,000.

**b. Dividends received from the investments during 2009**

**Lake Corp.**

Cash is received, so it is increased (a debit) by

$0.70 per share × 20,000 shares = $14,000

Under the equity method, we are trying to capture changes in Lake Corp.'s *equity,* or more accurately, its *retained earnings.* It is as if Unity has purchased a piece of Lake's retained earnings. As Lake's retained earnings change in value, so does Unity's investment in Lake Corp.

| | | |
|---|---|---|
| Cash ($0.70 × 20,000) | 14,000 | |
| Equity-Method Investment—Lake Corp. | | 14,000 |

When Lake Corp. pays a dividend, its retained earnings decrease. This means that the value of Unity's Lake Corp. Investment has also decreased (a debit) by $14,000.

| Lake Corp. Investment | | |
|---|---|---|
| Jan 1 | 60,000 | |
| | | 14,000 dividends received |
| Bal | 46,000 | |

**Drop Corp.**

Cash is received, so it is increased (a debit) by

$0.60 per share × 4,000 shares = $2,400

For available-for-sale investments, *Dividend Revenue* is also increased (a credit) by $2,400.

| | | |
|---|---|---|
| Cash ($0.60 × 4,000) | 2,400 | |
| Dividend Revenue | | 2,400 |

Notice that the Drop Corp. Investment (available-for-sale) recorded the dividends received as *Dividend Revenue,* while the value of the Lake Corp. Investment was decreased.

### c. Any adjustment for net income earned by the investments

**Lake Corp.**

When Lake Corp. earns net income, its retained earnings increases. This means that under the equity method, the value of Unity's investment in Lake Corp. *also* increases.

Equity-Method Investment—Lake Corp. is increased (a debit) by Unity's share of Lake's net income:

$$40\% \times \$120,000 = \$48,000$$

Unity's share of Lake's net income also impacts Unity's net income. The $48,000 is also recorded as Equity-Method Investment Revenue (a credit) on Unity's income statement.

| | | |
|---|---|---|
| Equity-Method Investment—Lake Corp. (40% × $120,000) | 48,000 | |
| Equity-Method Investment Revenue | | 48,000 |

**Lake Corp. Investment**

| | | | |
|---|---|---|---|
| Jan 1 | 60,000 | | 14,000 dividends received |
| | 48,000 net income | | |
| Bal | 94,000 | | |

### Drop Corp.

Available-for-sale investments do *not* adjust for net income. *Instead,* they adjust for year-end market price (see transaction **d**). There is no entry for Drop Corp.

### d. Any adjustment for the investments' year-end market price

**Lake Corp.**

Equity-method investments do *not* adjust for year-end market price. *Instead,* they adjust for net income (see transaction **c**). There is no entry for Lake Corp.

### Drop Corp.

We are required to adjust the value of available-for-sale investments to market price at year-end (for presentation on the balance sheet).

This means that we must adjust the Drop Corp. Investment from its original balance of $10,000 to its new fair market value:

$$\$3 \text{ market price per share} \times 4,000 \text{ shares} = \$12,000$$

The Drop Corp. Investment has increased in value by

$$\$12,000 - \$10,000 = \$2,000$$

However, instead of adjusting the investment account directly, we adjust an *allowance* account. In this way, we are able to keep a record of the original cost of the investment in the Drop Corp. Investment account, yet report the investment at market price on the balance sheet (by combining it with the allowance account).

So the Allowance to Adjust Investments to Market account is increased (a debit) by $2,000.

This increase is an *unrealized* gain (a credit) of $2,000. We know that the gain is unrealized because there is no cash involved in the transaction to ensure that the gain is "real." In the case of available-for-sale investments, we are uncertain because the stock was not actually sold. Market prices change constantly and today's gain could be tomorrow's loss. We emphasize this uncertainty on the income statement by highlighting this gain as an *unrealized* (paper) gain.

| | | |
|---|---|---|
| Allowance to Adjust Investment to Market | 2,000 | |
| Unrealized Gain [($3 × 4,000) − $10,000] | | 2,000 |

## Requirement 3

**What impact does the Lake Corp. investment have on Unity's investing cash flows for 2009?**

Purchases and sales of investments impact investing activities on the statement of cash flows. Because the Lake Corp. investment was purchased for $60,000, there would be an investing cash outflow of $60,000.

Note that the cash dividends received do *not* impact investing cash flows. Dividends received are dividend revenue, which is included as part of net income. Therefore, dividend revenues, through net income, are a part of *operating* cash flows.

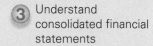

6 Report investing transactions on the statement of cash flows

## Requirement 4

**Suppose Unity purchased another 10,000 shares of Lake Corp. Would this still be the same kind of investment for Unity? Why or why not?**

If Unity purchased another 10,000 shares, then they would own a total of 20,000 + 10,000 = 30,000 shares. Because Lake only has 50,000 shares outstanding, this percentage ownership is now 30,000/50,000 = 60% ownership.

Ownership of greater than 50% of another business indicates complete control. This would now be a consolidation investment, and Unity would be required to consolidate Lake Corp.'s accounting information into their financial statements.

3 Understand consolidated financial statements

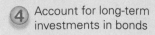

## Requirement 5

**Unity purchased a bond issued by Drop Corp. and intended to hold it until it matured in 2015. The bond had a face value of $3,000 and was priced at 102. Give the journal entry for the purchase of the bond with cash. Does this purchase impact the investment in Drop stock?**

Because Unity is planning on holding the bond until it matures, this would be classified as a held-to-maturity investment.

This investment is *not* the same as the available-for-sale investment in Drop Corp.'s stock, and would *not* impact the stock investment.

Unity purchased the bond at 102, which means that Unity paid 102% of face value for the bond. Therefore, $102\% \times \$3,000 = \$3,060$ of cash was paid for the bond investment. This results in a decrease to Cash of $3,060.

The bond is an investment asset, so Long-Term Investment in Bonds (an asset) would be increased by the purchase price of $3,060.

| | | |
|---|---|---|
| Long-Term Investment in Bonds | 3,060 | |
| Cash ($3,000 × 102%) | | 3,060 |

Notice that even though this bond was purchased at a premium, the premium is *not* recorded as a separate account. For bond investments, premiums and discounts are combined with the investment into a single, net, asset account.

### DEMO DOC COMPLETE

# Demo Doc 2

## Consolidations

*Learning Objective 3*

Nambu Corp. purchased all outstanding common stock (i.e., 100%) of Hakase, Inc., for $200,000 on January 1, 2009. On April 30, 2009, Hakase loaned $40,000 to Nambu. The two businesses' balance sheets are as follows:

### Nambu Corp. and Hakase, Inc.
### Balance Sheet
### December 31, 2009

|  | Nambu Corp. | Hakase, Inc. |
|---|---|---|
| Cash & Other Assets............................. | $600,000 dr | $190,000 dr |
| Loan Receivable from Nambu................ | — | 40,000 dr |
| Investment in Hakase............................ | 200,000 dr | — |
| | | |
| Loan Payable to Hakase......................... | 40,000 cr | — |
| Other Liabilities ..................................... | 200,000 cr | 30,000 cr |
| | | |
| Common Stock ....................................... | 160,000 cr | 50,000 cr |
| Retained Earnings ................................. | 400,000 cr | 150,000 cr |

## Requirement

1. Prepare the consolidated balance sheet of Nambu Corp.

# Demo Doc 2 Solutions

## Requirement 1

③ Understand consolidated financial statements

**Prepare the consolidated balance sheet of Nambu Corp.**

First, we need to eliminate all inter-company transactions. What are the inter-company transactions? We know that Hakase loaned money to Nambu. So we must get rid of the associated receivable and payable.

To eliminate/remove the Loan Receivable, which is a debit balance, we have to credit it. To eliminate/remove the Loan Payable, which is a credit balance, we have to debit it. So the journal entry to do this is

| 1. | Loan Payable to Hakase | 40,000 | |
|----|------------------------|--------|--------|
|    | Loan Receivable from Nambu | | 40,000 |

This journal entry is *not* recorded in Nambu's accounting books. It is *not* recorded in Hakase's accounting books. It is recorded in a special set of accounting books kept *only* for consolidating accounting records. In their own internal records, Hakase still has a receivable and Nambu still has a payable. It is *only* the consolidated records that eliminate these accounts.

Next, we have to remove/eliminate the equity accounts of the subsidiary company, Hakase. Hakase has Common Stock and Retained Earnings, which are credit balances. So to eliminate these accounts, we have to debit them:

| Common Stock | 50,000 | | (the amount of Hakase's common stock) |
|--------------|--------|-----|----------------------------------------|
| Retained Earnings | 150,000 | | (the amount of Hakase's retained earnings) |
| ??? | | ??? | |

Of course, this journal entry doesn't balance. We need some credits. What else do we have to do? We have to remove/eliminate the Investment in Hakase account from Nambu's records. Because this is an asset account, it has a debit balance, so to get rid of it we have to credit. Let's put this into our journal entry:

| 2. | Common Stock | 50,000 | |
|----|--------------|--------|---------|
|    | Retained Earnings | 150,000 | |
|    | Investment in Hakase | | 200,000 |

This balances, so our journal entry is complete. Again, this entry does *not* go into Nambu's books, nor does it go into Hakase's books. It goes into a special set of accounting books, which is kept *only* for consolidated financial statements.

Let's put these entries into an Eliminations column, on a consolidation work sheet. If you want, you can think of this as "posting" these entries. Next, we add all of the numbers across, to calculate the consolidated amounts. Remember that debits and credits are opposites, so they cancel each other out.

### Nambu Corp.
### Consolidated Worksheet
### December 31, 2009

| | Nambu Corp. | Hakase, Inc. | Eliminations Debit | Eliminations Credit | Consolidated |
|---|---|---|---|---|---|
| Cash & Other Assets............................. | $600,000 dr | $190,000 dr | | | $790,000 dr |
| Loan Receivable from Nambu................ | — | 40,000 dr | | 1.  40,000 | 0 |
| Investment in Hakase............................ | 200,000 dr | — | | 2. 200,000 | 0 |
| Loan Payable to Hakase......................... | 40,000 cr | — | 1.  40,000 | | 0 |
| Other Liabilities .................................... | 200,000 cr | 30,000 cr | | | 230,000 cr |
| Common Stock ...................................... | 160,000 cr | 50,000 cr | 2.  50,000 | | 160,000 cr |
| Retained Earnings ................................. | 400,000 cr | 150,000 cr | 2. 150,000 | | 400,000 cr |

Cash and Other Assets = 790,000 dr = 600,000 dr + 190,000 dr

Loan Receivable from Nambu = 0 = 40,000 dr + 40,000 cr

Investment in Hakase = 0 = 200,000 dr + 200,000 cr

Loan Payable to Hakase = 0 = 40,000 cr + 40,000 dr

Other Liabilities = 230,000 cr = 200,000 cr + 30,000 cr

Common Stock = 160,000 cr = 160,000 cr + 50,000 cr + 50,000 dr

Retained Earnings = 400,000 cr = 400,000 cr + 150,000 cr + 150,000 dr

# Demo Doc 3

## Foreign Currency Transactions

*Learning Objective 5*

Global Industries had the following transactions during 2009:

a. Performed services on account for a Jordanian company for 40,000 dinar. $1 U.S. = 2.00 dinar.

b. Purchased equipment from an Egyptian company on account for 300,000 Egyptian pounds. 1 pound = $0.17 U.S.

c. Adjusted for a change in the value of the dinar. $1 U.S. now = 1.60 dinar.

d. Paid for the equipment when 1 pound = $0.16 U.S.

e. Received cash from the Jordanian company when $1 U.S. = 2.50 dinar.

### Requirements

1. Journalize these transactions for Global Industries.

2. Based on these 2009 transactions, identify whether the dinar, the pound, and the U.S. dollar are strong or weak.

# Demo Doc 3 Solutions

**Journalize these transactions for Global Industries.**

(5) Account for international operations

**a. Performed services on account for a Jordanian company for 40,000 dinar. $1 U.S. = 2.00 dinar.**

For this *initial* transaction (that is, *before* there has been any fluctuation in exchange rates), we can simply journalize the entry as usual with the calculated U.S. dollar amount.

> $1 U.S. = 2.00 dinar
> therefore 1 dinar = $1/2.00 = $0.50 U.S.

When Global performs services, they are earning service revenue. This increases (a credit) Service Revenue by

> 40,000 × $0.50 = $20,000

Accounts Receivable is also increased (a debit) by $20,000.

| | | |
|---|---|---|
| Accounts Receivable (40,000 dinar × $0.50 U.S.) | 20,000 | |
| Service Revenue | | 20,000 |

**b. Purchased equipment from an Egyptian company on account for 300,000 Egyptian pounds. 1 pound = $0.17 U.S.**

Again, with this *initial* transaction, we can analyze the entry as usual.
Equipment is increased (a debit) by

> 300,000 × $0.17 = $51,000

Accounts Payable is also increased (a credit) by $51,000.

| | | |
|---|---|---|
| Equipment (300,000 pounds × $0.17 U.S.) | 51,000 | |
| Accounts Payable | | 51,000 |

**c. Adjusted for a change in the value of the dinar. $1 U.S. now = 1.60 dinar.**

An adjustment will obviously change the value of the account receivable; however, it will *not* change the value of the service revenue. No new revenue has been earned (or unearned); instead, this adjustment is due to foreign currency fluctuations beyond Global's control. Therefore, the balance to the Accounts Receivable adjustment will be a foreign-currency transaction gain or loss.

$$\begin{array}{c} \text{\$1 U.S. now} = 1.60 \text{ dinar} \\ \text{therefore 1 dinar} = \$1/1.60 = \$0.625 \text{ U.S.} \end{array}$$

The account receivable from the Jordanian company is now worth

$$40,000 \times \$0.625 = \$25,000$$

Because the receivable is recorded at \$20,000, we must increase Accounts Receivable (a debit) by

$$\$25,000 - \$20,000 = \$5,000$$

The corresponding credit (a balancing amount) goes to Foreign-Currency Transaction Gain (gain because it is a *credit*).

| | | |
|---|---|---|
| Accounts Receivable [(40,000 dinar × \$0.625) − \$20,000] | 5,000 | |
| Foreign-Currency Transaction Gain (to balance) | | 5,000 |

## d. Paid for the equipment when 1 pound = \$0.16 U.S.

The equipment was sold for 300,000 pounds and they expect to receive 300,000 pounds.

If 1 pound now = \$0.16 U.S., the amount of the account payable is now

$$300,000 \times \$0.16 = \$48,000$$

Therefore, Cash is decreased (a credit) by \$48,000.

The liability is completely satisfied, so Accounts Payable *must* be decreased (a debit) by the full \$51,000 (because there is no longer any liability to pay).

The difference is a balancing amount to Foreign-Currency Transaction Gain of

$$\$51,000 - \$48,000 = \$3,000$$

In this case, the balancing amount is a credit, which is a gain.

| | | |
|---|---|---|
| Accounts Payable | 51,000 | |
| Cash (300,000 pounds × \$0.16 U.S.) | | 48,000 |
| Foreign-Currency Transaction Gain (to balance) | | 3,000 |

Notice it is *not* that the contract has changed, it is the value of the *U.S. dollar* that has changed.

**e. Received cash from the Jordanian company when $1 U.S. = 2.50 dinar.**

$1 U.S. now = 2.50 dinar
therefore 1 dinar = $1/2.50 = $0.40 U.S.

If 1 dinar now = $0.40 U.S., the account receivable is now

40,000 × $0.40 = $16,000

Therefore, Cash is increased (a debit) by $16,000.

The receivable is completely collected, so Accounts Receivable *must* be decreased (a credit) by the full $25,000 (because there is no longer any further amount to collect).

The difference is a balancing amount to Foreign-Currency Transaction Loss of

$16,000 − $25,000 = −$9,000

In this case, the balancing amount is a debit, which is a loss.

| | | | |
|---|---|---|---|
| Cash (40,000 dinar × $0.40 U.S.) | 16,000 | |
| Foreign-Currency Transaction Loss (to balance) | 9,000 | |
| Accounts Receivable | | 25,000 |

## Requirement 2

**Based on these 2009 transactions, identify whether the dinar, the pound, and the U.S. dollar are strong or weak.**

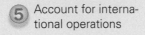
5  Account for international operations

The dinar went from $0.50 U.S. to $0.625 U.S. to $0.40 U.S. This means that over time, the dinar became less valuable as compared to the U.S. dollar. Therefore, the dinar is **weakening** when compared to the U.S. dollar.

The pound went from $0.17 U.S. to $0.16 U.S. This means that over time, the pound became less valuable as compared to the U.S. dollar. Therefore, the pound is **weakening** when compared to the U.S. dollar.

The U.S. dollar became more valuable relative to the pound, and more valuable as compared to the dinar. So the U.S. dollar is strong.

*DEMO DOC COMPLETE*

# Quick Practice Questions

## True/False

_____ 1. A stock investment could never be classified as a held-to-maturity investment.

_____ 2. Available-for-sale investments can only be classified as current assets.

_____ 3. The Allowance to Adjust Investment to Market account is a companion account that is used with the Short-Term Investment account to bring the investment's carrying amount to current fair market value.

_____ 4. An investor with a stock holding less than 20% of the investee's voting stock may significantly influence decisions on dividends, product lines, and other important matters.

_____ 5. Companies owning more than 50% of the outstanding stock in a subsidiary prepare consolidated financial statements.

_____ 6. Noncontrolling (minority) interest is that portion of a subsidiary's stock that is owned by stockholders other than the parent company.

_____ 7. Goodwill is the excess of the cost to acquire another company over the sum of the market value of its net assets.

_____ 8. Held-to-maturity investments are reported on the balance sheet at amortized cost.

_____ 9. A foreign-currency transaction gain or loss occurs when the exchange rate changes between the date an order is placed and the date the merchandise is received.

_____ 10. If the U.S. dollar value of a Russian ruble is $0.035 on January 1 and increases to $0.037 on February 1, the U.S. dollar has weakened.

_____ 11. Accounting for business activities across national boundaries is called international accounting.

# Multiple Choice

1. **How are available-for-sale securities reported on the balance sheet?**
   a. At fair market value as either current assets or long-term investments on the balance sheet
   b. At fair market value as current assets on the balance sheet
   c. At cost as current assets on the balance sheet
   d. At lower of cost or market as current assets on the balance sheet

2. **Where would a gain on the sale of an available-for-sale investment appear on the financial statements?**
   a. On the income statement as part of other gains and losses
   b. On the balance sheet as a current asset
   c. On the income statement as an operating revenue
   d. On the balance sheet as an equity account

3. **The entry to record dividends received from an available-for-sale investment includes which of the following?**
   a. A debit to Long-Term Investment
   b. A credit to Dividend Revenue
   c. A credit to Long-Term Investment
   d. A credit to Unrealized Gain on Investment

4. **A short-term investment has been properly classified by the investor as an available-for-sale investment. If the stock was bought on June 17, 2011, for $10,000, and it is now worth $13,500 on December 31, 2011, which of the following will occur?**
   a. A direct increase of $3,500 to Retained Earnings that is not reported on the income statement.
   b. Dividend Revenue of $3,500 is reported on the income statement.
   c. A $3,500 unrealized gain would appear on the balance sheet.
   d. The short-term investment will appear on the balance sheet at $10,000 on December 31.

5. **Which of the following accounting treatments for available-for-sale investments is in accordance with GAAP?**
   a. Available-for-sale investments are reported on the balance sheet at historical cost.
   b. Available-for-sale investments are reported at historical cost and adjusted to fair market value at year-end.
   c. Available-for-sale investments are reported on the balance sheet at fair market value.
   d. The Available-for-Sale Investment account should be adjusted to its fair market value on the balance sheet date and the realized gain or loss of adjusting from cost to market should be shown on the income statement.

6. **McGovern Corp. owns 45% of the stock of Mather Corp. Mather Corp. declares and pays cash dividends of $45,000 to McGovern Corp. Which of the following will occur on the books of McGovern Corp.?**
   a. The investment in Mather Corp. on the balance sheet will increase by $45,000.
   b. Dividend revenue of $45,000 will be reported on the income statement.
   c. The investment in Mather Corp. on the balance sheet will decrease by $45,000.
   d. A gain of $45,000 will be reported on the income statement.

7. **Which of the following is not true for available-for-sale investments?**
   a. Holding gains and losses on available-for-sale investments are not included as part of net income.
   b. Available-for-sale investments can be classified as short-term or long-term.
   c. Available-for-sale investments are intended to be sold in the very near future.
   d. Available-for-sale investments include all short-term stock investments other than trading securities.

8. **On January 1, 2011, Investor Company acquired 25% of the 20,000 shares of common stock of Investee Company and had significant influence over Investee Company. On December 31, 2011, Investee Company reported net income of $100,000. What account should Investor Company debit?**
   a. Long-Term Equity-Method Investment for $25,000
   b. Cash for $25,000
   c. Long-Term Equity-Method Investment for $100,000
   d. Cash for $100,000

9. **White Corp. purchased $20,000 of 8% bonds on March 1, 2011, for a purchase price of 90. White expects to hold the bonds until their maturity date, March 1, 2016. Interest on the bonds will be paid every March 1 and September 1 until maturity. Assuming the premium or discount is amortized every interest payment using straight-line amortization, how much interest revenue will be recorded by White on September 1, 2011?**
   a. $1,200
   b. $1,000
   c. $800
   d. $600

10. **A U.S. company sells merchandise to a British firm for 100,000 British pounds. Assume the exchange rates for the British pound were as follows:**

**Date of sale: $1.54**

**Date of collection: $1.53**

**Date merchandise resold by British firm: $1.52**

**What is the foreign-currency transaction gain or loss for the U.S. company on this transaction?**

a. $2,000 gain

b. $1,000 loss

c. $3,000 gain

d. $3,000 loss

## Quick Exercises

**10-1.** Zipper Corporation engaged in the following transactions involving long-term available-for-sale investments in 2011. Journalize these transactions.

**Jun 14** Purchased 3,500 shares of Button Corporation common stock for $13 per share.

| | General Journal | | |
|---|---|---|---|
| Date | Accounts | Debit | Credit |
| | | | |
| | | | |

**Sep 15** Button Corporation pays a $0.65 per share dividend to all common stockholders.

| | General Journal | | |
|---|---|---|---|
| Date | Accounts | Debit | Credit |
| | | | |
| | | | |

**Dec 31** The market price of Button Corporation stock is $13.75 per share.

| | General Journal | | |
|---|---|---|---|
| Date | Accounts | Debit | Credit |
| | | | |
| | | | |

**10-2.** John Corporation purchased 250,000 shares of Deere Corporation common stock on January 2, 2011, for $550,000. Deere Corporation has 625,000 shares outstanding. Deere Corporation earned net income of $330,000 and paid dividends of $100,000 during 2011.

a. What method should be used to account for the Deere Corporation investment?

b. How much revenue will be recorded by John Corporation in 2011 from its investment in Deere Corporation?

**c.** What is the balance in John Corporation's investment account at the end of 2011?

**d.** Assume all of the preceeding facts except that on January 2, 2011, John Corporation purchased 75,000 shares of Deere Corporation. How much revenue will be recorded by John Corporation in 2011 from its investment in Deere Corporation?

**10-3.** **On October 1, 2011, Ace Company paid $52,400 to purchase $50,000 of bonds that carry an 8% interest rate and will mature five years from the date of purchase. Interest on the bonds is paid September 30 and March 31 of each year. The company plans to hold the bonds until maturity and amortizes the premium or discount on bonds using the straight-line method each interest payment date. As of December 31, 2011, the bonds had a market value of $53,500.**

**1. Prepare all necessary journal entries for 2011 dealing with the investment in bonds.**

| | General Journal | | | |
|---|---|---|---|---|
| Date | Accounts | | Debit | Credit |
| | | | | |
| | | | | |
| | | | | |

| | General Journal | | | |
|---|---|---|---|---|
| Date | Accounts | | Debit | Credit |
| | | | | |
| | | | | |

| | General Journal | | | |
|---|---|---|---|---|
| Date | Accounts | | Debit | Credit |
| | | | | |
| | | | | |
| | | | | |

**2. Show how the bonds would be presented on the balance sheet at December 31, 2011.**

10-4. The Helms Company engaged in the following transactions during 2011.

1. Prepare the journal entries necessary to record each of the following transactions.

**Apr 1**  Purchased merchandise from a Mexican supplier at a cost of 100,000 pesos. The exchange rate on this date was $0.08 per peso.

| | Date | Accounts | Debit | Credit |
|---|------|----------|-------|--------|
| General Journal | | | | |
| | | | | |
| | | | | |
| | | | | |

**May 5**  Paid for the merchandise purchased on April 1. The exchange rate on this date was $0.07 per peso.

| | Date | Accounts | Debit | Credit |
|---|------|----------|-------|--------|
| General Journal | | | | |
| | | | | |
| | | | | |
| | | | | |

**Jun 10**  Sold goods to a Canadian buyer at a selling price of $83,000 Canadian dollars. The exchange rate on this date was $0.87 U.S. for each Canadian dollar.

| | Date | Accounts | Debit | Credit |
|---|------|----------|-------|--------|
| General Journal | | | | |
| | | | | |
| | | | | |

**Jul 30**  Received payment from the Canadian buyer for the goods sold on June 10. The exchange rate on this date was $0.85 U.S. for each Canadian dollar.

| General Journal | | | |
|---|---|---|---|
| Date | Accounts | Debit | Credit |
| | | | |
| | | | |
| | | | |

2. During the periods of time covered by the transactions, was the U.S. dollar getting stronger or weaker relative to the Mexican peso and the Canadian dollar?

# Do It Yourself! Question 1

## Long-Term Investments

On January 1, 2011, Giant Co. purchased the following investments for cash:

| | |
|---|---|
| 10,000 shares Rock Co. stock..................... | $15,000 |
| 40,000 shares Boulder Co. stock............... | $240,000 |

Both Rock and Boulder have 100,000 common shares outstanding.

During 2011, Rock and Boulder had the following information:

| | Net Income | Cash Dividends per Share | Market Price per Share at 12/31/11 |
|---|---|---|---|
| Rock Co..................... | $100,000 | $0.20 | $1.40 |
| Boulder Co................. | $350,000 | $0.50 | $6.50 |

## Requirements

1. What kind of investments are these?

2. For *each* investment, journalize the following transactions for Giant Co.:

    **a.** Purchase of investments on January 1, 2011

| General Journal | | | | |
|---|---|---|---|---|
| Date | Accounts | | Debit | Credit |
| | | | | |
| | | | | |
| | | | | |

| General Journal | | | | |
|---|---|---|---|---|
| Date | Accounts | | Debit | Credit |
| | | | | |
| | | | | |
| | | | | |

**b.** Dividends received from the investments during 2011

| General Journal | | | |
|---|---|---|---|
| Date | Accounts | Debit | Credit |
| | | | |
| | | | |
| | | | |
| | | | |

| General Journal | | | |
|---|---|---|---|
| Date | Accounts | Debit | Credit |
| | | | |
| | | | |
| | | | |
| | | | |

**c.** Any adjustment for net income earned by the investment

| General Journal | | | |
|---|---|---|---|
| Date | Accounts | Debit | Credit |
| | | | |
| | | | |
| | | | |
| | | | |

| General Journal | | | |
|---|---|---|---|
| Date | Accounts | Debit | Credit |
| | | | |
| | | | |
| | | | |
| | | | |

**d.** Any adjustment for the investment's year-end market price

| General Journal | | | | |
|---|---|---|---|---|
| Date | Accounts | | Debit | Credit |
| | | | | |
| | | | | |
| | | | | |
| | | | | |

| General Journal | | | | |
|---|---|---|---|---|
| Date | Accounts | | Debit | Credit |
| | | | | |
| | | | | |
| | | | | |
| | | | | |

# Do It Yourself! Question 2

## Foreign-Currency Transactions

### Requirement

1. Journalize the following transactions for Omni, Inc.:

    **a.** Performed services on account for a French company for 2,000 euro. 1 euro = $1.31 U.S.

| | General Journal | | | |
|---|---|---|---|---|
| Date | Accounts | | Debit | Credit |
| | | | | |
| | | | | |
| | | | | |
| | | | | |

    **b.** Purchased machinery from a Japanese company on account for 800,000 yen. 1 yen = $0.009 U.S.

| | General Journal | | | |
|---|---|---|---|---|
| Date | Accounts | | Debit | Credit |
| | | | | |
| | | | | |
| | | | | |
| | | | | |

    **c.** Adjusted for a change in the value of the euro. 1 euro now = $1.38 U.S.

| | General Journal | | | |
|---|---|---|---|---|
| Date | Accounts | | Debit | Credit |
| | | | | |
| | | | | |
| | | | | |
| | | | | |

    **d.** Paid for the machinery when 1 yen = $0.0089 U.S.

| | General Journal | | | |
|---|---|---|---|---|
| Date | Accounts | | Debit | Credit |
| | | | | |
| | | | | |
| | | | | |
| | | | | |

**e.** Received cash from the French company when 1 euro = $1.42 U.S.

| General Journal | | | |
|------|----------|-------|--------|
| Date | Accounts | Debit | Credit |
| | | | |
| | | | |
| | | | |
| | | | |

# Quick Practice Solutions

## True/False

**T**    1. A stock investment could never be classified as a held-to-maturity investment. (p. 617)

**F**    2. Available-for-sale investments can only be classified as current assets.

       False—Available-for-sale investments can be classified as current assets *or* long-term assets. (p. 606)

**F**    3. The Allowance to Adjust Investment to Market account is a companion account that is used with the Short-Term Investment account to bring the investment's carrying amount to current fair market value.

       False—The Allowance to Adjust Investment to Market account is a companion account that is used with the *Available-for-Sale account* to bring the investment's carrying amount to fair market value. (p. 608)

**F**    4. An investor with a stock holding less than 20% of the investee's voting stock may significantly influence decisions on dividends, product lines, and other important matters.

       False—An investor holding *between 20% and 50%* of an investee's voting stock has significant influence. (p. 610)

**T**    5. Companies owning more than 50% of the outstanding stock in a subsidiary prepare consolidated financial statements. (p. 613)

**T**    6. Noncontrolling (minority) interest is that portion of a subsidiary's stock that is owned by stockholders other than the parent company. (p. 616)

**T**    7. Goodwill is the excess of the cost to acquire another company over the sum of the market value of its net assets. (p. 616)

**T**    8. Held-to-maturity investments are reported on the balance sheet at amortized cost. (pp. 617–618)

**F**    9. A foreign-currency transaction gain or loss occurs when the exchange rate changes between the date an order is placed and the date the merchandise is received.

       False—A foreign-currency transaction gain or loss occurs when the exchange rate changes between the date of purchase and date of *payment*. (pp. 624–625)

____F____ 10. If the U.S. dollar value of a Russian ruble is $0.035 on January 1 and increases to $0.037 on February 1, the U.S. dollar has weakened.

False—If the U.S. dollar value of a Russian ruble is $0.035 on January 1 and increases to $0.037 on February 1, the U.S. dollar has *strengthened*. (pp. 624–625)

____T____ 11. Accounting for business activities across national boundaries is called international accounting. (p. 622)

# Multiple Choice

1. **How are available-for-sale securities reported on the balance sheet?** (p. 608)
   a. At fair market value as either current assets or long-term investments on the balance sheet
   b. At fair market value as current assets on the balance sheet
   c. At cost as current assets on the balance sheet
   d. At lower of cost or market as current assets on the balance sheet

2. **Where would a gain on the sale of an available-for-sale investment appear on the financial statements?** (pp. 609–610)
   a. On the income statement as part of other gains and losses
   b. On the balance sheet as a current asset
   c. On the income statement as an operating revenue
   d. On the balance sheet as an equity account

3. **The entry to record dividends received from an available-for-sale investment includes which of the following?** (p. 607)
   a. A debit to Long-Term Investment
   b. A credit to Dividend Revenue
   c. A credit to Long-Term Investment
   d. A credit to Unrealized Gain on Investment

4. **A short-term investment has been properly classified by the investor as an available-for-sale investment. If the stock was bought on June 17, 2011, for $10,000, and it is now worth $13,500 on December 31, 2011, which of the following will occur?** (p. 608)
   a. A direct increase of $3,500 to Retained Earnings that is not reported on the income statement.
   b. Dividend Revenue of $3,500 is reported on the income statement.
   c. A $3,500 unrealized gain would appear on the balance sheet.
   d. The short-term investment will appear on the balance sheet at $10,000 on December 31.

5. **Which of the following accounting treatments for available-for-sale investments is in accordance with GAAP?** (p. 609)
   a. Available-for-sale investments are reported on the balance sheet at historical cost.
   b. Available-for-sale investments are reported at historical cost and adjusted to fair market value at year-end.
   c. Available-for-sale investments are reported on the balance sheet at fair market value.
   d. The Available-for-Sale Investment account should be adjusted to its fair market value on the balance sheet date and the realized gain or loss of adjusting from cost to market should be shown on the income statement.

6. **McGovern Corp. owns 45% of the stock of Mather Corp. Mather Corp. declares and pays cash dividends of $45,000 to McGovern Corp. Which of the following will occur on the books of McGovern Corp.? (pp. 611–612)**
   a. The investment in Mather Corp. on the balance sheet will increase by $45,000.
   b. Dividend revenue of $45,000 will be reported on the income statement.
   c. The investment in Mather Corp. on the balance sheet will decrease by $45,000.
   d. A gain of $45,000 will be reported on the income statement.

7. **Which of the following is not true for available-for-sale investments? (pp. 606–607)**
   a. Holding gains and losses on available-for-sale investments are not included as part of net income.
   b. Available-for-sale investments can be classified as short-term or long-term.
   c. Available-for-sale investments are intended to be sold in the very near future.
   d. Available-for-sale investments include all short-term stock investments other than trading securities.

8. **On January 1, 2011, Investor Company acquired 25% of the 20,000 shares of common stock of Investee Company and had significant influence over Investee Company. On December 31, 2011, Investee Company reported net income of $100,000. What account should Investor Company debit? (pp. 611–612)**
   a. Long-Term Equity-Method Investment for $25,000
   b. Cash for $25,000
   c. Long-Term Equity-Method Investment for $100,000
   d. Cash for $100,000

9. **White Corp. purchased $20,000 of 8% bonds on March 1, 2011, for a purchase price of 90. White expects to hold the bonds until their maturity date, March 1, 2016. Interest on the bonds will be paid every March 1 and September 1 until maturity. Assuming the premium or discount is amortized every interest payment using straight-line amortization, how much interest revenue will be recorded by White on September 1, 2011? (pp. 617–618)**
   a. $1,200
   b. $1,000
   c. $800
   d. $600

10. **A U.S. company sells merchandise to a British firm for 100,000 British pounds. Assume the exchange rates for the British pound were as follows:**

**Date of sale: $1.54**

**Date of collection: $1.53**

**Date merchandise resold by British Firm: $1.52**

**What is the foreign-currency transaction gain or loss for the U.S. company on this transaction?** (pp. 624–625)
a. $2,000 gain
b. $1,000 loss
c. $3,000 gain
d. $3,000 loss

# Quick Exercises

**10-1. Zipper Corporation engaged in the following transactions involving long-term available-for-sale investments in 2011. Journalize these transactions.** (pp. 607–609)

**Jun 14    Purchased 3,500 shares of Button Corporation common stock for $13 per share.**

| General Journal | | | |
|---|---|---|---|
| Date | Accounts | Debit | Credit |
| Jun 14 | Long-Term Available-for-Sale Investment | 45,500 | |
| | Cash | | 45,500 |

**Sep 15    Button Corporation pays a $0.65 per share dividend to all common stockholders.**

| General Journal | | | |
|---|---|---|---|
| Date | Accounts | Debit | Credit |
| Sep 15 | Cash | 2,275 | |
| | Dividend Revenue | | 2,275 |

**Dec 31    The market price of Button Corporation stock is $13.75 per share.**

| General Journal | | | |
|---|---|---|---|
| Date | Accounts | Debit | Credit |
| Dec 31 | Allowance to Adjust Investment to Market | 2,625 | |
| | Unrealized Gain on Available-for-Sale Investment | | 2,625 |

**10-2. John Corporation purchased 250,000 shares of Deere Corporation common stock on January 2, 2011, for $550,000. Deere Corporation has 625,000 shares outstanding. Deere Corporation earned net income of $330,000 and paid dividends of $100,000 during 2011.** (pp. 610–612)

a. What method should be used to account for the Deere Corporation investment?

Equity method

b. How much revenue will be recorded by John Corporation in 2011, from its investment in Deere Corporation?

$$\$330,000 \times (250,000/625,000) = \$132,000$$

c. What is the balance in John Corporation's investment account at the end of 2011?

$$\$550,000 + \$132,000 - (\$100,000 \times 250,000/625,000) = \$682,000 - \$40,000 = \$642,000$$

**d.** Assume all of the preceeding facts except that on January 2, 2011, John Corporation purchased 75,000 shares of Deere Corporation. How much revenue will be recorded by John Corporation in 2011 from its investment in Deere Corporation?

$100,000 × (75,000/625,000) = $12,000

**10-3. On October 1, 2011, Ace Company paid $52,400 to purchase $50,000 of bonds that carry an 8% interest rate and will mature five years from the date of purchase. Interest on the bonds is paid September 30 and March 31 of each year. The company plans to hold the bonds until maturity and amortizes the premium or discount on bonds using the straight-line method each interest payment date. As of December 31, 2011, the bonds had a market value of $53,500.** (pp. 617–618)

**1. Prepare all necessary journal entries for 2011 dealing with the investment in bonds.**

| General Journal | | | |
|---|---|---|---|
| Date | Accounts | Debit | Credit |
| Oct 1 | Long-Term Investment in Bonds | 52,400 | |
| | Cash | | 52,400 |

| General Journal | | | |
|---|---|---|---|
| Date | Accounts | Debit | Credit |
| Dec 31 | Interest Receivable | 1,000 | |
| | Interest Revenue ($50,000 × 0.08 × 3/12) | | 1,000 |

| General Journal | | | |
|---|---|---|---|
| Date | Accounts | Debit | Credit |
| Dec 31 | Interest Revenue | 120 | |
| | Long-Term Investment in Bonds ($2,400 × 3/60) | | 120 |

**2. Show how the bonds would be presented on the balance sheet at December 31, 2011.**

The investment in bonds would be classified as a long-term investment on the balance sheet.

| | |
|---|---|
| Long-term investments: | |
| Long-term investment in bonds................. | $52,280 |

**10-4. The Helms Company engaged in the following transactions during 2011.** (pp. 624–625)

**1. Prepare the journal entries necessary to record each of the following transactions.**

**Apr 1**   **Purchased merchandise from a Mexican supplier at a cost of 100,000 pesos. The exchange rate on this date was $0.08 per peso.**

| General Journal | | | |
|---|---|---|---|
| Date | Accounts | Debit | Credit |
| Apr 1 | Inventory | 8,000 | |
| | Accounts Payable | | 8,000 |

**May 5**   **Paid for the merchandise purchased on April 1. The exchange rate on this date was $0.07 per peso.**

| General Journal | | | |
|---|---|---|---|
| Date | Accounts | Debit | Credit |
| May 5 | Accounts Payable | 8,000 | |
| | Foreign-Currency Transaction Gain | | 1,000 |
| | Cash | | 7,000 |

**Jun 10**   **Sold goods to a Canadian buyer at a selling price of $83,000 Canadian dollars. The exchange rate on this date was $0.87 U.S. dollars for each Canadian dollar.**

| General Journal | | | |
|---|---|---|---|
| Date | Accounts | Debit | Credit |
| Jun 10 | Accounts Receivable | 72,210 | |
| | Sales Revenue | | 72,210 |

**Jul 30** Received payment from the Canadian buyer for the goods sold on June 10. The exchange rate on this date was $0.85 U.S. dollars for each Canadian dollar.

| | General Journal | | |
|---|---|---|---|
| Date | Accounts | Debit | Credit |
| Jul 30 | Cash | 70,550 | |
| | Foreign-Currency Transaction Loss | 1,660 | |
| | Accounts Receivable | | 72,210 |

**2. During the periods of time covered by the transactions, was the U.S. dollar getting stronger or weaker relative to the Mexican peso and the Canadian dollar?**

During the periods of time covered by the transactions, the U.S. dollar strengthened relative to the Mexican peso and the Canadian dollar.

# Do It Yourself! Question 1 Solutions

## Long-Term Investments

### Requirements

1. What kind of investments are these?

The Rock Co. shares are an **available-for-sale investment**.

$$\% \text{ Ownership of Rock Co.} = \frac{10,000 \text{ shares}}{100,000 \text{ shares}}$$

$$= 10\%$$

The Boulder Co. shares are an **equity-method investment**.

$$\% \text{ Ownership of Boulder Co.} = \frac{40,000 \text{ shares}}{100,000 \text{ shares}}$$

$$= 40\%$$

2. For *each* investment, journalize the following transactions for Giant Co.:

### a. Purchase of investments on January 1, 2011

**Rock Co.**

| | | | |
|---|---|---|---|
| Available-for-Sale Investment—Rock Co. | | 15,000 | |
| Cash | | | 15,000 |

**Boulder Co.**

| | | | |
|---|---|---|---|
| Equity-Method Investment—Boulder Co. | | 240,000 | |
| Cash | | | 240,000 |

### b. Dividends received from the investments during 2011

**Rock Co.**

| | | | |
|---|---|---|---|
| Cash ($0.20 × 10,000) | | 2,000 | |
| Dividend Revenue | | | 2,000 |

**Boulder Co.**

| | | | |
|---|---|---|---|
| Cash ($0.50 × 40,000) | | 20,000 | |
| | Equity-Method Investment—Boulder Co. | | 20,000 |

### c. Any adjustment for net income earned by the investment

**Rock Co.**

No entry.

**Boulder Co.**

| | | | |
|---|---|---|---|
| Equity-Method Investment—Boulder Co. (40% × $350,000) | | 140,000 | |
| | Equity-Method Investment Revenue | | 140,000 |

### d. Any adjustment for the investment's year-end market price

**Rock Co.**

| | | | |
|---|---|---|---|
| Unrealized Loss [$15,000 – ($1.40 × 10,000)] | | 1,000 | |
| | Allowance to Adjust Investment to Market | | 1,000 |

**Boulder Co.**

No entry.

# Do It Yourself! Question 2 Solutions

## Foreign-Currency Transactions

1. Journalize the following transactions for Omni, Inc.:

a. **Performed services on account for a French company for 2,000 euro. 1 euro = $1.31 U.S.**

| | | |
|---|---|---|
| Accounts Receivable (2,000 euro × $1.31 U.S.) | 2,620 | |
| Service Revenue | | 2,620 |

b. **Purchased machinery from a Japanese company on account for 800,000 yen. 1 yen = $0.009 U.S.**

| | | |
|---|---|---|
| Machinery (800,000 yen × $0.009 U.S.) | 7,200 | |
| Accounts Payable | | 7,200 |

c. **Adjusted for a change in the value of the euro. 1 euro now = $1.38 U.S.**

| | | |
|---|---|---|
| Accounts Receivable (2,000 euro × $1.38 U.S. − $2,620) | 140 | |
| Foreign-Currency Transaction Gain (to balance) | | 140 |

d. **Paid for the machinery when 1 yen = $0.0089 U.S.**

If 1 yen now = $0.0089 U.S., the account payable is

$$800,000 \times \$0.0089 = \$7,120$$

| | | |
|---|---|---|
| Accounts Payable | 7,200 | |
| Cash (800,000 yen × $0.0089 U.S.) | | 7,120 |
| Foreign-Currency Transaction Gain (to balance) | | 80 |

**e. Received cash from the French company when 1 euro = $1.42 U.S.**

If 1 euro now = 1.42 U.S., the account receivable is

$$2,000 \times \$1.42 = \$2,840$$

| | | | |
|---|---|---|---|
| Cash (2,000 euro × $1.42 U.S.) | 2,840 | |
| Foreign-Currency Transaction Gain (to balance) | | 80 |
| Accounts Receivable (2,620 + 140) | | 2,760 |

# The Power of Practice

For more practice using the skills learned in this chapter, visit MyAccountingLab. There you will find algorithmically generated questions that are based on these Demo Docs and your main textbook's Review and Assess Your Progress sections.

Go to MyAccountingLab and follow these steps:

1. Direct your URL to www.myaccountinglab.com.
2. Log in using your name and password.
3. Click the MyAccountingLab link.
4. Click Study Plan in the left navigation bar.
5. From the table of contents, select Chapter 10, Long-Term Investments & International Operations.
6. Click a link to work tutorial exercises.

# 11 The Income Statement & the Statement of Stockholders' Equity

## WHAT YOU PROBABLY ALREADY KNOW

You already know that the income statement shows the calculation of income. However, it is possible to have *more than one* income number on the income statement.

Suppose you want to predict a company's income for next year. Where would you start? Most likely, you would want to begin with *this year's* income. However, the net income number for this year may include items that will *not* be present in next year's net income.

You probably already know that it can be helpful to look at past history to predict the future. Let's assume that you want to join a gym that will cost you $50 a month. You have decided that, although you have savings, you don't want to join if you can't afford to pay for it from your normal monthly earnings. Before you sign the contract, you may calculate your monthly finances. Assume you looked at the previous month's financial activity and found the following:

| Revenues: | | Expenses: | |
|---|---|---|---|
| Wages earned and received from employer .. | $ 850 | Rent and utilities............ | $625 |
| | | Insurance and gas .......... | 75 |
| Birthday gifts ............................................. | 200 | College application fee... | 100 |
| | | Food and entertainment. | 150 |
| Total revenues: ................................................ | $1,050 | Total Expenses: .................. | $950 |

Although there is an excess of revenues over expenses of $100, it cannot be assumed that this is what will occur in the future. The birthday gifts and the college application fee are unusual nonrecurring types of financial events. If those two items are eliminated, the recurring wage revenue of $850 equals the recurring monthly expenses of $850 and your conclusion would be that the gym membership is not affordable. The same concept holds for businesses. Those financial transactions that are nonrecurring should not be considered when making future projections; they should be identified and segregated from the routine operating results on the income statement.

## Learning Objectives

### Analyze a corporate income statement

The income statement reports **income from continuing operations,** which represents the results of operations that can be expected to continue (repeat) in the future. Below continuing operations, there may be special items that do not recur. These items, listed in the following list, are shown individually net of tax on the income statement after continuing operations but before net income.

- **Discontinued operations**—The financial results of a discontinued segment of the business. The segment must be able to be separately identified operationally and for reporting purposes from the remainder of the entity.
- **Extraordinary gains and losses**—The financial effect of events that are **both** unusual (not expected to occur again) and infrequent (not expected to recur in the near future).

**Earnings per share,** the net income earned per outstanding share of common stock, must be shown at the bottom of the income statement. This is probably the most important indicator used by analysts and investors for profitability analysis. *Review the multistep income statement containing special items in Exhibit 11-1 (p. 655).*

### Account for a corporation's income tax

There may be differences between pretax income on the income statement and taxable income on the income tax return for a corporation. The income tax expense on the income statement is based on the pretax income on the income statement. However, the income tax payable liability on the balance sheet is based on the taxable income on the tax return. The difference between these two amounts results in a *deferred tax asset* or *deferred tax liability.*

### Analyze a statement of stockholders' equity

When there have been multiple transactions impacting stockholders' equity during the year, a statement of stockholders' equity may be prepared. This statement is very similar to a statement of retained earnings, except that instead of only detailing the changes in Retained Earnings, it details the changes in *every* stockholders' equity account. *Observe the statement of stockholders' equity and calculation of comprehensive income in Exhibit 11-3 (p. 667).*

### Understand managers' and auditors' responsibilities for the financial statements

It is the managers of a company who are ultimately responsible for the numbers on financial statements. To help ensure that these numbers are correct, the shareholders, through the board of directors, hire auditors each year to examine the financial statements and accounting systems of the company. It is the auditor's job to express an opinion on these financial statements as to whether or not they have been prepared in accordance with GAAP. *Read Exhibits 11-5 (p. 669) and 11-6 (p. 671) to see examples of Management's Statement of Responsibility and an Auditor's Report.*

# Demo Doc 1

## Income Statement Presentation and Earnings per Share

*Learning Objectives 1, 3, 4*

Vater Industries had the following information for the year ended December 31, 2009:

| | |
|---|---:|
| Common stock, $0.50 par | $ 7,000 |
| Preferred stock, $20 par, 10% | 20,000 |
| Treasury stock (2,000 shares at cost) | 8,000 |
| Extraordinary items (before tax) | 30,000 |
| Tax impact of extraordinary items | (9,000) |
| Tax impact of income from continuing operations | (65,000) |
| Income from continuing operations (before tax) | 200,000 |
| Tax impact of discontinued operations | 11,000 |
| Discontinued operations (before tax) | (40,000) |

During 2009, Vater paid all required dividends for the preferred stock and also paid dividends of $1 per share on the common stock.

## Requirements

1. Prepare the lower portion of Vater's income statement for the year ended December 31, 2009, beginning with income from continuing operations, including earnings-per-share calculations.

2. Why are discontinued operations and extraordinary items not included as part of income from continuing operations?

3. The preferred stock was issued in January 2009, and the treasury stock was purchased in January 2009. How will these transactions impact Vater's statement of stockholders' equity for 2009? What other transactions would appear on Vater's statement of stockholders' equity?

4. In January 2010, auditors performed an examination of Vater's 2009 financial statements. They found no material errors in the accounting data. What type of opinion will the auditors give on the financial statements? Does giving this type of opinion mean that the auditor is responsible for the numbers that appear on those statements?

# Demo Doc 1 Solutions

## Requirement 1

1 Analyze a corporate income statement

**Prepare the lower portion of Vater's income statement for the year ended December 31, 2009, beginning with income from continuing operations, including earnings-per-share calculations.**

First, we must get the final numbers to be reported on the income statement for these items. Each of these items is reported *after tax,* so we must combine the pre-tax numbers with their tax impacts to get the after-tax numbers.

Income from continuing operations (after tax):

$$\$200,000 - \$65,000 = \$135,000$$

Discontinued operations (net of tax):

$$\$(40,000) + \$11,000 = \$(29,000)$$

Extraordinary items (net of tax):

$$\$30,000 - \$9,000 = \$21,000$$

Remember that discontinued operations and extraordinary items can be positive *or* negative. In this question, discontinued operations are negative and the extraordinary item is a gain, but either item could also be in the opposite direction. To help recall the order of presentation on this part of the income statement, remember that it is alphabetical: **CDE.**

**C** Income from **C**ontinuing Operations

**D** Income from **D**iscontinued Operations

**E** **E**xtraordinary Items

So the first part of the income statement is

### Vater Industries
### Income Statement (Partial)
#### Year Ended December 31, 2009

| | |
|---|---:|
| + Income from continuing operations | $135,000 |
| - Discontinued operations (net of tax) | (29,000) |
| + Extraordinary items (net of tax) | 21,000 |
| Net income | $127,000 |

Next, we must calculate the earnings per share (EPS) ratios for each of these items.

$$\text{Basic earnings per share} = \frac{\text{Net income} - \text{Preferred dividends}}{\text{Average number of common shares outstanding}}$$

Notice that there is *no mention* of *common* share dividends in the formula because it is *irrelevant* whether or not common share dividends are paid. Net income (after the preferred dividends) goes to the common shareholders. Whether they "receive" this income as an increase to Retained Earnings or as a cash dividend, it still belongs to the common shareholders.

Therefore, payment of common stock dividends is ignored in the EPS calculation.

It is *only* the preferred dividends (money that does *not* go to the common shareholders) that is subtracted.

So we ignore the common stock dividends in our earnings-per-share calculation.

We still need the number of common shares outstanding for the earnings-per-share calculation. The common stock account represents the par value of all issued shares.

So the number of issued common shares is

$$\$7{,}000/\$0.50 \text{ par per share} = 14{,}000 \text{ shares}$$

To get the number of outstanding common shares, we must take out the treasury stock:

Number of outstanding shares = Number of issued shares − Number of treasury shares

Number of outstanding shares =      14,000     −     2,000

= 12,000 shares of common stock outstanding

The $20,000 in the Preferred Stock account represents the par value of *all* preferred stock. Therefore, we can calculate the preferred share dividends paid in 2009:

$$10\% \times \$20{,}000 = \$2{,}000$$

### Income from Continuing Operations

For income from continuing operations, basic earnings per share is

$$\text{Basic earnings per share} = \frac{\text{Income} - \text{Preferred dividends}}{\text{Average number of common shares outstanding}}$$

$$= \frac{\$135{,}000 - \$2{,}000}{12{,}000 \text{ common shares}}$$

$$= \$11.08 \text{ per share}$$

### Income from Discontinued Operations

The portion of earnings per share relating to discontinued operations is

$$\text{Basic earnings (loss) per share} = \frac{\text{Income (Loss)}}{\text{Average number of common shares outstanding}}$$

$$= \frac{\$(29,000)}{12,000 \text{ common shares}}$$

$$= \$(2.42) \text{ per share}$$

### Income from Extraordinary Items

The portion of earnings per share relating to extraordinary items is

$$\text{Basic earnings (loss) per share} = \frac{\text{Income (Loss)}}{\text{Average number of common shares outstanding}}$$

$$= \frac{\$21,000}{12,000 \text{ common shares}}$$

$$= \$1.75 \text{ per share}$$

### Net Income

For net income, basic earnings per share is

$$\text{Basic earnings (loss) per share} = \frac{\text{Income (Loss)} - \text{Preferred dividends}}{\text{Average number of common shares outstanding}}$$

$$= \frac{\$127,000 - \$2,000}{12,000 \text{ common shares}}$$

$$= \$10.41 \text{ per share (rounded down)}$$

As a check, we can add up the portions of earnings per share from the other items:

$$\$11.08 - \$2.42 + \$1.75 = \$10.41$$

The full income statement, including earnings per share, is

**Vater Industries**
**Income Statement (Partial)**
Year Ended December 31, 2009

| | |
|---|---:|
| + Income from continuing operations | $135,000 |
| - Discontinued operations (net of tax) | (29,000) |
| + Extraordinary items (net of tax) | 21,000 |
| Net income | $127,000 |
| | |
| Income from continuing operations | $11.08 |
| Discontinued operations | (2.42) |
| Extraordinary items | 1.75 |
| Net income | $10.41 |

## Requirement 2

**Why are discontinued operations and extraordinary items not included as part of income from continuing operations?**

① Analyze a corporate income statement

Accountants must make financial statements helpful to investors (and other people) making decisions. One of the things the users of financial statements want to know is how much profit/income they can expect the business to make in the future. Income from *continuing* operations helps with estimating future profits because it involves income from business activities that will go on (that is, continue) into the future.

Discontinued operations are business activities that are ceasing (such as a subsidiary of the company that is in the process of being sold).

Extraordinary items are supposed to be one-time occurrences (by definition—unusual and infrequent) such as an earthquake.

These numbers are not helpful if you are trying to predict *future* profit levels. The discontinued operations will be gone in the future and the extraordinary events will not happen again. They will have *no* future impact.

These items are legitimately part of net income (and so are included there) but they are separated from income from continuing operations to make it easier for users of financial statements to understand what they can expect to see on future income statements. An analyst who is trying to predict *future* income would *only* use income from continuing operations because this is the only part of net income that will have a future impact (in other words, is *continuing* on into the future).

## Requirement 3

**The preferred stock was issued in January 2009, and the treasury stock was purchased in January 2009. How will these transactions impact Vater's statement of stockholders' equity for 2009? What other transactions would appear on Vater's statement of stockholders' equity?**

③ Analyze a statement of stockholders' equity

The statement of stockholders' equity shows all of the transactions that impacted stockholders' equity accounts during the year. When preferred stock is issued, the Preferred Stock account is increased, and likely Paid-In Capital in Excess of Par is increased as well. These increases would appear on the statement of stockholders' equity.

The purchase of treasury stock would increase the Treasury Stock account (decreasing stockholders' equity overall). This transaction would be displayed in the Treasury Stock column of the statement of stockholders' equity.

In addition, Vater's net income would appear as an increase in the Retained Earnings column, and the cash dividends paid (both to preferred and common shareholders) would appear as a decrease in the Retained Earnings column.

**④ Understand managers'
and auditors' responsi-
bilities for the financial
statements**

**In January 2010, auditors performed an examination of Vater's 2009 financial statements. They found no material errors in the accounting data. What type of opinion will the auditors give on the financial statements? Does giving this type of opinion mean that the auditor is responsible for the numbers that appear on those statements?**

If there are no material errors in the financial statements and they have been prepared under GAAP rules, then the auditors would give an unqualified (clean) opinion.

However, an unqualified opinion does *not* mean that the auditors are responsible for the financial statement numbers. Ultimate responsibility for the financial statements lies with management, as described in Management's Statement of Responsibility. See Exhibit 11-5 (p. 669) in the text for an example of this statement.

*DEMO DOC COMPLETE*

# Demo Doc 2

## Income Taxes

*Learning Objective 2*

Joe Danson owns all outstanding common shares of Joseph Corp. The corporation earned net income before tax of $80,000 in 2009 and has an income tax rate of 40%.

### Requirements

1. Is Joe Danson personally liable for the income taxes owed by Joseph Corp.?

2. Calculate the amount of income tax expense that will appear on Joseph Corp.'s 2009 income statement.

3. Joseph Corp.'s actual Income Tax Payable at December 31, 2009, should be $30,000. Assuming that the Income Tax Expense number you calculated for Requirement 2 is correct, give Joseph's journal entry to record the income taxes for 2009.

# Demo Doc 2 Solutions

### Requirement 1

2  Account for a corporation's income tax

**Is Joe Danson personally liable for the income taxes owed by Joseph Corp.?**

Corporations are liable for *their own* taxes. Even as the sole owner, Joe is not liable for the taxes of the corporation.

### Requirement 2

2  Account for a corporation's income tax

**Calculate the amount of income tax expense that will appear on Joseph Corp.'s 2009 income statement.**

$$\text{Income tax expense} = \text{Net income before tax} \times \text{Tax rate}$$
$$= \$80,000 \times 40\% = \$32,000$$

### Requirement 3

2  Account for a corporation's income tax

**Joseph Corp.'s actual Income Tax Payable at December 31, 2009, should be $30,000. Assuming that the Income Tax Expense number you calculated for Requirement 2 is correct, give Joseph's journal entry to record the income taxes for 2009.**

Income Tax Expense must be increased (a debit) by $32,000 (as calculated in Requirement 2). Income Tax Payable must be increased (a credit) by $30,000.

The difference between these two numbers is balanced to Deferred Taxes. So the journal entry to record Joseph Corp.'s income taxes for the year is

| | | |
|---|---|---|
| Income Tax Expense | 32,000 | |
| Deferred Taxes (to balance) | | 2,000 |
| Income Tax Payable | | 30,000 |

*DEMO DOC COMPLETE*

# Quick Practice Questions

## True/False

_____ 1. Discontinued operations are listed after extraordinary items on the income statement.

_____ 2. A loss due to a lawsuit would be considered an extraordinary item.

_____ 3. Preferred share dividends are considered to be part of income from continuing operations.

_____ 4. Earnings per share is computed by dividing net income less common stock dividends by the average number of common shares outstanding.

_____ 5. Dividends paid to common shares have no impact on the calculation of earnings per share.

_____ 6. Income Tax Expense and Income Tax Payable are not always the same amount.

_____ 7. Deferred Taxes can be either an asset or a liability account.

_____ 8. Management is ultimately responsible for the information released on the financial statements.

_____ 9. Prior-period adjustments adjust retained earnings for discontinued operations.

_____ 10. Comprehensive income is the company's change in total stockholders' equity from all sources other than from its owners.

_____ 11. The auditor's report includes a declaration of the auditor's responsibility for internal controls.

_____ 12. When a company has a change in accounting principle, all prior period amounts are retrospectively restated in the financial statements.

_____ 13. Revenue recognition remains one of the principal areas of difference between U.S. GAAP and IFRS.

# Multiple Choice

1. **Which of the following is the correct order of presentation for items on the income statement?**
   a. Income from continuing operations, then extraordinary items, then discontinued operations
   b. Discontinued operations, then extraordinary items, then income from continuing operations
   c. Income from continuing operations, then discontinued operations, then extraordinary items
   d. Extraordinary items, then income from continuing operations, then discontinued operations

2. **Earnings per share is defined as which of the following?**
   a. The amount of a company's dividends per share of its outstanding preferred stock
   b. The amount of a company's dividends per share of its outstanding common stock
   c. The amount of a company's net income per share of its outstanding preferred stock
   d. The amount of a company's net income per share of its outstanding common stock

3. **Which of the following statements about Deferred Taxes is true?**
   a. Deferred Taxes is the difference between Income Tax Expense and Income Tax Payable.
   b. Deferred Taxes is always an asset account.
   c. Deferred Taxes is always a liability account.
   d. Deferred Taxes must be paid to the government within one year.

4. **What is the correct calculation of Income Tax Payable?**
   a. Taxable Income / Income Tax Rate
   b. Taxable Income × Income Tax Rate
   c. Income before income tax / Income Tax Rate
   d. Income before income tax × Income Tax Rate

5. **Which of the following statements about prior period adjustments is true?**
   a. A prior period adjustment appears on the income statement.
   b. Prior period adjustments relate to a future accounting period.
   c. Neither (a) nor (b) is true.
   d. Both (a) and (b) are true.

6. **What impact will a stock split have on the statement of stockholders' equity?**
   a. There will be an increase in the Retained Earnings column.
   b. There will be an increase in the Treasury Stock column.
   c. There will be an increase in the Common Stock column.
   d. None of the above will occur.

7.  **When an auditor feels that a set of financial statements is materially correct and in accordance with GAAP, what type of opinion will he or she issue?**
    a.  Unqualified opinion
    b.  Qualified opinion
    c.  Adverse opinion
    d.  Disclaimer

8.  **The Gain on Sale of Machinery account would appear on the income statement as which of the following?**
    a.  Extraordinary gain
    b.  Component of income from discontinued operations
    c.  Component of net sales
    d.  Component of income from continuing operations

9.  **To be considered an extraordinary item on the income statement, the event must be which of the following?**
    a.  Unusual but not infrequent
    b.  Both infrequent and unusual
    c.  Neither infrequent nor unusual
    d.  Infrequent but not unusual

10. **Net income for a corporation for the current year amounts to $200,000. The corporation currently has outstanding 5,000 shares of 5%, cumulative $100 par preferred stock and 20,000 shares of $20 par common stock. What is the numerator to be used in the earnings-per-share calculation?**
    a.  $175,000
    b.  $195,000
    c.  $200,000
    d.  $225,000

11. **Which of the following income statement items does not exist under IFRS?**
    a.  Income from continuing operations
    b.  Income from discontinued operations
    c.  Extraordinary items
    d.  All of these are allowed on the income statement under IFRS.

12. **When recognizing revenue, which event must occur first?**
    a.  The seller delivers the product or service to the customer.
    b.  The customer takes possession and ownership of the product or service.
    c.  The seller is reasonably assured of collecting cash from the customer.
    d.  The seller collects cash from the customer.

## Quick Exercises

**11-1. Kamo, Inc., had the following information for the year ended December 31, 2011:**

| | |
|---|---:|
| Loss from extraordinary items (before tax) ............................ | $ 8,000 |
| Income from discontinued operations (before tax) ................ | 4,000 |
| Income from continuing operations (before tax) .................... | 20,000 |
| | |
| Tax savings from extraordinary loss ...................................... | 1,000 |
| Taxes on discontinued operations .......................................... | 2,000 |
| Taxes on income from continuing operations ........................ | 6,000 |

**1. Prepare the lower portion of Kamo's Income Statement for 2011.**

**11-2. Knoxville Corp. was incorporated into being on January 1, 2011, with an authorization of 100,000 $2 par common shares and 50,000 $8 par, 5% preferred shares. During the year, Knoxville had the following transactions:**

- Issued 40,000 common shares at $12 per share on January 1.
- Issued 5,000 preferred shares at $20 per share on January 2.
- Paid the preferred share dividends in cash on December 31.
- Paid common share dividends of $0.25 cash per share on December 31.

**1. If Knoxville's net income for the year was $47,000, calculate the company's basic earnings-per-share ratio.**

11-3. Bowen Corporation organized on January 1, 2011. Bowen Corporation has authorization for 90,000 shares of $10 par value common stock. As of December 31, 2011, Bowen had issued 50,000 shares of its common stock at an average issuance price of $15. Bowen also has authorization for 50,000 shares of 5%, $50 par value, noncumulative preferred stock. As of December 31, 2011, Bowen had issued 12,000 shares of preferred stock at an average issuance price of $68 per share. Bowen reported net income of $47,000 for its first year of operations ended December 31, 2011.

1. Prepare the stockholders' equity section of the balance sheet for Bowen Corporation dated December 31, 2011.

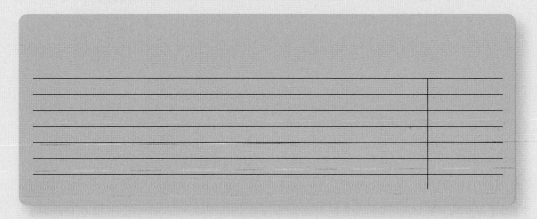

2. Prepare Bowen's statement of stockholders' equity for 2011.

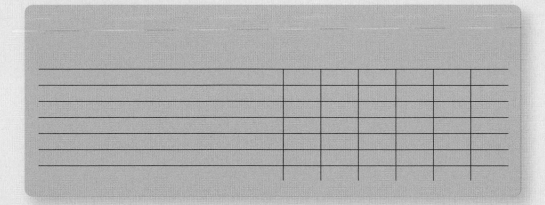

# Do It Yourself! Question 1

## Income Statement Presentation and Earnings per Share

Gate Corp. had the following information for the year ended December 31, 2011:

| | |
|---|---:|
| Common stock, $0.50 par | $ 200,000 |
| Preferred stock, $50 par, 8% | 500,000 |
| Tax impact of discontinued operations | (80,000) |
| Discontinued operations (before tax) | 400,000 |
| Extraordinary items (before tax) | (100,000) |
| Tax impact of extraordinary items | 30,000 |
| Tax impact of income from continuing operations | (750,000) |
| Income from continuing operations (before tax) | 2,500,000 |

During the year, Gate paid all required dividends for the preferred stock and also paid dividends of $1 per share on the common stock. Gate has no treasury stock.

## Requirement

1. Prepare the lower portion of Gate's income statement for the year ended December 31, 2011, beginning with income from continuing operations, including earnings-per-share calculations.

# Do It Yourself! Question 2

## Income Taxes

Gatcha, Inc., earned net income before tax of $200,000 in 2011 and has an income tax rate of 30%.

### Requirements

1. Calculate the amount of income tax expense that will appear on Gatcha's 2011 income statement.

2. Gatcha's actual Income Tax Payable at December 31, 2011, should be $50,000. Assuming that the Income Tax Expense number you calculated for Requirement 1 is correct, give Gatcha's journal entry to record the income taxes for 2011.

| Date | Accounts | Debit | Credit |
|------|----------|-------|--------|
|      |          |       |        |
|      |          |       |        |
|      |          |       |        |

# Quick Practice Solutions

## True/False

  F      1. Discontinued operations are listed after extraordinary items on the income statement.
False—Discontinued Operations are listed *before* extraordinary items on the income statement. (p. 660)

  F      2. A loss due to a lawsuit would be considered an extraordinary item.
False—A loss due to a lawsuit is *never* considered to be an extraordinary item. (p. 661)

  F      3. Preferred share dividends are considered to be part of income from continuing operations.
False—Dividends (including preferred) are not shown on the income statement, but are instead part of the statement of retained earnings or statement of stockholders' equity. (p. 667)

  F      4. Earnings per share is computed by dividing net income less common stock dividends by the average number of common shares outstanding.
False—Earnings per share is computed by dividing net income less *preferred* stock dividends by the average number of common shares outstanding. (pp. 662–663)

  T      5. Dividends paid to common shares have no impact on the calculation of earnings per share. (pp. 662–663)

  T      6. Income Tax Expense and Income Tax Payable are not always the same amount. (p. 665)

  T      7. Deferred Taxes can be either an asset or a liability account. (p. 665)

  T      8. Management is ultimately responsible for the information released on the financial statements. (pp. 669–670)

  F      9. Prior-period adjustments adjust retained earnings for discontinued operations.
False—Prior-period adjustments correct retained earnings for *errors made in prior periods.* (pp. 665–666)

  T    10. Comprehensive income is the company's change in total stockholders' equity from all sources other than from its owners. (pp. 666–667)

  F    11. The auditor's report includes a declaration of the auditor's responsibility for internal controls.
False—*Management's Statement of Responsibility* declares *management's* responsibility for internal controls. (p. 670)

  T    12. When a company has a change in accounting principle, all prior period amounts are retrospectively restated in the financial statements. (p. 661)

  T    13. Revenue recognition remains one of the principal areas of difference between U.S. GAAP and IFRS. (p. 656)

# Multiple Choice

1. **Which of the following is the correct order of presentation for items on the income statement?** (p. 655)
   a. Income from continuing operations, then extraordinary items, then discontinued operations
   b. Discontinued operations, then extraordinary items, then income from continuing operations
   c. Income from continuing operations, then discontinued operations, then extraordinary items
   d. Extraordinary items, then income from continuing operations, then discontinued operations

2. **Earnings per share is defined as which of the following?** (p. 662)
   a. The amount of a company's dividends per share of its outstanding preferred stock
   b. The amount of a company's dividends per share of its outstanding common stock
   c. The amount of a company's net income per share of its outstanding preferred stock
   d. The amount of a company's net income per share of its outstanding common stock

3. **Which of the following statements about Deferred Taxes is true?** (p. 665)
   a. Deferred Taxes is the difference between Income Tax Expense and Income Tax Payable.
   b. Deferred Taxes is always an asset account.
   c. Deferred Taxes is always a liability account.
   d. Deferred Taxes must be paid to the government within one year.

4. **What is the correct calculation of Income Tax Payable?** (p. 664)
   a. Taxable Income / Income Tax Rate
   b. Taxable Income × Income Tax Rate
   c. Income before income tax / Income Tax Rate
   d. Income before income tax × Income Tax Rate

5. **Which of the following statements about prior period adjustments is true?** (pp. 665–666)
   a. A prior period adjustment appears on the income statement.
   b. Prior period adjustments relate to a future accounting period.
   c. Neither (a) nor (b) is true.
   d. Both (a) and (b) are true.

6. **What impact will a stock split have on the statement of stockholders' equity?** (p. 667)
   a. There will be an increase in the Retained Earnings column.
   b. There will be an increase in the Treasury Stock column.
   c. There will be an increase in the Common Stock column.
   d. None of the above will occur.

7.  **When an auditor feels that a set of financial statements is materially correct and in accordance with GAAP, what type of opinion will he issue? (p. 672)**
    a. Unqualified opinion
    b. Qualified opinion
    c. Adverse opinion
    d. Disclaimer

8.  **The Gain on Sale of Machinery account would appear on the income statement as which of the following? (p. 661)**
    a. Extraordinary gain
    b. Component of income from discontinued operations
    c. Component of net sales
    d. Component of income from continuing operations

9.  **To be considered an extraordinary item on the income statement, the event must be which of the following? (p. 661)**
    a. Unusual but not infrequent
    b. Both infrequent and unusual
    c. Neither infrequent nor unusual
    d. Infrequent but not unusual

10. **Net income for a corporation for the current year amounts to $200,000. The corporation currently has outstanding 5,000 shares of 5%, cumulative $100 par preferred stock and 20,000 shares of $20 par common stock. What is the numerator to be used in the earnings-per-share calculation? (pp. 662–663)**
    a. $175,000
    b. $195,000
    c. $200,000
    d. $225,000

11. **Which of the following income statement items does not exist under IFRS? (p. 661)**
    a. Income from continuing operations
    b. Income from discontinued operations
    c. Extraordinary items
    d. All of these are allowed on the income statement under IFRS.

12. **When recognizing revenue, which event must occur first? (p. 655)**
    a. The seller delivers the product or service to the customer.
    b. The customer takes possession and ownership of the product or service.
    c. The seller is reasonably assured of collecting cash from the customer.
    d. The seller collects cash from the customer.

# Quick Exercises

**11-1. Kamo, Inc., had the following information for the year ended December 31, 2011:**

| | |
|---|---:|
| Loss from extraordinary items (before tax) ............................. | $ 8,000 |
| Income from discontinued operations (before tax) ................. | 4,000 |
| Income from continuing operations (before tax) .................... | 20,000 |
| | |
| Tax savings from extraordinary loss ...................................... | 1,000 |
| Taxes on discontinued operations ........................................... | 2,000 |
| Taxes on income from continuing operations ......................... | 6,000 |

**1. Prepare the lower portion of Kamo's Income Statement for 2011.** (p. 655)

**Kamo, Inc.**
**Income Statement**
**Year Ended December 31, 2011**

| | |
|---|---:|
| Income from continuing operations (before tax) ........................................ | $20,000 |
| Income tax expense ................................................................................... | (6,000) |
| Income from continuing operations........................................................... | 14,000 |
| Discontinued operations, $4,000, less income tax of $2,000.................... | 2,000 |
| Extraordinary items, $8,000, less income tax savings of $1,000 .............. | (7,000) |
| Net income................................................................................................ | $ 9,000 |

**11-2. Knoxville Corp. was incorporated into being on January 1, 2011, with an authorization of 100,000 $2 par common shares and 50,000 $8 par, 5% preferred shares. During the year, Knoxville had the following transactions:**

- Issued 40,000 common shares at $12 per share on January 1.
- Issued 5,000 preferred shares at $20 per share on January 2.
- Paid the preferred share dividends in cash on December 31.
- Paid common share dividends of $0.25 cash per share on December 31.

**1. If Knoxville's net income for the year was $47,000, calculate the company's basic earnings-per-share ratio.** ( pp. 662–663)

Preferred Share Dividends = 5,000 shares × $8 par × 5% = $2,000

$$\text{Earnings per Share} = \frac{\$47,000 \text{ Net Income} - \$2,000 \text{ Preferred Share Dividends}}{40,000 \text{ Common Shares Outstanding}}$$

= $1.125 per share

11-3. Bowen Corporation organized on January 1, 2011. Bowen Corporation has authorization for 90,000 shares of $10 par value common stock. As of December 31, 2011, Bowen had issued 50,000 shares of its common stock at an average issuance price of $15. Bowen also has authorization for 50,000 shares of 5%, $50 par value, noncumulative preferred stock. As of December 31, 2011, Bowen had issued 12,000 shares of preferred stock at an average issuance price of $68 per share. Bowen reported net income of $47,000 for its first year of operations ended December 31, 2011.

1. Prepare the stockholders' equity section of the balance sheet for Bowen Corporation dated December 31, 2011. (pp. 667–669)

### Bowen Corporation
### Stockholders' Equity
### December 31, 2011

| | |
|---|---:|
| Paid-in capital: | |
| Preferred stock, 5%, $50 par, 12,000 shares issued | $ 600,000 |
| Paid-in capital in excess of par—preferred | 216,000 |
| Common stock, $10 par, 90,000 shares authorized, 50,000 shares issued | 500,000 |
| Paid-in capital in excess of par—common | 250,000 |
| Total paid-in capital | $1,566,000 |
| Retained earnings | 47,000 |
| Total stockholders' equity | $1,613,000 |

2. Prepare Bowen's statement of stockholders' equity for 2011.

### Bowen Corporation
### Statement of Stockholders' Equity
### Year Ended December 31, 2011

| | Common Stock $10 par | Preferred Stock $50 par | Paid-In Capital in Excess of Par—Common | Paid-In Capital in Excess of Par—Preferred | Retained Earnings | Total Stockholders' Equity |
|---|---:|---:|---:|---:|---:|---:|
| 1. Balance, January 1, 2011 | $ 0 | $ 0 | $ 0 | $ 0 | $ 0 | $ 0 |
| 2. Issuance of Common Stock | 500,000 | | 250,000 | | | 750,000 |
| 3. Issuance of Preferred Stock | | 600,000 | | 216,000 | | 816,000 |
| 4. Net Income | | | | | 47,000 | 47,000 |
| 5. Balance, December 31, 2011 | $500,000 | $600,000 | $250,000 | $216,000 | $47,000 | $1,613,000 |

# Do It Yourself! Question 1 Solutions

## Income Statement Presentation and Earnings per Share

### Requirement

1. Prepare the lower portion of Gate's income statement for the year ended December 31, 2011, beginning with income from continuing operations, including earnings-per-share calculations.

Income from Continuing Operations (after tax):

$$\$2,500,000 - \$750,000 = \$1,750,000$$

Discontinued Operations (net of tax):

$$\$400,000 - \$80,000 = \$320,000$$

Extraordinary Items (net of tax):

$$\$(100,000) + \$30,000 = \$(70,000)$$

Net Income:

$$\$1,750,000 + \$320,000 - \$70,000 = \$2,000,000$$

Number of Common Shares Outstanding:

$$\$200,000/\$0.50 \text{ par per share} = 400,000 \text{ shares}$$

Preferred Share Dividends Paid:

$$8\% \times \$500,000 = \$40,000$$

For income from continuing operations, basic earnings per share is

$$\frac{\$1,750,000 - \$40,000}{400,000 \text{ shares}} = \$4.275 \text{ per share}$$

The portion of earnings per share relating to discontinued operations is

$$\frac{\$320,000}{400,000 \text{ shares}} = \$0.80 \text{ per share}$$

The portion of earnings per share relating to extraordinary items is

$$\frac{\$(70,000)}{400,000 \text{ shares}} = \$(0.175) \text{ per share}$$

For net income, basic earnings per share is

$$\frac{\$2,000,000 - \$40,000}{400,000 \text{ shares}} = \$4.90 \text{ per share}$$

**Gate Corp.**
**Income Statement (Partial)**
**Year Ended December 31, 2011**

| | |
|---|---:|
| + Income from continuing operations.................................................... | $1,750,000 |
| - Discontinued operations (net of tax)................................................. | 320,000 |
| + Extraordinary items (net of tax)....................................................... | (70,000) |
| Net income.................................................................................. | $2,000,000 |
| | |
| Income from continuing operations.................................................... | $4.275 |
| Discontinued operations................................................................... | 0.800 |
| Extraordinary items ........................................................................ | (0.175) |
| Net income..................................................................................... | $4.900 |

# Do It Yourself! Question 2 Solutions

## Income Taxes

Gatcha, Inc., earned net income before tax of $200,000 in 2011 and has an income tax rate of 30%.

### Requirements

1. Calculate the amount of income tax expense that will appear on Gatcha's 2011 income statement.

   $$\$200,000 \times 30\% = \$60,000$$

2. Gatcha's actual Income Tax Payable at December 31, 2011 should be $50,000. Assuming that the Income Tax Expense number you calculated for Requirement 1 is correct, give Gatcha's journal entry to record the income taxes for 2011.

| | | |
|---|---|---|
| Income Tax Expense | 60,000 | |
| Deferred Taxes (to balance) | | 10,000 |
| Income Tax Payable | | 50,000 |

# The Power of Practice

For more practice using the skills learned in this chapter, visit MyAccountingLab. There you will find algorithmically generated questions that are based on these Demo Docs and your main textbook's Review and Assess Your Progress sections.

Go to MyAccountingLab and follow these steps:

1. Direct your URL to www.myaccountinglab.com.
2. Log in using your name and password.
3. Click the MyAccountingLab link.
4. Click Study Plan in the left navigation bar.
5. From the table of contents, select Chapter 11, The Income Statement & the Statement of Stockholders' Equity.
6. Click a link to work tutorial exercises.

# 12 The Statement of Cash Flows

## WHAT YOU PROBABLY ALREADY KNOW

If you find yourself short of cash occasionally, it is not uncommon to wonder where all of the money has gone. You probably already know that you need to keep track of all cash received and spent for a period of time to find out the answer. Not only does that show you the *amount* of money coming in and going out, but you would also identify the *source* of the cash received and the *use* of the cash spent. Identifying the cash activities in your life helps you to predict your future cash flows based on past history, review the decisions you have made in your financial life that result in the creation and disbursement of cash, and assess your ability to meet future financial obligations. The same issues are important to a business. In this chapter, we will see how the statement of cash flows provides this information for an entity.

## Learning Objectives

 **Identify the purposes of the statement of cash flows**

The statement of cash flows helps to

- predict future cash flows. Recall from Chapter 11 the concept of income from continuing operations and special items. Those results are used to make predictions about the future.
- evaluate management decisions. The cash-flow result of management's decisions is reflected in the statement of cash flows.
- predict ability to pay debts and dividends. Investors and creditors will review past cash flows to assess the risk of nonpayment of debt and dividends.
- show the relationship of net income and cash flows.

 **Distinguish among operating, investing, and financing cash flows**

The statement of cash flows includes all transactions that increase or decrease Cash. These items are included in one of the following three categories:

- Operating—Activities that affect the income statement and current assets and current liabilities on the balance sheet. These transactions include inflows such as cash receipts from customers, interest, and dividends. *Outflows include cash paid to employees and suppliers. It is most important to have a positive net cash inflow for this activity.*
- Investing—Activities that affect long-term assets. These transactions include cash inflows from the sale of plant, property, and equipment;

investments; and the collection from long-term loans. Outflows include the cash payment to purchase plant, property, and equipment; make investments; and make loans.

- Financing—Activities that affect long-term liabilities and stockholders' equity. These transactions include cash inflows from the sale of stock and issuance of long-term debt. Cash outflows include the payment of dividends and the repayment of debt. Treasury stock transactions may be either inflows or outflows of cash.

*Refer to Exhibit 12-2 (p. 705) for the relationship between the activity categories and the balance sheet classifications.*

 **Prepare a statement of cash flows by the indirect method**

The **indirect method** reconciles from net income on the income statement to cash from operating activities. The schedule begins with accrual-basis net income and identifies the adjustments or items of difference to convert from the accrual basis of accounting to a cash basis for operating activities. Some of the adjustments include the following:

- Eliminating such noncash expenses as depreciation, depletion, and amortization—these expenses need to be added to net income to eliminate the expense from net income.
- Eliminating the gains or losses included in net income—gains need to be deducted from net income and losses need to be added to net income to eliminate these from net income. The gains and losses are deducted or added because the full proceeds of a sale are included as an investing activity.
- Changes in the current assets and current liabilities—review the "Changes in the Current Asset and the Current Liability Accounts" section in the text for the rules. Review the rationale for the rules.

*This can be a challenging concept. Review carefully the "Cash Flows from Operating Activities" section of the text and Exhibit 12-7 (p. 712).*

 **Prepare a statement of cash flows by the direct method**

The direct method lists the amount of cash receipts and cash payments from operating activities by major category. The FASB recommends the direct method, but most corporations use the indirect method, which requires less work. *Review the direct method of presenting operating activities in Exhibit 12-13 (p. 724).*

# Demo Doc 1

## Statement of Cash Flows (Indirect Method)

*Learning Objectives 2, 3*

### Indirect Method

Tanker, Inc., had the following information at December 31, 2011:

### Tanker, Inc.
### Balance Sheet
### December 31, 2011

| Assets | 2011 | 2010 | Change | Liabilities | 2011 | 2010 | Change |
|---|---|---|---|---|---|---|---|
| **Current:** | | | | **Current:** | | | |
| Cash.......................... | $ 700 | $1,160 | $(460) | Accounts payable ...................... | $ 680 | $ 530 | $150 |
| Accounts receivable............... | 300 | 420 | (120) | | | | |
| Inventory ............................... | 800 | 750 | 50 | Long-term notes payable............... | 660 | 815 | |
| Prepaid insurance................... | 120 | 90 | 30 | | | | |
| | | | | Total liabilities .............................. | $1,340 | $1,345 | |
| Furniture..................................... | 1,500 | 1,400 | | | | | |
| Less acc. depn. ...................... | (400) | (475) | | **Stockholders' Equity** | | | |
| Net............................................ | 1,100 | 925 | | Common stock (no par) ............... | $1,800 | $1,800 | |
| | | | | Retained earnings......................... | 880 | 200 | |
| Total assets............................. | $3,020 | $3,345 | | Less treasury stock ................... | (1,000) | 0 | |
| | | | | Total equity................................... | $1,680 | $2,000 | |
| | | | | Total liabilities and equity............... | $3,020 | $3,345 | |

### Tanker, Inc.
### Income Statement
### Year Ended December 31, 2011

| | |
|---|---|
| Sales revenue ..................................... | $ 3,400 |
| Less cost of goods sold .................... | (1,750) |
| Gross margin...................................... | $ 1,650 |
| | |
| Depreciation expense ...................... | $ (110) |
| Insurance expense ........................... | (230) |
| Other operating expenses................ | (390) |
| | |
| Gain on sale of furniture ................. | 80 |
| | |
| Net income....................................... | $ 1,000 |

**Other Information**

- Every year, Tanker declares and pays cash dividends.
- During 2011, Tanker sold old furniture for $90 cash. Tanker also bought new furniture by making a cash down payment and signing a $200 note payable.
- During 2011, Tanker repaid $500 of notes payable in cash and borrowed new long-term notes payable for cash.
- During 2011, Tanker purchased treasury stock for cash. No treasury stock was sold.

## Requirement

1. Prepare Tanker's statement of cash flows for the year ended December 31, 2011, using the indirect method.

# Demo Doc 1 Solutions

**Prepare Tanker's statement of cash flows for the year ended December 31, 2011.**

② Distinguish among operating, investing, and financing cash flows

③ Prepare a statement of cash flows by the indirect method

## Operating Activities

We first set up the statement of cash flows with the proper title and then start with operating activities.

## Net Income

The first item is net income. Because net income is positive, it is added to the Cash balance. Therefore, we add (that is, positive number) $1,000 on our cash-flow statement.

## Depreciation Expense

Net income includes depreciation expense, which must be removed because it is a 100% noncash item. Remember, no cash was "spent" for depreciation, yet it was still deducted to arrive at the net income number. Because depreciation expense was *subtracted* to calculate net income, we *add* it back to remove it.

## Gain on Sale of Furniture

After depreciation, we must look for gains and losses on disposal of long-term assets. These are treated in a manner similar to the depreciation. No cash was "earned" for the gain, yet it was still added to arrive at the net income number. The gain on sale of furniture was *added* to calculate net income, so we *subtract* it to remove it.

## Accounts Receivable

After looking at net income and the depreciation and gain adjustments, we need to incorporate the changes in current assets and current liabilities.

The increases and decreases in these accounts do not tell us whether to add or subtract these items on the statement of cash flows.

The first current asset (other than cash) is Accounts Receivable. On the balance sheet we see

| Assets | 2011 | 2010 | Change |
|---|---|---|---|
| Current: | | | |
| Cash | $700 | $1,160 | $(460) |
| Accounts receivable | 300 | 420 | (120) |

We must add the $120 decrease in Accounts Receivable. There are two ways to reason this out:

**1. Accounts Receivable went down. Why? Tanker collected more cash than its customers bought on account from Tanker during the year. How does this affect Cash? It increases Cash; therefore, we should add the number on the statement of cash flows.**

**2. Accounts Receivable went down. This is a decrease in an asset, which is a credit. If this credit is balanced out by the Cash account, that would be a debit to Cash, which is an increase. If Cash is increased, we should add the number on the statement of cash flows.**

Notice that in both of these cases, we are adding or subtracting on the cash-flow statement because of the item's effect on *cash flow. It doesn't matter if Accounts Receivable went up or down; what matters is how that affects cash flow.*

### Inventory

Let's try the two ways with the next current asset: Inventory. On the balance sheet, we see

| Assets | 2011 | 2010 | Change |
|---|---|---|---|
| Current: | | | |
| Cash...................................... | $700 | $1,160 | $(460) |
| Accounts receivable............... | 300 | 420 | (120) |
| Inventory................................ | 800 | 750 | 50 |

During the year, Inventory increased by $50.

**1. Why did Inventory increase? Tanker is purchasing inventory with cash. Therefore, this has a negative effect on cash flow.**

**2. If Inventory increased, this is an increase in an asset, which is a debit. If this is balanced out by Cash, then Cash is credited, which is a negative effect on cash flow.**

### Prepaid Insurance

The last current asset is Prepaid Insurance. On the balance sheet, we see

| Assets | 2011 | 2010 | Change |
|---|---|---|---|
| Current: | | | |
| Cash...................................... | $700 | $1,160 | $(460) |
| Accounts receivable............... | 300 | 420 | (120) |
| Inventory................................ | 800 | 750 | 50 |
| Prepaid insurance.................. | 120 | 90 | 30 |

During the year, Prepaid Insurance increased by $30.

**1. Why did Prepaid Insurance increase? Tanker paid more insurance costs in advance. This has a negative effect on cash flow.**

**2. If Prepaid Insurance is increased, this is an increase in an asset, which is a debit. If this is balanced out by Cash, then Cash is credited, which is a negative effect on cash flow.**

## Accounts Payable

The last part of operating activities is to look at the changes in current liabilities. The only current liability in this question is Accounts Payable. On the balance sheet, we see

| Liabilities | 2011 | 2010 | Change |
|---|---|---|---|
| Current: | | | |
| Accounts payable .................. | $680 | $530 | $150 |

During the year, Accounts Payable increased by $150.

1. **Why did Accounts Payable increase? Tanker is not paying all of its bills. This means that it is holding onto its cash, which is a positive effect on cash flow.**

2. **If Accounts Payable increased, this is an increase in a liability, which is a credit. If this is balanced out by Cash, then Cash is debited, which is a positive effect on cash flow.**

We total these numbers, and we are finished with operating activities. The completed operating activities section would appear as

| Operating Activities | | |
|---|---|---|
| Net income.......................................................................... | | $1,000 |
| Depreciation expense ....................................................... | $110 | |
| Gain on sale of furniture ................................................. | (80) | |
| Decrease in accounts receivable....................................... | 120 | |
| Increase in inventory ....................................................... | (50) | |
| Increase in prepaid insurance .......................................... | (30) | |
| Increase in accounts payable ........................................... | 150 | |
| Net cash flow provided by operating activities.................. | | $1,220 |

## Investing Activities

Investing activities looks at cash purchases and cash disposals of long-term assets. This means that we need to know how much cash was paid to purchase new furniture and how much cash was received when Tanker sold some of the old furniture. Do we have any of these numbers right away? Yes, we are told in the question that Tanker signed a $200 note payable to purchase new furniture. We also know that the old furniture was sold for $90 cash.

Before we do anything else, we should point out that the $200 note payable is a *noncash transaction*. Although we will *need* to use it in our analysis, it will *not* appear on the main body of the statement of cash flows. Instead, it will appear in a note for noncash investing and financing activities:

| Noncash Investing and Financing Activities | |
|---|---|
| Purchase of furniture with note payable ................ | $200 |

We need to calculate the *cash* Tanker paid to purchase new furniture. To do this, we need to analyze the Furniture (Net) T-account:

| Furniture (Net) | | |
|---|---|---|
| **Bal 12/31/10** | 925 | |
| | increases | decreases |
| Bal 12/31/11 | 1,100 | |

We know that the Furniture (Net) account increased and decreased. What caused that account to increase? Well, it would increase if Tanker bought new furniture. So obviously the cash paid *and* the note signed for new furniture went into this account.

What would cause the Furniture (Net) account to decrease?

If Tanker sold furniture, we would decrease the account, *but* it would be decreased by the *book* value (that is, the *net* amount) of the furniture sold. Remember, the book value is another term for *net* value. We are looking at net value in the T-account, so the Furniture (Net) account decreases by its *net/book* value.

We know that some furniture was sold, so obviously this decrease occurred.

We know that this furniture was sold for $90 cash, but this is *not* the net book value (NBV) of the furniture sold. This amount is still unknown.

However, we can calculate this amount using the gain/loss formula:

Gain or loss on sale of fixed assets
= Cash received on sale of fixed assets
− NBV of fixed assets sold

For this example, this becomes

Gain on sale of furniture
= Cash received on sale of furniture
− NBV of furniture sold

So $80 = $90 − NBV of furniture sold.

Therefore, the NBV of furniture sold is $10.

What else would decrease Furniture (Net)? Well, when Tanker takes depreciation expense, don't we decrease the net value of its assets? We know from the income statement that depreciation expense is $110. Let's now put all of the numbers in and see what comes out:

| Furniture (Net) | | | |
|---|---|---|---|
| **Bal 12/31/10** | 925 | | |
| **Cash Purchases** | X | | |
| **Noncash Purchases** | 200 | | |
| | | NBV Furniture Sold | 10 |
| | | Depreciation Expense | 110 |
| Bal 12/31/11 | 1,100 | | |

So $X$ = Cash paid to purchase furniture = $95.

To summarize, this is how we find missing information for long-term assets:

1. **Set up a T-account for the net value of the asset.**

2. **Fill in as much information as you can in the T-account (such as beginning and ending balances, depreciation expense, and purchases or net book value of disposals).**

3. **Solve for any missing information.**

4. **If there is more than one number missing, or if the missing information is not the number you need, use the gain/loss formula to calculate any remaining information.**

Now we can put our two numbers, $90 and $95, into the statement of cash flows. *Cash* purchases of equipment were $95. Did this cause Cash to increase or decrease? Obviously, it is a decrease because Tanker *paid* cash, so we will subtract it. Cash received on sale of equipment is $90, which is an increase to Cash, so we will add it.

Remember that for investing activities, we *cannot* combine these two items. They *must* be listed separately because they are two separate transactions.

Totaling these numbers completes investing activities.

The completed investing activities section would appear as

| Investing Activities | | |
|---|---|---|
| Cash paid to purchase new furniture........................... | $(95) | |
| Cash proceeds from sale of furniture........................... | 90 | |
| Net cash flow used for investing activities.................. | | $(5) |

## Financing Activities

Financing activities deals with long-term liabilities (debt) and equity accounts. First, we will look at long-term liabilities.

There are new notes payable (for which Tanker received cash) and Tanker repaid some other notes.

## Notes Payable

We need the cash numbers involved so that we can put them into the cash-flow statement. Do we have any of them immediately available to us?

Yes, we are told that Tanker repaid $500 of notes payable.

We also know that Tanker took out a noncash note (to purchase furniture) of $200. This noncash transaction has already been recorded in the note to the cash-flow statement (discussed under investing activities).

Knowing this, let us analyze the Notes Payable T-account:

| Notes Payable | | |
|---|---|---|
| | Bal 12/31/10 | 815 |
| decreases | increases | |
| | Bal 12/31/11 | 660 |

What would cause this account to increase? Well, it would increase if Tanker took out new notes payable. What would cause it to decrease? It would decrease if Tanker paid off some of the notes. Let's put in that information:

| Notes Payable | | | |
|---|---|---|---|
| | | Bal 12/31/10 | 815 |
| Note Repayments | 500 | | |
| | | New Cash Notes | $X$ |
| | | New Noncash Notes | 200 |
| | | Bal 12/31/11 | 660 |

So we can calculate that new cash notes = $X$ = \$145.

Now we can put these numbers into the cash-flow statement. *Cash* received from new notes was \$145. This increased Cash, so it has a positive effect on cash flow. Cash paid to repay old notes was \$500. This decreased Cash, so it has a negative effect on cash flow.

## Treasury Stock

Now we must analyze the changes in Tanker's equity. Tanker had some activity with treasury stock during the year. We know that Tanker purchased treasury stock.

| Treasury Stock | | | |
|---|---|---|---|
| Bal 12/31/10 | 0 | | |
| | increases | decreases | |
| Bal 12/31/11 | 1,000 | | |

What could cause this account to go up? It would go up if Tanker purchased treasury stock. What could cause it to go down? It would go down if treasury stock were sold. We know that there was no treasury stock sold, so looking at this again,

| Treasury Stock | | | |
|---|---|---|---|
| Bal 12/31/10 | 0 | | |
| Treasury Stock Purchased | $X$ | | |
| | | Treasury Stock Sold | 0 |
| Bal 12/31/11 | 1,000 | | |

So we can calculate that treasury stock purchased = $X$ = \$1,000. This means that cash was paid by Tanker, which is a negative effect on cash flow.

## Dividends

The other account in equity is Retained Earnings. The two major transactions impacting Retained Earnings are net income and dividends.

Net income was already listed in the operating activities section, so all that remains to be included in the financing activities section is dividend activity.

The Retained Earnings account looks like this:

| | Retained Earnings | |
|---|---|---|
| | Bal 12/31/10 | 200 |
| decreases | increases | |
| | Bal 12/31/11 | 880 |

What makes Retained Earnings go up? It goes up when Tanker earns net income. What makes it go down? It goes down when Tanker pays dividends. Putting this information in,

| | | Retained Earnings | |
|---|---|---|---|
| | | Bal 12/31/10 | 200 |
| | | New Income | 1,000 |
| Cash Dividends Paid | $X$ | | |
| | | Bal 12/31/11 | 880 |

So cash dividends paid = $X$ = \$320. These were paid in cash so this has a negative effect on Cash.

Totaling these numbers completes financing activities. The completed financing activities section would appear as

| Financing Activities | | |
|---|---|---|
| Cash proceeds from new notes | \$ 145 | |
| Cash repayment of old notes | (500) | |
| Cash purchase of treasury stock | (1,000) | |
| Cash dividends paid | (320) | |
| Net cash flow used for financing activities | | \$(1,675) |

Now we must combine operating activities, investing activities, and financing activities to get the total cash flow (the change in cash during the year).

Next, we show the Cash balance from the prior year (December 31, 2010) and add it to total cash flow to get this year's Cash balance (December 31, 2011).

**Tanker, Inc.**
**Statement of Cash Flows**
Year Ended December 31, 2011

**Operating Activities**

| | | |
|---|---:|---:|
| Net income | | $ 1,000 |
| + Depreciation expense | 110 | |
| – Gain on sale of furniture | (80) | |
| + Decrease in accounts receivable | 120 | |
| – Increase in inventory | (50) | |
| – Increase in prepaid insurance | (30) | |
| + Increase in accounts payable | 150 | |
| | | |
| Net cash flow provided by operating activities | | 1,220 |

**Investing Activities**

| | | |
|---|---:|---:|
| Cash paid to purchase new furniture | $ (95) | |
| Cash proceeds from sale of furniture | 90 | |
| | | |
| Net cash flow used for investing activities | | (5) |

**Financing Activities**

| | | |
|---|---:|---:|
| Cash proceeds from new notes | $ 145 | |
| Cash repayment of old notes | (500) | |
| Cash purchase of treasury stock | (1,000) | |
| Cash dividends paid | (320) | |
| | | |
| Net cash flow used for financing activities | | (1,675) |
| | | |
| Net decrease in Cash (change in Cash balance) | | $ (460) |
| | | |
| Cash, December 31, 2010 | | 1,160 |
| | | |
| Cash, December 31, 2011 | | $ 700 |

**Noncash Investing and Financing Activities**

| | | |
|---|---:|---:|
| Purchase of furniture with note payable | | $ 200 |

**DEMO DOC COMPLETE**

# Demo Doc 2

## Statement of Cash Flows (Direct Method)

*Learning Objectives 1, 2, 4*

### Direct Method

Use the information for Tanker, Inc., in the previous question:

### Tanker, Inc.
### Balance Sheet
### December 31, 2011

| Assets | 2011 | 2010 | Change | Liabilities | 2011 | 2010 | Change |
|---|---|---|---|---|---|---|---|
| Current: | | | | Current: | | | |
| Cash............................ | $ 700 | $1,160 | $(460) | Accounts payable ...................... | $ 680 | $ 530 | $150 |
| Accounts receivable............... | 300 | 420 | (120) | | | | |
| Inventory .............................. | 800 | 750 | 50 | Long-term notes payable............... | 660 | 815 | |
| Prepaid insurance.................. | 120 | 90 | 30 | | | | |
| | | | | Total liabilities ............................. | $1,340 | $1,345 | |
| Furniture................................. | 1,500 | 1,400 | | | | | |
| Less acc. depn. ...................... | (400) | (475) | | Owners' Equity | | | |
| Net.......................................... | 1,100 | 925 | | Common stock (no par) ............... | $1,800 | $1,800 | |
| | | | | Retained earnings.......................... | 880 | 200 | |
| Total assets............................... | $3,020 | $3,345 | | Less treasury stock ................... | (1,000) | 0 | |
| | | | | Total equity.................................... | $1,680 | $2,000 | |
| | | | | Total liabilities and equity............... | $3,020 | $3,345 | |

### Tanker, Inc.
### Income Statement
### Year Ended December 31, 2011

| | |
|---|---|
| Sales revenue .................................... | $ 3,400 |
| Less cost of goods sold................... | (1,750) |
| Gross margin.................................... | $ 1,650 |
| Depreciation expense ...................... | $ (110) |
| Insurance expense .......................... | (230) |
| Other operating expenses............... | (390) |
| Gain on sale of furniture ................ | 80 |
| Net income....................................... | $ 1,000 |

## Requirements

1. Prepare the operating activities section of Tanker's 2011 statement of cash flows using the direct method.

2. How is the information a statement of cash flows provides different from the information an income statement provides?

# Demo Doc 2 Solutions

## Requirement 1

**Prepare the operating activities section of Tanker's 2011 statement of cash flows using the direct method.**

We need to list all of the cash transactions involved in Tanker's day-to-day business operations. To do this, we should look at the income statement to get an idea of what these transactions are.

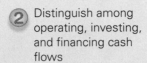

Distinguish among operating, investing, and financing cash flows

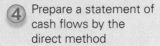

Prepare a statement of cash flows by the direct method

### Cash Received from Customers

What is the first item on the income statement? Revenues. How does this translate into a cash transaction? Revenues should result in customers giving Tanker cash, so the appropriate line on the direct method statement of cash flows is "cash received from customers."

For each income statement account that is not 100% cash, there is always a balance sheet account to record the related accrual. In this case, Accounts Receivable (on the balance sheet) takes care of revenues when cash has not yet been collected.

| Accounts Receivable | | | |
|---|---|---|---|
| Bal 12/31/10 | 420 | | |
| | increases | decreases | |
| Bal 12/31/11 | 300 | | |

What could cause this account to increase? It would increase if Tanker had more sales. What could cause it to decrease? It would decrease if Tanker collected the cash. We know from the income statement that sales were $3,400, so

| Accounts Receivable | | | |
|---|---|---|---|
| Bal 12/31/10 | 420 | | |
| Sales Revenue | 3,400 | | |
| | | Cash Collected | X |
| Bal 12/31/11 | 300 | | |

$X$ = cash collected from customers = $3,520. This is the amount for the direct method statement of cash flows.

### Cash Paid to Suppliers

The next line on the income statement is cost of goods sold. How does this relate to a cash transaction? In order to get the goods Tanker sold, it must buy the items from a supplier and pay for them. So the appropriate line on the statement of cash flows is "cash paid to suppliers." Accounts Payable is the balance sheet account that takes care of bills to suppliers that have not yet been paid.

| Accounts Payable | | | |
|---|---|---|---|
| | | Bal 12/31/10 | 530 |
| decreases | increases | | |
| | | Bal 12/31/11 | 680 |

What could cause this account to increase? It would increase if Tanker had more bills (that is, if Tanker were to purchase inventory from its suppliers). What could cause it to decrease? It would decrease if Tanker paid the cash it owed to the suppliers. However, we don't know how much inventory was purchased.

We can figure this out using the inventory formula from Chapter 6:

$$COGS = Beginning\ inventory + Purchases - Ending\ inventory$$

$$\$1,750 = \$750 + Purchases - \$800$$

$$Purchases = \$1,800$$

Putting this into the Accounts Payable T-account,

| Accounts Payable | | | |
|---|---|---|---|
| | | Bal 12/31/10 | 530 |
| Cash Payments | X | | |
| | | Inventory Purchases | 1,800 |
| | | Bal 12/31/11 | 680 |

$X$ = Cash payments to suppliers = $1,650. This is the amount for the direct method statement of cash flows.

The next item on the income statement is depreciation expense. Because we know that this is 100% noncash, we can ignore it for the direct method.

### Cash Paid for Insurance

Next is insurance expense. This would result in "cash paid for insurance." To calculate this number, we need to analyze the Prepaid Insurance account.

| Prepaid Insurance | | | |
|---|---|---|---|
| Bal 12/31/10 | 90 | | |
| increases | | decreases | |
| Bal 12/31/11 | 120 | | |

What could cause this account to increase? It would increase if Tanker paid more insurance in advance. What could cause it to decrease? It would decrease if Tanker incurred that insurance expense. We know from the income statement that insurance expense was $230.

| Prepaid Insurance | | | |
|---|---|---|---|
| Bal 12/31/10 | 90 | | |
| Cash Payments | X | | |
| | | Insurance Expense | 230 |
| Bal 12/31/11 | 120 | | |

$X$ = Cash paid for insurance = $260. This is the amount for the direct method statement of cash flows.

Following insurance expense are other expenses. Let's leave this until the end.

After this is the gain on sale of furniture. This is noncash and, therefore, does not impact a direct method statement of cash flows.

## Other Cash Expenses

Now we come back to other expenses. Are there any other current asset or current liability accounts with which we have not yet dealt? No, we have analyzed all of them. This means that there is no accrual portion (that is, no *noncash* portion) of these expenses. So we can just assume that they were *all paid in cash*. Therefore, the last line in the operating activities section is "other cash expenses" of $390.

| Operating Activities | | |
|---|---|---|
| Cash collected from customers................................... | | $3,520 |
| Cash paid to suppliers.............................................. | $(1,650) | |
| Cash paid for insurance............................................ | (260) | |
| Other cash expenses................................................. | (390) | |
| Net cash flow provided by operating activities.......... | | $1,220 |

Notice that the "net cash flow provided by operating activities" of $1,220 is the *same* total we calculated under the indirect method. It is *always* the case that cash flow from operating activities is the same under the direct and indirect methods. This is a good check to confirm that our calculations were correct.

Remember that the investing and financing activities are the same under both methods. So the rest of Tanker's statement of cash flows (investing activities to the end) would be identical to what is shown in Demo Doc 1.

## Requirement 2

**How is the information a statement of cash flows provides different from the information an income statement provides?**

> ① Identify the purposes of the statement of cash flows

The income statement shows the determination of net income. Net income is calculated on an accrual basis.

This means that net income not only includes cash transactions *but also* includes noncash transactions. We record revenue earned and expenses incurred *regardless* of whether or not cash has been received or paid.

The statement of cash flows shows the determination of cash flow (that is, the change in the Cash balance during the year). Because the statement of cash flows distills all transactions down to their cash components only, it is missing certain noncash transactions that are included in net income. Cash flow is actually net income *under the cash basis of accounting.*

So, the primary difference is that the income statement is prepared under the accrual basis of accounting whereas the statement of cash flows is prepared under the cash basis of accounting.

### DEMO DOC COMPLETE

# Quick Practice Questions

## True/False

_____  1. The statement of cash flows helps to inform the reader about all of the differences between net income and cash flows from operations.

_____  2. A company may have net income but still have a net cash outflow.

_____  3. Cash payments for interest expense would be classified as a financing activity.

_____  4. Free cash flow is a measure of cash adequacy that focuses on the amount of cash available from operations after paying for planned investments in long-term assets.

_____  5. Purchases of plant assets for cash would be classified as a financing activity.

_____  6. Under the indirect method, depreciation expense would be added to net income in the operating activities.

_____  7. The majority of U.S. corporations use the indirect method in preparing the statement of cash flows.

_____  8. Under the indirect method, the acquisition of land through the issuance of common stock would be an investing activity on the statement of cash flows.

_____  9. When using the direct method, a loss on sale of equipment is added to net income under the operating activities.

_____  10. Interest received on a bond investment would be shown as an investing cash inflow.

# Multiple Choice

1. **Which of the following statements is correct?**
   a. A statement of cash flows is an optional financial statement under GAAP.
   b. A statement of cash flows is dated at a point in time as opposed to over a period of time.
   c. One purpose of a statement of cash flows is to predict future cash flows.
   d. The statement of cash flows may be combined with the stockholders' equity section of the balance sheet.

2. **The investing activities section has a relationship with which part of the balance sheet?**
   a. Current assets and current liabilities
   b. Long-term assets
   c. Stockholders' equity and all liabilities
   d. Stockholders' equity and long-term liabilities

3. **Dividend payments would be included in which section of the statement of cash flows?**
   a. Operating activities
   b. Financing activities
   c. Investing activities
   d. Dividend payments are not included on the statement of cash flows.

4. **Cash dividends received would be included in which section of the statement of cash flows?**
   a. Operating activities
   b. Financing activities
   c. Investing activities
   d. Cash dividends received are not included on the statement of cash flows.

5. **The purchase of treasury stock would be included in which section of the statement of cash flows?**
   a. Operating activities
   b. Financing activities
   c. Investing activities
   d. The purchase of treasury stock is not included on the statement of cash flows.

6. **Activities that create revenues and expenses are included in which section of the statement of cash flows?**
   a. Investing activities
   b. Operating activities
   c. Financing activities
   d. Noncash investing and financing activities

7. **Where are noncash investing and financing activities reported?**
   a. The financing activities section of the statement of cash flows
   b. The investing activities section of the statement of cash flows
   c. Both (a) and (b) are correct.
   d. An accompanying schedule to the statement of cash flows

8. **Where is the loss resulting from the sale of equipment shown under the indirect method?**
   a. In the operating activities section as a deduction
   b. In the operating activities section as an addition
   c. In the investing activities section as an addition
   d. In the financing activities section as a deduction

9. **Wilson Company's 2011 income statement reports depreciation expense of $25,000. How would depreciation be shown on the statement of cash flows using the direct method for 2011?**
   a. As an addition under financing activities
   b. As a deduction under operating activities
   c. As an addition under operating activities
   d. It would not be reported.

10. **Which of the following would be shown as an addition to net income under the operating activities section using the indirect method?**
    a. Gain on sale of land
    b. Decrease in Accounts Payable account balance for the period
    c. Increase in Inventory balance for the period
    d. Decrease in Accounts Receivable account balance for the period

## Quick Exercises

12-1. Your best friend just lost his job because the company he was working for went bankrupt. He was complaining to you that even though the company had been profitable for three years in a row, it still went out of business. He asks you how this can happen.

1. Explain the most likely reason for the company's declaring bankruptcy. Could your friend have seen it coming? How?

2. Discuss the four purposes of the statement of cash flows.

12-2. State whether each of the following events should be classified as an operating activity (O), investing activity (I), financing activity (F), shown in a separate schedule of noncash investing and financing activities (N), or not disclosed on the statement of cash flows (NA).

_____ a. Received cash from sale of land
_____ b. Retired bonds payable by issuing common stock
_____ c. Paid for merchandise purchased on account
_____ d. Paid interest on a short-term note payable
_____ e. Received stock dividends
_____ f. Paid for a three-year insurance policy on property
_____ g. Issued preferred stock in exchange for land
_____ h. Issued common stock for cash
_____ i. Received cash dividends
_____ j. Purchased equipment for cash

**12-3.** Using the following data, prepare the operating activities section of a statement of cash flows for Virginia Corporation for the year ended December 31, 2011. Assume the indirect method is used.

| | |
|---|---:|
| Increase in salary payable | $ 1,500 |
| Decrease in accounts payable | 5,000 |
| Increase in accounts receivable | 3,500 |
| Net income | 98,000 |
| Decrease in inventory | 2,800 |
| Increase in prepaid expenses | 1,200 |
| Depreciation expense—equipment | 5,000 |
| Depreciation expense—buildings | 7,500 |
| Gain on sale of equipment | 1,300 |
| Loss on sale of patent | 2,500 |

**Virginia Corporation**
**Statement of Cash Flows**
Year Ended December 31, 2011

**12-4. For each of the following events, determine if it should be classified as an operating activity (O), investing activity (I), or financing activity (F). Then determine the cash inflow or (outflow).**

|  | Type of Activity | Cash Inflow (Outflow) |
|---|---|---|
| a. Declared cash dividends of $21,000 during the current period. Dividends payable on January 1 were $1,500; the December 31 balance was $2,300. | _____ | _____ |
| b. Interest income on the income statement for the current period is $22,000. Interest receivable on January 1 was $2,700; the December 31 balance was $2,250. | _____ | _____ |
| c. Issued $1,000,000, 10-year, 10% bonds at 102. | _____ | _____ |
| d. Sales on account for the current period amount to $160,000. The January 1 balance in Accounts Receivable was $95,000; the December 31 balance was $106,000. | _____ | _____ |
| e. Purchased equipment for $215,000 cash. | _____ | _____ |
| f. Sold 1,000 shares of $20 par common stock for cash at $29. | _____ | _____ |
| g. Salary expense on the income statement for the current year is $151,500. The Salary Payable balance on January 1 was $20,300; the December 31 balance was $17,800. | _____ | _____ |

**12-5.** Aycoth, Inc., gathered the following data from its accounting records for the year ended December 31, 2011:

| | |
|---|---:|
| Depreciation expense | $ 15,900 |
| Payment of income taxes | 24,500 |
| Collections of accounts receivable | 166,700 |
| Purchase of treasury stock | 40,000 |
| Declaration of stock dividend | 65,000 |
| Loss on sale of plant assets | 8,400 |
| Collection of dividend revenue | 13,800 |
| Payments of salaries and wages | 83,600 |
| Cash sales | 102,900 |
| Net income | 61,200 |
| Acquisition of land | 73,500 |
| Payment of interest | 19,400 |
| Interest received on investments | 3,100 |
| Issuance of bonds payable | 500,000 |
| Increase in accounts payable | 20,300 |
| Payments to suppliers | 170,300 |
| Acquisition of equipment by issuing long-term note payable | 50,000 |

**1. Prepare the operating activities section of the statement of cash flows using the direct method.**

Aycoth, Inc.
Partial Statement of Cash Flows
Year Ended December 31, 2011

| | | |
|---|---|---|
| | | |
| | | |
| | | |
| | | |
| | | |
| | | |
| | | |
| | | |
| | | |
| | | |
| | | |
| | | |
| | | |

# Do It Yourself! Question 1

## Indirect Method

Clean Co. had the following information at December 31, 2011:

### Clean Co.
### Balance Sheet
### December 31, 2011

| Assets | 2011 | 2010 | Change | Liabilities | 2011 | 2010 | Change |
|---|---|---|---|---|---|---|---|
| Current: | | | | Current: | | | |
| Cash.......................................... | $ 460 | $ 320 | $140 | Accounts payable ...................... | $ 800 | $ 540 | $260 |
| Accounts receivable............... | 510 | 420 | 90 | | | | |
| Inventory ................................. | 710 | 750 | (40) | Long-term notes payable .............. | 600 | 900 | |
| Prepaid rent .......................... | 170 | 250 | (80) | Total liabilities .............................. | $1,400 | $1,440 | |
| | | | | | | | |
| Equipment................................. | 1,350 | 1,500 | | Stockholders' Equity | | | |
| Less acc. depn. ...................... | (400) | (650) | | Common stock (no par) ............... | $ 200 | $ 150 | |
| Net............................................. | 950 | 850 | | Retained earnings.......................... | 1,200 | 1,000 | |
| | | | | | | | |
| | | | | Total equity.................................. | $1,400 | $1,150 | |
| | | | | | | | |
| Total assets................................. | $2,800 | $2,590 | | Total liabilities and equity............... | $2,800 | $2,590 | |

### Clean Co.
### Income Statement
### Year Ended December 31, 2011

| | |
|---|---|
| Sales revenue ..................................... | $1,800 |
| Less cost of goods sold .................... | (960) |
| Gross margin.................................. | $ 840 |
| | |
| Depreciation expense ...................... | $ (90) |
| Rent expense .................................... | (140) |
| Other operating expenses ................ | (195) |
| | |
| Loss on sale of equipment .............. | (55) |
| | |
| Net income....................................... | $ 360 |

## Other Information

- Every year, Clean declares and pays cash dividends.
- During 2011, Clean sold old equipment for cash. Clean also bought new equipment for $120 cash and a $140 note payable.
- During 2011, Clean repaid $600 of notes payable in cash and borrowed new long-term notes payable for cash.
- During 2011, new common stock was issued. No stock was retired.

## Requirement

1. Prepare Clean's statement of cash flows for the year ended December 31, 2011, using the indirect method.

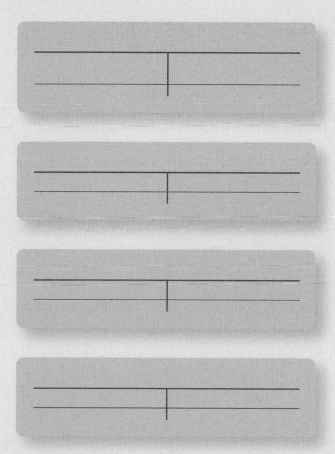

# Do It Yourself! Question 2

## Direct Method

Use the information for Clean Co. in the previous question.

### Clean Co.
### Balance Sheet
### December 31, 2011

| Assets | 2011 | 2010 | Change | Liabilities | 2011 | 2010 | Change |
|---|---|---|---|---|---|---|---|
| Current: | | | | Current: | | | |
| Cash......................................... | $ 460 | $ 320 | $140 | Accounts payable ...................... | $ 800 | $ 540 | $260 |
| Accounts receivable................ | 510 | 420 | 90 | | | | |
| Inventory .............................. | 710 | 750 | (40) | Long-term notes payable .............. | 600 | 900 | |
| Prepaid rent .......................... | 170 | 250 | (80) | Total liabilities ............................. | $1,400 | $1,440 | |
| | | | | | | | |
| Equipment................................. | 1,350 | 1,500 | | **Stockholders' Equity** | | | |
| Less acc. depn. ..................... | (400) | (650) | | Common stock (no par) ............... | $ 200 | $ 150 | |
| Net............................................ | 950 | 850 | | Retained earnings......................... | 1,200 | 1,000 | |
| | | | | | | | |
| | | | | Total equity................................... | $1,400 | $1,150 | |
| | | | | | | | |
| Total assets................................. | $2,800 | $2,590 | | Total liabilities and equity............... | $2,800 | $2,590 | |

### Clean Co.
### Income Statement
### Year Ended December 31, 2011

| | |
|---|---|
| Sales revenue .................................... | $1,800 |
| Less cost of goods sold ................... | (960) |
| Gross margin.................................... | $ 840 |
| | |
| Depreciation expense ...................... | $ (90) |
| Rent expense ................................... | (140) |
| Other operating expenses............... | (195) |
| | |
| Loss on sale of equipment .............. | (55) |
| | |
| Net income...................................... | $ 360 |

1. Prepare the operating activities section of Clean's 2011 statement of cash flows using the direct method.

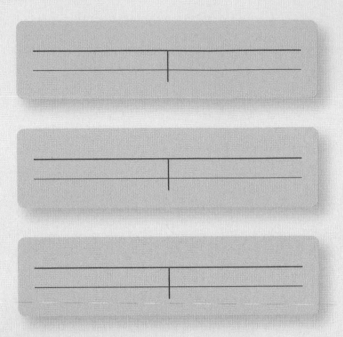

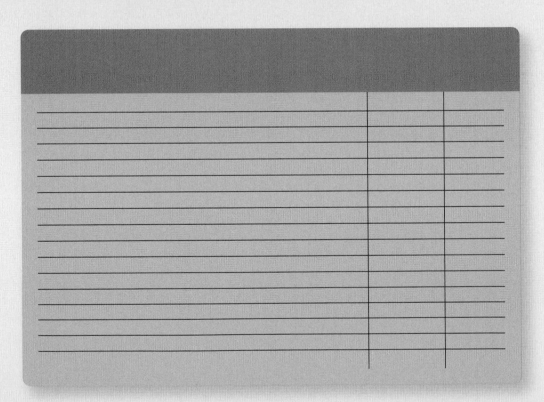

# Quick Practice Solutions

## True/False

_T_    1. The statement of cash flows helps to inform the reader about all of the differences between net income and cash flows from operations. (pp. 703–704)

_T_    2. A company may have net income but still have a net cash outflow. (p. 704)

_F_    3. Cash payments for interest expense would be classified as a financing activity.

     False—Cash payments for interest expense would be classified as an _operating_ activity. (p. 724)

_T_    4. Free cash flow is a measure of cash adequacy that focuses on the amount of cash available from operations after paying for planned investments in long-term assets. (p. 732)

_F_    5. Purchases of plant assets for cash would be classified as a financing activity.

     False—Purchases of plant assets for cash would be classified as an _investing_ activity. (p. 714)

_T_    6. Under the indirect method, depreciation expense would be added to net income in the operating activities. (p. 710)

_T_    7. The majority of U.S. corporations use the indirect method in preparing the statement of cash flows. (p. 720)

_F_    8. Under the indirect method, the acquisition of land through the issuance of common stock would be an investing activity on the statement of cash flows.

     False—Under the indirect method, the acquisition of land through the issuance of common stock would be a _noncash investing and financing_ activity. (p. 717)

_F_    9. When using the direct method, a loss on sale of equipment is added to net income under the operating activities.

     False—A loss on sale of equipment is added to net income under the operating activities using the _indirect_ method. Such losses are not reported on the statement of cash flows using the direct method. (p. 711)

_F_   10. Interest received on a bond investment would be shown as an investing cash inflow.

     False—Interest received on a bond investment would be shown as an _operating_ cash inflow. (p. 722)

# Multiple Choice

1. **Which of the following statements is correct?** (p. 703)
   a. A statement of cash flows is an optional financial statement under GAAP.
   b. A statement of cash flows is dated at a point in time as opposed to over a period of time.
   c. One purpose of a statement of cash flows is to predict future cash flows.
   d. The statement of cash flows may be combined with the stockholders' equity section of the balance sheet.

2. **The investing activities section has a relationship with which part of the balance sheet?** (p. 705)
   a. Current assets and current liabilities
   b. Long-term assets
   c. Stockholders' equity and all liabilities
   d. Stockholders' equity and long-term liabilities

3. **Dividend payments would be included in which section of the statement of cash flows?** (p. 708)
   a. Operating activities
   b. Financing activities
   c. Investing activities
   d. Dividend payments are not included on the statement of cash flows.

4. **Cash dividends received would be included in which section of the statement of cash flows?** (p. 722)
   a. Operating activities
   b. Financing activities
   c. Investing activities
   d. Cash dividends received are not included on the statement of cash flows.

5. **The purchase of treasury stock would be included in which section of the statement of cash flows?** (p. 708)
   a. Operating activities
   b. Financing activities
   c. Investing activities
   d. The purchase of treasury stock is not included on the statement of cash flows.

6. **Activities that create revenues and expenses are included in which section of the statement of cash flows?** (p. 708)
   a. Investing activities
   b. Operating activities
   c. Financing activities
   d. Noncash investing and financing activities

7. **Where are noncash investing and financing activities reported?** (p. 717)
   a. The financing activities section of the statement of cash flows
   b. The investing activities section of the statement of cash flows
   c. Both (a) and (b) are correct.
   d. An accompanying schedule to the statement of cash flows

8. **Where is the loss resulting from the sale of equipment shown under the indirect method?** (p. 711)
   a. In the operating activities section as a deduction
   b. In the operating activities section as an addition
   c. In the investing activities section as an addition
   d. In the financing activities section as a deduction

9. **Wilson Company's 2011 income statement reports depreciation expense of $25,000. How would depreciation be shown on the statement of cash flows using the direct method for 2011?** (p. 724)
   a. As an addition under financing activities
   b. As a deduction under operating activities
   c. As an addition under operating activities
   d. It would not be reported.

10. **Which of the following would be shown as an addition to net income under the operating activities section using the indirect method?** (p. 711)
   a. Gain on sale of land
   b. Decrease in Accounts Payable account balance for the period
   c. Increase in Inventory balance for the period
   d. Decrease in Accounts Receivable account balance for the period

# Quick Exercises

**12-1. Your best friend just lost his job because the company he was working for went bankrupt. He was complaining to you that even though the company had been profitable for three years in a row, it still went out of business. He asks you how this can happen.** (pp. 704–705)

**1. Explain the most likely reason for the company's declaring bankruptcy. Could your friend have seen it coming? How?**

A profitable company is one in which revenues exceed expenses on an accrual basis. This does not necessarily mean that the company is generating enough cash to pay its bills. The most likely reason your friend's company went bankrupt is the lack of cash. If your friend had access to the statement of cash flows, the cash-flow problems would have likely been evident.

**2. Discuss the four purposes of the statement of cash flows.**

The four purposes of the statement of cash flows are as follows:
1. To help predict future cash flows
2. To evaluate management decisions
3. To determine the company's ability to pay dividends to stockholders and interest and principal to creditors
4. To show the relationship of net income to changes in the business's cash

**12-2. State whether each of the following events should be classified as an operating activity (O), investing activity (I), financing activity (F), shown in a separate schedule of noncash investing and financing activities (N), or not disclosed on the statement of cash flows (NA).** (p. 708)

| | | |
|---|---|---|
| I | **a.** | Received cash from sale of land |
| N | **b.** | Retired bonds payable by issuing common stock |
| O | **c.** | Paid for merchandise purchased on account |
| O | **d.** | Paid interest on a short-term note payable |
| NA | **e.** | Received stock dividends |
| O | **f.** | Paid for a three-year insurance policy on property |
| N | **g.** | Issued preferred stock in exchange for land |
| F | **h.** | Issued common stock for cash |
| O | **i.** | Received cash dividends |
| I | **j.** | Purchased equipment for cash |

**12-3. Using the following data, prepare the operating activities section of a statement of cash flows for Virginia Corporation for the year ended December 31, 2011. Assume the indirect method is used.** (pp. 710–712)

| | |
|---|---:|
| Increase in salary payable............................. | $ 1,500 |
| Decrease in accounts payable ....................... | 5,000 |
| Increase in accounts receivable.................... | 3,500 |
| Net income................................................. | 98,000 |
| Decrease in inventory ................................. | 2,800 |
| Increase in prepaid expenses......................... | 1,200 |
| Depreciation expense—equipment .............. | 5,000 |
| Depreciation expense—buildings.................. | 7,500 |
| Gain on sale of equipment........................... | 1,300 |
| Loss on sale of patent.................................. | 2,500 |

### Virginia Corporation
### Statement of Cash Flows
### Year Ended December 31, 2011

| | | |
|---|---:|---:|
| Cash flows from operating activities: | | |
| Net income.................................................................. | | $ 98,000 |
| Adjustments to reconcile net income to | | |
| net cash provided by operating activities: | | |
| Depreciation on equipment .......................................... | $5,000 | |
| Depreciation on buildings ........................................... | 7,500 | |
| Loss on sale of patent.................................................. | 2,500 | |
| Gain on sale of equipment .......................................... | (1,300) | |
| Increase in accounts receivable ................................... | (3,500) | |
| Increase in prepaid expenses ....................................... | (1,200) | |
| Decrease in inventory.................................................. | 2,800 | |
| Increase in salary payable............................................ | 1,500 | |
| Decrease in accounts payable ...................................... | (5,000) | 8,300 |
| Net cash inflow from operating activities............... | | $106,300 |

**12-4. For each of the following events, determine if it should be classified as an operating activity (O), investing activity (I), or financing activity (F). Then determine the cash inflow or (outflow).** (p. 708)

| Transaction Description | Type of Activity | Cash Inflow (Outflow) |
|---|---|---|
| a. Declared cash dividends of $21,000 during the current period. Dividends payable on January 1 were $1,500; the December 31 balance was $2,300. | F | $ (20,200) |
| b. Interest income on the income statement for the current period is $22,000. Interest receivable on January 1 was $2,700; the December 31 balance was $2,250. | O | $ 22,450 |
| c. Issued $1,000,000, 10-year, 10% bonds at 102. | F | $1,020,000 |
| d. Sales on account for the current period amount to $160,000. The January 1 balance in Accounts Receivable was $95,000; the December 31 balance was $106,000. | O | $ 149,000 |
| e. Purchased equipment for $215,000 cash. | I | $ (215,000) |
| f. Sold 1,000 shares of $20 par common stock for cash at $29. | F | $ 29,000 |
| g. Salary expense on the income statement for the current year is $151,500. The Salary Payable balance on January 1 was $20,300; the December 31 balance was $17,800. | O | $ (154,000) |

**12-5. Aycoth, Inc., gathered the following data from its accounting records for the year ended December 31, 2011:** (pp. 720–724)

| | |
|---|---|
| Depreciation expense | $ 15,900 |
| Payment of income taxes | 24,500 |
| Collections of accounts receivable | 166,700 |
| Purchase of treasury stock | 40,000 |
| Declaration of stock dividend | 65,000 |
| Loss on sale of plant assets | 8,400 |
| Collection of dividend revenue | 13,800 |
| Payments of salaries and wages | 83,600 |
| Cash sales | 102,900 |
| Net income | 61,200 |
| Acquisition of land | 73,500 |
| Payment of interest | 19,400 |
| Interest received on investments | 3,100 |
| Issuance of bonds payable | 500,000 |
| Increase in accounts payable | 20,300 |
| Payments to suppliers | 170,300 |
| Acquisition of equipment by issuing long-term note payable | 50,000 |

**1. Prepare the operating activities section of the statement of cash flows using the direct method.**

| | | |
|---|---:|---:|
| **Aycoth, Inc.** | | |
| **Partial Statement of Cash Flows** | | |
| **Year Ended December 31, 2011** | | |
| Cash flows from operating activities: | | |
| Receipts: | | |
| Collections from customers........................................... | $ 269,600* | |
| Interest received .......................................................... | 3,100 | |
| Dividends received ...................................................... | 13,800 | |
| Total cash receipts.................................................. | | $ 286,500 |
| Payments: | | |
| To suppliers................................................................ | $(170,300) | |
| To employees ............................................................. | (83,600) | |
| For interest................................................................. | (19,400) | |
| For income tax............................................................ | (24,500) | |
| Total cash payments............................................... | | (297,800) |
| Net cash outflow from operating activities...................... | | $ (11,300) |

*($166,700 + $102,900 = $269,600)

# Do It Yourself! Question 1 Solutions

## Indirect Method

### Requirement

1. Prepare Clean's statement of cash flows for the year ended December 31, 2011, using the indirect method.

### Calculations: Investing Activities

The $140 note payable is a *noncash transaction*.

|  | Equipment (Net) |  |  |  |
| --- | --- | --- | --- | --- |
| Bal 12/31/10 | 850 |  |  |  |
| Cash Purchases | 120 |  |  |  |
| Noncash Purchases | 140 |  |  |  |
|  |  | NBV Equipment Sold | $X$ |  |
|  |  | Depreciation Expense | 90 |  |
| Bal 12/31/11 | 950 |  |  |  |

$X$ = NBV of equipment sold = $70
Loss = −$55 = Cash received − $70
Cash received on sale of equipment = $15

# Calculations: Financing Activities

## Notes Payable

| | | | |
|---|---|---|---|
| | | Bal 12/31/10 | 900 |
| Note Repayments | 600 | | |
| | | New Cash Notes | $X$ |
| | | New Noncash Notes | 140 |
| | | Bal 12/31/11 | 600 |

New cash notes = $X$ = $160

## Common Stock

| | | | |
|---|---|---|---|
| | | Bal 12/31/10 | 150 |
| Retirements | 0 | | |
| | | New Stock Issued | $X$ |
| | | Bal 12/31/11 | 200 |

New stock issued = $X$ = $50

## Retained Earnings

| | | | |
|---|---|---|---|
| | | Bal 12/31/10 | 1,000 |
| Cash Dividends Paid | $X$ | | |
| | | Net Income | 360 |
| | | Bal 12/31/11 | 1,200 |

Cash dividends paid = $X$ = $160

**Clean Co.**
**Statement of Cash Flows**
Year Ended December 31, 2011

**Operating Activities**

| | | |
|---|---:|---:|
| Net income.................................................................... | | $ 360 |
| + Depreciation expense ................................................. | $ 90 | |
| + Loss on sale of equipment ........................................... | 55 | |
| – Increase in accounts receivable ................................... | (90) | |
| + Decrease in inventory.................................................. | 40 | |
| + Decrease in prepaid rent............................................. | 80 | |
| + Increase in accounts payable ....................................... | 260 | |
| | | |
| Net cash flow provided by operating activities.................. | | 795 |

**Investing Activities**

| | | |
|---|---:|---:|
| Cash paid to purchase new equipment ............................. | $(120) | |
| Cash proceeds from sale of equipment ............................. | 15 | |
| | | |
| Net cash flow used for investing activities........................ | | (105) |

**Financing Activities**

| | | |
|---|---:|---:|
| Cash proceeds from new notes........................................ | $ 160 | |
| Cash repayment of old notes........................................... | (600) | |
| Cash proceeds from new stock issue................................ | 50 | |
| Cash dividends paid ....................................................... | (160) | |
| | | |
| Net cash flow used for financing activities ....................... | | (550) |
| | | |
| Net increase in Cash (change in Cash during year)........... | | $ 140 |
| | | |
| Cash, December 31, 2010 ............................................... | | 320 |
| | | |
| Cash, December 31, 2011 ............................................... | | $ 460 |

**Noncash Investing and Financing Activities**

| | | |
|---|---:|---:|
| Purchase of equipment with note payable ........................ | | $ 140 |

# Do It Yourself! Question 2 Solutions

## Direct Method

1. Prepare the operating activities section of Clean's 2011 statement of cash flows using the direct method.

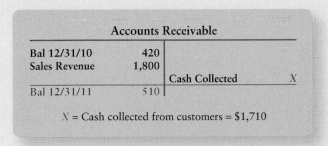

**Accounts Receivable**

| | | | |
|---|---|---|---|
| Bal 12/31/10 | 420 | | |
| Sales Revenue | 1,800 | | |
| | | Cash Collected | X |
| Bal 12/31/11 | 510 | | |

$X$ = Cash collected from customers = $1,710

**Accounts Payable**

| | | | |
|---|---|---|---|
| | | Bal 12/31/10 | 540 |
| Cash Payments | X | | |
| | | Inventory Purchases | 920* |
| | | Bal 12/31/11 | 800 |

$X$ = Cash payments to suppliers = $660
*COGS = $960 = $750 + Purchases − $710
Purchases = $920

**Prepaid Rent**

| | | | |
|---|---|---|---|
| Bal 12/31/10 | 250 | | |
| Cash Payments | X | | |
| | | Rent Expense | 140 |
| Bal 12/31/11 | 170 | | |

$X$ = Cash paid for rent = $60

### Clean Co.
### Statement of Cash Flows (Partial)
### Year Ended December 30, 2011

**Operating Activities**

| | | |
|---|---|---|
| Cash collected from customers | | $1,710 |
| Cash paid to suppliers | $(660) | |
| Cash paid for rent | (60) | |
| Other cash expenses | (195) | |
| Net cash flow from operating activities | | $ 795 |

# The Power of Practice

For more practice using the skills learned in this chapter, visit MyAccountingLab. There you will find algorithmically generated questions that are based on these Demo Docs and your main textbook's Review and Assess Your Progress sections.

Go to MyAccountingLab and follow these steps:

1. Direct your URL to www.myaccountinglab.com.
2. Log in using your name and password.
3. Click the MyAccountingLab link.
4. Click Study Plan in the left navigation bar.
5. From the table of contents, select Chapter 12, The Statement of Cash Flows.
6. Click a link to work tutorial exercises.

# 13 Financial Statement Analysis

## WHAT YOU PROBABLY ALREADY KNOW

For years now, you have been a student and have taken many exams. You probably already know that there may be typical responses you have upon receiving your grade. Your first reaction may be the level of satisfaction you have with your grade compared to your previous grades received in that class and the established grading norms for your institution. You may then ask your friends what grade they received so that you can compare your results to theirs. The instructor may announce the average exam results and you could then determine if you performed better or worse than the average. Students often like to assess their performance by comparing their grade to a standard, their peers, and the average. Businesses often do the same thing. In this chapter, you study various techniques and ratios that a business will use to assess its performance using comparisons to previous results, competitors, and the industry average.

## Learning Objectives

 **Perform a horizontal analysis of financial statements**

**Horizontal analysis** provides comparisons of financial information over time. To analyze a line item in the financial statements, the difference between the current and earlier time period amounts is computed. The dollar amount change of the line item between the periods is useful, but it is more informative to determine the percentage change by dividing the dollar change (current period amount, or this year's balance minus earlier period amount, or last year's balance) by the earlier ("base") period amount. *Review the horizontal analysis of the income statements and the balance sheets in Exhibits 13-2 and 13-3 (pp. 779–780).*

 **Perform a vertical analysis of financial statements**

**Vertical analysis** provides comparisons of individual items on a financial statement to a relative base. The base, which serves as the denominator, is usually net sales for the income statement and total assets for the balance sheet. The vertical analysis percentage is calculated by dividing each financial statement item amount by the relevant base of net sales *or* total assets.

The vertical analysis percentage is shown next to the item amount on the financial statement. *Review the vertical analysis of the income statements and the balance sheets in Exhibits 13-4 and 13-5 (pp. 783–784).*

**3** **Prepare common-size financial statements**

A **common-size statement** is similar to the vertical analysis but shows only the vertical analysis percentages of each item in the financial statement. This presentation permits ready comparisons between companies of various sizes. *Review the common-size comparison of Amazon.com versus Walmart in Exhibit 13-6 (p. 786).*

**4** **Use the statement of cash flows for decisions**

Examining the statement of cash flows can provide much information about a company. Cash flows from operations are usually expected to be positive and equal to or greater than net income. If this is not the case, the company may be in trouble.

In a healthy company, we expect investing activities and financing activities to provide low or negative cash flows. *Review the cash-flow signs of a healthy company on p. 787.*

**5** **Compute the standard financial ratios**

Financial ratios are helpful to assess a company's performance and financial position. Trends can be determined and comparisons to competing companies can be made. Various ratios are presented to measure the following:

- Ability to pay current liabilities
- Ability to sell inventory and collect receivables
- Ability to pay debts
- Profitability
- Return on stock investment

*Review "Using Ratios to Make Business Decisions" in the text for descriptions and formulas for the financial ratios on pp. 790–798.*

**6** **Use ratios in decision making**

When used properly, ratios can be very helpful in evaluating stock investment options. The price/earnings ratio shows the market price of $1 of earnings. Dividend yield is the ratio of dividends per share of stock to the stock's market price. Book value per share of common stock is the accounting value of the company for each individual common share. *Review the calculation of these ratios on pp. 798–799.*

**7** **Measure the economic value added by operations**

Economic value added (EVA) is an accounting and finance measure used to evaluate company performance. A high EVA indicates that shareholder wealth has increased. *Review the calculation of economic value added on pp. 799–800.*

# Demo Doc 1

## Financial Statement Analysis

*Learning Objectives 1–7*

MeMe Co. had the following information at December 31, 2011:

| MeMe Co. Balance Sheet December 31, 2011 and 2010 | | |
|---|---|---|
| *(Dollar amounts in millions)* | 2011 | 2010 |
| **Assets** | | |
| Cash.................................................. | $150 | $130 |
| Accounts receivable......................... | 80 | 145 |
| Inventory.......................................... | 130 | 190 |
| Total assets...................................... | $360 | $465 |
| **Liabilities** | | |
| Accounts payable............................. | 90 | 140 |
| Loans payable.................................. | 140 | 220 |
| Total liabilities................................ | $230 | $360 |
| **Stockholders' Equity** | | |
| Common stock.................................. | 20 | 10 |
| Retained earnings............................ | 110 | 95 |
| Total stockholders' equity............... | $130 | $105 |
| Total liabilities and equity.............. | $360 | $465 |

| MeMe Co. | | |
|---|---|---|
| Income Statement | | |
| Years Ended December 31, 2011 and 2010 | | |
| *(Dollar amounts in millions)* | 2011 | 2010 |
| Sales revenue..................................... | $650 | $580 |
| Less cost of goods sold.................... | 430 | 350 |
| Gross profit....................................... | $220 | $230 |
| Salary expense................................. | 120 | 140 |
| Rent expense..................................... | 70 | 80 |
| Net income...................................... | $ 30 | $ 10 |

At December 31, 2009, MeMe's inventory was $160 and total equity was $95.

## Requirements

1. **Prepare horizontal and vertical analyses for MeMe's financial statements.**

2. **Calculate MeMe's inventory turnover and rate of return on stockholders' equity ratios for both years.**

3. **Calculate MeMe's book value per share of common stock for 2011, assuming that MeMe has 50 million common shares outstanding.**

4. **Calculate MeMe's cash flow from operating activities using the indirect method. Does this number indicate that MeMe is in good financial health?**

5. **Calculate MeMe's economic value added (EVA) for 2011, assuming a cost of capital of 10%.**

# Demo Doc 1 Solutions

## Requirement 1

**Prepare horizontal and vertical analyses for MeMe's financial statements.**

> ① Perform a horizontal analysis of financial statements

### Horizontal Analysis

As its name implies, horizontal analysis goes *across* the rows of the financial statements, looking at *one* account and how it has changed.

For *each* number on the balance sheet and income statement, we calculate the *dollar change* and the *percent change*.

> Dollar change = This year's balance − Last year's balance

So in the dollar change of Accounts Receivable and Sales Revenue:

> Accounts Receivable = \$80,000,000 − \$145,000,000 = \$(65,000,000) change
> Sales Revenue = \$650,000,000 − \$580,000,000 = \$70,000,000 change

Notice that the negative value on the change in Accounts Receivable indicates that this account has decreased, whereas the positive value on the change in Sales Revenue indicates that this account has increased.

Extra care must be taken when using this calculation on expenses (because they are presented as subtracted/negative numbers on the income statement). The *absolute value* of the expense (that is, ignoring the fact that it is already a negative number) must be used to calculate dollar change. In the dollar change of COGS and Rent Expense

> COGS = \$430,000,000 − \$350,000,000 = \$80,000,000 change
> Rent Expense = \$70,000,000 − \$80,000,000 = \$(10,000,000) change

Again, the positive value indicates that COGS increased and the negative value indicates that Rent Expense decreased.

$$\text{Percent change} = \frac{\text{Dollar change}}{\text{Last year's balance}}$$

So in the percent changes of Accounts Receivable and Sales Revenue

$$\text{Accounts Receivable} = \frac{\$(65,000,000)}{\$145,000,000}$$
$$= (44.8)\% \text{ change}$$

$$\text{Sales Revenue} = \frac{\$70,000,000}{\$580,000,000}$$
$$= 12.1\% \text{ change}$$

Again, the percent change numbers are negative for Accounts Receivable (which decreased in 2011) and positive for Sales Revenue (which increased in 2011). The percent change is calculated the same way for expenses, again using the *absolute value* of the expenses. In the percent changes of COGS and Rent Expense

$$COGS = \frac{\$80,000,000}{\$350,000,000}$$
$$= 22.9\% \text{ change}$$

$$Rent\ Expense = \frac{\$(10,000,000)}{\$80,000,000}$$
$$= (12.5)\% \text{ change}$$

### MeMe Co.
### Horizontal Analysis of Balance Sheet
### Years Ended December 31, 2011 and 2010

| (Dollar amounts in millions) | 2011 | 2010 | Increase (Decrease) Amount | Percent |
|---|---|---|---|---|
| **Assets** | | | | |
| Cash.................................................. | $150 | $130 | $ 20 | 15.4 % |
| Accounts receivable......................... | 80 | 145 | (65) | (44.8) |
| Inventory.......................................... | 130 | 190 | (60) | (31.6) |
| Total assets...................................... | $360 | $465 | $(105) | (22.6) |
| **Liabilities** | | | | |
| Accounts payable ............................ | 90 | 140 | (50) | (35.7) |
| Loans payable ................................. | 140 | 220 | (80) | (36.4) |
| Total liabilities ............................... | $230 | $360 | $(130) | (36.1) |
| **Stockholders' Equity** | | | | |
| Common stock................................. | 20 | 10 | 10 | 100.0 |
| Retained earnings............................ | 110 | 95 | 15 | 15.8 |
| Total stockholders' equity............... | $130 | $105 | $ 25 | 23.8 |
| Total liabilities and equity............... | $360 | $465 | $(105) | (22.6)% |

**MeMe Co.**
**Horizontal Analysis of Comparative Income Statement**
**Years Ended December 31, 2011 and 2010**

| (Dollar amounts in millions) | 2011 | 2010 | Increase (Decrease) | |
|---|---|---|---|---|
| | | | Amount | Percent |
| Sales revenue............................. | $650 | $580 | $ 70 | 12.1 % |
| Less cost of goods sold.................. | 430 | 350 | 80 | 22.9 |
| Gross profit.................................. | $220 | $230 | (10) | (4.3) |
| Salary expense............................. | 120 | 140 | (20) | (14.3) |
| Rent expense................................ | 70 | 80 | (10) | (12.5) |
| Net income.................................. | $ 30 | $10 | $ 20 | 200.0 % |

## Vertical Analysis

As its name implies, vertical analysis takes *each* number on the financial statements and compares it to others in the same year (that is, *down* the columns of the financial statements). Vertical analysis is sometimes called *common-size analysis* because it allows two companies of different sizes to be compared (through the use of percentages).

2 Perform a vertical analysis of financial statements

3 Prepare common-size financial statements

### Balance Sheet Vertical Analysis

On the **balance sheet,** each number, whether it is an asset, a liability, or an equity account, is calculated as a percentage of *total assets.*

$$\text{Vertical analysis percent (balance sheet)} = \frac{\text{Account balance}}{\text{Total assets}}$$

So in the case of Accounts Receivable

$$\text{Vertical analysis percent (2011 Accounts Receivable)} = \frac{\$80,000,000}{\$360,000,000}$$
$$= 22.2\%$$

In other words, about 22% of all the assets in 2011 are in Accounts Receivable.

### Income Statement Vertical Analysis

On the **income statement,** each number is calculated as a percentage of **net sales revenues.**

$$\text{Vertical analysis percent (income statement)} = \frac{\text{Account balance}}{\text{Net sales revenues}}$$

So in the case of Gross Profit

$$\text{Vertical analysis percent (2011 Gross Profit)} = \frac{\$220,000,000}{\$650,000,000}$$
$$= 33.8\%$$

This means that for every dollar in sales revenues, \$0.338 went to Gross Profit.

For expenses, the calculation is the same. So in the cases of COGS and Rent Expense:

$$\text{Vertical analysis percent (2011 COGS)} = \frac{\$430,000,000}{\$650,000,000}$$
$$= 66.2\%$$

$$\text{Vertical analysis percent (2011 Rent Expense)} = \frac{\$70,000,000}{\$650,000,000}$$
$$= 10.8\%$$

### MeMe Co.
### Vertical Analysis of Balance Sheet
### December 31, 2011 and 2010

| (Dollar amounts in millions) | 2011 | 2011 % | 2010 | 2010 % |
|---|---|---|---|---|
| **Assets** | | | | |
| Cash.............................................. | $150 | 41.7% | $130 | 28.0% |
| Accounts receivable......................... | 80 | 22.2 | 145 | 31.1* |
| Inventory........................................ | 130 | 36.1 | 190 | 40.9 |
| Total assets..................................... | $360 | 100.0% | $465 | 100.0% |
| **Liabilities** | | | | |
| Accounts payable............................ | 90 | 25.0% | 140 | 30.1% |
| Loans payable................................. | 140 | 38.9 | 220 | 47.3 |
| Total liabilities............................... | $230 | 63.9% | $360 | 77.4% |
| **Stockholders' Equity** | | | | |
| Common stock................................ | 20 | 5.5*% | 10 | 2.2% |
| Retained earnings........................... | 110 | 30.6 | 95 | 20.4 |
| Total stockholders' equity............... | $130 | 36.1% | $105 | 22.6% |
| Total liabilities and equity............... | $360 | 100.0% | $465 | 100.0% |

*Rounded down to balance.

**MeMe Co.**
**Vertical Analysis of Comparative Income Statement**
**Years Ended December 31, 2011 and 2010**

|  | 2011 | 2011 % | 2010 | 2010 % |
|---|---|---|---|---|
| Net sales revenue............................. | $650 | 100.0% | $580 | 100.0% |
| Less cost of goods sold.................... | 430 | 66.2 | 350 | 60.3 |
| Gross profit...................................... | $220 | 33.8% | $230 | 39.7% |
| Salary expense................................. | 120 | 18.4* | 140 | 24.2 (rounded) |
| Rent expense.................................... | 70 | 10.8 | 80 | 13.8 |
| Net income...................................... | $ 30 | 4.6% | $ 10 | 1.7% |

*Rounded to balance.

## Requirement 2

**Calculate MeMe's inventory turnover and rate of return on stockholders' equity ratios for both years.**

⑤ Compute the standard financial ratios

Remember that "average" (when used in a financial ratio) generally means the beginning balance plus the ending balance divided by 2.

$$\text{Inventory turnover} = \frac{\text{COGS}}{\text{Average inventory}}$$

$$2011 \text{ Inventory turnover} = \frac{\$430,000,000}{[\frac{1}{2}(\$190,000,000 + \$130,000,000)]}$$
$$= 2.7 \text{ times}$$

$$2010 \text{ Inventory turnover} = \frac{\$350,000,000}{[\frac{1}{2}(\$160,000,000 + \$190,000,000)]}$$
$$= 2 \text{ times}$$

$$\text{Rate of return on stockholders' equity} = \frac{\text{Net income} - \text{Preferred dividends}}{\text{Average common stockholders' equity}}$$

$$2011 \text{ Rate of return on stockholders' equity} = \frac{[\$30,000,000 - \$0]}{[\frac{1}{2}(\$105,000,000 + \$130,000,000)]}$$
$$= 25.5\%$$

$$2010 \text{ Rate of return on stockholders' equity} = \frac{[\$10,000,000 - \$0]}{[\frac{1}{2}(\$95,000,000 + \$105,000,000)]}$$
$$= 10\%$$

## Requirement 3

⑥ Use ratios in decision making

**Calculate MeMe's book value per share of common stock for 2011, assuming that MeMe has 50 million common shares outstanding.**

$$\text{Book value per share of common stock} = \frac{\text{Total stockholders' equity} - \text{Preferred equity}}{\text{Number of shares of common stock outstanding}}$$

$$\text{2011 Book value per share of common stock} = \frac{\$130,000,000 - 0}{50,000,000 \text{ shares}}$$

$$= \$2.60$$

## Requirement 4

④ Use the statement of cash flows for decisions

**Calculate MeMe's cash flow from operating activities using the indirect method. Does this number indicate that MeMe is in good financial health?**

If necessary, review the preparation of the statement of cash flows in Chapter 12.

Using the indirect method, we begin with net income, which is $30,000,000. Because MeMe has no depreciation expense or gains or losses on its income statement, we do not have to make any adjustments to net income.

The non-cash current assets are accounts receivable and inventory, which both decreased. These decreases (calculated in Requirement 1 of this question) would increase cash flow.

The only current liability is accounts payable, which decreased (decrease calculated in Requirement 1 of this question). This would decrease cash flow.

So, cash flow from operating activities would be calculated as follows:

| | |
|---|---:|
| Net income..................................................... | $ 30,000,000 |
| Decrease in accounts receivable...................... | 65,000,000 |
| Decrease in inventory..................................... | 60,000,000 |
| Decrease in accounts payable ......................... | (50,000,000) |
| Net cash flow from operating activities........... | $105,000,000 |

The cash flow from operating activities is positive, and significantly higher than net income. This would indicate that MeMe is in good financial health.

## Requirement 5

⑦ Measure the economic value added by operations

**Calculate MeMe's economic value added (EVA) for 2011, assuming a cost of capital of 10%.**

$$\text{Economic value added} = \text{Net income} + \text{Interest expense} - \text{Capital charge}$$
$$\text{where}$$
$$\text{Capital charge} = [\text{Notes payable} + \text{Long-term debt} + \text{Stockholders' equity}] \times \text{Cost of capital}$$
$$\text{2011 Capital charge} = [\$140,000,000 \text{ Loans Payable} + \$130,000,000 \text{ Total Equity}] \times 10\%$$
$$= \$27,000,000$$
$$\text{2011 EVA} = \$30,000,000 \text{ Net Income} - \$27,000,000 = \$3,000,000$$

## *DEMO DOC COMPLETE*

# Quick Practice Questions

## True/False

_____ 1. It is generally considered less useful to know the percentage change in financial statement amounts from year to year than to know the absolute dollar amount of their change.

_____ 2. Benchmarking may be done against an industry average or against a key competitor.

_____ 3. Horizontal analysis of financial statements reveals changes in items on the financial statements over time.

_____ 4. Inventory turnover is the ratio of average inventory to cost of goods sold.

_____ 5. Book value per share of common stock has no relationship to market value.

_____ 6. A high current ratio means that a company's current assets represent a relatively large portion (or ratio) of current liabilities.

_____ 7. The debt ratio measures the ability to pay current liabilities.

_____ 8. The acid-test (quick) ratio includes the sum of Cash, Net Accounts Receivable, and Inventory in the numerator.

_____ 9. Earnings per share indicates the net income earned for each share of common and preferred stock.

_____ 10. A signal of financial trouble may include cash flow from operations being lower than net income from period to period.

# Multiple Choice

1.  **Vertical analysis can be described as which of the following?**
    a. Percentage changes in various financial statement amounts from year to year
    b. The changes in individual financial statement amounts as a percentage of some related total
    c. The change in key financial statement ratios over a certain time frame or horizon
    d. None of the above

2.  **Trend percentages can be considered a form of which of the following?**
    a. Ratio analysis
    b. Vertical analysis
    c. Profitability analysis
    d. Horizontal analysis

3.  **In 2010, net sales were $1,600,000 and in 2011, net sales were $1,750,000. How is the percent change calculated?**
    a. Divide $1,600,000 by $1,750,000
    b. Divide $1,750,000 by $1,600,000
    c. Divide $150,000 by $1,750,000
    d. Divide $150,000 by $1,600,000

4.  **Horizontal analysis can be described as which of the following?**
    a. Percentage changes in the balances shown in comparative financial statements
    b. The change in key financial statement ratios over a specified period of time
    c. The dollar amount of the change in various financial statement amounts from year to year
    d. Individual financial statement items expressed as a percentage of a base (which represents 100%)

5.  **What is the base that is used when performing vertical analysis on an income statement?**
    a. Net sales
    b. Gross sales
    c. Gross profit
    d. Total expenses

6.  **What is the base that is used when performing vertical analysis on a balance sheet?**
    a. Total assets
    b. Stockholders' equity
    c. Total liabilities
    d. Net assets

7. **Which ratio measures the ability to cover interest expense with current operating income?**
   a. Rate of return on net sales
   b. Earnings per share
   c. Times-interest-earned ratio
   d. Acid-test (quick) ratio

8. **Which of the following would be most helpful in the comparison of different-sized companies?**
   a. Performing horizontal analysis
   b. Looking at the amount of income earned by each company
   c. Comparing working capital balances
   d. Preparing common-size financial statements

9. **Which ratio(s) help(s) in the analysis of working capital?**
   a. Current ratio
   b. Acid-test ratio
   c. Debt ratio
   d. Both a and b are correct.

10. **Assume that collections from customers on account are being received faster. Which of the following would be true?**
    a. The accounts receivable turnover would be higher.
    b. The days' sales in receivables would be higher.
    c. The current ratio would be higher.
    d. None of the above is true.

# Quick Exercises

**13-1. Selected items from the balance sheet and income statement follow for the Brothers Company for 2011 and 2010.**

    **1. Calculate the amount of the change and the percentage of change for each item.**

| | 2011 | 2010 | $ Change | % Change |
|---|---|---|---|---|
| Cash.............................................. | $121,000 | $100,000 | _____ | _____ |
| Accounts receivable..................... | 117,000 | 125,000 | _____ | _____ |
| Merchandise inventory................ | 70,000 | 85,000 | _____ | _____ |
| Accounts payable ........................ | 63,500 | 50,000 | _____ | _____ |
| Sales............................................ | 144,000 | 135,000 | _____ | _____ |
| Cost of goods sold....................... | 74,000 | 67,500 | _____ | _____ |

**13-2. Using the following data for Dream Corporation for 2011, calculate the ratios that follow:**

| | |
|---|---|
| Market price per share of common stock at 12/31/11 .............. | $ 9.00 |
| Net income............................................................................. | 50,000.00 |
| Number of common shares outstanding.................................... | 25,000.00 |
| Dividend per share of common stock ....................................... | $ 0.71 |

    **a.** earnings per share of common stock

    **b.** price/earnings ratio

    **c.** dividend yield

**13-3.** The income statement for Science Corporation for the year
ended December 31, 2011, follows:

Science Corporation
Income Statement
Year Ended December 31, 2011

| | | |
|---|---:|---:|
| Net sales..................................... | | $661,000 |
| Expenses: | | |
| Cost of goods sold ................. | $268,500 | |
| Selling expenses...................... | 35,000 | |
| General expenses.................... | 49,300 | |
| Interest expenses ................... | 45,000 | |
| Income tax expense............... | 30,000 | |
| Total expenses........................... | | 427,800 |
| Net income................................. | | $233,200 |

1. **Prepare a vertical analysis of the income statement showing appropriate percentages for each item listed.**

Science Corporation
Income Statement
Year Ended December 31, 2011

2. **What additional information would you need to determine whether these percentages are good or bad?**

**13-4. Match the function with the appropriate ratio.**

**Functions:**

a. Gives the amount of net income earned for each share of the company's common stock

b. Measures the number of times operating income can cover interest expense

c. Shows ability to pay all current liabilities if they come due immediately

d. Shows the percentage of a stock's market value returned to stockholders as dividends each period

e. Measures ability to collect cash from credit customers

f. Measures ability to pay current liabilities with current assets

g. Indicates the market price of $1 of earnings

h. Measures the difference between current assets and current liabilities

i. Indicates percentage of assets financed with debt

j. Shows the percentage of each sales dollar earned as net income

**Ratios:**

1. _____ Dividend yield
2. _____ Rate of return on net sales
3. _____ Accounts receivable turnover
4. _____ Working capital
5. _____ Debt ratio
6. _____ Current ratio
7. _____ Price/earnings ratio
8. _____ Times-interest-earned ratio
9. _____ Acid-test ratio
10. _____ Earnings per share of common stock

**13-5.** Following are selected data from the comparative income statement and balance sheet for Deerfield Corporation for the years ended December 31, 2011 and 2010:

|  | 2011 | 2010 |
|---|---|---|
| Net sales (all on credit)................... | $97,600 | $93,000 |
| Cost of goods sold........................... | 53,500 | 52,500 |
| Gross profit...................................... | 44,700 | 40,500 |
| Income from operations ................. | 16,300 | 15,000 |
| Interest expense.............................. | 3,100 | 3,500 |
| Net income...................................... | 9,800 | 9,000 |
| Cash................................................. | 7,700 | 7,500 |
| Accounts receivable, net................. | 10,700 | 12,500 |
| Inventory......................................... | 20,000 | 26,000 |
| Prepaid expenses ............................ | 1,000 | 900 |
| Total current assets ........................ | 39,400 | 46,900 |
| Total long-term assets .................... | 50,000 | 67,000 |
| Total current liabilities................... | 32,000 | 44,500 |
| Total long-term liabilities............... | 11,000 | 39,800 |
| Common stock, no par*................. | 10,000 | 10,000 |
| Retained earnings............................ | 25,400 | 19,600 |

*Note: Two thousand shares of common stock have been issued and outstanding since the company started operations. During the entire fiscal year ended December 31, 2011, the stock was selling for $45 per share.

## 1. Calculate the following ratios at December 31, 2011:

**a.** Acid-test ratio

**b.** Inventory turnover

**c.** Days' sales in receivables

**d.** Book value per share of common stock

**e.** Price/earnings ratio

**f.** Rate of return on total assets

**g.** Times-interest-earned ratio

**h.** Current ratio

**i.** Debt ratio

# Do It Yourself! Question 1

Tykes, Inc., had the following information at December 31, 2011:

## Tykes, Inc.
### Balance Sheet
#### December 31, 2011 and 2010

| (Dollar amounts in millions) | 2011 | 2010 |
|---|---|---|
| **Assets** | | |
| Cash | $400 | $300 |
| Accounts receivable | 290 | 350 |
| Inventory | 150 | 220 |
| Total assets | $840 | $870 |
| **Liabilities** | | |
| Accounts payable | $140 | $ 75 |
| Loans payable | 450 | 600 |
| Total liabilities | 590 | 675 |
| **Stockholders' Equity** | | |
| Common stock | 40 | 40 |
| Retained earnings | 210 | 155 |
| Total stockholders' equity | 250 | 195 |
| Total liabilities and equity | $840 | $870 |

## Tykes, Inc.
### Income Statement
#### Years Ended December 31, 2011 and 2010

| (Dollar amounts in millions) | 2011 | 2010 |
|---|---|---|
| Sales revenue | $1,200 | $1,000 |
| Less cost of goods sold | 800 | 600 |
| Gross profit | 400 | 400 |
| Insurance expense | 200 | 190 |
| Interest expense | 60 | 80 |
| Net income | $ 140 | $ 130 |

At December 31, 2009, Tykes' inventory was $200 million and total equity was $165 million.

## Requirements

1. Prepare a horizontal analysis of Tykes' financial statements.

### Tykes, Inc.
### Horizontal Analysis of Balance Sheet
### December 31, 2011 and 2010

| (Dollar amounts in millions) | 2011 | 2010 | Increase (Decrease) Amount | Percent |
|---|---|---|---|---|
| **Assets** | | | | |
| Cash.................................................. | $400 | $300 | | |
| Accounts receivable.......................... | 290 | 350 | | |
| Inventory.......................................... | 150 | 220 | | |
| | | | | |
| Total assets...................................... | $840 | $870 | | |
| | | | | |
| **Liabilities** | | | | |
| Accounts payable............................. | $140 | $ 75 | | |
| Loans payable.................................. | 450 | 600 | | |
| | | | | |
| Total liabilities ............................... | 590 | 675 | | |
| | | | | |
| **Stockholders' Equity** | | | | |
| Common stock................................. | 40 | 40 | | |
| Retained earnings............................ | 210 | 155 | | |
| | | | | |
| Total stockholders' equity............... | 250 | 195 | | |
| | | | | |
| Total liabilities and equity............... | $840 | $870 | | |

### Tykes, Inc.
### Horizontal Analysis of Comparative Income Statement
### Years Ended December 31, 2011 and 2010

| (Dollar amounts in millions) | 2011 | 2010 | Increase (Decrease) | |
| --- | --- | --- | --- | --- |
| | | | Amount | Percent |
| Sales revenue | $1,200 | $1,000 | | |
| Less cost of goods sold | 800 | 600 | | |
| Gross profit | 400 | 400 | | |
| Insurance expense | 200 | 190 | | |
| Interest expense | 60 | 80 | | |
| Net income | $ 140 | $ 130 | | |

## 2. Prepare a vertical analysis of Tykes' financial statements.

### Tykes, Inc.
### Vertical Analysis of Balance Sheet
### December 31, 2011 and 2010

| (Dollar amounts in millions) | 2011 | 2011 % | 2010 | 2010 % |
| --- | --- | --- | --- | --- |
| **Assets** | | | | |
| Cash | $400 | | $300 | |
| Accounts receivable | 290 | | 350 | |
| Inventory | 150 | | 220 | |
| Total assets | $840 | | $870 | |
| **Liabilities** | | | | |
| Accounts payable | $140 | | $ 75 | |
| Loans payable | 450 | | 600 | |
| Total liabilities | 590 | | 675 | |
| **Stockholders' Equity** | | | | |
| Common stock | 40 | | 40 | |
| Retained earnings | 210 | | 155 | |
| Total stockholders' equity | 250 | | 195 | |
| Total liabilities and equity | $840 | | $870 | |

**Tykes, Inc.**
**Vertical Analysis of Comparative Income Statement**
**Years Ended December 31, 2011 and 2010**

| (Dollar amounts in millions) | 2011 | 2011 % | 2010 | 2010 % |
|---|---|---|---|---|
| Net sales revenue.............................. | $1,200 | | $1,000 | |
| Less cost of goods sold.................... | 800 | | 600 | |
| Gross profit...................................... | 400 | | 400 | |
| Insurance expense ........................... | 200 | | 190 | |
| Interest expense............................... | 60 | | 80 | |
| Net income...................................... | $ 140 | | $ 130 | |

3. **Calculate Tykes' inventory turnover and rate of return on stockholders' equity ratios for both years.**

4. **Calculate Tykes' book value per share of common stock for 2011, assuming that Tykes has 40 million common shares outstanding.**

5. **Calculate Tykes' economic value added (EVA) for 2011, assuming a cost of capital of 15%.**

# Quick Practice Solutions

## True/False

<u> F </u>   1. It is generally considered less useful to know the percentage change in financial statement amounts from year to year than to know the absolute dollar amount of their change.

        False—It is generally considered *more* useful to know the percentage change in financial statement amounts than to know the absolute dollar amount of their change. (p. 778)

<u> T </u>   2. Benchmarking may be done against an industry average or against a key competitor. (pp. 785–786)

<u> T </u>   3. Horizontal analysis of financial statements reveals changes in items on the financial statements over time. (p. 782)

<u> F </u>   4. Inventory turnover is the ratio of average inventory to cost of goods sold.

        False—Inventory turnover is the ratio of *cost of goods sold to average inventory*. (p. 793)

<u> T </u>   5. Book value per share of common stock has no relationship to market value. (p. 799)

<u> T </u>   6. A high current ratio means that a company's current assets represent a relatively large portion (or ratio) of current liabilities. (pp. 790–792)

<u> F </u>   7. The debt ratio measures the ability to pay current liabilities.

        False—The debt ratio measures the ability to pay *total* liabilities. (p. 795)

<u> F </u>   8. The acid-test (quick) ratio includes the sum of Cash, Net Accounts Receivable, and Inventory in the numerator.

        False—The acid-test (quick) ratio includes the sum of *Cash, Short-Term Investments, and Net Receivables* in the numerator. (p. 792)

<u> F </u>   9. Earnings per share indicates the net income earned for each share of common and preferred stock.

        False—Earnings per share indicates the net income earned for each share of the company's *common* stock. (pp. 797–798)

<u> T </u>  10. A signal of financial trouble may include cash flow from operations being lower than net income from period to period. (p. 787)

## Multiple Choice

1. **Vertical analysis can be described as which of the following? (p. 782)**
   a. Percentage changes in various financial statement amounts from year to year
   b. The changes in individual financial statement amounts as a percentage of some related total
   c. The change in key financial statement ratios over a certain time frame or horizon
   d. None of the above

2. **Trend percentages can be considered a form of which of the following? (p. 781)**
   a. Ratio analysis
   b. Vertical analysis
   c. Profitability analysis
   d. Horizontal analysis

3. **In 2010, net sales were $1,600,000 and in 2011, net sales were $1,750,000. How is the percent change calculated? (p. 778)**
   a. Divide $1,600,000 by $1,750,000
   b. Divide $1,750,000 by $1,600,000
   c. Divide $150,000 by $1,750,000
   d. Divide $150,000 by $1,600,000

4. **Horizontal analysis can be described as which of the following? (p. 778)**
   a. Percentage changes in the balances shown in comparative financial statements
   b. The change in key financial statement ratios over a specified period of time
   c. The dollar amount of the change in various financial statement amounts from year to year
   d. Individual financial statement items expressed as a percentage of a base (which represents 100%)

5. **What is the base that is used when performing vertical analysis on an income statement? (p. 782)**
   a. Net sales
   b. Gross sales
   c. Gross profit
   d. Total expenses

6. **What is the base that is used when performing vertical analysis on a balance sheet? (p. 783)**
   a. Total assets
   b. Stockholders' equity
   c. Total liabilities
   d. Net assets

7. **Which ratio measures the ability to cover interest expense with current operating income? (p. 795)**
   a. Rate of return on net sales
   b. Earnings per share
   c. Times-interest-earned ratio
   d. Acid-test (quick) ratio

8. **Which of the following would be most helpful in the comparison of different-sized companies? (p. 784)**
   a. Performing horizontal analysis
   b. Looking at the amount of income earned by each company
   c. Comparing working capital balances
   d. Preparing common-size financial statements

9. **Which ratio(s) help(s) in the analysis of working capital? (pp. 790–792)**
   a. Current ratio
   b. Acid-test ratio
   c. Debt ratio
   d. Both a and b are correct.

10. **Assume that collections from customers on account are being received faster. Which of the following would be true? (p. 794)**
    a. The accounts receivable turnover would be higher.
    b. The days' sales in receivables would be higher.
    c. The current ratio would be higher.
    d. None of the above is true.

# Quick Exercises

**13-1.** Selected items from the balance sheet and income statement follow for the Brothers Company for 2011 and 2010. (pp. 778–779)

1. Calculate the amount of the change and the percentage of change for each item.

|  | 2011 | 2010 | $ Change | % Change |
|---|---|---|---|---|
| Cash | $121,000 | $100,000 | $ 21,000 | 21.0 % |
| Accounts receivable | 117,000 | 125,000 | (8,000) | (6.4)% |
| Merchandise inventory | 70,000 | 85,000 | (15,000) | (17.6)% |
| Accounts payable | 63,500 | 50,000 | 13,500 | 27.0 % |
| Sales | 144,000 | 135,000 | 9,000 | 6.7 % |
| Cost of goods sold | 74,000 | 67,500 | 6,500 | 9.6 % |

**13-2.** Using the following data for Dream Corporation for 2011, calculate the ratios that follow: (pp. 797–799)

| | |
|---|---|
| Market price per share of common stock at 12/31/11 | $ 9.00 |
| Net income | 50,000.00 |
| Number of common shares outstanding | 25,000.00 |
| Dividend per share of common stock | $ 0.71 |

**a.** earnings per share of common stock

$50,000/25,000 = $2.00

**b.** price/earnings ratio

$9.00/$2.00 = 4.5

**c.** dividend yield

$0.71/$9.00 = 0.08

**13-3. The income statement for Science Corporation for the year ended December 31, 2011, follows: (pp. 782–783)**

Science Corporation
Income Statement
Year Ended December 31, 2011

| | | |
|---|---:|---:|
| Net sales.................................... | | $661,000 |
| Expenses: | | |
| Cost of goods sold ................. | $268,500 | |
| Selling expenses...................... | 35,000 | |
| General expenses................... | 49,300 | |
| Interest expenses ................... | 45,000 | |
| Income tax expense............... | 30,000 | |
| Total expenses............................ | | 427,800 |
| Net income................................. | | $233,200 |

**1. Prepare a vertical analysis of the income statement showing appropriate percentages for each item listed.**

Science Corporation
Income Statement
Year Ended December 31, 2011

| | Amount | Percentage |
|---|---:|---:|
| Net sales................................... | $661,000 | 100.0% |
| Expenses | | |
| Cost of goods sold................. | 268,500 | 40.6 |
| Selling expenses...................... | 35,000 | 5.3 |
| General expenses................... | 49,300 | 7.5 |
| Interest expense...................... | 45,000 | 6.8 |
| Income tax expense............... | 30,000 | 4.5 |
| Total expenses........................ | 427,000 | 64.7 |
| Net income.............................. | $233,200 | 35.3% |

**2. What additional information would you need to determine whether these percentages are good or bad?**

Additional information to determine whether these percentages are good or bad might include the following:

- Industry averages to compare to Science Corporation
- The change in each line item percentage over a relevant period of time

## 13-4. Match the function with the appropriate ratio. (pp. 790–799)

**Functions:**

a. Gives the amount of net income earned for each share of the company's common stock
b. Measures the number of times operating income can cover interest expense
c. Shows ability to pay all current liabilities if they come due immediately
d. Shows the percentage of a stock's market value returned to stockholders as dividends each period
e. Measures ability to collect cash from credit customers
f. Measures ability to pay current liabilities with current assets
g. Indicates the market price of $1 of earnings
h. Measures the difference between current assets and current liabilities
i. Indicates percentage of assets financed with debt
j. Shows the percentage of each sales dollar earned as net income

**Ratios:**

1. __d__ Dividend yield
2. __j__ Rate of return on net sales
3. __e__ Accounts receivable turnover
4. __h__ Working capital
5. __i__ Debt ratio
6. __f__ Current ratio
7. __g__ Price/earnings ratio
8. __b__ Times-interest-earned ratio
9. __c__ Acid-test ratio
10. __a__ Earnings per share of common stock

**13-5. Following are selected data from the comparative income statement and balance sheet for Deerfield Corporation for the years ended December 31, 2011 and 2010: (pp. 790–799)**

|  | 2011 | 2010 |
|---|---|---|
| Net sales (all on credit).................... | $97,600 | $93,000 |
| Cost of goods sold........................... | 53,500 | 52,500 |
| Gross profit.................................... | 44,700 | 40,500 |
| Income from operations ................. | 16,300 | 15,000 |
| Interest expense............................. | 3,100 | 3,500 |
| Net income.................................... | 9,800 | 9,000 |
| Cash.............................................. | 7,700 | 7,500 |
| Accounts receivable, net ................ | 10,700 | 12,500 |
| Inventory....................................... | 20,000 | 26,000 |
| Prepaid expenses ........................... | 1,000 | 900 |
| Total current assets ....................... | 39,400 | 46,900 |
| Total long-term assets ................... | 50,000 | 67,000 |
| Total current liabilities.................. | 32,000 | 44,500 |
| Total long-term liabilities............... | 11,000 | 39,800 |
| Common stock, no par*................. | 10,000 | 10,000 |
| Retained earnings........................... | 25,400 | 19,600 |

*Note: Two thousand shares of common stock have been issued and outstanding since the company started operations. During the entire fiscal year ended December 31, 2011, the stock was selling for $45 per share.

## 1. Calculate the following ratios at December 31, 2011:

**a.** Acid-test ratio

$$(\$7,700 + \$10,700)/\$32,000 = 0.58$$

**b.** Inventory turnover

$$\frac{\$53,500}{(\$20,000 + \$26,000)/2} = 2.33$$

**c.** Days' sales in receivables

$$\frac{(\$10,700 + \$12,500)/2}{\$97,600/365} = 43.4 \text{ days}$$

**d.** Book value per share of common stock

$$\frac{\$10,000 + \$25,400}{2,000} = \$17.70$$

**e.** Price/earnings ratio

$$\frac{\$45}{\$9,800/2,000} = 9.18$$

**f.** Rate of return on total assets

$$\frac{\$9,800 + \$3,100}{(\$39,400 + \$50,000 + \$46,900 + \$67,900)/2} = 0.13$$

**g.** Times-interest-earned ratio

$$\frac{\$16,300}{\$3,100} = 5.26 \text{ times}$$

**h.** Current ratio

$$\frac{\$39,400}{\$32,000} = 1.23$$

**i.** Debt ratio

$$\frac{\$32,000 + \$11,000}{\$39,400 + \$50,000} = 0.48$$

# Do It Yourself! Question 1 Solutions

## Requirements

1. Prepare a horizontal analysis for Tykes' financial statements.

### Tykes, Inc.
### Horizontal Analysis of Balance Sheet
### December 31, 2011 and 2010

| (Dollar amounts in millions) | 2011 | 2010 | Increase (Decrease) Amount | Percent |
|---|---|---|---|---|
| **Assets** | | | | |
| Cash.................................... | $400 | $300 | $ 100 | 33.3 % |
| Accounts receivable......................... | 290 | 350 | (60) | (17.1) |
| Inventory........................................ | 150 | 220 | (70) | (31.8) |
| Total assets..................................... | $840 | $870 | $ (30) | (3.4) |
| **Liabilities** | | | | |
| Accounts payable............................ | $140 | $ 75 | $ 65 | 86.7 |
| Loans payable ................................. | 450 | 600 | (150) | (25.0) |
| Total liabilities ............................... | 590 | 675 | (85) | (12.6) |
| **Stockholders' Equity** | | | | |
| Common stock................................ | 40 | 40 | 0 | 0.0 |
| Retained earnings............................ | 210 | 155 | 55 | 35.5 |
| Total stockholders' equity............... | 250 | 195 | 55 | 28.2 |
| Total liabilities and equity............... | $840 | $870 | $ (30) | (3.4)% |

**Tykes, Inc.**
**Horizontal Analysis of Comparative Income Statement**
**Years Ended December 31, 2011 and 2010**

| (Dollar amounts in millions) | 2011 | 2010 | Increase (Decrease) Amount | Percent |
|---|---|---|---|---|
| Sales revenue............................... | $1,200 | $1,000 | $200 | 20.0 % |
| Less cost of goods sold................... | 800 | 600 | 200 | 33.3 |
| Gross profit.................................... | 400 | 400 | 0 | 0.0 |
| Insurance expense ........................... | 200 | 190 | 10 | 5.3 |
| Interest expense.............................. | 60 | 80 | (20) | (25.0) |
| Net income..................................... | $ 140 | $ 130 | $ 10 | 7.7 % |

## 2. Prepare a vertical analysis for Tykes' financial statements.

**Tykes, Inc.**
**Vertical Analysis of Balance Sheet**
**December 31, 2011 and 2010**

| (Dollar amounts in millions) | 2011 | 2011 % | 2010 | 2010 % |
|---|---|---|---|---|
| **Assets** | | | | |
| Cash.................................................. | $400 | 47.6% | $300 | 34.5% |
| Accounts receivable......................... | 290 | 34.5 | 350 | 40.2 |
| Inventory.......................................... | 150 | 17.9 | 220 | 25.3 |
| Total assets...................................... | $840 | 100.0% | $870 | 100.0% |
| **Liabilities** | | | | |
| Accounts payable ............................ | $140 | 16.7% | $ 75 | 8.6% |
| Loans payable ................................. | 450 | 53.5 | 600 | 69.0 |
| Total liabilities ............................... | 590 | 70.2 | 675 | 77.6 |
| **Stockholders' Equity** | | | | |
| Common stock................................. | 40 | 4.8 | 40 | 4.6 |
| Retained earnings............................ | 210 | 25.0 | 155 | 17.8 |
| Total stockholders' equity............... | 250 | 29.8 | 195 | 22.4 |
| Total liabilities and equity............... | $840 | 100.0% | $870 | 100.0% |

### Tykes, Inc.
### Vertical Analysis of Comparative Income Statement
### Years Ended December 31, 2011 and 2010

| (Dollar amounts in millions) | 2011 | 2011 % | 2010 | 2010 % |
|---|---|---|---|---|
| Net sales revenue............................ | $1,200 | 100.0% | $1,000 | 100.0% |
| Less cost of goods sold................... | 800 | 66.7 | 600 | 60.0 |
| Gross profit...................................... | 400 | 33.3 | 400 | 40.0 |
| Insurance expense .......................... | 200 | 16.6 | 190 | 19.0 |
| Interest expense.............................. | 60 | 5.0 | 80 | 8.0 |
| Net income...................................... | $ 140 | 11.7% | $ 130 | 13.0% |

## 3. Calculate Tykes' inventory turnover and rate of return on stockholder's equity ratios for both years.

$$2011 \text{ Inventory turnover} = \frac{\$800,000,000}{[\frac{1}{2}(\$220,000,000 + \$150,000,000)]}$$
$$= 4.3 \text{ times}$$

$$2010 \text{ Inventory turnover} = \frac{\$600,000,000}{[\frac{1}{2}(\$200,000,000 + \$220,000,000)]}$$
$$= 2.9 \text{ times}$$

$$2011 \text{ Rate of return on stockholders' equity} = \frac{[\$140,000,000 - \$0]}{[\frac{1}{2}(\$195,000,000 + \$250,000,000)]}$$
$$= 62.9\%$$

$$2010 \text{ Rate of return on stockholders' equity} = \frac{[\$130,000,000 - \$0]}{[\frac{1}{2}(\$165,000,000 + \$195,000,000)]}$$
$$= 72.2\%$$

## 4. Calculate Tykes' book value per share of common stock for 2011, assuming that Tykes has 40 million common shares outstanding.

$$2011 \text{ Book value per share of common stock} = \frac{\$250,000,000 - 0}{40,000,000 \text{ shares}}$$
$$= \$6.25$$

## 5. Calculate Tykes' economic value added (EVA) for 2011, assuming a cost of capital of 15%.

$$2011 \text{ Capital charge} = [\$450,000,000 \text{ Loans Payable} + \$250,000,000 \text{ Total Equity}] \times 15\%$$
$$= \$105,000,000$$

$$2011 \text{ EVA} = \$140,000,000 \text{ Net Income} - \$105,000,000 = \$35,000,000$$

# The Power of Practice

For more practice using the skills learned in this chapter, visit MyAccountingLab. There you will find algorithmically generated questions that are based on these Demo Docs and your main textbook's Review and Assess Your Progress sections.

Go to MyAccountingLab and follow these steps:

1. Direct your URL to www.myaccountinglab.com.
2. Log in using your name and password.
3. Click the MyAccountingLab link.
4. Click Study Plan in the left navigation bar.
5. From the table of contents, select Chapter 13, Financial Statement Analysis.
6. Click a link to work tutorial exercises.

# Index